Cambridge Studies in

CHEAP PRINT AND POPULAR PIETY, 1550–1640

This book looks at popular belief through a detailed study of the cheapest printed wares produced in London in the century after the Reformation. It investigates the interweaving of the printed word with the existing oral and visual culture, as well as the general growth of literacy. Part I deals with the broadside ballad as song, disseminated by a widening network of minstrels and pedlars; Part II looks at the broadside picture as an image for the wall, placed against a background of domestic wall painting and domestic cloth. Part III examines the development of cheap print intended primarily for reading, and traces for the first time the beginnings of the chapbook trade in the early seventeenth century.

Protestantism is seen, in common with print, as modifying rather than as replacing traditional culture. Although reformers stopped using the ballad as an evangelical medium in the 1580s, some of their 'godly songs' found commercial success and offer us insights into the moderate piety of 'honest householders' in the seventeenth century. Although there was increasing suspicion of some types of religious imagery, English walls were still decorated with little woodcut Christs and biblical tales. The extent of national 'iconophobia' should not be exaggerated.

Both Protestantism and print have been credited by recent historians with enormous, even 'revolutionary' impact upon popular culture. The Protestant hostility towards traditional recreations is said to have 'inserted a cultural wedge' in village society, while its logo-centrism took the English people across a watershed 'from a culture of orality and image to one of print culture'. This study challenges these confrontational models, showing instead how traditional piety could be gradually modified to create a religious culture which was distinctively post-Reformation, if not thoroughly 'Protestant'.

Cambridge Studies in Early Modern British History

Series editors

ANTHONY FLETCHER
Professor of Modern History, University of Durham

JOHN GUY
Professor of Modern History, University of St Andrews

and JOHN MORRILL
Lecturer in History, University of Cambridge, and Fellow and Tutor of Selwyn College

This is a series of monographs and studies covering many aspects of the history of the British Isles between the late fifteenth century and the early eighteenth century. It includes the work of established scholars and pioneering work by a new generation of scholars. It includes both reviews and revisions of major topics and books which open up new historical terrain or which reveal startling new perspectives on familiar subjects. All the volumes set detailed research into our broader perspectives and the books are intended for the use of students as well as of their teachers.

For a list of titles in the series, see end of book.

CHEAP PRINT
AND POPULAR
PIETY
1550–1640

TESSA WATT

CAMBRIDGE
UNIVERSITY PRESS

Published by the Press Syndicate of the University of Cambridge
The Pitt Building, Trumpington Street, Cambridge CB2 1RP
40 West 20th Street, New York, NY 10011–4211, USA
10 Stamford Road, Oakleigh, Melbourne 3166, Australia

First published 1991
First paperback edition 1994
Reprinted 1996

Printed and bound in Great Britain by Woolnough Bookbinding Ltd,
Irthlingborough, Northamptonshire

British Library cataloguing in publication data

Watt, Tessa
Cheap print and popular piety, 1550–1640.
1. Great Britain. Christianity, history
I. Title
209.41

Library of Congress cataloguing in publication data

Watt, Tessa.
Cheap print and popular piety, 1550–1640/Tessa Watt.
p.   c. – (Cambridge studies in early modern British history)
Includes bibliographical references.
ISBN 0 521 38255 6
1. Christian literature, English – History and criticism.
2. Street literature – Great Britain – History and criticism.
3. English literature – Early modern, 1500–1700 – History and
criticism. 4. Ballads, English – History and criticism. 5. Chapbooks,
English – History and criticism. 6. Broadsides – Great Britain.
7. Great Britain – Popular culture – History – 17th century.
8. Great Britain – Popular culture – History – 16th century. 9. Books
and reading – Great Britain – History. 10. Printing – Great Britain –
History.   I. Title.   II. Series.
PR428.C48W38   1991
820.9' 382' 09031 – dc20   90-1581 CIP

ISBN 0 521 38255 6 hardback
ISBN 0 521 45827 7 paperback

*For June Gabriel
and F. W. W.*

CONTENTS

vii

ILLUSTRATIONS

FIGURES

TABLES

ACKNOWLEDGEMENTS

I would like to thank the following for permission to reproduce copyright material: The Ashmolean Museum; Bibliothèque Nationale, Paris; Bodleian Library, Oxford; The British Library; The Trustees of the British Museum; The Earl of Crawford; The Folger Shakespeare Library; Guildhall Library, City of London; The Huntington Library, San Marino, California; The Master and Fellows, Magdalene College, Cambridge; The Royal Commission on the Historical Monuments of England; Rutgers University Press; The Society of Antiquaries of London; The Board of Trustees of the Victoria and Albert Museum.

This study has taken me into a number of fields, where I would often have been lost without the help of others. For information on matters of bibliography, I am indebted to Katherine Pantzer, David McKitterick, Sheila Lambert and the staff of the Rare Books room in the Cambridge University Library. In the search for broadsides and woodcut pictures I have been aided by Betty Ingram, Chantal Ratcliffe, Morris Martin, Anthony Griffiths, Marianne Grivel, Mireille Galinou, Elizabeth Miller and Tamsyn Williams. On decorative painting, I was advised by David Park and Joseph Michel, with further help from E. Clive Rouse, Muriel Carrick and John Mitchell. Robert Thomson, Richard Rastall, Helena Shire and Rivkah Zim were helpful on balladry, music and literature.

A number of historians have given me suggestions, information or encouragement, including Peter Burke, Eamon Duffy, Paul Hopkins, Andrew Pettegree, Judith Richards, Bob Scribner and Peter Spufford. I owe particular thanks to Ian Green, who gave up valuable time to sift through file cards on my behalf.

Eric Carlson and Anthony Milton have been scholars-of-all-trades, supplying me with a flow of helpful references. I would especially like to thank Amy Erickson, Chris Marsh, Judith Maltby, Derek Plumb, Helen Weinstein and the other 'Spuffordians' for their encouragement and help in many forms.

From 1984 to 1987, while working towards my doctorate, I was supported by a Commonwealth Scholarship. I am also grateful to the Commission for a grant to purchase photographs, later supplemented by a grant from the Prince Consort and Thirlwall Fund. Corpus Christi College, Cambridge, and the staff of Leckhampton provided a wonderful setting in which to work during these years.

From 1987 to 1989 I was supported by a Drapers' Company Research Fellowship at Pembroke College, Cambridge. I am very grateful to the Master and Fellows for their warm welcome and their support.

This book is based on my PhD thesis, 'Cheap print and religion *c*. 1550 to 1640' (Cambridge, 1988). In the task of transforming the thesis into book form, I have been helped by the comments of my examiners Patrick Collinson and Keith Wrightson, and of series editors Anthony Fletcher and John Morrill.

I cannot adequately thank my PhD supervisor, Margaret Spufford, not only for her invaluable guidance and criticism, but also for her constant enthusiasm, often under circumstances which would have defeated a lesser scholar or human being.

Finally I am grateful to my husband, Richard Woolley, for putting up with me and it over the past five years.

ABBREVIATIONS

Arber
: Edward Arber, ed., *A transcript of the registers of the Company of Stationers of London 1554–1640* (5 vols., 1875–94).

BL
: British Library.

BM Prints
: Department of Prints and Drawings, British Museum.

BM Satires
: Collection of prints in the Department of Prints and Drawings, British Museum. All pre-1640 prints described in *Catalogue of prints and drawings in the British Museum. Division 1. Satires. Vol. 1. 1320–1689*, ed. Frederic G. Stephens (1870).

Child
: F. J. Child, *The English and Scottish popular ballads* (5 vols., 1882–98).

Collmann
: H. L. Collmann, ed., Ballads and broadsides chiefly of the Elizabethan period . . . now in the library at Britwell Court (1912). Collection now in the Huntington Library, California.

Crawford
: Collection of ballads and broadsides owned by the Earl of Crawford, on deposit at the John Rylands Library, Manchester. Listed in *Bibliotheca Lindesiana: catalogue of a collection of English ballads of the XVIIth and XVIIIth centuries* (1890; facs. edn, 1962).

Dicey catalogue 1754
: William and Cluer Dicey, *A catalogue of maps, histories, prints, old ballads, copy-books, broadsheets and other patters, drawing-books, garlands &c.* (1754). Reprinted in R. S. Thomson, 'The development of the broadside ballad trade and its influence upon the transmission of English folksongs' (Cambridge PhD, 1974), App. C.

DNB	The Dictionary of National Biography.
Douce	Francis Douce collection of ballads in the Bodleian Library, Oxford.
ent.	Entry in Stationers' Register.
Euing	Collection of ballads in Glasgow University Library. Reprinted in John Holloway, ed., *The Euing collection of English broadside ballads* (Glasgow, 1971).
Eyre	G. E. B. Eyre, ed., *A transcript of the registers of the worshipful Company of Stationers 1640–1708* (3 vols., 1913–14).
Hind	Arthur M. Hind, *Engraving in England in the sixteenth and seventeenth centuries* (3 vols., vol. III compiled by M. Corbett and M. Norton, Cambridge, 1952–64).
Huth. 50	Collection of ballads in the British Library. Reprinted by Joseph Lilly, 1867.
Lilly	Joseph Lilly, ed., *A collection of 79 black-letter ballads and broadsides printed in the reign of Queen Elizabeth* (1867). Now in the British Library, Huth. 50.
Manchester	Manchester Central Library, collection of ballads, 2 vols.
MS Ashmole 48	Manuscript volume of ballads in the Bodleian Library, Oxford. Reprinted in Wright. ed., *Songs and ballads, with other short poems, chiefly of the reign of Philip and Mary* (1860).
Norris and Brown 1712	List of stock ballads and chapbooks registered on 20 September 1712 to Thomas Norris and Charles Brown. Reprinted in Thomson, 'Development of the broadside ballad trade', App. B.
'partners'	The 'ballad partners' syndicate (with changing membership) for the publication and distribution of ballads throughout much of the seventeenth century.
Pepys	Ballad collection of Samuel Pepys, Magdalene College, Cambridge, 5 vols.
PRO	Public Record Office.
Rawlinson 566	Rawlinson Collection of ballads in the Bodleian Library, Oxford.
RB orig.	Roxburghe collection of ballads in the British Library, 3 vols. Virtually all pre-1640 items have

been reprinted in 'RB repr.'.

RB repr.
William Chappell and J. Woodfall Ebsworth, eds., *The Roxburghe Ballads* (8 vols., 1871–97).

RCHM
Royal Commission on the Historical Monuments of England.

REED
Records of Early English Drama (Toronto, 1979–   ).

Rollins Index
Hyder E. Rollins, *An analytical index to the ballad-entries in the Stationers' Registers: 1557–1709* (1924; 2nd edn with intro. by Leslie Shepard, Hatboro, 1967).

SA
Collection of Broadsides in the Society of Antiquaries, London. Catalogue by Robert Lemon, 1866.

Seng
Peter Joseph Seng, ed. *Tudor songs and ballads. From MS Cotton Vespasian A-25* (Cambridge, Mass., 1978).

Shirburn
Andrew Clark, ed., *The Shirburn ballads* (Oxford, 1907). From a MS in the library of Shirburn Castle, Oxfordshire.

Simpson
Claude M. Simpson, *The British broadside ballad and its music* (New Brunswick, New Jersey, 1966).

STC
A short-title catalogue of books printed in England, Scotland & Ireland and of English books printed abroad 1475–1640 (first compiled by A. W. Pollard and G. R. Redgrave; 2nd edn, revised and enlarged, begun by W. A. Jackson and F. S. Ferguson, completed by Katherine F. Pantzer, 2 vols., 1976–86).

Wing
Short-title catalogue of books printed in England, Scotland, Ireland, Wales and British North America and of English books printed in other countries 1641–1700 (compiled by Donald Wing, vol. III, New York, 1951; 2nd edn, revised and enlarged by the Index Committee of the Modern Language Association of America, vols. I–II, New York, 1972–82).

Wood
Anthony Wood's collection of ballads in the Bodleian Library, Oxford.

Wright
Thomas Wright, ed., *Songs and ballads, with other short poems, chiefly of the reign of Philip and Mary* (1860).

NOTE FOR THE READER

The place of publication for all printed works referred to in the footnotes and appendices is London, unless otherwise stated.

Dates in round brackets (1570) are given in the work itself, or (ent. 1570) refer to a definite entry in the Stationers' Register.

Dates in square brackets [1570] have been deduced from probable identification with a Register entry, or from other sources, usually following the judgement of the STC.

INTRODUCTION

My decision to begin research in early modern English history was inspired by studies published over the past fifteen years which are loosely described as works on 'popular culture'.[1] Margaret Spufford's work on the late seventeenth-century chapbook trade, in particular, raised a challenging set of questions.[2] How far back could this trade be traced? When did publishers begin to produce and distribute reading material consciously aimed at the humblest members of the literate public? The criterion of 'cheapness' seemed the best place to start, since price was the major constraining factor in book buying, after literacy. In this period up to 75% of the cost came from the paper, so the shortest works were the cheapest works: the one-page broadside and the tiny octavo chapbook.[3] This 'cheap' print, once identified, would provide an insight into popular culture and popular religion.

To some extent, these expectations were satisfied. There was, indeed, an increasing degree of specialization at the bottom end of the publishing trade in the decades before 1640, reaching, it would appear, a rapidly widening market. However, it would be misleading to describe this as a 'popular' printed culture, if 'popular' is taken to imply something exclusive to a specific social group. Ballads were hawked in the alehouses and markets, but in the same period they were sung by minstrels in the households of the nobility and gentry, who copied them carefully into manuscripts. Pictorial themes which appeared in the crudest woodcuts were also painted on the walls of manor houses. Chapbooks which sold for twopence, and appealed to 'honest folks that have no lands', were also bought by a Staffordshire lady

---

[1] For example, Robert W. Malcolmson, *Popular recreations in English society 1700–1850* (Cambridge, 1973); Keith Thomas, *Religion and the decline of magic* (1971); Natalie Zemon-Davis, *Society and culture in early modern France* (Stanford, 1982 edn); Robert Scribner, *For the sake of simple folk* (Cambridge, 1981). Not all of these historians have used the term 'popular culture' themselves.

[2] Margaret Spufford, *Small books and pleasant histories. Popular fiction and its readership in seventeenth-century England* (1981).

[3] Philip Gaskell, *A new introduction to bibliography* (Oxford, 1972), p. 177.

1

and carefully left in her will to her clergyman son.[4] In the process of research, 'cultural homogeneities' appeared as often as cultural divisions.[5]

The model of a binary opposition of 'popular' and 'elite' has already been criticized, modified and sometimes disowned by recent social historians. Tim Harris points out that the two-tiered model fails to match the reality of a multi-tiered social hierarchy, with substantial numbers of households in the 'middling' levels. He argues that 'vertical antagonisms', especially the divisions caused by religion, were as important as horizontal divisions in seventeenth-century London.[6] Martin Ingram emphasizes the converse argument, describing areas of cultural 'consensus' which united those at all social levels.[7] While these critics doubt the explanatory value of the model, Roger Chartier attacks the theoretical premise which underlies it: the assumption 'that it is possible to establish exclusive relationships between specific cultural forms and particular social groups'. This assumption has led historians to pre-define certain cultural cleavages, which they have then proceeded to describe.[8]

Should we completely abandon the concept of 'popular culture', or can we find a more constructive way of using it? Peter Burke's 'asymmetrical' definition provides a start: for him, the 'great' tradition was the closed culture of the educated elites, while the 'little' (or popular) tradition was open to everyone, including those elites.[9] This inclusive definition is helpful, but, as Bob Scribner points out, the language tends to reduce the 'little' tradition to a 'residual or marginalized category'. Scribner suggests that we must think of popular culture as a 'total, unified culture': a system of shared attitudes and values, and the performances or artefacts in which they are embodied.[10] We cannot ignore the existence of social stratification, nor of subcultural identities (such as apprentices or vagrants), but we must see how these overlapping segments somehow made up a functional whole.[11]

Scribner's concept of culture is harder to grasp and to use than the model

---

[4] See chs. 1, 5, 8.

[5] Martin Ingram, 'Ridings, rough music and the "reform of popular culture" in early modern England', *Past and Present*, 105 (Nov. 1984), p. 113.

[6] Tim Harris, 'The problem of "popular political culture" in seventeenth-century London', *History of European Ideas*, 10 (1989), pp. 43–58.

[7] Ingram, 'Ridings, rough music and the "reform of popular culture"', pp. 79, 112–13; Martin Ingram, *Church courts, sex and marriage in England, 1570–1640* (Cambridge, 1987), p. 167.

[8] Roger Chartier, *The cultural uses of print in early modern France*, trans. Lydia C. Cochrane (Princeton, 1987), p. 3; Roger Chartier, *Cultural history. Between practices and representations*, trans. Lydia C. Cochrane (Cambridge, 1988), p. 30.

[9] Peter Burke, *Popular culture in early modern Europe* (1978), p. 28.

[10] Bob Scribner, 'Is a history of popular culture possible?', *History of European Ideas*, 10 (1989), pp. 181–2. The definition is that used by A.L. Kroeber to define 'culture' as a whole.

[11] *Ibid.*, pp. 183–4.

of simple binary opposition, but it is more faithful to the complexities of past societies. In the present study, I will try to explore what we may describe as 'shared values', 'widespread attitudes' or 'commonplace mentalities': not a homogeneous, articulated set of doctrines, but a mosaic made up of changing and often contradictory fragments.

We may choose to call this mosaic 'popular' belief, but only if the term is understood inclusively. As historians used to the 'almost tyrannical pre-eminence of the social dimension'[12] we may be uncomfortable with the lack of evidence to pinpoint the audience for cheap print, and to locate it precisely on the social scale. We may be frustrated with the inability of the printed artefacts to help us differentiate between the views of the gentry, the 'middling sort' and the labouring poor. But this idea that the broadsides and chapbooks were aimed at and consumed by a definable social group may be a myth. The audience presupposed within the cheap print itself appears to be inclusive rather than exclusive, addressed both as 'readers' and as 'hearers'; as substantial householders expected to employ labourers, and as couples 'whose whole stocke could hardly purchase a wedding ring'.[13] Of course, this cheap print is not homogeneous: some items like the copper engravings and plague broadsides appear to have been produced for a market of middling Londoners, while other ballads and chapbooks inhabit the world of poor Northumberland men, west-country lasses, serving-men, chambermaids and 'poor and plaine people' living in 'remote' parts of the country.[14] As literacy increased, the market for cheap print expanded, and there may sometimes have been gaps between authorial intention and audience consumption. But the buyers remained socially variegated: in the early seventeenth century gentry collectors were still copying ballads into their commonplace books; probably the same ballads which were to be found on the walls of 'honest alehouses', in 'the shops of artificers' and in 'the cottages of poor husbandmen'.[15]

Admittedly, no matter how we define 'popular belief', it is impossible for the historian to get 'directly at' this mosaic of values and attitudes. Bob Scribner is particularly sceptical about the source materials used in studies of popular culture (including printed broadsides and chapbooks),

---

[12] Chartier, *Cultural history*, p. 30.

[13] John Andrewes, *The converted mans new birth: describing the direct way to heaven* (1629), sig.A2. 'A most excellent new dittie, wherein is shewed the sage sayings, and wise sentences of Salomon' (1586). *Cupids schoole: wherein, yongmen and maids may learne divers sorts of complements* (1632), sig.C3. See pp. 311, 100, 295.

[14] Engravings and broadsides discussed in ch. 6. Martin Parker, *The king and a poore northerne man* (1633). 'The crafty lass of the west', Pepys, IV, 7. *Cupids schoole*. Richard Hawes, *The poore-mans plaster-box* (1634). See pp. 299, 294–5.

[15] B M Addit. MS 15,225; Shirburn. Izaak Walton, *The complete angler; or, the contemplative man's recreation* (1653), facs. edn (1976), p. 49. Nicholas Bownde, *The doctrine of the sabbath* (1595), p. 242.

arguing that they reveal only 'forms of downward mediation by educational or literate elites'.[16] The present study is more positive about the value of looking at printed wares, provided they are set in their cultural context. In our approach to printed sources, Roger Chartier's notion of cultural 'consumption' may be useful. For Chartier 'consumption' should be taken as 'a form of production which, to be sure, manufactures no object, but which constitutes representations that are never identical to those that the producers (the authors or artists) have introduced into their works'.[17] Although we cannot recover the reaction of the individual buyer, we will be looking at how the collective responses of cheap-print 'consumers' exercised an influence on what was printed, and especially what was reprinted. For example, in chapter 3 we will look at a body of long-enduring ballads which was to some extent 'produced' by the consumers through the process of selection. This examination will suggest ways in which the propaganda of Protestant reformers was modified by the more conservative religious outlook of the larger public.

There are undoubtedly certain sources which can bring us closer to ordinary people as cultural 'creators' rather than as creative 'consumers'.[18] Historians are paying increasing attention to records of slanderous rhymes, skimmingtons and other ritualized protests or festivities which show people using established symbols in a resourceful way.[19] However, the ballads, woodcuts and chapbooks provide a window on a particular element in the 'process of culture formation':[20] the role of print. This is an important issue in an era of increasing literacy, and in a country whose religion placed so much emphasis on words and reading. The past decades have seen a number of influential studies on the impact of print in the early modern period.[21] But we still need more careful investigation of the ways in which print interacted with other forms of communication in the specific cultural context of post-Reformation England.

Clearly not all printed sources are equally good as windows on the process by which cultural values were disseminated and absorbed (or modified)

---

[16] Scribner, 'Is a history of popular culture possible?', p. 177.

[17] Chartier, *Cultural history*, p. 40.

[18] Bob Scribner criticizes Chartier's theory of 'consumption' for its failure to show ordinary people as creators. Scribner, 'Is a history of popular culture possible?', p. 184.

[19] For example, Ingram, 'Ridings, rough music and the "reform of popular culture"', pp. 79–113; Buchanan Sharp, 'Popular political opinion in England 1660–1685', *History of European Ideas*, 10 (1989), pp. 13–29; David Underdown, *Revel, riot and rebellion. Popular politics and culture in England 1603–1660* (Oxford, 1985).

[20] Scribner, 'Is a history of popular culture possible?', p. 184.

[21] Elizabeth L. Eisenstein, *The printing press as an agent of change* (2 vols. in 1, Cambridge, 1980 edn). Marshall McLuhan, *The Gutenberg galaxy* (Toronto, 1962). Walter J. Ong, *Rhetoric, romance and technology* (1971); Walter J. Ong, *Orality and literacy: the technologizing of the word* (1982).

by the wider society. The notion of 'cheap print' is a valid one, if used as a neutral category, not as a genre aimed exclusively at a definable social group. Although we should try to avoid assumptions about the readership, we must also take account of the basic social and economic realities which limited contact with printed texts for much of the populace. These realities included the cost of a work, its geographical distribution, and the level of reading skills which it presupposed. During our period, publishers themselves were increasingly adopting strategies to match these realities: by organizing a syndicate for the distribution of ballads, by using woodcut pictures to appeal to those on the fringes of literacy, by condensing longer stories into an inexpensive 24-page octavo format.[22]

The growing specialization of publishers in printed works targeted for humble readers could be seen as an agent of 'polarization'; of a growing gap between patrician and plebeian culture, as described by Anthony Fletcher and John Stevenson.[23] Yet, if the culmination of this process was the creation of a separated body of 'chap' literature for an identifiably 'plebeian' audience, this did not occur within the period under study here, and possibly not until the eighteenth century. Before 1640, it is likely that a large proportion of the buyers were drawn from the middling ranks of yeomen, husbandmen and tradespeople, and that even gentry readers were not uncommon.[24] If publishers did increasingly 'target' humbler readers, this should not necessarily be seen as a divisive phenomenon. Cheap print in this period was just as likely to be an instrument of social cohesion, as more people were brought into the reading public, and as stories, images and values permeated the multiple tiers of English society.

This 'shared culture' was disseminated along lines of communication which connected the country, both socially and geographically. The distribution of cheap print relied especially on a network of wayfarers: minstrels, broadside ballad sellers, interlude players, petty chapmen. Texts and their effects radiated outward to local communities from certain focal points: the marketplace, the parish church, the godly household, the inn or alehouse.[25]

The cultural historian Roger Chartier, while attacking the elite–popular divide, has set up a new dichotomy which seems equally rigid: that of city versus country. In the cities, print was 'everywhere present, posted, exhibited, cried in the streets, and highly visible'; but in the seventeenth century this 'familiarity that was the beginning of literacy' was almost exclusively

---

[22] See chs. 3, 4, 7.
[23] A.J. Fletcher and J. Stevenson, 'A polarised society?', in Fletcher and Stevenson, eds., *Order and disorder in early modern England* (Cambridge, 1985), pp. 1–15.
[24] See Frances Wolfreston, pp. 315–17.
[25] See chs. 1, 5.

the privilege of urban dwellers.[26] This may well be true of France, but
in England there can be no doubt that texts of one kind or another were
familiar in all parts of the realm. From the beginning of Elizabeth's reign,
injunctions required that the Lord's Prayer and other biblical sentences be
painted in every parish church, and this order was reinforced by visitations.[27]
In a Protestant country there was greater incentive to encourage
literacy, and most parishioners had some contact with bibles, catechisms,
prayer books or psalters, which were read aloud in church, and probably
handled, if not actually owned.[28] Broadside ballads were commonplace
from deepest Cambridgeshire to Lancashire, to the western counties; and
literature of the period most typically depicts the ballad seller in a rural
setting. Although early Elizabethan ballads were sometimes billed as 'A
warning to London' or addressed to 'London dames', by the second quarter
of the seventeenth century they were much more commonly given titles
like 'The cooper of Norfolke' or 'A pleasant new northerne song, called
the two York-shire lovers'.[29]

Some of these stories and their tunes may well have been picked up in
the alehouses of Norfolk and Yorkshire by the same pedlars and travelling
performers who later disseminated the printed ballads.[30] Even when they
were concocted in London by an anonymous hack, these printed wares
were not finished products like gloves or combs, to be used in much the
same way by each purchaser. If we are to choose a metaphor from the
chapman's pack, print was more like the 'scotch cloth' or 'coarse linen',
sold by the yard, to be made into something by the buyer.[31] In the parlance
of the new cultural history, we should not look at print in isolation, but
at how it was 'appropriated'.[32] Much of this study will focus on the single-
sheet broadside, chosen at first because, at a penny or less, it was the cheapest
form of print. Yet the broadside was not only a text to be read. It was
also, in fact primarily, a song to be sung, or an image to be pasted on

---

[26] Chartier, *The cultural uses of print*, pp. 347, 158–9, 166, 176.

[27] See pp. 217–18.

[28] On the importance of the Book of Common Prayer as a unifying force and an encouragement
to literacy, see John N. Wall jnr, 'The Reformation in England and the typographical
revolution: "By this printing ... the doctrine of the Gospel soundeth to all nations"', in
Gerald P. Tyson and Sylvia Wagonheim, eds., *Print and culture in the Renaissance: essays
on the advent of printing in Europe* (1986).

[29] 'A warning to London by the fall of Antwerp' [1577?], Collmann no. 69. 'A proper new
balade expressyng the fames, concerning a warning to al London dames' [1571], Collmann
no. 71. 'The cooper of Norfolke' [*c.* 1627], Pepys, I, 400. 'A pleasant new northerne song'
[*c.* 1630], Pepys, I, 240.

[30] John Taylor collected anecdotes from victualling houses for his *Wit and mirth. Chargeably
collected out of tavernes, ordinaries, innes ...* (1626).

[31] On the contents of the pedlar's pack, see Margaret Spufford, *The great reclothing of rural
England: petty chapmen and their wares in the seventeenth century* (1984).

[32] Chartier, *The cultural uses of print*, p. 6.

the wall. In these oral and visual forms, it had the potential to reach a much wider audience than its original buyers and its 'literate' readers.

The question of literacy is, of course, central to any study of print in this period. We know that by the 1640s roughly 30% of adult males in rural England could sign their names, with up to 78% fully 'literate' in London.[33] David Cressy's evidence shows how the ability to sign one's name was closely tied to social status, with marked differences across geographical regions. In 1600, 52% of East Anglian tradesmen and craftsmen could sign, compared with 80% in London. East Anglian yeomen and husbandmen were 61% and 21% 'literate', while in Durham and Northumberland the figures were much lower, at 23% and 13% respectively. Statistics for labourers are thin on the ground, but in the diocese of Norwich over the entire period 1580–1700, 15% could sign their names. This was a little better than the women, whose showing was only 11%.[34]

However, as Margaret Spufford has convincingly argued, these statistics are probably gross underestimates of *reading* ability.[35] Reading was taught before writing, and it is likely that many more rural people could get through the text of a broadside ballad than could sign their names to a Protestation Oath. In Sweden, a tradition of teaching reading alone, without writing, survived well into the nineteenth century, and the gap between these skills is verified in church examination registers.[36] Cressy's figures for early modern England may only represent the proportion of each group which remained in school from age seven to eight when writing was taught. Amongst husbandmen and labourers especially, there may be a large number who attended school up to the age of six, and learnt the primary skill of reading, but who were whisked away to join the labour force 'as soon as they were strong enough to contribute meaningfully to the family economy'.[37] The 'literacy' statistics should be taken as minimum figures, not as certainties.

Nevertheless, in a partially literate society, the most influential media were those which combined print with non-literate forms. Recent studies on the impact of the printing press have viewed the sixteenth and seventeenth centuries as a period in which oral and literate modes of communication

---

[33] David Cressy, *Literacy and the social order. Reading and writing in Tudor and Stuart England* (Cambridge, 1980), p. 72.

[34] *Ibid.*, pp. 146, 150, 152, 119.

[35] Margaret Spufford, 'First steps in literacy: the reading and writing experiences of the humblest seventeenth-century autobiographers', *Social History*, 4 (1979), pp. 407–35. See also Keith Thomas, 'The meaning of literacy in early modern England', in Gerd Baumann, ed., *The written word. Literacy in transition* (Oxford, 1986), p. 103.

[36] Egil Johansson, 'The history of literacy in Sweden', in Harvey J. Graff, ed., *Literacy and social development in the West: a reader* (Cambridge, 1981), pp. 181–2.

[37] Spufford, *Small books*, p. 26.

were closely intertwined.[38] Printed works were disseminated by word of mouth, transforming the culture of the 'illiterate', and oral modes of communication shaped the structure of printed works. The interesting process was not only the spread of literacy and readership, but the complex interweaving of the printed word with existing cultural practices. In Part I, we will look at how the broadside ballad interacted with oral and musical traditions. In Part II, we will see the broadside picture against the visual background of domestic wall painting and painted cloth. Only in Part III will we follow the development of 'cheap print' intended primarily for reading; first surveying a variety of short pamphlets, and then charting the beginnings of the 'penny chapbook' as a specialized product.

The dissemination of Protestant ideas will be used as a focus for this investigation. However, to describe these ballads, woodcuts and chapbooks as thoroughly 'Protestant' would be to overlook the way they blended the new ideas with older attitudes to religion and morality, just as they embraced existing oral and visual traditions. Protestant concepts and images were, like printed texts, the raw material which the purchaser could choose and shape as he wanted, according to his own needs and beliefs. We can only approach the buyer's perspective indirectly, by comparing the initial polemic of Protestant reformers with the religious ballads and chapbooks which found long-lasting commercial success.

There is little in this cheap godly print (and therefore in this study) about double predestination, ecclesiastical vestments, the position of the altar, or the prerequisites for communion. We should not assume that the audience had no interest in these matters, but that, when they did, it was satisfied elsewhere; in black-letter sermons and treatises, or discussions with neighbours, or catechizing sessions. The printed works in this study operated largely outside the sphere of the church. They were bought for entertainment, or to satisfy needs which the reader might not necessarily have defined as 'religious': the need for role models, for inspirational stories, for behavioural rules to give to their children, for guidance on the approach to death. As the cheap print trade developed and became more specialized, it seems to have become increasingly responsive to these needs, and therefore of particular interest to the 'social and cultural' historian, as well as to the historian of 'religion'.

---

[38] Eisenstein, *The printing press as an agent of change*, p. 129. Roger Chartier, 'Culture as appropriation: popular cultural uses in early modern France', in Stephen L. Kaplan ed., *Understanding popular culture: Europe from the middle ages to the nineteenth century* (Berlin, 1984), pp. 229–53. Ong, *Rhetoric, romance and technology*, pp. 23–47; Ong, *Orality and literacy*. Tyson and Wagonheim, eds., *Print and culture in the Renaissance*.

I

THE BROADSIDE BALLAD

Small and popular music

Any study of the impact of printing in England must take account of the fact that one of the first widespread and widely affordable forms of the printed word was the song. Thousands of ballads were churned from the London printing presses, not only to be read, but to be sung to popular tunes. There were roughly 3,000 distinct ballads published in the second half of the sixteenth century, the period when the Stationers' Register is most complete.[1] If we take 200 copies as the smallest run for which a printer would set up type, this would give us an absolute minimum of 600,000 ballads circulating in the second half of the sixteenth century.[2] If the runs were closer to 1,000 or 1,250, normal runs for a book in this period, the total number of copies would reach between 3 and 4 million.[3] These figures take no account of the possibility of numerous editions of the more popular ballads.

The printed broadside was the cheapest and most accessible form of print. In the year 1520, the Oxford bookseller John Dorne sold 170 ballads at a halfpenny each, with concessions for batches such as 7 for 3d. or 12 for 5d.[4] By 1641, the standard price was a penny: 'For a peny you may have all the Newes in England, of Murders, Flouds, Witches, Fires, Tempests, and what not, in one of Martin Parkers Ballads.'[5] Historians have assumed a standard penny price throughout our period, but it is possible

---

[1] For calculations see below, p. 42.

[2] In the very early days of printing, book editions of only 200–300 copies were common, although by the sixteenth century runs of 1,000 to 1,500 became the norm. (Philip Gaskell, *A new introduction to bibliography* (Oxford, 1972), pp. 160–1.)

[3] In 1587, an impression of 1,250 for Bullinger's *Decades* was taken as the norm. William A. Jackson, ed., *Records of the Court of the Stationers' Company 1602 to 1640* (1957), p.22.) In 1651, John Harris, the printer of a pamphlet called *The accuser sham'd* said that 'he knows not how many of them he printed; their ordinary Number of such Things, as they print, being One thousand'. (D.F. McKenzie, 'The London trade in the later seventeenth century' (Sandars Lectures, typescript on deposit in Cambridge University Library, 1976), p. 29.)

[4] F. Madan, ed., 'The day-book of John Dorne, bookseller in Oxford 1520', *Collectanae*, Proceedings of the Oxford Historical Society, 1st series (1885), pp. 71–178.

[5] Henry Peacham, *The worth of a penny* (1641), sig.D1.

that the rise only came around 1635, when book prices in general leapt by 40%.[6] In 1630, the leading ballad publishers (the 'partners') sold their ballads to hawkers at 13s4d. per ream, or a third of a penny each.[7] At a penny each to the customer, the ballad singer would have had to sell only a dozen ballads in a day to make 8d., the wage of a labourer in the building trades.[8] At a halfpenny to the public he would have had to sell forty-four ballads a day for the same wage; quite possible (one would think) at busy fairs, but high for an ordinary day on the road. The association of ballad sellers with petty crime does suggest that they had need to supplement their profits from legitimate sales. Probably the price was somewhere between a halfpenny and a penny, with room for haggling and concessions.

Scores of contemporary references in plays, diaries, and polemical tracts indicate the ubiquity of the ballad at all social levels.[9] As Nicholas Bownde commented in 1595: 'You must not onely look into the houses of great personages ... but also in the shops of artificers, and cottages of poor husbandmen, where you shall sooner see one of these newe Ballades ... than any of the Psalmes, and may perceive them to be cunninger in singing the one, than the other.'[10] For every ballad sold, any number of people could have come in contact with it. Reformers replying to 'popish rhymes' tell us that polemical ballads were 'scattered abroad' in places as diverse as Northampton in 1570, Lancashire in 1601, and 'the west parts' in 1604.[11] Ballads were stuck up on the walls in alehouses and private homes.[12] Bownde claims to have witnessed the interesting situation of illiterate cottagers pasting up ballads in order to 'learne' them later: 'and though they cannot read themselves, nor any of theirs, yet will have many Ballades set up in their houses, that so might learne them, as they shall have

---

[6] The penny price is assumed in Hyder E. Rollins, 'The black-letter broadside ballad', *Publications of the Modern Language Association*, 34 (1919), p. 296; R.S. Thomson, 'The Development of the broadside ballad trade and its influence upon the transmission of English folksongs' (Cambridge PhD, 1974), p. 42. On book prices, see Francis R. Johnson, 'Notes on English retail book-prices, 1550–1640', *The Library*, 5th ser., 5 (1950), pp. 89–90.

[7] Testimony of John Hamond in Chancery Interrogatories over the Symcocke patent (see ch. 3). Cited in Jackson, ed., *Records of the Court of the Stationers' Company*, p. xxi.

[8] Labourers' wages in 1580–1626 were 8d. per day; in 1626–39, from 8d. to 10d. (E.H. Phelps Brown and Sheila V. Hopkins, 'Seven centuries of building wages', in Eleanor M. Carus-Wilson, ed., *Essays in economic history II* (1962), p. 177.)

[9] A number of passages from contemporary literature which refer to ballads are reproduced in the appendix to Natascha Wurzbach, *Die englische straßenballade 1550–1650* (Munich, 1981).

[10] Nicholas Bownde, *The doctrine of the sabbath* (1595), p. 242.

[11] 'An answer to a papisticall byll, cast in the streetes of Northampton...' (Collmann, p. 171). 'A short poeme conteyning an answere to certen godles and seditious balledes spred abroad in Lancashire' (Arber, III, p. 187). 'An Answere to a popishe Rime latelie scatered abroade in the weste partes ...' (Arber, III, p. 209).

[12] See pp. 148–9, 194.

occasion'.[13] There was theoretically no man, woman or child who could not have access to a broadside ballad, at least in its oral form, when it was sung aloud.

In what way did the broadside's status as song restrict and shape what could be said with it? We need to know how the medium of song was used in ways specific to early modern England. The same ballad might have had quite a different meaning when chanted by a vagrant ballad singer, or drunken dancers on the village green, from that it acquires within the repertory of the twentieth-century 'folksinger'. It would appear that the 'ballad' was once performed in a wider variety of circumstances, including minstrelsy, dance, theatrical jigs, three-man-songs and other recreational forms now extinct. This set of associations of balladry affected the reformers' attitudes to be discussed in chapter 2. In this chapter I will try to map out the routes by which the printed broadside infiltrated the existing musical culture.

Like the modern 'folksong', the early modern notion of a 'ballad' concealed a wide variety of song-types, from courtly wooing song to Scottish battle legend. Such distinctions were constantly breaking down as a natural result of the process of oral dissemination. 'Once the ballad style had crystallized in the late Middle Ages, it was the cumulative variations over decades and centuries that remade all manner of diverse poetry – carols, episodes from romances, debates, coronachs, and the multifarious poetry of the minstrel repertory – into ballads.'[14]

The advent of print must have accelerated the divorce of a song's form and content from any specialized social function. The broadside ballad publishers borrowed tunes and stories from court, city and country without discrimination, and distributed them to an equally varied audience. George Puttenham, writing around 1570, described several situations in which popular song was performed:

[so doth] the over busie and too speedy returne of one maner of tune, too much annoy & as it were glut the eare, unlesse it be in small & popular Musickes
[1] song by these *Cantabanqui* upon benches and barrels heads where they have none other audience than boys or countrey fellowes that passe by them in the streete, [2] or else by blind harpers or such like taverne minstrels that give a fit of mirth for a groat, & their matters being for the most part stories of old time, as the tale of Sir Topas, the reports of Bevis of Southampton, Guy of Warwicke, Adam Bell and Clymme of the Clough, & such other old romances or historical rimes, [3] made purposely for recreation of the common people at Christmasse diners and brideales, and in tavernes & alehouses, and such other places of base resort,

[13] Bownde, *Doctrine of the sabbath*, p. 241.
[14] Albert B. Friedman, 'The oral-formulaic theory of balladry – a re-rebuttal', in James Porter, ed., *The ballad image: essays presented to Bertrand Harris Bronson* (Los Angeles, 1983), p. 218.

[4] also they be used in Carols and rounds and such light or lascivious Poems, which are commonly more commodiously uttered by these buffons or vices in playes then by any other person.[15]

Puttenham's description provides a good starting point for distinguishing between the major possible contexts in which the ballad could be used, if we may take a few liberties with his categories and expand on them from other sources. He begins by making a clear distinction between two types of professional or semi-professional ballad singers: the '*Cantabanqui* upon benches and barrels heads' versus the 'blind harpers or such like taverne minstrels' with their 'historical rimes'. The former we may, perhaps, equate with the Autolycus-style broadside ballad singers-and-sellers so complained of in other contemporary treatises.[16] Puttenham's reference to 'recreation of the common people' may be extended to include not only paid performances of 'old romances', but also amateur song and dance. Finally, ballads could be dramatized in various ways; incorporated into the antics of the 'buffons or vices' in moral interludes, or sung in dialogue form at the local alehouse.

BLIND HARPERS AND TAVERN MINSTRELS

Puttenham's harpers and minstrels are the best starting point, since with their 'stories of old time' they might appear to represent a traditional, orally transmitted form of music. However, it can be no coincidence that the titles he mentions – 'Sir Topas', 'Bevis of Southampton', 'Guy of Warwicke', 'Adam Bell' and 'Clymme of the Clough' – are stories which had been in print in quarto form since 1500, and which more recently had begun to appear in broadside ballad form.[17] Their origins are literary and genteel, in the chivalric romances of the thirteenth and fourteenth centuries.[18] These stories may also have been passed around orally by the minstrels, but their structure, shape and very preservation cannot have been unaffected by the circulation of printed copies. The minstrels seem to have occupied a position as mediators between older musical traditions and the London printing press.

---

[15] George Puttenham, *The arte of English poesie* (1589), ed. G.D. Willcock and A. Walker (2nd edn, Cambridge, 1970), sig.M1 of first edn. The editors date the likely composition of Puttenham's first draft to c. 1569. Bracketed letters and spacing are my own.

[16] In Italian 'cantabanchi' are strolling players, buskers; charlatans.

[17] STC 1987, 12540, 1805.7. 'Guy of Warwicke' was first registered to Richard Jones in 1592, 'to the tune of, Was ever man soe tost in love' (Rollins Index no. 2117). 'Adam Bell' was entered as a ballad to John King in 1557–8 (Rollins Index no. 10). See also Table 4.

[18] 'Guy of Warwicke' appeared in France in 1232–42, and in England around 1300. 'Bevis of Hampton' appeared in France around 1200 (as 'Boeve de Haumtone') and in England around 1300. From Lee C. Ramsay, *Chivalric romances: popular literature in medieval England* (Bloomington, Indiana, 1983), p. 232.

The term 'minstrel' did not mean the same thing in 1570 as it had a century earlier. Puttenham's derogatory attitude to 'taverne minstrels that give a fit of mirth for a groat' bears witness to the sixteenth-century descent of the 'minstrel' from respected professional musician to the status of vagabond. The official seal on this debasement was Elizabeth's statute of 1572, which applied the vagrancy laws to all 'common players in interludes and minstrels' who were not under aristocratic or royal patronage.[19] There had always been a hierarchy of music makers, based on both patronage and skill, from the king's trumpeters down through the minstrels attached to noble households to the independent wayfarers. However, by the sixteenth century there was another factor: musical literacy. To merit the newer respectable term 'musician', one now had to be able to read music, to sing as well as play, to teach wealthy amateurs, and even to compose part-music for domestic recreation.[20] The madrigal writer and music teacher Thomas Whythorne had an inflated expectation of the skills required of 'musicians', writing of 'minstrels' with contempt (*c.* 1576):

I kannot heer leav out or let pas to speak of an other sort that do lyv by miuzik and yet ar no miuzisians at all. And thos be thei, who after thei hav learned A littl to sing priksong, or els hav either learned by hand, or by ear, or els by tabulatiur, to play or sownd on miuzikall instriuments, such miuzik az hath bin and iz mad by otherz and not by them bianby thei will ywzurp on miuzik, and akkownt and kall them selvz miuzisians, of the which petifoggers of miuzik, ther be both skoolmasterz, singing-men, and minstrels.[21]

Despite Whythorne's obvious derogatory bias, he was probably correct in his estimate of the minstrels' relative lack of familiarity with written music or 'priksong', and of the common practice of learning an instrument 'by hand, or by ear'. An authority on late medieval music writes that 'throughout the Middle Ages minstrelsy was performed according to an aural tradition, a minstrel being taught his craft without the aid of written music and performing from memory in the same way'.[22] Large numbers of the wandering harpers and fiddlers 'such as range the country, riming and singing songs in taverns, ale-houses, inns and other public assemblies'[23] must have continued within this aural tradition.

The aural transmission of the *music* did not, of course, preclude the use

---

[19] The provisions of this statute were reiterated in a Vagrancy Act of 1597. (A.L. Beier, *Masterless men: the vagrancy problem in England 1560–1640* (1985), p. 96.)

[20] I am grateful to Richard Rastall of the Department of Music at Leeds University for correspondence on the different skills of 'musicians' and 'minstrels' in the sixteenth century. His comments were very tentative, and any misinterpretations are my own.

[21] *The autobiography of Thomas Whythorne*, ed. James M. Osborn (Oxford, 1961), p. 246.

[22] Richard Rastall, 'Alle hefne makyth melody', in Paula Neuss, ed., *Aspects of early English drama* (Cambridge, 1983), p. 8.

[23] Philip Stubbes, *Anatomy of abuses* (1583), cited in William Chappell, *Popular music of the olden time* (2 vols., 1853–9), p. 406.

of written or printed song *texts* as an aid to the memory. That these were common by the mid-sixteenth century is indicated in the interrogation of a Norfolk minstrel whose apprentices were accused of singing a song against the mass in 1554. James Wharton was immediately asked 'if they had eny bookes of songes', which indeed they did.[24] There is no indication that these books also contained music.

Descriptions of minstrels singing anti-papist songs or 'stories of old time' indicate another way in which the meaning of the term had changed from medieval usage. Until the early sixteenth century 'minstrel' had referred to an instrumental musician, while professional vocalists were called 'singing men'.[25] Many instruments used by minstrels, such as bagpipes, trumpets and other wind instruments, had precluded singing.[26] But in the sixteenth century the term was increasingly applied to musicians using harps, lutes or fiddles to accompany vocal performance.[27] Eventually these minstrels were lumped together with unskilled performers such as broadside ballad singers.

Broadly, the sixteenth-century 'minstrel' may still be distinguished from the broadside ballad singer-and-seller, in that his living was based primarily on the performance rather than its printed artefact. One would expect from a minstrel the presence (or at least greater importance) of musical accompaniment on harp or fiddle, and a greater role of songs learnt or 're-created' from oral tradition. However, there must have been a continuum from the most unmusical pedlar-cum-ballad-seller, through minstrels using broadside texts to various degrees, to the 'blind harper' whose reliance on oral transmission probably represented an extreme (though not total) immunity from print.[28] Ballads passed down from years of tradition could co-exist in the minstrel's repertory with songs originating from manuscripts or printed texts, the latter either learnt directly from a broadside, or via any number of oral mediators.

We have evidence for this variety of sources in the repertory of one such minstrel, Richard Sheale of Tamworth in Staffordshire, recorded in a collection of 'songs and ballads' compiled between 1557 and 1565.[29] Historians, succumbing to wishful thinking, have long supposed the entire manuscript to be Sheale's notebook of songs from his repertory; however, Hyder E.

[24] REED Norwich, p. 34.
[25] John Stevens, *Music and poetry in the early Tudor court* (1961), p. 320.
[26] Richard Leighton Greene, *The early English carols* (2nd edn, Oxford, 1977), pp. cxxxv–vi
[27] For example, Richard Sheale (below, pp. 16–21), James Wharton's apprentices (above).
[28] Peter Burke, *Popular culture in early modern Europe* (1978), p. 255. The blind harper was not only a character of legend, but appears in civic and household account books throughout our period. (See Walter Lincoln Woodfill, *Musicians in English Society from Elizabeth to Charles I* (Princeton, 1953), pp. 257, 262.)
[29] MS Ashmole 48. Reprinted in Wright.

Rollins argued convincingly years ago that MS Ashmole 48 is an ordinary commonplace book copied largely from broadsides.[30] Such commonplace books show that the broadside was familiar amongst the most 'elite' groups of sixteenth-century society, yet, at the same time, suggest an ambivalent attitude to print. Rather than pasting the broadsides in, the songs were copied out longhand, 'as if the action of writing were a condition of personal appropriation'.[31] This act transformed an ephemeral, commercial product into a private or household possession, preserved for posterity in a bound volume.

Although not his own notebook, the manuscript does contain five pieces credited to Richard Sheale, which provide us with a glimpse of the kinds of songs he sang. They include an autobiographical ballad which vividly illustrates the role such a minstrel could play as a cultural conduit, spanning great geographical and social distances. According to Sheale's account, he still belonged to the medieval system of patronage of minstrels, for he was under the protection of the Earl of Derby. This association would guarantee him immunity from the vagabondage laws, and apparently an audience amongst the earl's acquaintances:

> And my lord Strang also on me dyde tak compassion.
> For whos sakys I thank Gode I have ben well regardyde,
> And among ther lovyng frenddes I have ben well rewardyde.[32]

However, their payments were not enough to keep body and soul together, and Sheale fell into a relationship of increasing debt to some 'frenddes in London'. The purpose of Sheale's autobiographical song was to illicit sympathy after he was allegedly robbed on the highway of £60 in gold which he and his wife had collected together to clear his debts.

At the least, Sheale's contacts in London show that he had a high degree of mobility, and the probability of contact with the broadside ballad trade. But it also seems that Sheale was involved in the chapman's trade himself:

> But I hade frenddes in London whos namys I can declare,
> That at all tymys wolde lende me xx[lds] worth off ware.[33]

Sheale may have been buying silks and linen for his wife, who was a specialized chapwoman. Her route covered fairs and markets in Staffordshire, especially at Lichfield and Atherstone, both within 10 miles of Tamworth:

---

[30] Wright, p. iv. Thomson, 'Development of the broadside ballad trade', ch. 2. Hyder E Rollins, 'Concerning Bodleian MS Ashmole 48', *Modern Language Notes*, 34 (1919), pp. 340–51.

[31] Roger Chartier, *The cultural uses of print in early modern France*, trans. Lydia C. Cochrane (Princeton, 1987), p. 234. Chartier is here describing how a textile worker of Lille in the 1680s used to copy the news from printed *canards* into his journal.

[32] Wright, p. 160.

[33] *Ibid.*, p. 157.

> My wyff in dede ys a sylke woman be her occupacion,
> And lynen clothe moste cheffly was here greatyste trayd,
> And at fearis and merkyttes she solde sale-war that she made,
> As sherttes, smockys, partlyttes, hede clotthes, and other thingges,
> As sylk threde, and eggynges, shurte banddes, and stringes.
> At Lychfelde merkyte and Addarston good costomars she fownde;
> And also in Tamworth, wher I dwell, she took may a j¹.[34]

They may have travelled to markets as a pair, he singing and she selling. Given Sheale's involvement with both minstrelsy and peddling, it is quite likely that some of the wares he picked up in London included broadside ballads. It was common for the trade to be conducted on a sale-or-return basis, and as a sideline for a chapman dealing chiefly in other goods.[35] The suggestion that our 'minstrel' was also a 'ballad seller' must remain speculation, but some contact with broadsides during his travels will be apparent from the discussion of his songs below.

Not only did Sheale's work take him over 100 miles south-east to London, but also some 80 miles in the opposite direction, north-west to Ormskirk in Lancashire. He attended the Countess of Derby's funeral there, as we know from his eye-witness account.[36] As he travelled in this great diagonal swathe across the country, he must have stopped over at victualling houses or at the households of his patron's 'lovyng frenddes', performing along the way. The contacts of Sheale and his wife between them covered the entire social scale, from the noble Lancashire household, to the shops of London tradesmen, to the Staffordshire markets, to the world of the local alehouse-keepers in Tamworth:

> My neabors dyd caus me to mayk a pot off ale,
> And I think God off his goodnes, I had a very good sale.
> Fur a bushell off malt, I do put youe owt off dowte,
> I had fyv pownd off mony, or nyghe thereabowte.[37]

Sheale's misfortunes forced him into ale-brewing, one of the last resorts of the poor, and into begging for help 'abrowde among the congrigacion' by way of his song. His story shows the medieval-style earl's minstrel slipping down the social scale towards the nether world of broadside ballad sellers who were persecuted as vagrants and often forced into petty crime. He commented that his sorry economic state was not uncommon among minstrels:

---

[34] *Ibid.*, p. 158.
[35] Margaret Spufford, *Small books and pleasant histories. Popular fiction and its readership in seventeenth-century England* (1981), pp. 91, 102–3 n. 9; Margaret Spufford, *The great reclothing of rural England: petty chapmen and their wares in the seventeenth century* (1984), pp. 57, 62.
[36] Wright, p. 181.
[37] *Ibid.*, p. 160.

> I thought beth reason of my harpe no man wolde me susspecte;
> For minstrels offt with mony the be not moche infecte.[38]

The account in a minstrel's own words puts flesh on a picture confirmed in other records, such as that of John Parkins who 'had purportedly served Lord Stafford, but was playing at fairs in Essex in 1634, and four years earlier had petitioned Stafford quarter sessions for poor relief'.[39]

How did Sheale's compositions come to be included in the commonplace book? Rollins suggested that Sheale sent written copies of his songs to the compilers. Another possibility might be that these five songs (unlike most of the rest of the manuscript) were copied down from an oral performance by Sheale, accompanied on his harp. The compilers may have belonged to the household of Sheale's patron, or a neighbouring household which might take an interest in his personal accounts of fortune and mishap. Whether these songs reached the compilers in oral or manuscript form, they still retain elements of orality. The irregular metre, the repetition of ideas, abundance of 'filler' phrases, and begging of money from the audience all communicate the flavour of a semi-extemporized performance.

Sheale's five songs show varying degrees of personal creativity as opposed to the influence of commercial broadsides. At the extreme of individuality is the account of his robbery, just described, which appears to be entirely his own composition. In a less idiosyncratic piece, Sheale thanked his host or patron for his hospitality. This reads more like a standard formula of gratitude to the host, cobbled together from commonplace rhymes and clichés:

> I perseve withowt phable,
> Ye kepe a good table;
> Sum tym I wyll be your gest,
> Or els I wear a beaste,
> Knowyng yore mynd,
> Yf I wolde not be so kynde,
> Sum tym to tast your cuppe,
> And with youe dyne and suppe.[40]

At the other extreme from these personal songs is the grand historical ballad of which Sheale was certainly not the creator, but only the transmitter. Sheale's famous legacy is the earliest known version of 'Chevy Chase'.[41] He may have learnt this ballad from oral tradition, but it is also likely

---

[38] *Ibid.*, p. 158.
[39] Beier, *Masterless men*, p. 97.
[40] Wright, p. 162.
[41] *Ibid.*, p. 24. Thomson, 'Development of the broadside ballad trade', ch. 2. Simpson, p. 99.

that there was a broadside copy in circulation of which we have no record.[42] This ballad fits into our stereotypical picture of the minstrel's repertory, Puttenham's 'old romances or historicall rimes'.

Sheale's fourth song, a godly song, has less in common with narrative tradition than with the literacy compositions produced especially for the London printing press. It is impossible to know whether this reflected Sheale's own piety, or if it was brought out specially for the benefit of the manuscript's compiler, whose biases can be seen in the predominance of the religious and moral in over half the pieces of his collection. The song begins 'Remember man thy frayle estate, repent thy folles past', and is similar to many other Protestant ballads written early in Elizabeth's reign, containing the usual exhortations to live by Scripture, renounce worldly joy and pray for grace.[43] It may have been composed by Sheale, but the relative complexity of vocabulary and ideas compared with his other pieces suggests that it was probably learnt from a broadside or manuscript copy.

The last composition bearing Sheale's name, an epitaph for his patroness Lady Margaret, Countess of Derby, as Rollins has already remarked, 'bears every sign of having been composed for publication by the ballad press'.[44] It is headed with a long-winded title in typical broadside form: 'the epith off the dethe off the ryghte honorable lady Margrete countes of Darbe, which departyde this world the xix[th] day off January, and was buryede the xxiii[ti] off Phebruary, in anno Domini 1558, on whosse soll God have mercye, Amen, quothe Rycharde Sheale'.[45] Sheale would certainly have been capable of composing this rather homely account of the countess's last farewells to her family and household, and of her good character:

> When that he [the earl] saw that she was dede, he wept and mad gret mone,
> For he lovyde here well, and she lovyde him, all this ys ryght well knowen.[46]

Epitaphs of nobility and gentry make up a substantial proportion of surviving sixteenth-century broadsides.[47] With the growing importance of the printed word, it was no longer enough for a death to be marked by an oral tribute from the household's minstrel: now there was apparently a desire to have this eulogy legitimized in print, and distributed in broadside form. The responsibility fell to minstrels like Sheale, who had one foot in London and the other in noble households in the provinces. Minstrels and ballad hacks could be overlapping categories.

---

[42] The first entry to the 'ballad partners' in 1624 (Arber, IV, p. 131) almost certainly records a transfer of a ballad already in print.
[43] Wright, p. 54.
[44] Rollins, 'Concerning Bodleian MS Ashmole 48', p. 351.
[45] Wright, p. 179.
[46] *Ibid.*, p. 180.
[47] See Rollins Index nos. 725–71.

Whether or not Sheale's epitaph was ever brought to print, his appropriation of broadside style for the title suggests that the repertory of this
minstrel was influenced by broadside ballads. The fact that the compilers
of MS Ashmole 48 included Sheale's own compositions mixed up with pieces
copied from broadsides also indicates that contemporaries did not perceive
any firm distinction between minstrelsy and broadside balladry.

Richard Sheale, with his pedlar wife and his broadside connections, represents an impecunious minstrel who lived close to the fringe world of the
itinerant ballad seller. However, there were others still described as minstrels
who were more financially secure, and more musically versatile. These minstrels had begun to acquire the skills approaching those demanded of a
'musician' by Whythorne.[48] In the will of John Lancaster of Great Yar-
mouth, 'minstrel' (1558), he leaves to his two apprentices 'my two basse
vialles' and 'all my smalle Instrumentes that lieth abought in my howse
& my pricksonge bookes evenlye to parte betwyne them'.[49] The skills
required before obtaining the respected position of a city wait are outlined
in the apprenticeship indenture of Thomas Knott, son of a husbandman
of Catton, Norfolk, to one Michael Knott, rowmason and Norwich wait:
'Also the sayede Michaell Knote further grauntithe to teache the sayed Thomas Knott to play in and uppon the vyoll vyolettes and harpe as allso to
synge playnesonge & pryksonge at his owne proper costes and charges.'[50]

Yet even the civic music of the waits was not so far removed from the
written or printed ballad. We have records of the role of waits in performing
and disseminating 'filthy songes or sonnettes'. In the House Books of the
York city council for 1611 is a case brought by the religious fraternity
of St Anthony (taken over by the city at dissolution in 1547):

against Richard Bradley and his associates waites of this Cittye alledginge thereby
that the waites have [nowe] of late devised certaine scandelous libells songes or
sonnettes against the saide Auncient Guild and fraternitye and the same have publike-
lie sounge in diverse places ... [Richard Bradley] saieth that he & his wief beinge
at Lowth [Louth] in Lincolnshire at Easter next shalbe thre yeres had the same
& diverse other songes given hym by the waites ther, and saieth, that he did not
singe it in disgrace of the saide guild or in discreditt of the Maister and the keepers
thereof.[51]

The exact nature of Bradley's libel is lost, but the interesting point is the
exchange of songs between waits of different cities; songs which were 'given'
rather than just taught, and therefore must have been recorded in script

---

[48] Rastall roughly dates this shift to 'after about 1530, when the old-style minstrel began
to be superseded by musically-literate instrumentalists (such as the Coventry wait James
Hewet)'. Rastall, in Neuss, ed., *Aspects of early English drama*, p. 142 n. 6.
[49] REED Norwich, p. 44.
[50] *Ibid.*, p. 46.
[51] REED York, p. 535.

or print. Only politically or morally dangerous examples reach the record books, but, as Bradley says, 'diverse other songes' were disseminated this way. A similar case in Norwich in 1554 involved the exchange between two ordinary minstrels of a song 'against the Masse and the godly procedinges of the Catholike faythe of the churche, touching therein the homnor and dignytie of the Quenes highnes'.[52] James Wharton, a minstrel from East Winch, near King's Lynn, obtained a copy of the anti-Catholic song from 'a Mynstrell at Wyndham at one castelten hows at the signe of the Wastell xiiij daies now passed Which Mynstrell playeth uppon a Harpe, and is called Robert Gold. and further he knoweth ain not'.[53]

The high degree of mobility amongst waits and other minstrels meant that the songs they performed were disseminated to all corners of England, including the far north. In Newcastle, between February and August 1562, the Chamberlains' Account Books record payment to the waits of Darlington in county Durham, Cockermouth and Carlisle in Cumberland, Leeds and Thirsk in Yorkshire; and to minstrels from Ireland and Scotland.[54] Over the Christmas season in 1614–15, Carlisle was visited not only by the waits of various other towns in Cumberland and Westmorland, but also those from Lancaster, Lincoln and even Bristol.[55] Between these relatively official visits, there were many wanderers. The accounts of Carlisle and of neighbouring Naworth Castle show a number of payments each year to musical nomads such as 'a piper that came out of Lankyshire', 'two fiddlers at the gate', 'a knightes musicions yat came oute of Yorkshyer' and 'j scotes gentlewomanminstrell'.[56]

Not only did the Bristol waits make the long voyage north to Cumberland, but northern waits came south. In 1633, Coventry was a stop-over for the waits of Preston, Halifax, Ripon and Kendal, as well as, more predictably, from cities with a radius of about 50 miles, like Shrewsbury, Derby, Nottingham and Newark.[57] Nor was the music of the waits heard only in the major towns and cities. In 1511, twenty-eight townships of western Cambridgeshire contributed sums toward a pageant of St George, held at the village of Bassingbourn. Minstrels and waits were hired, for a lump sum of 5s.11d., to come out into the countryside from Cambridge for three days.[58]

[52] REED Norwich, p. 34.
[53] *Ibid.*, pp. 34–5.
[54] REED Newcastle, pp. 30–2. In these examples, I am choosing peak periods of the year, but not exceptional years.
[55] REED Cumberland, Westmorland, Gloucestershire, pp. 80–1.
[56] Woodfill, *Musicians in English Society*, p. 261. REED Cumberland, Westmorland, Gloucestershire, pp. 90, 66.
[57] REED Coventry, p. 434.
[58] Margaret Spufford, *Contrasting communities. English villagers in the sixteenth and seventeenth centuries* (Cambridge, 1974), p. 248; Spufford, *Small books*, p. 229.

The minstrels and waits were by no means a class apart from the rest of society, but on the contrary could come from the humblest social levels. Walter Woodfill has described the background of most professional musicians (somewhat anachronistically) as 'lower middle class'. He draws from the Register of the Freemen of the City of York, which records the sons of a grocer, a wright, a tailor, a porter, a labourer and two tapissers becoming musicians in Elizabeth's reign. In turn, the sons of a minstrel free in Mary's reign (to give just one example) became a tailor, a glover and a goldsmith.[59] The songs and perhaps some of the musical skills of the minstrels must have permeated the lives of their families, neighbours and friends in these other trades. Some professional musicians were only part-time, such as the Norwich apprentice Thomas Knott who was also to learn the trade of a rowmason. At the end of his term, his master was to present him with the following goods: 'iij li a suffycient vyoll a vyolet and a harpe one trowell onn plumbe rewle on hameraxe on square and doble apparell &c. in Wollen & lynnen &c'.[60] And, of course, our minstrel Richard Sheale was also of humble origins, married to a pedlar woman. The minstrels' texts and tunes must have travelled extensively; not only to the distant regions of Lancashire, Yorkshire and Norfolk via a network of itinerant minstrels, but also to the nether regions of society via a network of their familial and social contacts.

The performances of waits and minstrels were probably the most musical context in which ordinary people would encounter popular songs. The versions played and sung by musically literate professionals would be the closest most people would hear to the tunes as we have received them, recorded in lute, cittern and virginal manuscripts, complete with ornamentations, variations and adaptations to the tastes of the elite.[61] In the performance of able musicians, the music could have been the most important feature of the ballad, invested with a large part of its atmosphere, emotion and meaning. At the other end of the spectrum, we have the performance of the unskilled ballad seller, where the text became all-important, and the tune little more than a hook upon which to hang it.

CANTABANQUI UPON BENCHES

Unlike the skilled minstrel, the broadside ballad seller used his vocal performance primarily as a sales pitch for the printed text. William Brown described in 1616 how the technique of suspense was used in a marketplace performance:

[59] Woodfill, ed., *Musicians in English society*, p. 244.
[60] REED Norwich, p. 46.
[61] See the tunes in Simpson.

> Ballad-mongers on a Market-day
> Taking their stand, one (with as harsh a noyce
> As ever Cart-wheele made) squeakes the sad choice
> Of Tom the Miller with a golden thumbe,
> Who crost in love, ran mad, and deafe, and dumbe,
> Halfe part he chants, and will not sing it out,
> But thus bespeakes to his attentive rout:
> Thus much for love I warbled from my brest,
> And gentle friends, for mony take the rest.[62]

Even if the seller could do more than 'squeake' or 'chant' the story, it was still an indispensable part of his trade, necessary for drawing in the customers and getting them 'hooked' by the plot. There was no question of just setting the ballad sheets out in a stall like books; they were written for oral performance.

The dubious musical quality of such performances is not surprising. It appears that most ballad sellers, unlike minstrels, were not primarily musicians at all, but pedlars, either working independently, in the style of Autolycus, or in the hire of the ballad publishers. A passage from Henry Chettle's *Kind-harts dreame* [1593?] describes the latter type of arrangement:

no stationer, who after a little bringing them uppe to singing brokerie, takes into his shop some fresh men, and trusts his olde searvantes of a two months standing with a dossen groates worth of ballads. In which, if they proove thrifty, hee makes them prety chapmen, able to spred more pamphlets by the state forbidden then all the booksellers in London.[63]

The inventories of the post-Restoration cheap print publishers substantiate this picture of a close economic relationship with some of their distributors.[64] From the government's point of view, the closer the better: a Star Chamber decree of 1637 required that all distributers of print must serve a seven years' apprenticeship within the Stationers' Company.[65] However, as one would expect, this decree was a response to an existing problem. Ballad sellers were more often guildless, 'masterless' men, and our records of them come almost solely from their prosecutions as vagrants.

The most frequent references to 'ballad singers', as such, outside London can be found in Norwich, the second city of the realm. A half-dozen ballad singers appear in the Norwich Court Books from 1600 to 1640, with orders forbidding them to practise their trade and sometimes exiling them from the city. On 9 August 1600, the ballad singer Richard Rogers was com-

[62] William Brown, *Britannia's pastorals. The second booke* (1616), p. 11.
[63] Henry Chettle, *Kind-harts dreame. Conteining five apparitions, with their invectives against abuses raigning* [1593?], sig.C2v.
[64] Spufford, *Small books*, p. 91. I have checked the records of the Prerogative Court of Canterbury, the Archdeaconry and Commissary Courts, but have found no inventory for a pre-1640 publisher of ballads or chapbooks.
[65] Beier, *Masterless men*, p. 92.

manded to depart from the city before Saturday on pain of whipping. By 13 September he had found a widow who was willing to marry him, and who went to the mayor for permission. But the ruse was unsuccessful: 'mr mayor answered he hadd nothing to doe with making of marriages but willed hir to follow hir husbonde & that neyther of them after marriage shall tarry in Norwiche/ he being no better then a rogishe vagrante.'[66]

In the Norwich records the singing and selling of ballads are invariably mentioned together. William Nynges was part of a husband-and-wife team, both ordered in 1605 not to 'singe nor sell any Ballettes within this Cytty after this day upon payne of whippynge'. In 1614, James Dickon was 'Inioyned not to singe Ballades nor to sell eyther Ballades or Alminackes in the market after this day.' Alexander Lawes was 'forbidden to use sellynge or singinge of Balletes' in 1629, but was apprehended again thirteen years later, when the authorities seized 'thirty Libellous & scandalous ballettes which he was singinge of in this Citty & puttinge to sale which were burned in the open market'.[67] These real-life balladeers may have had no more musical talent than the squeaking ballad monger with his performance of 'Tom the Miller'. But the fact that they did sing confirms again that the ballad was considered to be a performance, and not just a printed text to be sold and read, detached from its tune.

Ballad sellers also reached the Wiltshire record books, which include the rare survival of a 'register of passports' for vagrants apprehended in Salisbury.[68] In 1616 'Apprice Williams, a ballad-singer and vagrant' was sent home from Salisbury to Goldhanger in Essex. In 1630 'Edward Kerbye, a ballad-seller, wandering' claimed he came from Holborne, London.[69] Another London man, Walter Plummer of Southwark was stopped at Trowbridge fair in 1620, 'carrying with him a store of ballads to sing in his travels'. And in the 1650s, when ballads were banned, singers were arrested in Devizes and Bristol.[70]

Ballads were even to be found lying about on the roads of Wiltshire, according to a petty chapman at Stalbridge fair accused of stealing money: 'he sayeth that he found itt folded up in a Ballad in the highway neare Warminster'.[71] Even if this is a fabrication, the fact that such a story sprang immediately to mind shows how commonplace ballads were in this region. Ballad sellers apprehended in this area were quite likely to be on their way from London heading further south and west. Of those vagrants described

---

[66] REED Norwich, p. 115.
[67] *Ibid.*, pp. 126, 141, 200–1, 237.
[68] 'Register of passports for vagrants 1598–1669', in Paul Slack, *Poverty in early-Stuart Salisbury*, Wiltshire Record Society, vol. 31 (Devizes, 1975).
[69] *Ibid.*, pp. 49, 58.
[70] Beier, *Masterless men*, p. 98.
[71] BL Harleian MS 6715, fol. 98v.

as 'chapman', 'chapwoman' or 'petty chapman' caught in Salisbury between 1598 and 1640, most were either from London (four of them) or from the southern and western counties of Hampshire, Somerset, Dorset and Devon (eight).[72] These chapmen probably plied their wares at least as far as the towns they described as home; and some of them may have been carrying ballads among the other trinkets in their packs.

Unfortunately nothing like the Salisbury register appears to survive for the midlands or the north, and other sources for the history of vagrancy are sparse in these areas.[73] My search through a number of the quarter sessions records available in print yielded nothing on 'ballad singers' or 'ballad sellers'.[74] This may be partly a problem of terminology: very few of the vagrants appear to have called themselves 'ballad sellers' as such. In A.L. Beier's statistics on the occupations of vagrants, they may be among the 7–10% of vagrants described as 'petty chapmen'.[75] Others may be hidden among the 'apprentices and servants' who made up almost a quarter of Beier's masterless men *c.* 1620–*c.* 1640.[76] Still others, trained in any number of trades, may have sold ballads on the side, or for brief periods between other jobs. The fluidity of 'occupations' is epitomized by the Wiltshire man who was 'sometimes a weaver, sometimes a surgeon, sometimes a minstrel, sometimes a dyer, and now a bullard'.[77]

The paucity of 'ballad singers' or 'ballad sellers' in the records is not just a semantic problem, then, but may tell us something about the degree

---

[72] Slack, *Poverty in early-Stuart Salisbury.* From London and environs: Register nos. 82, 152, 288, 476. From the south and west: nos. 144, 156, 192, 293, 344, 366, 387, 551.

[73] Beier, *Masterless men,* p. 35. Excepting Cheshire and Somerset, Beier's statistics on vagrants' occupations do not stretch more than 100 miles from London. (Table XI is drawn from London, Wiltshire, Essex, Leicester, Norfolk, Somerset and Chester.)

[74] The following records were covered: J.C. Atkinson, ed., *Quarter sessions records 1605–47,* The North Riding Record Society, vols, 1–4 (1884–6). J.H.E. Bennett and J.C. Dewhurst, eds., *Quarter sessions records with other records of the justices of the peace for the county palatine of Chester 1559–1760,* Record Society of Lancashire and Cheshire, vol. 94 (1940). S.A.H. Burne, ed., *Quarter sessions rolls 1581–1606,* William Salt Archeological Society: Collections for a History of Staffordshire (5 vols., Kendal, 1931–40). John F. Curwen, ed., *Records relating to the barony of Kendale,* Cumberland and Westmorland Antiquarian and Archeological Society, Record or Chartulary Series, vol. 6 (Kendal, 1926). James Tait, ed., *Lancashire quarter sessions records 1590–1606,* Chetham Society (Manchester, 1917). For the south, I looked at John Cordy Jeaffreson, ed., *Middlesex county records,* Middlesex County Record Society (4 vols., 1886–92). H.C. Johnson, ed., *Minutes of proceedings in sessions, 1563 and 1574 to 1592,* Wiltshire County Records (Devizes, 1949).
After this sampling, the negligible returns for the volume of material covered did not seem to justify visits to the various county record offices on speculation. I have therefore been forced to rely on the long-term and wide-ranging work on poverty and vagrancy by scholars like Paul Slack and A.L. Beier.

[75] Beier, *Masterless men,* Table XI. 7.7% of vagrants were listed as petty chapmen in *c.* 1520–*c.* 1600; 7.1% in *c.* 1600–*c.* 1620; 9.8% in *c.* 1620–*c.* 1640.

[76] *Ibid.* 16.3% in *c.* 1520–*c.* 1600; 21.9% in *c.* 1600–*c.* 1620; 23.2% in *c.* 1620–*c.* 1640.

[77] Woodfill, *Musicians in English society,* p. 128.

of specialization in the trade. Pedlars carrying just ballads were probably much less common in this period than those carrying ballads as a sideline with other wares, like Shakespeare's Autolycus.[78] Cases in the Court of Requests from the 1590s on show that chapmen from the midlands and south-west, as well as the home counties, were following regular trade routes to and from London. In 1595, a Leicester chapman had been bringing the wares of a London haberdasher to a local cordwainer for twenty years.[79] Another Leicestershire chapman fell in debt to a silkman and various other London merchants before 1599, while in 1608, a Nottingham chapman in the haberdashery trade owed £15 to his London supplier.[80] A chapman of Taunton in Somerset had, by 1623, run up a similar bill in silks worth some £120.[81]

The chapmen were given wares on credit because they were regular customers, as a London linen draper testified in 1603: 'having dealinge wth divers chapmen in the countrey by whome the chiefest and greatest parte of his gaine and comoditie doth arrise and growe, and usinge to deliver and suffer unto his saide chapmen oftentymes divers of his wares uppon their wordes and creditts wth out takinge any bonde bill or other assurance for the same'.[82] One of the draper's chapmen was William Greenstreet of Shoreham in Sussex, who made his living 'buying & sellinge of lynnen clothe and divers other smale wares'.[83] Chapmen trading in linen, haberdashery and silks, the merchandise mentioned most often in the Court of Requests cases, were especially likely to carry 'divers other smale wares', which might include books and ballads.[84] The most famous ballad seller of all, Autolycus, carried linen as his main stock-in-trade.[85]

The Court of Requests cases for this period yield no information about trade between London and the far north, but by the 1570s there were chap-

---

[78] William Shakespeare, *The winter's tale* [written 1610–11], especially IV, iii–iv. In *Great reclothing*, pp. 88–9, Margaret Spufford examines the items in Autolycus' pack, which included linen, cambrics and lawns, haberdashery and small courtship gifts, as well as ballads.

[79] PRO, Req. 2 259/64.

[80] PRO, Req. 2 293/27, Req. 2 394/22.

[81] PRO, Req. 2 397/67.

[82] PRO, Req. 2 198/54.

[83] Greenstreet died in 1603 leaving a supposed debt to the linen draper for £12, although there was no written proof of it.

[84] See the post-Restoration inventories in Spufford, *Great reclothing*, pp. 149–235. For example, George Pool of Brampton, Cumberland (d. 1695), a pedlar on foot, left stock in Scotch cloth, silk handkerchiefs and lace, as well as '11 books att 9d per piece'. Robert Griffin of Canterbury (d. 1707), a mounted chapman, dealt in laces, linens, small looking glasses and books. (*Ibid.*, pp. 154–5, 167–8.)

[85] *Ibid.*, p. 88.

men following a route between King's Lynn and Westmorland.[86] They
were almost certainly bringing cloth woven around Kendal for export or
distribution in East Anglia, and perhaps taking 'small wares' with them
on the journey home.[87] Even if the particular chapmen who reached the
record books were not ballad sellers, they indicate the existence of a network
for the distribution of goods, on a credit system, ready to be exploited
by enterprising publishers. Ballads and pamphlets may also have travelled
north with the carriers, who left regularly from specific inns in London,
bound for Halifax, Wakefield, Doncaster, Preston and many other towns
in between.[88] For example, according to the list compiled by John Taylor
in 1637, the carriers of York arrived at the sign of the Bell outside Ludgate
every Friday, and left again on Saturday or Monday. Goods sent to York
could then be sent on 'any waies north, broad and wide as farre or further
than Barwicke', while from Lancaster they could be 'conveyd to Kendall,
or Cockermouth'.[89] The existence of regular carrier services, together with
the evidence that chapmen's routes to the extreme north and south-west
were already well established in Elizabeth's reign, suggests that we should
think of a national market for cheap print, and not merely a metropolitan
area.

Waits from the south travelled as far as Carlisle (as we have seen), and
alehouse-keepers in villages of the North Riding were prosecuted for harbouring fiddlers and pipers.[90] Some of these may have transmitted the
broadside ballads, at least in oral form. Whether they came with the minstrel,
the carrier or the petty chapman, by 1624 a fondness for broadside ballads
was said to be particularly typical of 'North-Villages', where 'o're the Chym-
ney they some Ballad have / Of Chevy-Chase, or of some branded slave

---

[86] There are twenty-seven cases involving 'chapmen' during the reigns of Elizabeth and James
   I, although some of these are family disputes with no information about trade routes.
   In 1577, three merchants of King's Lynn became bound jointly in debt to a Westmorland
   chapman for a sum of up to £120. (PRO Req. 2 239/23.) In 1588, a chapman of King's
   Lynn was bound to a Kendal man for the sum of £40. (PRO, Req. 2 272/15.)
[87] Kendal cloth was exported to Italy and Spain, and Kendal merchants had business contacts
   across the country. (Joan Thirsk, 'The farming regions of England' in Thirsk, ed., *The
   agrarian history of England and Wales, vol. IV: 1560–1640* (Cambridge, 1967), pp. 20–1.)
[88] John Taylor, *The carriers cosmographie; or a briefe relation of the innes in and neere
   London* (1637), sig.B2, B3, C, C3.
[89] *Ibid.*, sig.C3, A2v.
[90] On 1 July 1614, a Kirkby Misperton alehouse-keeper was presented for having 'in his
   house a piper, one Henry Foster, being no inhab.' there but a wanderer'. On 4 October
   1631, a widow who ran an alehouse in Farlington was presented 'for keeping disorders
   in her house and harbouring of fiddlers, pipers, tinkers and wanderers &c'. (Atkinson,
   ed., *Quarter sessions records 1605–47*, II, p. 51, III, p. 322.) See also Peter Clark, *The
   English alehouse: a social history 1200–1830* (1983), pp. 152–3.

/ Hang'd at Tyborne'.[91] If the author of *The downefall of temporizing poets* was right in his count of 277 ballad sellers in London in 1641, it is likely that by then these London-based pedlars alone covered much of the country in their wanderings.[92]

Like the minstrels, the pedlars were not 'moche infecte' with money, and according to contemporary writers, they often used their ballad selling as a pretext for more lucrative activities. The playwrights and pamphleteers loved to conjure up scenes from the ballad sellers' 'vagrant and vicious life' drifting into the underworld of petty crime.[93] Autolycus's pick-pocketing stunts are only the most famous example. Robert Greene's *The second part of conny-catching* (1591) describes this as a regular practice in London:

divers honest Cittizens and daylabouring men, that resort to such places as I am about to speake of, onely for recreation as opportunity serveth, have bin of late sundry times deceived of their purses. This trade, or rather unsufferable loytring qualitie, in singing of Ballets and songs at the doores of such houses where plaies are used, as also in open markets and other places of this Cittie, where is most resort: which is nothing els but a sly fetch to draw many togeather, who listning unto an harmelesse dittie, afterward walke home to their houses with heavie hearts.[94]

Chapmen in general were often accused of theft at fairs and markets. At Chester fair in 1616, one Richard Cokley who came to do singing, dancing and tricks was accused of stealing a purse containing £5.[95] A peddling couple from Thame, picked up in 1624 on suspicion of pickpocketing, were in turn looking for a chapman they thought had stolen £30 of their own goods at Bicester market.[96]

The youthfulness of the ballad sellers is another characteristic repeatedly emphasized by Chettle: 'As vile it is that boyes, of able strength and agreeable capacity, should bee suffered to wrest from the miserable aged the last refuge in their life (beggery excepted) the poore helpe of ballad-singing.'[97] General statistics for the vagrant population indicate that two-thirds were single, primarily male, and that (between 1570 and 1622) an astonishing two-thirds were under the age of twenty-one.[98] There may be some truth in the image of ballad-singing youths flooding the countryside, sometimes coming into

---

[91] A[braham] H[olland], 'A continued inquisition against paper-persecutors', in John Davies, *A scourge for paper-persecutors, or papers complaint, compil'd in ruthfull rimes, against the paper-spoylers of these times* (1624), sig.A2v of the section by Holland.

[92] Cited in Thomson, 'Development of the broadside ballad trade', p. 178.

[93] Chettle, *Kind-harts dreame*, sig.C1.

[94] Cited in Wurzbach, *Die englische straßenballade*, p. 389.

[95] Beier, *Masterless men*, p. 97.

[96] BL Harleian MS 6715, fol. 98v.

[97] Chettle, *Kind harts-dreame* [1592?], sig.C3v.

[98] This fell from 67% to 47% for the years 1623–39. Beier, *Masterless men*, pp. 51–5, Tables III and IV.

conflict with the older tradition of the blind harpers or minstrels singing 'romances or historicall rimes' as described by Puttenham.

BUFFOONS OR VICES IN PLAYS

Petty chapmen were the primary distributors of the broadside, but there were myriad ways in which a ballad could travel when it was cut loose from its printed form. Puttenham mentions the performances of 'buffons or vices in playes'. Interludes, in which ballads (or fragments of ballads) played an important part, were by no means confined to London or the south-east. Professional troupes of interlude players, protected from prosecution by their noble patrons, travelled as far north as Carlisle and Kendal on their summer tours.[99] In February 1636 the Earl of Cumberland's accounts record payment of £1.0.0 to 'a certain company of roguish players who presented A New Way to Pay Old Debts'. On the same day, 5s. was paid to 'Adam Gerdler whom my lord sent for from York to act a part in The Knight of the Burning Pestle'.[100]

Such performances were not only to be seen in noble households and major cities, but in the alehouses of remote villages in the North Riding, where groups of craftsmen travelled as 'common Players of Enterludes' during the spring and summer months. One such troupe, with a fluctuating membership of up to eight players, appears in the quarter sessions records for July 1612, April 1616, and both April and July 1619. The company was made up of weavers, shoemakers and tailors, primarily from several villages between Pickering and Scarborough, but also drawn from Egton and Staithes (some 25 miles north), and from Bridlington (15 miles south, on the coast). Presentments of alehouse-keepers who received the players show them travelling large distances to perform, in an area marked out roughly by Thirsk in the west, Skelton in the north, the coastline on the east and Malton in the south.[101]

This group appears to have been an offshoot of an earlier company, first heard of in 1595, which is familiar to historians of northern recusancy because of performances at the houses of known Catholic gentlemen and yeomen. Sir John Yorke of Nidderdale was brought before the Star Chamber for a seditious interlude performed by the players at his house in 1609, during the Christmas season. The offending entertainment was a dialogue between a Catholic priest and a Protestant minister, which ended with the

---

[99] Kendal accounts show forty visits from groups of players between 1585 and 1637. Carlisle accounts show thirty-four visits from players between 1602–3 and 1639. REED Cumberland, Westmorland, Gloucestershire, p. 27.
[100] Woodfill, *Musicians in English Society*, p. 260. The accounts relate to activities at the Cliffords' northern castles in Westmorland and Yorkshire.
[101] Atkinson, ed., *Quarter Sessions Records 1605–47*, I, p. 260, II, pp. 119, 197, 205.

minister being carried off by devils, amidst flashes of fire. The travelling company was not, however, solely a vehicle for popish polemic. The main entertainment that day was an old morality called 'St Christopher' which was apparently considered harmless by the authorities, and the players also offered an up-to-date repertory including Shakespeare's *King Lear* and *Pericles, Prince of Tyre*.[102] Another group of northern interlude players, from Warrington in Cheshire, performed a 'play called Henry the Eight' in an alehouse loft during Sunday service in 1632.[103]

The use of popular music to liven up the drama came from a long tradition stretching back to the medieval miracle and morality plays. In the former, music was most often the heavenly chorus of the angels, but in the latter, it was the vices who came to be identified with song and dance.[104] This standard association was continued in the Tudor interludes which portrayed the struggle between heaven and hell for the soul of a young man. Like the dance, this drama contributed to a set of associations whereby popular song could eventually be equated with immorality and ungodliness. In the mid-sixteenth-century interludes *Lusty Juventus, Nice Wanton* and *Youth*, the musical characters are called Pride, Riot, Hypocrisy, Fellowship and Abominable Living.[105] These vices sang the most catchy and popular tunes of the day. In *The Four Elements* (*c.* 1517?), Sensual Appetite enters singing a jumble of clichéd popular refrains:

> Make room, sirs, and let us be merry,
> With huffa gallant sing, tirl on the berry,
> And let the wide world wind!
> Sing, frisky jolly, with hey troly lolly.[106]

Numerous scraps like this can be found in the interludes, and sometimes more substantial ballad excerpts. The medley sung by the foolish young man Moros in the first scene of Wager's *The longer thou livest, the more foole thou art* could be used as a catalogue of popular ballad titles.[107] The use of well-known songs was a clever trick to draw in the audience, making them identify closely with vice, and thus take to heart the warning message

---

[102] Christopher Howard, *Sir John Yorke of Nidderdale 1565–1634* (1939), pp. 20–6. Hugh Aveling, *Northern Catholics. The Catholic recusants of the North Riding of Yorkshire 1558–1790* (1966), pp. 193, 288–90.

[103] Clark, *The English alehouse*, p. 153.

[104] Rastall, 'Alle hefne makyth melody', in Neuss, ed., *Aspects of early English drama*, pp. 1–12.

[105] Stevens, *Music and poetry in the early Tudor court*, p. 252.

[106] *The Four Elements* (*c.* 1517?), cited in *ibid.*, p. 252. 'Huff! a galawnt' (originally a falconer's cry) was the refrain of a fourteenth-century carol, which became an identifying catchphrase for proud and foolish young men in the morality plays and interludes. (Tony Davenport, '"Lusty fresche galaunts"', in Neuss, ed., *Aspects of early English drama*, pp. 113–14.)

[107] William Wager, *A very mery and pythie commodie called the longer thou livest, the more foole thou art* [1569], sig.A3. First performed *c.* 1559–68.

which followed. But the attitude of the interlude writers to music presents an obvious paradox: popular song was used to represent a worldly life which was thoroughly condemned, yet at the same time was vital to the play's success as entertainment. This ambiguity would be echoed later in the century in the Protestant reformers' relationship to the broadside ballad, discussed in chapter 2.

Printed interludes, complete with the ballad-singing character of the vice, were published for use by groups like the weavers and shoemakers of the Northern Riding. Title-pages carried directions such as 'eight persons may easely play this Commody', although sometimes these were false claims to sell the play to smaller companies than it was written for.[108] Popular songs travelled across the country within the plays acted by these professional and semi-professional troupes. But the ballads also constituted a kind of 'dramatic performance' in their own right. Broadside ballads printed in dialogue form, sometimes called 'jigs', were (according to their titles) to be acted out at the local and amateur level: 'A Country new Iigge betweene *Simon* and *Susan*, to be sung in merry pastime by Bachelors and Maydes';[109] 'Clods Carroll: or, A proper new Iigg, to be sung Dialogue wise, of a man and a woman that would needs be married'.[110] If this was a gimmick, it was a persistent one. In 1611 Shakespeare arranged a pedlar and shepherdesses in a three-part song 'to the tune of "Two maids wooing a man"'. Some seventy years later, courtship ballads were printed either as dialogues, or in the form of a 'first part' and a 'reply'.[111]

While the 'jig' was invariably comic, other kinds of dialogue ballad could be polemical. The Stationers' Register of 1561–2 records a ballad 'intituled Rusticus and Sapyence', and in 1588 a 'proper new ballad dialoguewyse betwene Syncerytie and Wilful Ignorance'.[112] Extant examples include two pieces in Sloane MS 1896, compiled before 1576: 'A dialogue betwene death and youthe' and 'A dialogue betwene Christe and the pore oppressed synner'.[113] The 'New notborune mayd upon the passion of Cryste' was a drama

---

[108] T.W. Craik, *The Tudor interlude. Stage, costume and acting* (Leicester, 1958), p. 29.

[109] Pepys, I, 278. Reproduced in Charles Read Baskervill, *The Elizabethan jig. And related song drama* (Chicago, 1929), p. 382.

[110] RB repr. I, p. 201. Reproduced in Baskervill, *The Elizabethan jig*, p. 389. Of the twenty-four English texts printed in Baskervill's study, sixteen, or two-thirds are from broadside ballads. (*Ibid.*, pp. 375–490.)

[111] Shakespeare, *The winter's tale*, IV, iv, 289. Courtship ballads include 'The two loyal lovers, Sweet William and Coy Susan' (for J. Blare, [post-1682]), RB repr. VII, pp. 499–500; 'The constant maiden's resolution' (J. Lock for J. Clark), RB repr. VII, pp. 539–40.

[112] Baskervill, *The Elizabethan jig*, p. 49.

[113] Reprinted in Hyder E. Rollins, *Old English ballads 1553–1625* (Cambridge, 1920), nos. 44, 48. The former contains the implication of performance: 'For he that doth us now behold – / perusing this our talke.'

between Jesus and Mary.[114] Dialogues like this may have been sung at 'Christmasse diners and brideales, and in tavernes & alehouses' by local people whose performance, perhaps rewarded with a pot of ale, was unlikely to reach the record books.

RECREATION OF THE COMMON PEOPLE

A ballad might arrive in a town or village in a pedlar's pack, or in the repertory of travelling performers. From here, it could spread around the community in varying degrees of fragmentation or permutation, according to local memories and talents. The popular musical memory was retentive: the singers in town and country had a large stock of tunes which could be brought to mind with the instruction 'to the tune of –' on each new broadside. Claude Simpson argues that about 1,000 different broadside ballad tunes were current in the sixteenth and seventeenth centuries, of which over 400 have survived.[115]

Disbelief in the sponge-like qualities of the musical memory can lead to the mistaken assumption that printed music and musical literacy were common. The oral transmission of tunes, even when the song *texts* were increasingly disseminated by literacy, has its most obvious proof in the absence of musical notation from the ballad sheets. For a brief period at the end of the seventeenth century a small percentage of broadside ballads included music. There are 156 with musical notation in Pepys volume V, but more than 100 of these tunes are corrupt; often completely meaningless.[116] Most of Simpson's 400-odd broadside tunes have been painstakingly collected from instrumental variations for keyboard, lute or viols, and from Playford's country dance manuals designed for the gentry.[117]

At the lower social level, amongst the artisans, labourers, husbandmen and lesser yeomen, musical literacy was probably rare, except for those apprenticed to waits or minstrels. Margaret Spufford has tried to illuminate seventeenth-century musical culture by looking at nineteenth-century evidence that knowledge of musical notation was common amongst masons and agricultural labourers.[118] But this evidence is unfortunately inappropriate: Thomas Hardy and John Clare lived in a musical climate that had undergone great change over the previous two centuries. The growing use

---

[114] W. Carew Hazlitt, ed., *Remains of the early popular poetry of England* (4 vols., 1864–6), III, pp. 2–22. The original 'Nutbrown mayde' was an early ballad printed in 'chapbook' form, sold by John Dorne for a penny in 1520. (Madan, ed., 'The day-book of John Dorne'.)

[115] Simpson, p. xv.

[116] *Ibid.*, p. xii.

[117] *Ibid.*, pp. xii–xiii and throughout.

[118] Spufford, *Small books*, pp. 171–3.

of musical notation can be traced in the development of parish church music. In the seventeenth century, metrical psalms were sung unaccompanied and in unison. In the eighteenth, church bands and choirs were formed, using printed part-music.[119]

It would be a mistake, however, to take musical literacy as the major measure of musical talent. There is evidence at the humblest levels of the ability to improvise vocal harmony. The most ubiquitous form of part-singing was the 'three-man song'. This seems to have involved the improvisation of two extra parts to a well-known tune, although it may also have been used more loosely to mean the simple 'round'.[120] Three-man songs were staple fare on stage in the Tudor interludes, and were sung at the court by Henry VIII and his favourites, but they were also popular amongst ordinary people.[121] The city of London felt the need in 1553 to prohibit craftsmen (and especially tailors and shoemakers) from singing three-man songs for profit: 'leaving the use and exercise of their crafts and manual occupations and giving themselves wholly to wandering abroad, riot, vice, and idleness, to commonly use now adays to sing songs called three men's songs in the taverns, alehouses, inns, and other such places of this city'.[122] Thomas Deloney included singing in his set of rules for cobblers: 'what Journey-man so-ever he be hereafter, that cannot handle his Sword and Buckler, his long sword or a Quarterstaffe, sound the Trumpet, or play upon the flute, and bear his part in a three-mans song, and readily reckon up his tools in Rime . . . shall forfeit and pay a pottle of wine'.[123]

Three-part harmony was one form of creative response to popular song. Another response was a physical one: the invention of dances to fit the ballad tunes. In the second half of the sixteenth century, a new type of 'figure' dance began to appear in the English countryside, which had a close relationship with the broadside ballad.[124] These dances were gentrified,

---

[119] Vic Gammon, '"Babylonian performances": the rise and suppression of popular church music, 1660–1870', in Eileen Yeo and Stephen Yeo, eds., *Popular culture and class conflict 1590–1914: explorations in the history of labour and leisure* (1981), pp. 61–82.

[120] Stevens, *Music and poetry in the early Tudor court*, p. 286.

[121] In the *Castle of perseverance* (*c.* 1425): the people are reproved because they would rather 'syttyn at the ale, iij mens songys to syngyn lowde, thanne towarde the chyrche for to crowde'. (Cited in Stevens, *Music and poetry in the early Tudor court*, p. 287.) Three-man songs were used in *The Tudor interludes Nice Wanton and Impacient Poverty* (ed. Leonard Tennenhouse, 1984 edn), pp. 73, 99; and *The Interlude of Youth. Hick Scorner* (ed. Ian Lancashire, Manchester, 1980 edn), pp. 133, 138. Their use at court is recorded in *The Life of Sir Peter Carew* (cited in Stevens, *Music and poetry in the early Tudor court*, p. 286).

[122] Common council of city of London, ordinance of 1553 (cited in Woodfill, *Musicians in English society*, p. 14).

[123] Cited in Bruce Pattison, *Music and poetry of the English Renaissance* (2nd edn, 1970), p. 13.

[124] Older and simpler forms of dance were the round, hey and farandole. (Frances Rust, *Dance in society* (1969), pp. 35–44.)

nationalized and preserved for posterity by John Playford, but originally their form was probably much more fluid, with versions specific to each local community.[125]

The figure dances were performed to the same tunes used by the ballad writers. The names of the dances mentioned by Thomas Nashe in *Have with you to Saffron-Walden* (1596) are some of the tunes cited most frequently on the broadside ballads:

Who ... would ... doo as Dick Harvey did ... that, having preacht and beat downe three pulpits in inveighing against dauncing, one Sunday evening, when hys Wench or Friskin was footing it aloft on the Greene, with foote out and foote in, and as busie as might be at Rogero, Basilino, Turkeloney, All the flowers of the broom, Pepper is black, Green sleeves, Peggy Ramsey, he came sneaking behind a tree and lookt on, and though hee was loth to be seene to countenance the sport, having laid Gods word against it so dreadfully, yet, to shew his good-will to it in hart, hee sent her 18 pence, in hugger mugger, to pay the fiddlers.[126]

'All the flowers of the broom' apparently had particular powers of seduction for the clergy. In Essex in 1566, Joan Porter reported that 'John Clarck rector would have her dance upon the green at their door and took her by the hand and kissed her and whistled the dance with his mouth in the presence of goodman John Paprell and Edmund Fuller, which was but in pastime, and the dance was the flowers in the broom.'[127]

There seems to have been a two-way flow of influence, as some dance tunes inspired broadside ballads and shaped their structure; while other tunes first popularized by ballads were formed into new dances.[128] But the relationship may also have gone beyond this sharing of tunes to the actual singing or chanting of the broadside ballads during the dance itself. Contemporary comments often suggest that the general habit of singing ballads and dancing at one time was common in the sixteenth and seventeenth centuries. In 1577, John Northbrooke described his contemporaries as dancing 'with disordinate gestures, and with monstrous thumping of the feete, to pleasant soundes, to wanton songs, to dishonest verses'.[129] Further evi-

---

[125] John Playford, *The English dancing master* (1651), ed. M. Dean-Smith (facs. edn, 1957). Cecil J. Sharp, *The country dance book* (3 vols, in 6 pts, Wakefield, 1972 edn), pt 2, pp. 8–10.

[126] Thomas Nashe, *Have with you to Saffron-Walden* (1596), in R.B. McKerrow, ed., *The works of Thomas Nashe*, 2nd edn, revised by F.P. Wilson (5 vols., Oxford, 1958), III, p. 122.

[127] F.G. Emmison, 'Tithes, perambulations and sabbath-breach in Elizabethan Essex', in F.G. Emmison and Roy Stephens, eds., *Tribute to an antiquary. Essays presented to Marc Fitch by some of his friends* (1976), p. 203.

[128] Tunes like 'Wigmore's Galliard' and 'The Spanish pavan' probably began life in the service of the dances for which they are named. 'Rogero' was first a vocal tune: an Italian ground bass used for extemporization in the chanting of epic poetry. (Simpson, p. 612.)

[129] John Northbrooke, *A treatise wherein dicing, dauncing, vaine playes or enterluds ... are reproved* [1577?], sig.S4v. Ent. 2 December 1577.

dence can be found in a group of wedding and May-day ballads, which sound very much like the patter of a caller.[130] In the early Elizabethan manuscript containing Richard Sheale's five pieces is a song beginning 'Our Jockye sale have our Jenny' which describes the couple's wedding festivities. At the end is the dance, re-created through a running commentary of instructions, stock 'filler' phrases and jokes:

> Halfe torne Jone, haffe nowe, Jocke!
> Well dansyde, be sent Dennye!
> And he that breakys the firste strocke,
> Sall gyve the pypar a pennye.
>
> In with fut, Robsone! owt with fut, Byllynge!
> Here wyll be good daunsyng belyve;
> Daunsyng hath cost me forty good shyllynge,
> Ye forti shillynge and fyve.[131]

Over a century later, a similar kind of patter appeared in broadside form as 'The west country jigg, or a Trenchmore galliard' [*c.* 1672], in which new characters are slotted into each stanza:

> Jonny he plaid with Jenny, and Jenny she plaid with Jock;
> And he pull'd out a Guinney, to buy her a Holland smock:
> Then up with Aley, Aley, up with Sue and Siss
> And in came wanton Willy, and then they mump and kiss.[132]

These ballads may be the result of professional hacks imitating a tradition of improvised verse monologue which was once common, and is otherwise lost to us. As the broadside became more ubiquitous, it seems possible that a ballad like the 'West country jigg' could have been used as a set text into which local names and jibes were dropped in at the appropriate places.[133]

The writers and publishers of these bawdy callers' patters, like those of the courtship 'jigs', apparently expected a high degree of participation on the part of the ballad buyers. This active response to songs could sometimes be subversive. A libel investigation in Oxfordshire in 1584 records what

---

[130] Such a caller was described by Cecil Sharp after witnessing the Appalachian 'running set' early this century: '[he] recites certain prescribed verbal phrases, a mixture of prose and doggerel rhyme that in the course of time has become stereotyped. He does not always, however, restrict himself exclusively to the use of these, but will sometimes improvise remarks of his own, after the manner of the chantey-man, and crack jokes, chaff the dancers, and so forth.' Sharp believed that this 'running set' pre-dated the Playford dances, which replaced it in southern England in the seventeenth century. The older form lasted on in the north, and was brought to America in the eighteenth century. (Sharp, *Country dance book*, pt 5, pp. 9, 19.)

[131] Wright, p. 123.

[132] RB repr. VII, p. 342.

[133] See also Thomas D'Urfey's 'Winchester wedding', RB repr. VII, p. 208; and 'The May-Day country mirth', RB repr. VII, p. 81.

appears to be a standardized song which allowed local names to be slotted into a formula:

> Yf I had as faire a face as John Willms
> his daughter Elizabeth hasse,
> Then wold I were a taudrie lace as Goodman
> bolts daughter Marie dosse.[134]

Incidents recording the use of popular songs for insult and gossip show a creative attitude towards ballads: the people who sang them were not the passive conduits of a fixed tradition. When studying broadside texts it is worth bearing in mind the myriad ways in which they may have been dramatized, localized and personalized by the singers.

The printed broadside ballad was only the visible tip of an iceberg. Ballads could be chanted out by petty chapmen, performed by travelling players, danced to at bride-ales, harmonized, or shouted as insults. The relationship between the singer and the printed text could take many forms, from direct reading or singing from a broadside, to improvisation from half-remembered verses heard from a minstrel at the alehouse.

The ballad seems to have satisfied different demands in its functions as reading matter and as song. With the dissemination of fixed printed texts came an emphasis on specific facts, dates and places which is a feature of broadside balladry and not of 'traditional' oral ballads. The broadside could satisfy a demand for news and information, for veracity and detail: the shepherdess Mopsa loved 'a ballet in print, a-life, for then we are sure they are true'.[135] But as singers, most people appear to have been inefficient conduits of these printed texts. Tristram Potter Coffin has argued that folk-singers are most interested in a song's 'emotional core' rather than the details of the action in themselves.[136] Coffin provides a convincing theory of how the printed ballad could be transformed into oral folksong as we know it today. First a poem or broadside entered the oral tradition. Gradually some of the frills of literary style and details of plot were worn way until it became a 'traditional' ballad of the kind collected by Francis Child. Left to oral transmission, a narrative ballad eventually drifted toward lyric, or even nonsense song.[137]

The broadside ballads which were successful as *songs* were those with certain simple qualities to make them stick in the popular memory. The patchwork of half-remembered ballads sung by the fool in Wager's *The*

---

[134] J.W. Ebsworth, ed., *The Bagford ballads* (2 vols., 1878), I, pp. xviii–xix.

[135] Shakespeare, *The winter's tale*, IV, iv, 260.

[136] Tristram Potter Coffin, *The British traditional ballad in North America* (1977 edn), pp. 165–6.

[137] *Ibid.*, pp. 166–7.

longer thou livest is distinguished by repetitive refrains: 'Brome, Brome on
hill', 'Robin lende to me thy Bowe, thy Bowe', 'Deintie love, deintie love'.[138]
A ballad might survive as song because of its tune, a catchy refrain, the
appeal of a striking character or event, the strength of the dramatic or
'emotional' core. In chapter 2 we will look at the ballads churned out by
the presses, at the instigation of Protestant reformers, in the first decades
of Elizabeth's reign. These ballads made use of popular tunes, but often
the text had more in common with pamphlets and printed treatises than
with oral balladry. In chapter 3 we will examine those godly ballads which
appear to have had more success as songs, and whose survival over a period
of time gave them a status approaching 'folksong'.[139]

---

[138] Wager, *The longer thou livest, the more foole thou art*, sig.A3.
[139] The term 'folksong' in this study is used to describe any song which was sung for several
generations, whether or not its survival was reinforced by printed versions. It is not intended
to imply any theory of 'popular' or 'communal' origins.

2

A godly ballad to a godly tune

In 1624, the year in which the formation of a syndicate called the 'ballad partners' marked the coming of age of the trade, Abraham Holland satirized the appetite for these penny sheets:

> As in North-Villages, where every line
> Of Plumpton Parke is held a work divine.
> If o're the Chymney they some Ballad have
> Of Chevy-Chase, or of some branded slave
> Hang'd at Tyborne, they their Mattins make it
> And Vespers too, and for the Bible take it.[1]

Holland was a versifier, not an evangelist, but he chose religious metaphors for his lampoon of plebeian taste. By 1624 it was a commonplace to situate the ballads in cultural opposition to the Bible; to portray them as an alternative sort of religion. While for Holland this cliché was just a vehicle for satire, he had absorbed the language used by reformers attacking popular recreations over the past half-century. For Edward Dering, writing in 1572, stories of Guy of Warwicke and Robin Hood were at best 'childish follye' and 'witless devices'; at worst the tools of the devil and the pope:

And yet of all the residue the most dronken imaginations, with which [our forefathers] so defiled their Festival and high hoydaies, their Legendawry, theyr Saintes lyves, their tales of Robyn Goodfellow, and of many other Spirites, which Satan had made, Hell had printed, and were warranted unto sale under the Popes priviledge, to kindle in mens hartes the sparkes of superstition, that at last it might flame out into the fire of Purgatorie.[2]

The convention that traditional stories were incompatible with Protestantism could be adopted by recusants themselves. It was used as an expression

---

[1] A[braham] H[olland], 'A continued inquisition against paper-persecutors', in John Davies, *A scourge for paper-persecutors, or papers complaint, compil'd in ruthfull rimes, against the paper-spoylers of these times* (1624), sig. A2v of the section by Holland.
[2] Edward Dering, *A briefe and necessary instruction* (1572), sig. A2v.

of religious protest in the late 1620s by a recusant widow in county Durham. Margerie Stobbes, visiting her Protestant neighbours on Sunday, gave this advice to the young daughter who was going to be catechized: 'that she might tell them a taile, whoe examined her, of Robin Hoode, worth foure and twentie of that, meaneinge of the chatichisme'.[3]

The language of conflict between Protestant culture and popular culture was by no means the universal discourse of early Elizabethan reformers. From the 1550s to the 1570s, the writers of metrical psalms and 'moralized' ballads borrowed the tunes of secular song as their route to the people's hearts. Certainly there were zealous reformers like Miles Coverdale and John Hall who did seek to replace rather than supplement profane poetry. However, the relationship between the godly ballad writers and the popular songs they moralized cannot always be reduced to this simple formula. As Rivkah Zim has recently argued, it is misleading to view the metrical psalms simply 'as part of a general determined effort to displace love poetry'. The great sixteenth-century poets like Wyatt and Surrey wrote both. Their interest in biblical literature was a consequence of humanist trends, not a puritanical reaction against them.[4]

The broadside ballads, like the psalms, were written from both ends of this spectrum of motivation. The Protestant divine Thomas Brice ventured into balladry out of a concern to clean up 'filthy writing' and provide something more edifying for the public. A recent ballad by William Elderton called 'The gods of love' prompted a specific attack from Brice:

> Tell me is Christ, or Cupide Lord?
>   doth God or Venus reigne?
> And whose are wee? whom ought wee serve?
>   I ask it, answer plaine.[5]

Yet Elderton himself, a professional writer, wrote several ballads of impeccable Protestant fervour.[6] No doubt the controversy between godly and profane was sometimes artificially fuelled to sell more print and make a profit. This device of 'flyting' is suggested by the situation whereby the

[3] W.H.D. Longstaff, ed., *The acts of the High Commission within the diocese of Durham*, Publications of the Surtees Society, vol. 34 (Durham, 1858), pp. 52–3. Testimony of November 1633, about an incident some five years earlier. Stobbes also said 'that they did God good service that killed a Protestant'.

[4] Rivkah Zim, *English metrical psalms: poetry as praise and prayer 1535–1601* (Cambridge, 1987), pp. 4, 6.

[5] Thomas Brice, 'Against filthy writing, and such like delighting' (1561-2), Collmann no. 13.

[6] 'A ballat intituled Northomberland newes' [1570], Collmann no. 41; 'A ballad intituled, A newe well a daye, as playne maister papist as Donstable waye' [1570], Lilly p. 1; 'Prepare ye to the plowe' [1570], Lilly, p. 174.

same publisher, William Pickering, registered 'Row well ye Mariners' in 1565–6 and 'Roo well ye marynors moralyzed' the next year.[7] Other publishers followed suit in 1567–8 with 'Row well, God's Mariners', and 'Row well, ye Christ's Mariners'.[8] If zealous reformers initiated the moralizing vogue, a host of writers and publishers of varying sincerity were quick to join the bandwagon.

The godly parody was not a Protestant invention; the clerics who wrote medieval carols were adept at borrowing tunes and burdens from popular dance song.[9] Nor was it solely an English phenomenon, but a feature of the Reformation across Europe, and north of the border in Scotland.[10] Hymns based on secular melodies were one of the most powerful tools of the early Lutheran Reformation. In Germany they were printed, not on broadsides, but in small octavo pamphlets, most containing only one or two hymns each.[11] The moralized song-pamphlet was also tried in Henrician England: 'The new notborune mayd upon the passion of Cryste' (1535?) replaced the original 'Nutbrown mayde' which had sold for a penny in 1520.[12]

The first generation of Protestant reformers in England made no sharp break with pre-Reformation attitudes to traditional recreations. Their ballads, metrical psalms, interludes and martyrologies were all attempts to appropriate pre-Reformation cultural forms in the service of Protestantism, and as such have been well studied by literary historians.[13] What has only recently been noted, however, is that the writing of godly ballads was on the wane by the middle of Elizabeth's reign. This discovery was published by Patrick Collinson in his Stenton lecture at Reading, in which he looked at drama and graphic images, as well as the ballads. Collinson described a general shift, taking place around 1580, from 'iconoclasm' (that is, attacks

---

[7] Arber, I, pp. 305, 340.

[8] *Ibid.*, pp. 360, 362.

[9] Richard Leighton Greene, *The early English carols* (2nd edn, Oxford, 1977), pp. clxv–viii.

[10] A.F. Mitchell, ed., *A compendious book of godly and spiritual songs commonly known as 'The gute and godlie ballatis' reprinted from the edition of 1567* (Edinburgh, 1897).

[11] Kyle C. Sessions, 'Song pamphlets: media changeover in sixteenth-century publicization', in Gerald P. Tyson and Sylvia S. Wagonheim, eds., *Print and culture in the Renaissance: essays on the advent of printing in Europe* (1986), pp. 110–19. Of 851 hymnals analysed by Sessions, 56% contained from 1 to 4 hymns; and of these, 89% contained only 1 or 2 hymns. Like the English broadside ballads, most had no printed music but only a designated tune name.

[12] 'The new notborune mayd' is reprinted in W. Carew Hazlitt, ed., *Remains of the early popular poetry of England* (4 vols., 1864–6), III, p. 2. This was a long poem in chapbook form which looks likely to have been sung. The secular 'Nutbrown mayde' is recorded in F. Madan, ed., 'The day-book of John Dorne, bookseller in Oxford 1520', *Collectanae*, Proceedings of the Oxford Historical Society, 1st series (1885), pp. 71–178.

[13] John King, *English Reformation literature: the Tudor origins of the Protestant tradition* (Princeton, 1982); Zim, *English metrical psalms*.

on certain unacceptable images) to 'iconophobia' (hostility to all images, to art in general).[14]

We shall have cause to come back to this proposition in relation to the woodcut pictures discussed in chapter 4. The task here will be first to establish the chronology of the 'decline' of the godly ballad as precisely as possible through an analysis of titles in the Stationers' Register, and then to look at the reasons for the widening rift between the Protestant reformers and the broadside ballad.

STATIONERS' REGISTER TITLE STUDY

A major obstacle to the study of the ballad is the extremely low survival rate of sixteenth-century broadsides: only some 250 exist in black-letter copies.[15] The Stationers' Registers give us the closest reflection we have of total output, which can be estimated roughly as follows. A comparison of the Registers with the surviving sixteenth-century ballads shows that approximately 65% were recorded. This fits in well with the calculations of the bibliographer W.W. Greg, who suggested that 60 to 70% of all printed works were registered in this period.[16] I have counted just over 1,500 ballads registered before the year 1600. Assuming 65% registration, and allowing for a constant output during the years for which there is no Stationers' Register (1550–7 and 1571–6), this figure represents probably 3,000 distinct ballads in the second half of the sixteenth century.

If we wish to form any idea of the subject matter of sixteenth-century ballads we must clearly turn to the Registers rather than to the small sample of accidental survivals. An examination of the licensing patterns of ballad publishers suggests that the Registers are a fairly reliable tool for this purpose.

The control of the broadside press was a matter of particular concern to the Tudor rulers, who were sensitive to the power of ballads to influence

---

[14] Patrick Collinson, *From iconoclasm to iconophobia: the cultural impact of the second English Reformation*, Stenton lecture 1985 (Reading, 1986); re-stated in Patrick Collinson, *The birthpangs of Protestant England. Religious and cultural change in the sixteenth and seventeenth centuries* (1988), pp. 94–126.

[15] Carole R. Livingston, 'The provenance of three early broadsheets', *The Library*, 6th ser., 2 (1980), pp. 53–60. Livingston's estimate seems to be accurate on the basis of the major sixteenth-century collections: Society of Antiquaries, London; Huth Collection, British Library; Huntington Library, California. (The last two once made up a single collection, but unfortunately nothing is known of its originator.) There are also a few sixteenth-century broadsides scattered amongst the enormous collections of predominately seventeenth-century ballads, such as the Roxburghe Collection, British Library.

[16] W.W. Greg, *Some aspects and problems of London publishing between 1550 and 1650* (Oxford, 1956), p. 7.

their subjects, particularly in the area of religion. Henry VIII issued the first proclamations which specifically banned offensive ballads, in 1533 and 1542, and there were similar proclamations under Edwards VI and Mary.[17] The latter had her own propagandist in the form of her chaplain, William Forrest, who praised the queen in 'A new ballad of the marigolde'.[18] By Elizabeth's reign, the system of censorship was more effective. Elizabeth does not appear to have commissioned most of ballads glorifying England's Protestant destiny, and attacking the papist enemy. However, the licensing procedures ensured that these sincere effusions of her zealous subjects would pass, while Catholic or dangerously sectarian ballads would be forced underground, printed at great risk on foreign or clandestine presses.

The lynchpin of the Elizabethan system was the Stationers' Company, granted its charter in 1557, which required that all printers must be members of the London company (except for the printers to the Crown and the universities). From 1557, we have the first Stationers' Company Register, in which copies of all books and ballads were supposed to be entered. This registration served two functions: as a record of the licensing of the production and as evidence of the publisher's copyright. There were elaborate provisions and distinctions about the licensing of various types of publication; but essentially ballads were to be perused by the Archbishop of Canterbury, or the Bishop of London.[19] These gentlemen were unlikely to sit down and read each broadside that passed through their hands: no doubt they put their names to most works at the recommendation of their chaplains and secretaries. Such delegation of authority became official under Archbishop Whitgift. Around 1588 he named a panel of twelve 'preachers and others' whose signatures (some alone, some in pairs) would be sufficient to license a publication for print.[20]

We have a second-hand story of a High Commission case which hints at the practical problems of enforcing the licensing process.[21] In 1631–2, articles were brought against one of the leading ballad publishers, Henry Gosson for printing a ballad 'wherin all the histories of the bible were scurrilously abused'. Gosson defended himself saying the ballad 'was printed before he was born and he hath but renewed it, and is very sorry for it, and that this was never called in'. The Bishop of London was aware of

---

[17] R.S. Thomson, 'The development of the broadside ballad trade and its influence upon the transmission of English folksongs' (Cambridge PhD, 1974), p. 29. Cyprian Blagden, *The Stationers' Company. A history, 1403–1959* (1960), ch.1.

[18] 'A new ballad of the marigolde' [1553?], SA no. 36, repr. Thomas Park, ed., *Harleian miscellany* (10 vols., 1808–13), X, p. 253.

[19] Greg, *Some aspects and problems of London publishing*, p. 6.

[20] *Ibid.*, p. 9.

[21] From Bodleian Library, Oxford, MS Rawlinson A128, printed in Samuel Rawson Gardiner, ed., *Reports of cases in the courts of Star Chamber and High Commission* (Camden Society, 1886), p. 314.

the problem: 'There was a parish clarke chosen to view all the balletts before they were printed, but he refuseth to doe it, let be ordered that he shall undertake it by commaundment from this Court.'

The licensing procedure was not complete until the publication had been 'allowed' by the Wardens of the Stationers' Company and duly entered into the Company Register. In practice, the Wardens acted as the chief licensing agents: on their own judgement they sometimes permitted the entrance of a copy lacking official sanction (at the author's own peril) or accepted the recommendation of ministers who were not officially recognized as licensers. The Company officials were periodically reminded of their responsibility to ensure authorization.[22]

Figs. 1 and 2 show the numbers of ballads recorded in the Stationers' Registers each year from 1557 to 1641. After an initial spurt in the first year the numbers are low: certainly a total of four ballads in 1559–60 does not reflect the output of the press, but rather the reticence of publishers to adapt themselves to the new system of registration. However, the fee for registering a ballad was 4d.; the fine for failure to do so could be anywhere from 1s. to 5s. The Stationers' Company officials made their serious intentions clear early on: in 1558–9 the Court fined three stationers up to 2s. each for printing ballads without license, and another stationer was 'sent to warde' for the same offence.[23] After this, the numbers of ballads registered rose, and were not to fall below the forty-ballad mark for the rest of the 1560s.

The peak in 1569–70 was a reaction to two big events: the Catholic uprising in the north, and the execution of John Felton, who posted the papal bull of excommunication against the queen.[24] The even higher peak in the mid-1580s resulted from the Star Chamber decree of 1586. This decree was a response to problems with clandestine presses in the 1580s, both Catholic and radical Protestant.[25] The decree set up a more rigid control of the system: it named twenty master printers (plus the Queen's Printer) and specified the number of presses allowed to each.[26] Authorization was re-emphasized, and printers were meant to bring in any old stock

---

[22] Greg, *Some aspects and problems of London publishing*, ch. 3. Hyder E. Rollins, 'William Elderton: Elizabethan actor and ballad-writer', *Studies in Philology*, 17 (1920), pp. 212–13.

[23] Rollins Index, nos. 128, 178, 130, 753.

[24] See ballad titles in Arber, I, pp. 405–6, 408, 414–16.

[25] On Catholic printers and distributors see J.R. Dasent, ed., *Acts of the Privy Council* (1890–1907), XIII, pp. 154, 186, 264; Leona Rostenberg, *The minority press and the English crown 1558–1625* (Nieuwkoop, 1971), ch. 3. Imported sectarian publications provoked a royal proclamation banning the works of the Family of Love in October 1580, and another against the Brownists in June 1583. (*Ibid.*, ch. 13.)

[26] Arber, II, pp. 807–12.

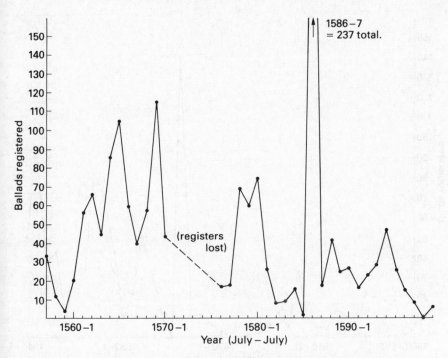

Fig. 1 Yearly total of ballads in Stationers' Registers (1557–1600)

which had not been properly licensed. We see an immediate response in the number of ballads registered, which leapt to 237 in 1586–7.[27]

As the graph shows, by the end of the century the Stationers' Company lost its hold on registration enforcement. There was little change in this situation until the second quarter of the seventeenth century, when the formation of a syndicate called the 'ballad partners' marked a new stage in the organization of the trade. On 14 December 1624 the Register records the accumulation by the 'partners' of 128 ballads.[28] From here on, the yearly totals of ballads registered are dominated by large entries to the 'partners'.[29] Their competitors also began to register their ballads in batches to ensure copyright, and from 1632-3 it became a policy to bring in a list in July of all ballads printed 'this yeare now past'.[30]

[27] This included a very large entry of 123 ballads to Richard Jones, unfortunately listed on a separate sheet which is now lost. (Arber, II, pp. 452.)

[28] On 6 November 1624, the Court of the Stationers' Company ordered Pavier and his partners to enter the ballads they had so far been publishing without license. (William A. Jackson, ed., *Records of the Court of the Stationers' Company 1602 to 1640* (1957), p. 171.)

[29] Arber, IV, pp. 213, 216, 260, 268, 278, 299, 323, 366.

[30] *Ibid.*, pp. 299, 323, 366.

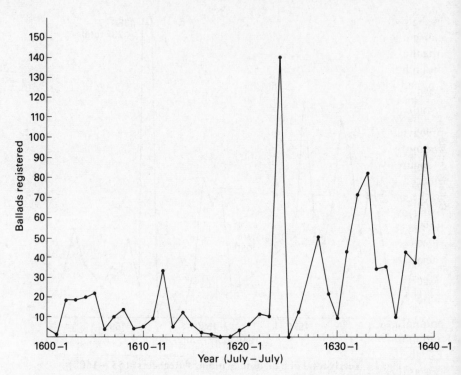

Fig. 2   Yearly total of ballads in Stationers' Registers (1600–41)

Throughout most of our period, the Registers provide a good source from which to gauge the proportion of religious and of secular ballads. The weakest link is the thirty years from 1595 to 1624, but the stretch of high registration both before and after this period should give a reliable indication of the long-term trends. While recognizing the existence of a variable unregistered element each year, there is no reason to believe that more religious than secular ballads should be unregistered, or vice versa. Of 200 extant ballads in the periods before 1600 for which the registers survive, 34% of the secular ballads were unlicensed and 39% of the religious and moralizing ballads; a difference slim enough to dismiss, given the small size of the sample and the difficulty of categorizing any given ballad as 'secular' or 'religious'.

This line between the godly and the worldly was far from clear-cut in our period. Every event was still seen as the active work of God's hand in the world, and it is almost impossible to find a straight 'news' ballad

in the sixteenth century which does not refer to the greater 'religious' significance of the individual 'secular' event. Political ballads, dealing with events
like the 'northern rebellion' of 1569, also straddled the line between secular
and religious concerns. When faced with the title in the Stationers' Register,
I aimed for consistency: if the title mentioned God, religion, the pope or
papists it was recorded as a religious ballad. Thus 'A lamentation from
Rome, how the pope, doth bewayle, That the rebelles in England can not
prevayle' was classified as a religious ballad, while 'Northumberland newes'
was not.

Figures 3 and 4 show the percentage of religious and moralizing ballads
entered yearly in the Stationers' Registers to 1640. The study shows that
in the early Elizabethan period a minimum of over one third of the ballads
being produced were 'godly' ballads, as compared with under one tenth
by the second quarter of the seventeenth century. For the period 1560–88
the average was 35%; for 1588–1625 it was 19% (15% if we discount
the year 1624); for 1625–40 only 9%.[31] The decisive drop occurred in
the 1580s; this chronology agrees fairly well with Collinson's estimate of
a break with the past around 1580.[32]

The year of the big entry to the 'partners' in 1624–5 stands out as an
anomaly: in this year there were 139 ballads registered, with a high religious
and moralizing proportion of 30%. Their own entry of 128 ballads, mostly
Elizabethan, contained fully one third 'godly' ballads. This figure is striking:
it is as high as the percentage in the original 'gospelling' period before 1588.
With this re-registration of 'stock' the Registers are able for the first time
to show the longevity and popularity of ballad titles. Before this, (apart
from the smaller scale 'stock' entries of 1586) the Registers yield a picture
primarily of the new ballads written in any given year, not of ballads being
reprinted and still circulating. The 'stock' ballads tell much about the
audience, and will form the basis of chapter 3. In this chapter, we concentrate
on what the Registers show about the new religious ballads being written.

The decline in religious ballads appears to have continued throughout
the seventeenth century. The 'partners' entry of 1675 still contains a fairly
respectable proportion of almost one fifth godly ballads, of which almost

---

[31] Only the output of those years with a total registration of at least twenty ballads has been
recorded on the graph, since the smaller samples sometimes yielded absurd results.

[32] The religious content remained relatively high in the 1580s because of two unusual years:
1586–7, when the Star Chamber decree ordered publishers to bring in their old unregistered
ballads; and 1588–9, when the Armada victory inspired the production of numerous godly
ditties.

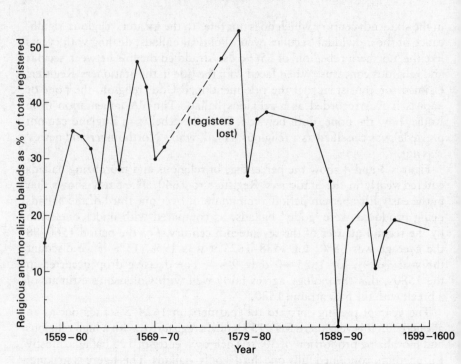

Fig. 3   Yearly percentage of religious and moralizing ballads in Stationers' Registers
(1557–1600)

Period	% religious and moralizing
1560–88	35
1588–1625	19
1625–40	9

half are pre-1640 stock.[33] But these later 'partners' had less of a monopoly
on the trade than their predecessors, and it appears from the extant collections that their competitors had even less to offer for their customers' souls.
Of the sixteenth-century ballads I examined, almost half could be classified
as religious. This contrasts sharply with the great seventeenth-century collections, primarily post-Restoration, like the Roxburghe and the Pepys. In

[33] Some 35 of 196 titles (18%) are religious or moralizing.

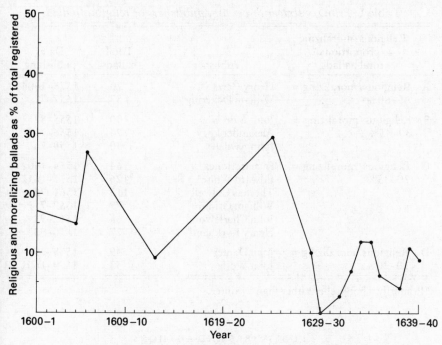

Fig. 4 Yearly percentage of religious and moralizing ballads in Stationers' Registers (1600–40)

the printed volumes of the Roxburghe collection, not one in ten ballads deals with religious subjects.[34] In the collection of Samuel Pepys, begun by John Selden, the ballads on 'Devotion and Morality' fit into 130 pages out of 2,000: that is, taking up only 6.5% of the total space.[35]

---

[34] RB repr. There are, very roughly, 120 religious or moralizing ballads, in a collection of 1,466 ballads.

[35] Samuel Pepys Library, Magdalene College, Cambridge. The personal tastes of the collector do not account for such a low figure: in his chapbook collection 24% are 'penny godlinesses'. (Margaret Spufford, *Small books and pleasant histories. Popular fiction and its readership in seventeenth-century England* (1981), p. 197.) This figure is indeed somewhat lower than the selection of godlies on the publishers' trade lists (32%), since Pepys was not especially attracted to pious books. But if we were to assume a bias of the same proportion for the ballads, that would still leave us with a projected figure for religious ballads of only 9%.

Table 1. *Primary sixteenth-century publishers of religious ballads*

Religious/moralizing as proportion of total ballads		Publisher	Total ballads	Dates publishing
A	Religious/moralizing = 45–60%	Henry Carr[a]	70	1578–1604
		William Pickering[a]	57	1557–71
B	Religious/moralizing = 30–45%	John Alde	100	1555–82
		Alexander Lacy	74	1556–71
		John Awdeley	30	1559–75
C	Religious/moralizing = 20–35%	Richard Jones	164	1564–1602
		Edward White[a]	126	1577–1612
		Thomas Colwell	113	1561–75
		William Griffith	79	1552–71?
		John Charlewood	66	1562–93
		Henry Kyrkham[a]	27	1570–93
D	Religious/moralizing = 10–20%	John Danter	49	1589–99
		John Wolfe	53	1579–1601

[a] Primarily a bookseller rather than a printer.

PUBLISHERS AND AUTHORS

Before we can attempt to explain the decline of religious ballads at the end of the sixteenth century we must first look at the earlier period. Why were there so many godly ballads published, and was there a market for them? We must first consider the possibility that these ballads were not profitable: that the printers were zealous puritans with evangelical motives, as was sometimes the case with weightier and more controversial theological works.[36] Were there stationers who specialized in godly ballads, whose personal zeal could account for the high percentage in the early Elizabethan period?

Table 1 shows all the major sixteenth-century publishers of religious ballads, as established by their entries in the Stationers' Company Register. Only two middling publishers, Henry Carr and William Pickering, showed an especially high level of religious and moralizing ballads. Most of the major publishers, including the ballad giant Richard Jones, published a mix of secular and religious ballads that fell roughly in line with the yearly average. The one stationer who appears to have had more than a commercial

---

[36] A number of printers who appear to have been motivated by their religion are discussed in W. Calderwood, 'The Elizabethan Protestant press: a study of the printing and publishing of Protestant religious literature in English, excluding Bibles and liturgies 1558–1603' (London PhD, 1977).

interest in the godly ballad was John Awdeley. He published religious ballads written by himself, of which four survive; with titles like 'Remember death, and thou shalt never sinne' (1569). His will was prefaced with a lengthy and thoroughly Protestant preamble.[37] Yet even Awdeley's presses produced the same variety of secular ballads as the other publishers.

There seems to have been no sense of contradiction about printing bawdy ballads together with calls to repentance. In 1578 Edward White was fined for printing an 'undecent ballat' called 'the Jocund joy of the meetinge of ij Lovers'. Payment of the fine was recorded in the same entry as White's registration fee for two other ballads, including 'a penitent confession to the tune of thaged mans dump'.[38]

Publishers like Edward White do not seem to have had any special interest in their readers' souls, but only in their purses: they printed what they thought would sell. George Wither (in *Schollers Purgatory, c.* 1625) lamented the flexible religious stance of the typical stationer: 'to a Papist he rails upon Protestants; to a Protestant he speaks ill of Papists; and to a Brownist, he reviles them both'.[39]

Admittedly Wither was a biassed reporter, being in the midst of a quarrel with the Stationers' Company over the publication of his own *Godly hymns and spiritual songs*. But there is abundant evidence to show that stationers' religious opinions were often easily adjusted. John Charlewood published puritan writers like Robert Crowley, Edward Dering and William Fulke, as well as various rabidly anti-Catholic works.[40] Yet his press was brought to Acton for the use of the Jesuit Robert Southwell.[41] John Wolfe also published Father Southwell's devotional works, as well as Protestant literature of both the established church and the puritan opposition.[42] John Danter published anti-papist ballads, yet in 1596 his presses were seized for printing a popular Catholic book of devotion, the *Jesus Psalter*.[43] There is evidence that Catholic books were extremely overpriced: in 1624 a Douai

---

[37] Collmann no. 2. PRO, Prerogative Court of Canterbury, Prob. 11. 57. Dated 22 June 1575.

[38] Arber, II, p. 336. The fine was 4s.4d.

[39] Quoted in Hyder E. Rollins, 'The black-letter broadside ballad', *Publications of the Modern Language Association*, 34 (1919), p. 296.

[40] Calderwood, 'Elizabethan Protestant press', p. 209.

[41] Rostenberg, *Minority press*, p. 57.

[42] Calderwood, 'Elizabethan Protestant press', pp. 213–14. The same man was in 1588 an official searcher for secret presses. (W.W. Greg and E. Boswell, eds., *Records of the Court of the Stationers' Company 1576 to 1602* (1930), p. 27.)

[43] Arber, II, p. 657. R.B. McKerrow, *A dictionary of printers and booksellers in England, Scotland and Ireland, and of foreign printers of English books 1557–1640* (1910), pp. 83–4.

Bible could cost up to 40s. and a Rheims New Testament 16s. or 20s.[44] It is unlikely that these printers harboured recusant sentiments: they took the risk of printing papist literature because of the highly lucrative nature of the trade.

If these publishers were businessmen, not evangelists, then the godly ballads must have been saleable. This impression is confirmed by the involvement of semi-professional ballad writers like John Barker or the popular William Elderton, who also produced secular love ballads and news ballads.[45] Elizabethans were apparently willing to spend their money on ballads about religious issues. However, we must be wary of taking every Elizabethan ballad as direct evidence of wide popular opinion. Later, when the 'partners' joined forces on distribution, it is probable that all of their ballads had print runs of at least 1,000 copies and reached a wide market. The reprinting of stock ballads also provides us with a way to measure popularity. In the sixteenth century, print runs may have varied greatly; ballads by Deloney and Elderton may have been widely distributed, while the first effort of an unknown clergyman may have been run off in only a few hundred copies.[46] This would have been economically feasible, since the overheads were almost non-existent, apart from the cost of paper. Type for a single sheet was easily set up, and the author writing out of a sense of mission would presumably expect no payment.

As a prolific and profit-making ballad writer, then, William Elderton was an exception in the Elizabethan period. The majority of authors seem to have written no more than one or two ballads, and these for evangelical rather than financial motives. The writers were not a separate breed of journalists, but came from a cross-section of respectable professions. We have ballads written by a merchant-tailor of London (William Fulwood), a silk-weaver (Thomas Deloney), as well as dramatists and stationers

---

[44] John Gee, *The foot out of the snare* (1624), cited in Rostenberg, *Minority press*, p. 107. These may have been particularly lavish bound volumes, although Gee gives a long list of high prices for Catholic works.

[45] Barker wrote 'A balade declaryng how neybourhed, love and trew dealyng is gone' [1561], Lilly, p. 134; 'The plagues of Northumberland' [1570]?; Lilly, p. 56; 'Of the horyble and woful destrucion of Jerusalem' [1569?], Collmann no. 5. He was also the author of several news ballads in the Huth collection, British Library. Surviving ballads by Elderton include half a dozen dealing with religious themes, and a dozen in a more secular vein (STC 7552.5 to 7565).

[46] Thomson comments that 'composition was an expensive portion of the overall printing charge involved in producing a few hundred copies of a ballad', and that the shared use of a warehouse by the 'partners' made large print runs possible. But he gives no evidence for size of print runs either before or after the formation of the 'partners'. (Thomson, 'Development of the broadside ballad trade', p. 66.)

(Thomas Preston, John Awdeley).[47] Most of the ballads, when not anonymous, were signed with initials only, or credited to names now unknown and meaningless. For this reason it is impossible to draw up a league table of godly ballad-writing occupations, but it appears that if we could, clergymen would come somewhere near the top.

William Kethe was a Protestant divine and a Marian exile. He was one of the translators of the Geneva Bible and wrote some of the metrical psalms that were adopted in the *English Psalter* of 1562. With his personal experience of the Marian persecution, it is not surprising to see him the author of several anti-papist ballads.[48] Thomas Brice was another clergyman very committed to the Protestant cause in the Marian period: he risked his life smuggling Protestant books from Wesel into Kent and London.[49] When safer days came he spent his energies on a metrical account of the Marian martyrs, a ballad 'against filthy writing', and moralizations of the two great collections of courtly love poetry, *The courte of Venus* (*c.* 1538) and *Songes and sonnettes* ('Tottel's miscellany', 1557).[50] Thomas Broke was the son of the alderman of Calais, a prominent sectary. Broke the younger wrote a ballad on Bishop Bonner, comparing his persecution of the Protestants with Herod's slaughter of the innocents.[51] John Cornet was another ballad-writing minister, and Laurence Ramsay was a prominent anabaptist who versified against the Catholics.[52]

The social and educational status of these reforming versifiers is a stark

[47] For the merchant-tailor William Fulwood see Rollins, 'William Elderton', p. 213. His ballads are broadly moralizing. (STC 11485, 'The shape of ii monsters'; 'A new ballad against unthrifts' [1562], Lilly, p. 153.) Thomas Preston was the author of 'A lamentation from Rome, how the pope, doth bewayle, That the rebelles in England can not prevayle' (1570), Collmann no. 75. Thomas Deloney wrote 'a proper new ballade dyaloguewyse betwene Syncerytie and Wilfull Ignorance' (ent. 1588), in *The garland of good will* (1631); 'The overthrow of proud Holofernes ...' (ent., 1588), in *ibid.*; 'The Duchess of Suffolk' in *Strange histories* (1602). John Awdeley wrote and published godly ballads like 'The cruel assault of Gods fort' [*c.* 1560], Collmann no. 3.

[48] *DNB*. 'A ballet declaring the fal of the whore of Babylone' (a thirty-two page pamphlet, described in *DNB*) and 'Of misrules contending with Gods worde by name' [1553?], SA no. 16.

[49] *DNB*.

[50] Brice's *A compendious regester in metre, conteinyng the names, and pacient suffrynges of the members of Jesus* (1559) may have been a source for John Foxe. (Collmann, p. 36.) Brice's 'Courte of Venus moralized' was registered in 1566-7. *The courte of Venus*, which contained five poems by Wyatt, had been through its third edition in *c.* 1563. A better known moralization is John Hall's *The court of virtue* (1565). Tottel's *Songes and sonnettes*, by Wyatt, Surrey and others, must have been the inspiration for Brice's 'Songes and Sonnettes' which appeared in 1567-8. The latter entry does not specify a moralization, but given Brice's opinions on love poetry it could not have been anything else. Neither of Brice's collections survive.

[51] 'An epitaphe declarynge the lyfe and end of D. Edmund Boner &c.' (1569), Collman no. 14.

[52] John Cornet, 'An admonition to Doctor Story', Collmann no. 33. Laurence Ramsey discussed in Collmann, p. 225.

contrast to that of the ballad writers half a century later. In the early Elizabethan period, the closest thing to a ballad hack was William Elderton,
famed for his drinker's red nose. Yet this prolific writer was also a respectable
professional: he was an attorney at the Sheriff's Court in London, in 1562.
A decade later he was Master of the Boy Actors of Eton College, and then
the Children of Westminster School, posts of some importance. Elderton's
counterpart in Charles' reign was Martin Parker, the most famous and popular ballad writer of the seventeenth century. Parker seems to have been
an alehouse-keeper, a steep drop from an attorney on the social scale.[53]
As respectable godly writers began opting out of the ballad scene, presumably
this trend made more room for ballad hacks of dubious character, whose
increase, in turn, must have accelerated the rush of the godly to disassociate
themselves from the medium.

Why did the ballad cease to be an acceptable vehicle for the Protestant
message? A general change in the attitude of reformers to 'popular culture'
is only a broad description: a result rather than a cause. The process itself
was made up of interrelated developments, musical, ideological, social and
literary. Here I will attempt to disentangle a few of them from this complex
web.

The emphasis will be on changing perceptions of 'godly' and 'ungodly'
activities; however, it would be wrong to think that the desertion of the
ballad by the educated elite was purely on moral grounds. The changing
literary taste associated with the 'English Renaissance' meant the rejection
of the 'rude & homely maner of vulgar Poesie' in favour of the 'sweete
and stately measures and stile of the Italian Poesie'.[54] By the 1580s, poets
like Sidney had little respect for native verse, with its unsophisticated metre.[55]
The importation of Continental models occurred throughout the
arts; and as we can see in decorative wall painting, a sense of Italianate
fashion reached down at least as far as the solid middle ranks of society.[56]
The ballads did continue to gain in popularity with singers and buyers,
but their rejection as poetry in literary circles cannot but have affected the
educated Protestant gentlemen, clergymen and professionals who once put
their pens to religious ballads. The religious reaction against certain aspects
of 'popular culture' coincided with a changing 'Renaissance' aesthetic, and
the two movements were inextricably intertwined.

---

[53] Rollins, 'William Elderton', pp. 205–6, 216. Susan Aileen Newman, 'The broadside ballads
     of Martin Parker: a bibliographical and critical study' (Birmingham PhD, 1975), I, p. 2.
[54] George Puttenham, quoted in King, *English Reformation literature*, pp. 11–12.
[55] Sir Philip Sidney, *An apologie for poetrie* (1595).
[56] See p. 214.

DECLINE OF THE GODLY BALLAD[57]

Rise of the psalm

In the 1550s and 60s the godly ballads and metrical psalms were all facets of one endeavour: the creation of a body of religious song based on the metre and tunes of mid-sixteenth-century courtly music. However, by the 1570s and 80s the psalms were becoming firmly established as the definitive godly songs, to the exclusion of the ballads. The circumstances which combined in the psalms' favour included their scriptural authority which recommended them to Calvinists; their musical simplicity which endeared them to ordinary people; and their use in the parish church service, which established a weekly context in which they would be learnt throughout the country. *The whole book of psalms*, the version used universally in worship (first printed by John Day in 1562), ran to nearly 500 editions over 125 years.[58]

The Calvinist tenor of English Protestantism was a major factor restricting the development of religious song. Calvin was clear in his preference for the pure word of God: 'Look where we may, we will never find songs better, nor more suited to the purpose, than the Psalms of David; which the Holy Ghost himself composed. And so, when we sing them, we are certain that God puts the words in our mouth, as if he himself sang in us to magnify his praise.'[59] The ballads, with the exception of the metrical paraphrases of Scripture, were human creations, and as such immediately inferior on this textual basis. Even apart from this principle, the psalms were obviously better poetry than anything the versifying reformer could produce, and their qualities to comfort and inspire were recognized by all the great contemporary poets.[60]

The Calvinist emphasis on the precedence of the scriptural text had a musical corollary. The psalm tune must be sober and clear, with a quality of 'poids et majesté'; not only out of reverence, but so that the words might

---

[57] Many of these points have already been put very succinctly by Patrick Collinson in his Stenton lecture *(From iconoclasm to iconophobia*, pp. 17–21); re-stated in *Birthpangs of Protestant England*, pp. 106–12. Here I have more room to expand on some of these issues (such as the relationship between psalms and ballads, based on the work of Nicholas Temperley), and to add a closer examination of the ballad tunes.

[58] The psalms sung by Sternhold at the Edwardian court, and augmented by Hopkins, were the basis of the Genevan service book used by the Marian exiles. This in turn developed into *The whole book of psalms*. Influenced by courtly music, Sternhold used the simple 'common metre' (then known as 'Sternhold's metre'), departing from Continental precedents. (Nicholas Temperley, *The music of the English parish church* (2 vols., Cambridge, 1979), I, pp. 30, 53–4, 26.)

[59] Quoted in *ibid.*, p. 20.

[60] See Zim, *English metrical psalms*.

be understood.[61] This principle was embedded in the 1559 Act of Uniformity, which permitted non-liturgical music in church so long as it were 'a modest and distinct song, so used in all parts of the common prayers in the church, that the same may be as plainly understood as if it were read without singing'.[62] Plainness also required the general rule of one syllable per note, of which Thomas Cranmer had declared himself an early exponent.[63] Polyphony was still used in cathedrals, but from the 1570s all music began to disappear from the parish churches save unison congregational psalm singing.[64] For some committed Protestants this simplicity became a kind of musical aesthetic akin to the whitewashing of images; a reaction against all superfluous religious expressions in favour of internalized faith. One expression of this reaction can be found in Thomas Becon's *The jewell of joye* [1550?]: 'A Christian man's melody, after St. Paul's mind, consisteth in heart, while we recite psalms, hymns, and spiritual songs, and sing to the Lord in our hearts ... All other outward melody is vain and transitory, and passeth away and cometh to nought.'[65]

The success of the psalms was not only a matter of religious principle, but also of their practical features of memorability. While the psalm book contained sixty-seven tunes at its fullest, it appears that the psalms made their way into popular tradition on the backs of a very small number of shorter 'common' tunes which did not appear in print until the 1590s. These melodies were already well established orally; their first publisher Thomas East wrote in 1594 that all of the psalms were sung to one of four tunes 'in most churches of this realm'.[66] By 1620 there were at least ten such tunes in currency, known by the names of the towns and regions they came from (or were reputed to have come from): for example, the Oxford tune, the Scottish tune, the Cheshire tune.[67] Playford printed ten of these short tunes in his *Introduction to the skill of musick* (1660), and only seven of the official tunes.[68] The common tunes were only three lines long instead

---

61 Jean Calvin, *Institutes of the Christian religion* (1536), trans. Ford Lewis Battles, ed. John T. McNeill (2 vols., Library of Christian Classics, vol. XX, 1961), Book III, ch. 20, section 32. Discussed in Collinson, *From iconoclasm to iconophobia*, p. 21

62 Temperley, *Music of the English parish church*, I, p. 39.

63 Letter to Henry VIII, quoted in Peter Le Huray, *Music and the Reformation in England 1549–1660* (1967), p. 7.

64 Temperley, *Music of the English parish church*, I, pp. 42–6. Temperley attributes this disappearance to other factors as well as 'Puritan propaganda', including the lack of money to support professional music.

65 Quoted in Le Huray, *Music and the Reformation*, p. 12.

66 Temperley, *Music of the English parish church*, I, p. 68.

67 H. Dod wrote of 'at the least X or XI other usual & good tunes, which were never entered into the said common book ...' in his edition of *Al the psalmes of David* (1620), cited in *ibid.*, p. 69.

68 John Playford, *A brief introduction to the skill of musick*, 3rd edn (1660). In the 1674 edition he printed twenty short tunes and nine long.

of eight; they had a square rhythm, small range, two standard cadence points (one on the dominant or supertonic, the other on the tonic). Some were derived from court song or dance music; others developed out of the first half of a long tune, or from the descant sung in certain churches.[69] These common tunes, easily memorized, and reinforced by use in church, account for much of the success of the psalm. For the seventeenth-century public the common tunes became the definitive religious tunes.

The godly tune

Were the godly ballads not also sung to catchy and popular melodies? Were they even sung at all? Unfortunately we have little 'hard' evidence referring to the singing of godly broadside ballads, which may be suggestive about their lack of success in comparison with the psalms. But at first, terms like 'psalm', 'ballad' and 'song' were used so vaguely and interchangeably that we cannot always be sure to which genre contemporary comments referred.[70] There is no reason to believe that the persistent practice of labelling the godly broadsides 'to the tune of –' was an artificial device maintained over years and generations. The ballad tunes have survived for posterity in instrumental variations which often include added ornamentation. This hinders attempts to measure correlation with the text. Yet it is clear in most cases that the godly lyrics do match the tunes, in rhythm, length and number of measures, and often in tone or mood as well. Thus a rousing patriotic ballad like Elderton's 'Prepare ye to the plowe' was sung to the up-beat dance tune 'Pepper is black'; a gloomy tune like 'Fortune my foe' was used for St Bernard's vision of death.

There is some evidence that the ballads sold by the 'partners' were in currency as song: almost half the godly ballads were listed by their first lines in the 1624 entry.[71] This contrasts with original entries of new, unfamiliar ballads, almost always by title. One would not normally enter a book or pamphlet by its opening phrase, but it is precisely this beginning which one best remembers in a song.

The 1624 ballads preserved tunes which were now half a century old,

---

[69] Temperley, *Music of the English parish church*, I, pp. 70–5.

[70] Miles Coverdale, *Goostly psalmes and spirituall songes drawen out of the holy scripture* [1535?]. We have evidence about the early spread of congregational psalm singing in *The diary of Henry Machyn*, ed. J.G. Nichols (1848), p. 212; and in a letter from John Jewel, cited in Temperley, *Music of the English parish church*, I, p. 43.

[71] For example, 'When Jesus Christ was 12', 'Good Lord what a wicked world', 'I am a poore woman and blinde'. (See App. A.)

many of which appear to have been introduced first at the Tudor Court.[72] Their use as dance music by travelling musicians rapidly spread these tunes far beyond 'elite' or 'polite' circles; their coupling with favourite ballads helped to ensure their staying power. However, if we compare the most common tunes in the 'partners' 1624 godly ballad stock with those which found favour in the early Elizabethan years, we see a process of selection. First, amongst the merrier tunes we see a preference for simplicity of metre and melody. Secondly, we see a growing bias towards the slow, sombre tune, which we can also relate to transitions in the tempo of psalmody.

Only a third of the sixteenth-century godly ballads included tune directions,[73] leaving us with just over a dozen melodies named on extant broadsides. The most common Elizabethan tunes were 'The Black Almain' and 'Row well ye Mariners', which appear three times each. In the seventeenth-century popular stock, 'Rogero', 'Wigmore's Galliard' and 'Fortune my foe' were used three times each, while 'O man in desparation' is named five times. All of these tunes are reproduced in Fig. 5, together with a stanza of a corresponding godly ballad for each.[74]

The almain was a courtly dance performed by couples in a circular procession: like the pavan it had a dignified, stately quality. Morley described it as a 'more heavie daunce' than the galliard, 'so that no extraordinarie motions are used in dauncing of it'.[75] The almain was never popularized like the livelier galliard, which was primarily a solo dance and which became mixed up with the 'jig'.[76] We have sixteenth-century godly ballads written to 'The Black Almain' and 'The Queen's Almain', but none of these survived in the popular stock.

An examination of 'The Black Almain' suggests why. It is a complex melody of four four-measure phrases plus a two-bar coda. Steven Peel's 'warning to al London dames', set to this tune, uses a twelve-line stanza as opposed to the four- or eight-line units which later became standard ballad fare.[77] The range covers one and a half octaves; the melody would originally have been written for instrumental accompaniment to the dance,

---

[72] We know that the galliards and almains were danced at Court, and that some tunes like the Italian 'Rogero' (originally 'Ruggiero') and 'The Spanish pavin' were imported from the Continent. The inclusion of tunes in such manuscripts as 'My Ladye Nevells book' and 'The Fitzwilliam virginal book' shows their currency in aristocratic circles. (Simpson, pp. 612–14, 678–81, xxi.)

[73] See below, p. 79.

[74] Ballad excerpts are from Collmann no. 71, 75; Shirburn, p. 43; Collmann no. 84; Shirburn, pp. 170, 72. Tunes are from Simpson, pp. 43, 618, 612, 783, 535, 227.

[75] Cited in Bruce Pattison, *Music and poetry of the English Renaissance* (2nd edn, 1970), p. 184.

[76] Charles Read Baskervill, *The Elizabethan jig. And related song drama* (Chicago, 1929), pp. 143, 364.

[77] Ballads of twelve-line stanzas set to this tune require a repetition of the first strain and of the coda. (Simpson, p. 43.)

Fig. 5   Most popular godly ballad tunes: Elizabethan favourites compared with
1624 'stock'

Elizabethan tunes

'A Proper new balade expressying the fames, concerning a warning to al London
dames'

To the tune of 'The blacke Almaine'

You London dames, whose passying fames
  Through out the worlde is spread,
In to the skye, ascendyng hye
  To euery place is fled:
For thorow each land and place,
For beauties kyndely grace:
  You are renowned ouer all,
  You haue the prayse and euer shall.
What wight on earth that can beholde
More dearer and fayrer dames than you?
  Therfore to extoll you I may be bolde,
  Your paces and graces so gay to vieu.

'A lamentation from Rome, how the pope, doth bewayle, That the rebelles in England can not prevayle'

To the tune of 'Rowe well ye Mariners'

All you that newes would here,
Geue eare to me poore Fabyn Flye,
At Rome I was this yere,
And in the Pope his nose dyd lye,
But there I could not long abide,
He blew me out of euery side:
For surst when he had harde the newes,
That Rebelles dyd their Prince misuse,
Then he with ioye,
Did sporte him selfe with many a toye,
He then so stout,
From that his nose he blew me out.

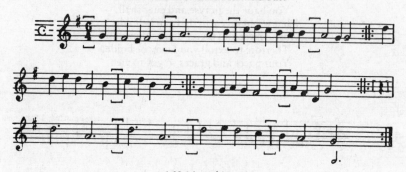

1624 'stock' tunes

'A right Godly and Chresteane a.b.c. Shewinge the dewty of every degre'

To the tune of 'Rogero'

Arise, and walke from wickedness;
    repent, and thow shalt lyve,
or else, with sword and pestilence,
    the Lord God will the[e] grieve.

Beware of lust and Letchery;
    keepe thow they body chast,
or else frequent the remedy
    that Paule doth say thow maist.

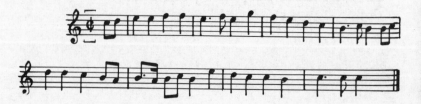

'A most excellent new dittie, wherein is shewed the sage sayings, and wise sentences of Salomon: wherein each estate is taught his duetie, with singular counsell to his comfort and consolation'

To the tune of 'Wigmoores Galliard'

Those that will run a Vertuous race,
  and learne the Precepts of the sage:
Those that true wisedome will imbrace
  and learne to liue in youth and age:
Let him approach hereto with speed,
And to these Lessons give good heed:
  for bearing well these thinges away,
  the Lord will blesse them night & day.

'The zealous Querister's songe of Yorke, in the prayse of heaven, to all faithfull singers and godlye readers in the world'

To the tune of 'O man in desparation'

Jerusalem, my happy home,
  when shall I come to thee?
When shall my sorrowes have an end:
  thy ioyes then shall I see?
When happy harbour is of Saints,
  with sweete and pleasant soyle.
In thee noe sorrowes ever were found,
  no griefe, no care, nor toyle.

'The judgment of God shewed upon one John Faustus, Doctor in Divinity'

To the tune of 'Fortune my Foe'

All Christian men, give ear a while to me,
How I am plung'd in pain but cannot die;
I liv'd a life the like did none before,
Forsaking Christ, and I am damn'd therefore.

At Wittenburge, a town in Germany,
There was I born and bred of good degree,
Of honest Stock, which afterwards I shamed,
Accurst therefore, for Faustus was I named.

Source: The music is from Claude M. Simpson, *The British broadside ballad and its music* (New Brunswick, New Jersey, 1966), pp. 43, 227, 535, 612, 618, 783. Copyright by Rutgers, The State University, reprinted by permission of Rutgers University Press.

not for vocal performance. The syncopated rhythm does not easily accommodate words, which have to be sung at two notes to the syllable ('You Lo-ondon da-ames, whose pa-assyng fames ...'). 'Row well ye Mariners' is also a complex melody which calls for a twelve-line stanza, 'each quatrain of which is metrically distinctive'.[78] All of the sixteenth-century ballads which name this tune may, as Simpson comments, 'be sung very smoothly to it'; yet the fact that it went out of fashion may indicate that the melody was not easily remembered. Certainly the dominance of the 'common' psalm tunes indicates that people coped best with a short, simple melodic line.

This principle is well illustrated by the tune of 'Rogero', a cheerful melody of four brief phrases, popular in 1624.[79] The 'Christians ABC' is in ballad metre (8.6.8.6.), and the words fit to the tune note-for-syllable, producing a jogging or marching effect which after much repetition could tend to 'annoy and as it were glut the ear', in Puttenham's words.[80] The four-square melody seems suited to the mnemonic purpose of the 'ABC', with its platitudinous aphorisms. Another long-lasting aphoristic ballad, 'Solomon's sentences', was set to 'Wigmore's Galliard'. Unfortunately the lute version we possess fits very awkwardly with all the extant texts; however, it appears that the running passages are purely ornamental, written to fill the vacuum left by long notes.[81] If this is so, we can hear a very simple and repetitive melody underneath the ornamentation.[82]

These lively tunes for godly lyrics, while memorable and obviously acceptable to many seventeenth-century ballad buyers, were something of an anachronism. The most commonly named tune in the 1624 religious stock, 'O man in desparation', is a much more solemn tune, described by the pamphleteer John Davies as 'light Notes and sad'.[83] The tune which appears to match this title can only be sung in a slow, ponderous manner. Its doleful

---

[78] *Ibid.*, p. 618. The first quatrain, as we see from Preston's 'Lamentation from Rome', requires a reversal of the normal ballad metre: here it is a three-beat followed by a four-beat line.

[79] The tune was of Italian origin. *Ibid.*, p. 612.

[80] Quoted on pp. 13–14. 'Christians ABC' was the common short form used for this ballad and its tune. See, for example, Arber, IV, pp. 131–2.

[81] Simpson, pp. 784–5. Apart from 'O man in desparation' it is the only ballad in Fig. 5 for which we do not have several variants to compare.

[82] Each verse of 'Solomon's sentences', with its eight lines in ballad metre, requires a repetition of the entire air.

[83] John Davies, *The scourge of folly* [1611], sig.Q3v:

> Yea Ballet-mongers make my sheetes to shake,
> To beare Rimes-doggrell making dogs perbrake;
> Whereto (ay me) grosse Burthens still they adde,
> And to that put againe, light Notes and sad:
> O Man in desperation, what a dewce
> Meanst thou such filth in my white face to sluce?

octave drops emphasize lament rather than hope in 'Jerusalem, my happy home':

> When shall my sorrowes have an end:
> thy ioyes when shall I see?

Another tune in the godly stock, 'Fortune my foe', was the most often-used seventeenth-century melody for ballads of murders, disasters and death-bed repentance. Its association with the story of Doctor Faustus, damned and 'plung'd in pain', led to the naming of 'Doctor Faustus' as the tune for other ballads.[84] 'Fortune' may have been played at a lively pace by Elizabethans, but in the seventeenth century it became a gloomy tune. The use of minims in the notation, as in 'O man in desparation', indicates the slow tempo.

'O man in desparation' and 'Fortune my foe' were, for seventeenth-century singers, specifically godly tunes. But in the early days of psalmody and balladry, there was no sense that religious tunes should not be lively: the psalms were known as Geneva 'jigs' and were written to 'galliards and measures'.[85] By the seventeenth century the tempo of psalm singing was slowing down as a natural result of oral transmission. The pace became more and more sluggish with the 'drag' of the less musical singers waiting for the pitch, the absence of instrumental accompaniment to keep up the tempo, and the echoing church building prolonging the sound.[86] Thomas Ravenscroft used crotchets when he printed secular folk tunes (1609–11) and minims for his psalms (1621), a differentiated notation which was continued throughout the latter half of the century in the editions of Playford's *Introduction to the skill of musick*.[87] By the time Shakespeare wrote *The winter's tale* (in 1610–11) the image of a puritan who 'sings psalms to hornpipes' was a source of amusement.[88] According to Temperley's estimate, the psalms were sung in the early seventeenth century at the tortoise-like speed of almost two seconds per note.[89]

With these ponderous psalms setting the standard for religious song, it is not surprising that dance tunes began to seem inappropriate for godly ballads. In 1588, just as godly ballad writing was going out of fashion, John Rhodes wrote his *Countrie mans comfort* for 'the poore Countrieman and his familie, who wil ask these vain questions, sometimes saying: what shall we doe in the long winter nights: how shall we passe away the time

[84] Simpson, p. 228.
[85] Howe's preface to Stowe's survey, 1615. The description is omitted in 1631. (Temperley, *Music of the English parish church*, I, p. 36.)
[86] *Ibid.*, pp. 64, 92.
[87] Playford printed psalms in minims and semibreves, songs and dances in crotchets and quavers. (Discussed in *ibid.*, p. 64.)
[88] Shakespeare, *A winter's tale*, IV, iii, 43–5.
[89] Temperley, *Music of the English parish church*, I, p. 64.

on Sundayes, what wold you have us doe in the Christmas Holydayes. . . .'.[90]
The recreation Rhodes offered consisted of the Creed, Ten Commandments
and Lord's Prayer in meter; versified graces, prayers and moral aphorisms;
carols for Christmas and other occasions; songs on the transience of worldly
pleasure. The ballad tunes to which Rhodes set his verses were almost all
associated with religious song: 'O Lord of whom I doe depend', 'Fortune
my foe', 'Labandala Shot' (originally a dance tune, but best known coupled
with a ballad beginning 'I Waile in wo, I plunge in pain').[91] Other tune
directions were 'the 15. Psalme', 'the 25. Psalme' and 'to the tune of any
ordinary Psalme'. It may be that this latter direction was taken as the accepted
procedure when no tune was named, as is the case for the majority of
Rhodes' pieces. The whole collection was in ballad metre, and could easily
be sung to any of the 'common tunes'.

Rhodes' choice of tunes tells us much about the growing sense of an
appropriate 'godly' melody. So does an examination of the tunes chosen
for new religious ballads written in the seventeenth century, which was
a diminishing genre, as we have seen. A trickle of religious texts continued
to be set to secular tunes. But most writers of godly ballads began to operate
within a closed world, naming the titles of other godly ballads as their
tunes. In fact, many of the post-Restoration pious ballads can be located
within one chain, all sung to the lugubrious 'Fortune my foe'. 'Fortune'
was named as the tune for an ABC ballad, 'An excellent song wherein you
shall finde / Great consolation for a troubled minde' [1628–9].[92] The first
line of this ballad 'Ayme not too hie', was the most popular alternate name
for the tune, and was used for 'The godly man's instructions' [post-1670].
'The godly mans instruction [*sic*]' was named as the tune for 'A letter for
a Christian family' [1684–6]; itself the tune for 'A lesson for all true Christians' [post-1692]. This ballad, in turn, provided the tune for 'A godly song
for all penitent sinners', 'The troubles of these times' and 'The youth's
guide'.[93]

One would think that this endless repetition of 'Fortune my foe' would
make the ballads tedious and unsaleable. However, perhaps this makes more

---

[90] John Rhodes, *The countrie mans comfort. Or religious recreations. Printed in 1588, and
since corrected by the author*, 2nd edn (1637), p. 1.

[91] Simpson, p. 419. Rhodes used two other ballad tunes. 'Rogero' was lively, but possibly
by then associated with moralizing songs like the 'Christians ABC'. 'In Crete when Daedalus
. . .', which Rhodes named twice, was used for such songs as 'The sinner's redemption'.
Thomas Nashe derided this tune in *Have with you to Saffron-Waldon* (1596), charging
that Gabriel Harvey looked upon it 'as food from heaven, and more transporting and ravish-
ing, than Platoes Discourse of the immortalitie of the soule was to Cato'. (Cited in Simpson,
p. 364.)

[92] RB repr. I, p. 325. Later ent. to 'partners', 13 March 1656.

[93] RB repr. VII, pp. 830, 811, 814, 692. Pepys, II, 50. Crawford 1014. Disentangled in
Simpson, pp. 229–30.

sense if we see it as a movement away from 'song' and back in the direction of 'chant'. Crowley, in his psalter of 1549, had seen no problem in setting all 150 psalms to one tune, based on the Gregorian reciting tones.[94] The primacy of words over musical variety in these seventeenth-century ballads was a logical extension of Calvinist thinking, even if the words themselves, lacking scriptural authority, would not have met with Calvin's approval.

The ungodly performers

Solemn tunes were for solemn themes. Dance tunes were for dancing. No doubt for some of the ballad writers and singers this was a matter of changing fashion: the hundredth psalm to the tune of 'Greensleeves' was out of style.[95] For others, any possible connection of religious themes with the activity of dancing was increasingly objectionable. William Perkins associated dancing with popish ceremony and argued that it was contrary to the second commandment; a ring of dancers round the maypole was 'a circle whose centre was the devil'.[96] Others worried primarily about licentiousness; William Prynne described how all Ten Commandments were breached in dancing.[97] Church court records do suggest that a certain amount of sexual play was normally tolerated as a part of the dance. A woman in Wiltshire who was seen to 'kiss and coll' with a married man, and with 'many others of the parish' while they were dancing, was said by the rector to have done nothing which did not become 'the modesty of a maid'.[98] The broadside ballads were closely linked with dance: they shared the same tunes, were often accompanied by the same wandering musicians, and were performed in the same public places. Some dance ballads explicitly encouraged participants to the sins the reformers abhorred, usually on the very day of the week which was supposed to be reserved for preaching and prayer.[99]

John Northbrooke refuted the argument that dancing is sanctioned in

[94] Robert Crowley, trans., *The psalter of David newely translated into Englysh metre. Where-unto is added a note of four partes* (1549).
[95] Mistress Ford: 'they do no more adhere and keep place together than the hundred Psalms to the tune of "Greensleeves"'. Shakespeare, *Merry Wives of Windsor* (written 1597, revised 1600–1), II, i, 62–3. The words of the hundredth psalm actually fit very poorly to the tune of 'Greensleeves', and Mistress Ford is referring primarily to this awkwardness. But Shakespeare may also be poking fun at the whole godly ballad genre, as with the puritan who sings psalms to hornpipes, above.
[96] Cited in Jeremy Goring, *Godly exercises or the devil's dance? Puritanism and popular culture in pre-Civil War England*. Friends of Dr William's Library, 37th lecture (1983), p. 22.
[97] Prynne, *Histrio-mastix* (1633), p. 231. Cited in *ibid.*, p. 12.
[98] Martin Ingram, *Church courts, sex and marriage in England, 1570–1640* (Cambridge, 1987), p. 241.
[99] See 'The west country jigg' on p. 36, above. On dancing as a pastime which lured young people away from church on Sunday, see Patrick Collinson, *The religion of Protestants. The church in English society 1559–1625*, The Ford Lectures 1979 (Oxford, 1982), pp. 224–30.

the Scriptures: holy women like Miriam, Jephthah's daughter and Judith danced together with other women, not wantonly with men. 'Also their daunces were spirituall, religious, and godly, not after our hoppings, and leapings, and interminglings men with women & c (dauncing every one for his part) but soberly, gravely, and matronelyke, moving scarce little or nothing in their gestures at all, eyther in countenance or bodie.'[100] This notion of a 'godly' form of dance appears to be the physical corollary of the 'poids et majesté' prescribed by Calvin as the criterion for religious music.

Reformers objected not only to the associations with the dance, but to the general bawdiness of the ballads themselves and the dubious character of their performers. There were tales of amorous exploits which remained gleefully outside the realm of religious teleology. 'Watkins Ale' was a bawdy allegory for the male generative fluid:

> He took her by the middle small,
> And gave her more of Watkins ale . . .
> Her colour waxed wan and pale
> With taking much of Watkins ale.[101]

When the travelling ballad singers had a collection like this, one can begin to imagine how reformers like Nicholas Bownde did not want the word of God sung in the same context. In 1595 he considered the possibility of printing the psalms as broadsides, but rejected it on these grounds: 'Indeed, many of the common singing men are so ungodly, that it were better for them to leave their mouths stopped, then once to open them to pollute such holy and sacred songs.'[102]

These ungodly singing men were, of course, the minstrels and pedlars discussed in chapter 1, often living a vagrant life on the fringes of poverty and petty crime. In Ben Jonson's fictionalized presentation of this lifestyle, the ballad singer Nightingale performs a 'Caveat against cutpurses' as a diversion while his partner picks pockets in the crowd. Godly words are merely a pretext for vice.

> But O, you vile nation of cutpurses al
> Relent and repent and amend and be sound.[103]

It was not only the ballad singers who had a reputation for an ungodly lifestyle. The ballad writers were associated with drunkenness in the pamphlet literature. In the 1560s, Elderton was lampooned for having a red nose;

---

[100] John Northbrooke, *A treatise wherein dicing, dauncing, vaine playes or enterluds .. are reproved* [1577?], sig. Q3v.

[101] 'A ditty delightfull of Mother Watkins ale' [c. 1590], Lilly, p. 251.

[102] Nicholas Bownde, *The doctrine of the sabbath* (1595), p. 241. A few 'psalms' did appear in broadside form, but these were psalms reworked as political propaganda for Elizabeth. (Zim, *English metrical psalms*, pp. 251, 257.)

[103] Ben Jonson, *Bartholomew Fair* (1614), III, v.

in the 1630s, Parker was an alehouse-keeper.[104] Thomas Nashe complained in 1596 about Thomas Deloney, 'the Balleting Silke weaver'. Apparently it was because Deloney's muse had been so deprived of ale that year that 'not one merrie Dittie will come from him, but *The Thunderbolt against Swearers, Repent, England Repent*, and *The Strange judgements of God*'.[105] In satirical writing, then, the alehouse hack was associated less with bawdy ballads than with false godly ones. If many of the early religious ballads had been written by sincere and zealous reformers, the typical pot-poet described by John Earle in 1628 is a mere hypocrite: 'sitting in a bawdy house he writes God's judgements'.[106]

Eventually, for some of these hacks, God's judgements would be left out entirely. Martin Parker's corpus, dating from 1624 to 1643, shows a marked absence of religious ballads. His new ballads are filled with physical details instead of with religious lessons.[107] Even a promising title like the 'Whoremonger's conversion' bases its warning on this-worldly punishment: the loss of money and the danger of catching diseases.[108] Religion comes in briefly with the lame threat 'or else you'll sayle th'infernall lake', then the ballad goes on to delight in the subject it has chosen to denounce.

The repertoire of ballad writers and singers was at best hypocritical; at worst it was outrightly immoral. Or so it appeared to the second generation of reformers and educated Protestants. Even those who wrote in defence of poetry, like Thomas Lodge in 1579, were intent on disassociating themselves from the ballads: 'Believe mee the magestrats may take advice, (as I knowe wisely can) to roote out those odde rymes which runnes in every rascales mouth. Savoring of rybaldry, those foolishe ballets, that are admitted, make poets good and godly practises to be refused.'[109] For Nicholas Bownde, ballad singing was in direct competition with psalm singing:

For as when the light of the Gospel came first in, the singing of ballads (that was rife in Poperie) began to cease, and in time was cleane banished away in many places: so now the sudden renewing of them, and hastie receiving of them everywhere, maketh me to suspect, least they should drive away the singing of Psalms again, seeing they can so hardly stand together.[110]

[104] Rollins, 'William Elderton'; Newman, 'The broadside ballads of Martin Parker', I, p. 2.
[105] Nashe, *Have with you to Saffron-Waldon*, in R.B. McKerrow, ed., *The works of Thomas Nashe* (1904–10), III, p. 84.
[106] John Earle, 'Micro-cosmographie' (1628). Quoted in Natascha Wurzbach, *Die englische straßenballade 1550–1650* (Munich, 1981), pp. 403–4.
[107] Of three murder ballads, only one mentions in passing that the culprit has forfeited his soul; and God is left entirely out of the ballad of a monstrous fish. (Newman, 'The broadside ballads of Martin Parker', II, ballads nos. 1, 44.)
[108] Ibid., II, ballad no. 24.
[109] Thomas Lodge, [A defence of poetry, music and stage plays] [1579].
[110] Bownde, *Doctrine of the sabbath*, p. 242.

The two activities were now mutually exclusive, and (at least for the reformers) there could be no such thing as a 'godly' ballad.

Serious professors and the heathenish ignorant[111]

The reformers were cutting some of their links with traditional recreations. Not only were they distancing themselves from the ballads, but also from drama and from certain types of graphic art.[112] Many Stuart writers were still concerned with their mission to evangelize and instruct the poor.[113] However, they transferred their efforts to other forms of print, to be used in very different contexts. We know that despite the decline of religious ballads, the total output of religious print remained very high: 42% of the STC works published in 1640 can be classified as religious.[114] While the number of works printed per year had almost tripled since 1550, the religious percentage had kept pace, remaining roughly the same as in the Elizabethan period. There was a growth in the production of prayer books, psalters, catechisms, sermons and treatises, versified biblical paraphrases, moralizing pamphlets, handbooks to devotion.[115]

Some of these forms were, like the ballads, still designed for both oral and literate modes of communication. Prayer books were read in church; sermons were first heard aloud; catechisms were based on memorization, and taught through verbal question-and-answer sessions. Buf if this was 'oral culture', it was of a very different sort: centred around parish priest and church, possibly with a radius extending to the satellite station of the 'good household'.[116] Religious treatises could be read aloud to the unlettered, but could never spread through the countryside as effectively as a broadside ballad could, once it was cut loose from the printed page, and fixed to a tune in the popular memory. The ballad was a very public medium: performed to gathered crowds, passed around in taverns, sung at work or in holiday festivities. If Protestant ballads had never really achieved this kind of ubiquity, they at least represented a broader vision and a wider range of potential appeal.

---

[111] Richard Baxter, *Confirmation and restauration, the necessary means of reformation and reconciliation* (1658), pp. 157–65.

[112] Collinson, *From iconoclasm to iconophobia.*

[113] Eamon Duffy, 'The godly and the multitude in Stuart England', *Seventeenth Century Journal*, 1 (1986), pp. 31–55.

[114] Calculated from figures given in Edith L. Klotz, 'A subject analysis of English imprints for every tenth year from 1480 to 1640', *Huntington Library Quarterly*, 1 (1938), p. 418.

[115] Louis B. Wright, *Middle-class culture in Elizabethan England* (Ithaca, 1958 edn), pp. 228–96. Sandra Clark, *The Elizabethan pamphleteers. Popular moralistic pamphlets 1580–1640* (1983). Ian Green's *Religious instruction in early modern England c. 1540–1740* (in progress) will for the first time properly quantify these developments.

[116] See ch. 6.

The changing media also expressed changing concerns of the reformers. While early Elizabethan ballads had focussed on the broad social reform and conversion from popery, later clerical authors had high demands about the people's understanding of sacramental doctrine and the need for spiritual self-examination. Many of the parish clergy began to expect more knowledge from their catechumens than was found in the official Edwardian catechism, and to publish alternative versions to this end.[117] Ian Green shows a barrage of alternative catechisms after 1570, reaching their first peak in the 1580s, just as the ballad was declining. He identifies over 250 independent catechetical works: with repeat editions, Green calculates that 'over three-quarters of a million copies of these works were in circulation by the early seventeenth century', in addition to perhaps half a million copies of the official forms'.[118]

Protestant reformers directed their energies increasingly within a closed godly culture centred on the church and private household, rather than more public and 'popular' forms of recreation. The decline of religious ballad writing is evidence of a growing gap which they perceived between certain 'godly' and 'ungodly' spheres of activity, each sphere with its own exclusive type of music: the godly psalms and the ungodly ballads. Richard Baxter's description of his childhood in Shropshire shows the important part music could play in causing a keen sense of separation of 'the saints' from 'the rest'. Each Sunday the villagers spent dancing under a maypole near Baxter's house: 'So that we could not read the Scripture in our family without the great disturbance of the tabor and pipe and noise in the street. Many times I was inclined to be among them ... But when I heard them call my father Puritan it did much to cure me and alienate me from them.'[119] 'Puritan' separatists could bring this alienation on themselves by encouraging social segregation of the elect from the irreligious majority within the parish. From the other side, the cultural rift was widened by playwrights and pamphleteers who made 'precise' religion (along with 'godly ballads') the butt of mockery, and a threat to 'good fellowship'. In 1639 Beaumont and Fletcher satirized the godly gentleman who was no longer a good fellow. His former friend complains:

> ... thou hast marr'd him,
> Thou and thy prayer-books. I do disclaim him.
> Did not I take him singing yesternight
> A godly ballad, to a godly tune too,
> And had a certain catechism in's pocket, damsel?
> One of your dear disciples, I perceive it.

[117] Ian Green, "For children in yeeres and children in understanding": the emergence of the English catechism under Elizabeth and the early Stuarts', *Journal of Ecclesiastical History*, 37 (1986), pp. 397–425.

[118] *Ibid.*, p. 425.

[119] *The autobiography of Richard Baxter*, ed. N.H. Keeble (1974), p. 6.

When did he ride abroad since he came over?
What tavern has he used to? what things done
That shew a man and mettle? When was my house
At such a shame before, to creep to bed
At ten o'clock, and twelve, for want of company?
No singing, nor no dancing, nor no drinking?[120]

Court records show that tensions between 'the precise' and the rest of the
community played a genuine part in many local conflicts, and that popular
music could be used as a weapon. A case brought to the Star Chamber
in 1632 records a libellous song composed extempore by a servant in a
Rymes alehouse, and set to the ballad tunes of 'The watch currants' and
'Tom of Bedlam'. The song implied adultery between two of the town's
godly sort, and was well received in the alehouse. One listener paid a quart
of wine to a scribe for a written copy, which he showed to various people
about town.[121]

However, dislike of the self-styled 'godly sort' is no evidence that those
who danced under maypoles never worried about their souls. Religion was
still an inescapable presence in ordinary people's lives. A full exploration
of their beliefs has been hampered by the tendency of historians to see
religious culture in terms of a binary opposition. In their study of Terling
in Essex, Keith Wrightson and David Levine drew a picture of a village
community which was becoming increasingly divided in the early seventeenth
century. Religion was a form of cultural differentiation which helped the
parish elite – the yeomen, substantial tradesmen and husbandmen – to detach
themselves from their poorer neighbours.[122] Protestant codes of behaviour
were imposed from above on 'a popular culture of communal dancings,
alehouse sociability and the like', which was being transformed into 'a culture
of poverty'.[123] Anthony Fletcher and John Stevenson have taken up this
theory of increasing 'polarisation' between polite and plebeian culture in
the seventeenth century. Although they caution against a 'rigid dichotomy
between classes', they accept the basic division between a Protestantized
culture of the gentry and some of the middling ranks, and a 'traditional
culture' of the labourers and the poor.[124]

[120] Francis Beaumont and John Fletcher, *Monsieur Thomas* (1639), in *Beaumont and Fletcher*,
ed. A. Glover and A.R. Waller (10 vols., Cambridge, 1905–12), IV, p. 134.

[121] Gardiner, ed., *Reports of cases in the courts of Star Chamber and High Commission*,
pp. 149–53. A version of 'Tom a Bedlam' is in Simpson, p. 711. A similar incident took
place at a Lincolnshire victualling house in James I's reign, when a piper was encouraged
to sing a song libelling the 'Puritans of Nottingham'. (Peter Clark, *The English alehouse:
a social history 1200–1830* (1983), p. 156.)

[122] Keith Wrightson and David Levine, *Poverty and piety in an English village. Terling, 1525–
1700* (1979), pp. 17–18, 176.

[123] *Ibid.*, pp. 171, 182.

[124] A.J. Fletcher and J. Stevenson, 'A polarised society?', in Fletcher and Stevenson, eds.,
Order and disorder in early modern England (Cambridge, 1985), p. 3.

This view of cultural division has been attacked from several angles. Margaret Spufford criticizes the equation of religious belief with a particular social or economic status, suggesting that we may have underestimated the existence of 'puritanism' amongst humbler villagers.[125] Martin Ingram argues not only that any rift between 'godly' and 'ungodly' was not necessarily along class lines, but also that the divisions themselves were not so clear-cut. His exploration of church court records in Wiltshire suggests a broad consensus of values on issues of sexual morality and social behaviour. The church and religion were touchstones of respectability for 'honest householders' at all social levels, including the poorer sort.[126] Rather than looking for binary opposition, we should recognize a 'broad spectrum' of religious belief, including many shades of 'unspectacular orthodoxy'.[127] A helpful contemporary source, from this point of view, is Richard Baxter's description of his parish at Kidderminster, which has been used by Eamon Duffy to show popular piety in an 'altogether more three-dimensional picture than any two-culture polarity'.[128]

Baxter described twelve different types of parishioner, in a subtle range of distinctions between degrees of religious commitment, understanding of doctrine and morality of lifestyle. About a third of the 1,800 communicants in Baxter's parish constitued the inner core, most of them 'such as the vulgar call precise, that are rated to be serious Professours of Religion'. But amongst the rest of the parishioners, there was no one described as being completely lacking in religious knowledge or opinions. Some of 'tractable dispositions' had problems grasping the meaning of 'Sanctification, Faith, or Justification', and even seemed not to know the story of Christ's life, death and resurrection. Yet they believed in 'their good serving' of God, which meant 'saying every night and morning in bed, or as they undress them, the Lords Prayer and the Creed for a Prayer, and comming to Church'. Others who lived 'in idle or tipling company' took the trouble to read 'all the books that are written for admitting all to the Lord's Table, that they can light of'. Even those 'hardened in ungodliness' justified their behaviour with the conviction that all is predestined by God, and therefore 'they cannot do nothing of themselves'.

Baxter's account is twenty years out of our period, and the proportion he places in each category of parishioner may be biassed or atypical. Nevertheless, his wide spectrum of popular belief makes some sense out of the evidence of the broadside ballads. If reformers had stopped writing godly

[125] M. Spufford, 'Puritanism and social control?' in *ibid.*, pp. 44–7.
[126] Ingram, *Church courts, sex and marriage*, pp. 118, 123–4.
[127] *Ibid.*, p. 94.
[128] Baxter, *Confirmation and restauration*, pp. 157–65. Discussed in Duffy, 'The godly and the multitude', pp. 38–40.

ballads, the evidence of the 'partners' ballad stock shows that somebody was still buying them. These ballads sometimes tended towards the same 'erroneous' opinions described by Baxter and by William Perkins, such as pelagianism, or a belief in universal redemption.[129] It is very likely that the godly ballad buyers were not solely, not even primarily, the 'serious Professours' at the core of the parish. This well-catechized group would probably have demanded more sophisticated forms of religious print, such as sermons and guides to devotion. If they could afford it, they might have saved their money for a testament or psalter; if not, psalm singing and sermon going were always free.

Meanwhile, the group Baxter called 'secret Heathens', who made a show of religion for respectability, might well have liked to display '100 godly lessons' stuck up prominently on their wall. They could be seen publicly buying a godly ballad as they filed out after the sermon: Fletcher writes of 'church corners where "Dives" and the suff'ring Ballads hang'.[130] Those whom Baxter said had yet to absorb the Protestant doctrine of salvation may have found 'St Bernard's vision' appealing. The hardened drunks and infidels might at least enjoy 'David and Bethsheba', if they did not break down and purchase 'The dying teares of a penitent sinner' in a moment of weakness.[131]

The contradiction between godly and ungodly spheres of activity was not as clear-cut to the pre-1640 ballad-buying public as it was to some Protestant ministers and writers (and to some twentieth-century historians). The surviving ballads reflect a spectrum of belief throughout the whole parish, not only the consistent, considered doctrine of the godliest sort. The activities of the more zealous reformers had not succeeded in catechizing ordinary people out of an interest in their eternal salvation, despite their unwillingness to give up a merry tune.

---

[129] Perkins' list of errors is quoted in Green, 'For children in yeeres and children in understanding', p. 414.

[130] John Fletcher (and Thomas Middleton), *Nice Valour* (1647), IV, i, in *Beaumont and Fletcher*, ed. Glover and Waller, X, p. 181. 'Dives' refers to the parable of 'Dives and Lazarus', first registered as a ballad in 1557–8, and possibly surviving in the form of Child ballad no. 56. (Rollins Index no. 2293.)

[131] Ballads discussed below, pp. 108, 117.

3

The 1624 stock

In 1631–2, one of the leading ballad publishers, Henry Gosson, was brought before the High Commission for printing a 'scurrilous' ballad, of which one stanza was recorded: 'Jacob came to Heaven gate, and Adam kept the doore, thou art a sinner, Adam said, but thou (saith Jacob) wast the causer of our woe, wherat he runnes away for woe'. Gosson accepted responsibility for the ballad reluctantly, replying that it was 'printed before he was born and he hath but renewed it, and is very sorry for it.'[1] Although we have only a few scraps of information about the incident, it illustrates the change in the ballad trade from half a century earlier. The Elizabethan authorities normally had a living author at whom to point the finger, and a printer who was fully accountable as the author's accomplice. Now, Gosson claimed, he was only reproducing old stock from 'before he was born'. The ballad publisher had become a custodian of tradition. He printed songs (whether religious or irreligious), which had proven themselves saleable, and with whose authors and origins he had, in many cases, lost contact.

The decline of godly ballad writing coincided with changes in the structure of the broadside ballad trade. These developments were not unrelated. To expand the market, the publishers needed to organize themselves properly for distribution, to which end a syndicate was created. The success of the 'ballad partners' at infiltrating rural musical culture, by way of an increasing number of vagrant ballad sellers, could only have exacerbated the objections of the reformers. Meanwhile, as ballad writing went out of style in educated Protestant circles, this may have encouraged the publishers' tendency to rely increasingly on the reproduction of old favourites for their godly stock. This continual reprinting gained its own momentum, as the audience apparently came to demand the familiar ballads in a familiar format.

[1] Samuel Rawson Gardiner, ed., *Reports of cases in the courts of Star Chamber and High Commission* (Camden Society, 1886), p. 314. Based on abstracts from Bodleian Rawlinson MS A128 (see above, p. 43).

TRANSITION IN THE TRADE

Specialization

In the early Elizabethan years, most of the stationers of London dealt in the occasional ballad. Some forty stationers registered at least one broadside with the Stationer's Company during its first ten years.[2] But in the same period, only seven published ballads as their main staple, while another five published up to several dozen ballads.[3] In the second and third generations of ballad publishers, the number of stationers heavily involved in the ballad trade remained comparable; however, it became much rarer for other publishers to put out the odd ballad or two.[4] In 1612 a Stationers' Company order limited the *printing* of ballads to five stationers.[5] Meanwhile, during James' reign, a group of the poorer booksellers gradually accumulated the copyright to the popular stock ballads.

The new 'ballad partners' were Thomas Pavier, John Grismond, Henry Gosson and the three brothers John, Cuthbert and Edward Wright. A court order of 6 November 1624 ordered 'Pavier and partners' to register their ballads 'heretofore disorderly printed without entrance or allowance'.[6] In 1625 Thomas Pavier died and was succeeded by Francis Coules in 1626. The growing domination of the trade by the 'partners' was interrupted in 1628–9 by the misuse of a patent for the printing of broadsides operated by Thomas Symcocke, who began to publish ballads on his own behalf, disregarding copyrights.[7] Several ballad publishers still operated independently outside the partnership, notably Thomas Lambert, John Trundle

---

[2] Hyder E. Rollins, 'The black-letter broadside ballad', *Publications of the Modern Language Association*, 34 (1919), p. 260. He found thirty more names on unregistered extant copies before 1580.

[3] Richard Jones registered 164 separate titles during his career, not including 123 entered in 1586 which were listed on a sheet of paper now lost. Following Jones were Thomas Colwell (113 titles), John Aldee (100), William Griffith (79), Alexander Lacy (74), John Charlewood (66) and William Pickering (57). Those who produced ballads as a sideline included John Awdeley, Henry Kyrkham, Thomas Purfoote, Richard Lante and Hugh Singleton.

[4] The generation which set up shop in the late 1570s and 1580s was headed by Edward White (126 registered titles), Henry Carr (70), John Wolfe (53) and John Danter (49).

[5] These were Edward Allde, George Elde, William White, Symon Stafford, Ralph Blore. (William A Jackson, ed., *Records of the Court of the Stationers' Company 1602 to 1640* (1957), pp. 54–5.) On 23 January 1621 ballad sellers were again allowed to employ any printing establishment. (*Ibid.*, p. 33.)

[6] *Ibid.*, p. 171.

[7] According to Jackson's count from the original STC, of thirty-nine ballads printed for Symcocke at this time at least ten were covered by the 'partners' entry of 1624. (*Ibid.*, pp. xvi–xxii.)

and Francis Grove. However, by the 1630s the 'partners' had a near monopoly on the publication and distribution of the most popular ballad titles.[8]

The 'ballad partners' were booksellers, not printers.[9] The primary function of the partnership does not appear to have been collaboration in the
actual production of the ballads, but rather, their distribution.[10] While
some of the 'partners' were more involved in the publication process, all
may have taken part in the distribution of the thousands of ballad sheets
which bore the imprint of one of the members.[11]

There are various indications that distribution was a particular skill of
these booksellers. John Wright, for example, sold a number of titles (at
least seventeen) published by other stationers; an indication of his access
to markets which they could not reach from their own shops.[12] His shop
was located on Guiltspur Street just outside Newgate, well placed for carriers
going west or north-west from the city. It was near the market at West
Smithfield, where chapmen gathered to purchase wares of all kinds. Smithfield was still the main neighbourhood for ballad and chapbook publishers
in the late seventeenth century. Routes to the south were covered by another
cluster of shops on London Bridge, where Henry Gosson was now set up.[13]
Francis Coules and Francis Grove were also located just outside Newgate:
Coules in the Old Bailey and Grove on Snowhill. In 1624 John Trundle,
another ballad publisher who had kept shop at his famous sign of the
'Nobody' in Barbican, moved down the road to Smithfield, the centre of
the ballad trade.[14]

Apart from ballads, Henry Gosson's staple products were the pamphlets
of John Taylor the Water Poet, of which he published thirty.[15] Taylor
sheds light on the distribution network in the early seventeenth century.
In *The carriers cosmographie* (1637), Taylor listed the inns around London

[8] A detailed account of the events leading up to the formation of the partnership has already
     been given in R.S. Thomson, 'The development of the broadside ballad trade and its influence
     upon the transmission of English folksongs' (Cambridge PhD, 1974), Part I, chs. 1–2.
[9] The only exception was John Grismond.
[10] Cyprian Blagden, 'Notes on the ballad market in the second half of the seventeenth century',
     Papers of the Bibliographical Society of the University of Virginia, 6 (1953–4), p. 167.
     Gerald D. Johnson, 'John Trundle and the book-trade 1603–1626', *Studies in Bibliography*,
     39 (1986), p. 189.
[11] Henry Gosson, John Wright and Francis Coules appear to have been most active in the
     ballad trade (see ch. 7). Only a few ballad imprints survive for Cuthbert and Edward
     Wright, Thomas Pavier and John Grismond. R.S. Thomson claims that both Grismond
     and Cuthbert Wright were sleeping partners ('Development of the broadside ballad trade',
     p. 57), but Cuthbert's name appears alone on several ballads (e.g. RB orig. I, 134–5;
     Pepys, I, 59) as does Grismond's (e.g. Pepys, I, 242–3.)
[12] Johnson, 'John Trundle', p. 189.
[13] Margaret Spufford, *Small books and pleasant histories. Popular fiction and its readership
     in seventeenth-century England* (1981), map 1 on p. 114.
[14] Johnson, 'John Trundle', p. 181.
[15] See p. 291.

where carriers could be found on specific days of the week, bound for over 200 towns across Britain (with any number of stops in between), and able to deliver goods and letters to the remotest regions of Scotland, Wales and Cornwall. Taylor's own pamphlets travelled some of these routes. While apologizing for any mistakes in the list, the author quips: 'I hope I shall give none of my Readers cause to curse the carrier that brought me [ie. this pamphlet] to towne.'

The 'partners' first entry of 14 December 1624 records the accumulation of 127 ballads, consisting largely of old Elizabethan stock. In this entry, more than two-thirds of the religious titles which can be traced are of six-teenth-century origin. And of these, two-thirds had been published by the year 1586, when the Star Chamber decree ordered stationers to bring in their old copies which had not been properly authorized.[16]

It is in 1586 that the records first show the accumulation of large numbers of 'stock' ballads in a few hands. The largest entry of 123 ballads to Richard Jones was unfortunately listed on a separate sheet which is now lost.[17] It is possible that many of the 'partners' 1624 titles were on that list. In 1598, Jones sold his business to William White, who was one of the official printers of ballads from 1612 to 1620.[18] White was printing ballads for the senior 'partner' Thomas Pavier around 1615.[19] The future 'partners' may have acquired ballad copyrights from William or from his son John who succeeded him in 1618.[20]

R. S. Thomson may have overemphasized the importance of Jones' stock, for quite a number of the 1624 ballads were owned by stationers other than Jones in 1586.[21] The second largest entry in 1586 was one of thirty-six ballads to Edward White, whose titles were luckily entered directly into the register. One fifth of the 1624 godly ballads were from Edward White's stock.[22] Here we have several definite links between these two generations in the ballad trade (see publishers' genealogy, Fig. 6). John Wright was apprenticed to Edward White in 1594, and was one of the senior

---

[16] Six godly ballads in the 1624 entry were registered in the 1560s, two in the 1570s, seven more by 1586. The five ballads entered in August 1586, in response to the Star Chamber decree, were probably of earlier origin. (See App. A.) The 'secular' ballads are also primarily Elizabethan.

[17] Arber, II, p. 452.

[18] Arber, III, p.702.

[19] For example, 'A most excellent new dittie, wherein is shewed the sage sayings, and wise sentences of Salomon' [c. 1615], Collmann no. 84.

[20] Information from Katherine Pantzer, Houghton Library.

[21] Thomson suggests a very close relationship between Jones' missing list of 123 ballads and the 'partners' 128. ('Development of the broadside ballad trade', p. 54.)

[22] 'Rogers will', 'John Carelesse', 'From sluggish sleepe', 'When Jesus Christ was 12', 'Christians ABC', 'Proverbs of Salomon', 'Good Lord what a wicked world'. (See App. A nos. 2, 3, 5, 7, 8, 10, 11.)

'partners'.[23] When Edward died around 1613 he was succeeded by his son Edward (2), who passed the shop to another 'partner', John Grismond, in 1618. The son Edward died in 1624, the year of the large ballad entry, and his widow assigned her property in a number of copies to the printer Edward Allde. Allde had close ties with the 'partners' as official ballad printer from 1612 to 1620, and with his career stretching back to 1584, he may provide another strong personal link in the ballad chain.[24]

R. S. Thomson has already impressively illustrated the importance of the broadside 'stock' in the transmission and survival of folksong. Thomson showed how ballads collected from the oral tradition by folk enthusiasts in the last two centuries in fact owe their survival to the reinforcement of the printed word.[25] He traced the titles of many 'familiar folksongs' which appear and reappear in the 'partners' batch entries of 1624,1656 and 1675; and later, in ballad sellers' catalogues of the eighteenth century.[26] I will follow his example, using inclusion in the 1624 stock list (and reappearance in the later 'partners' entries) as the best measure of success for the 'godly' ballads.

'Packaging' the ballad

The consolidation of copyrights to the popular ballad titles was accompanied by a new emphasis on what we would now call 'marketing strategy'. The most striking change was the institution of woodcut pictures as a standard feature. In the sixteenth century, apart from borders and initial letters, woodcut embellishment was not the norm. Only one fifth of surviving sixteenth-century religious ballads are illustrated.[27] Taking the sixteenth-century collections as a whole ('secular' as well as 'religious' ballads), no more than roughly one quarter have some kind of woodcut decoration.

In the seventeenth century, the proportion of ballads with woodcuts was completely reversed. For the period 1600–40, more than five-sixths of extant religious ballads are illustrated.[28] There was also more of an attempt than in the sixteenth century to achieve some correlation between text and

---

[23] John Wright was apprenticed to Edward White 24 June 1594, and gained his freedom on 28 June 1602. (Arber, II, pp. 194, 732.) I am grateful to Sheila Lambert for this information. Blagden and Thomson both mistakenly state that John was an apprentice of Windet, but this apprentice was another, unconnected Wright. (Blagden, 'Notes on the ballad market', p. 180; Thomson, 'Development of the broadside ballad trade', ch. 2.)

[24] 29 June 1624 (Arber, IV, p. 120). See Tessa Watt, 'Cheap print and religion c. 1550 to 1640' (Cambridge PhD, 1988) p. 104 nn. 28, 29.

[25] Thomson, 'Development of the broadside ballad trade', especially map.

[26] See Table 2 below.

[27] Fourteen out of sixty-six ballads.

[28] There are woodcuts on thirty-eight of forty-five broadsides. The same trend can be confirmed for the secular ballads (Watt, 'Cheap print and religion', p. 105 n. 34).

image.[29] The importance placed on the woodcuts is one of the best indications of a growing commercial sense in the ballad trade, and an awareness
of the demands of the public.

Unfortunately, this change of visual appearance cannot be dated precisely
because of a gap in the surviving broadsides: the sixteenth-century collections
are mostly concentrated in the period from around 1550 to 1572, while
the seventeenth-century collections do not begin in full force until 1624–5.[30]
Woodcuts may have become a regular feature at the instigation of the leading
'partners'-to-be who began their careers at the turn of the century.[31] Or
it may have been an innovation of the small group of printers to whom
ballad printing was officially delegated in 1612. Illustration was accompanied by a standardization of format, with the growing prevalence
of the style which dominated for most of the seventeenth century: the two-
part folio sheet with a row of woodcuts along the top.[32]

If the ballad buyers were growing to expect a familiar format with familiar
illustrations, they could also now expect the name of a tune to appear on
the ballad sheet. For the sixteenth century, tunes are named on only a quarter
to a third of surviving religious broadside ballads.[33] On secular ballads
the percentage is slightly higher, between a third and a half. When no tune
was named, this did not necessarily mean that no particular tune was implied.
In a couple of cases the ballad was meant to be sung to its *own* tune,
sometimes labelled 'to a pleasant new tune'. Others have distinctive refrains
which hint at specific tunes.[34] Some of the religious ballads are parodies
of popular songs which we no longer know, and were meant to be sung
to the same melody.[35] If there were no internal clues, the ballad singer-sellers
may have passed on the tunes by word of mouth.

In the early seventeenth century this situation changes. Tunes are named

[29] See p. 149.
[30] Watt, 'Cheap print and religion', p. 106. From the point of view of the ballad *texts*, this
gap is filled by manuscript collections (see App. C).
[31] Thomas Pavier was free of the Stationers' Company in 1600, Henry Gosson in 1601 and
John Wright in 1602. (R.B. McKerrow, *A dictionary of printers and booksellers in England,
Scotland and Ireland, and of foreign printers of English books 1557–1640* (1910), with
corrections from Sheila Lambert and Katherine Pantzer.)
[32] On format see Watt, 'Cheap print and religion', p. 107 n. 40; Thomson, 'Development
of the broadside ballad trade', p. 64.
[33] Tunes are named directly on eighteen of the sixty-six religious ballads from the sixteenth-
century.
[34] For example, 'The constancy of Susanna' (Pepys, I, 33) has the refrain 'Lady, lady' which
indicates that it should be sung to King Solomon. (Simpson, pp. 410–12.)
[35] When contemporaries read 'The complaint of a sinner, vexed with paine' (Collmann no.
7) they could tell from the first line it was to be sung to the tune of Elderton's 'Gods
of love'. 'A ballad intituled, A newe well a daye, as playne, maister papist, as Donstable
waye' (Lilly, p. 1) obviously went to the tune 'Welladay'. (Simpson, pp. 261, 747.)

directly on roughly four-fifths of surviving broadsides.[36] This helps us to
establish the seventeenth-century ballad more firmly as song, and to distinguish it from the broadside meant only to be read or looked at. The
naming of tunes also suggests that the publishers could no longer rely on
subtle clues or word of mouth; that the ballads were reaching a wider public.
A tune stated clearly in print would either be known already in the countryside, or could be enquired of by name from the ballad seller or other travel-
lers. In *The winter's tale*, when Autolycus produces a ballad to the tune
of 'Two maids wooing a man', the shepherdess Dorcas assures him that
'we had the tune on't a month ago'.[37]

After woodcuts, format and tune, the final indication of the transformed
ballad was a negative one: the absence of an author. In the sixteenth century,
almost three-quarters of extant 'religious' ballads named the author on the
broadside, either by full name or initials.[38] Broadsides were often used
for flyting: for contrived literary invective like the Churchyard–Camel controversy of 1552 which produced over a dozen ballads, probably indecipherable to those outside a small London-centred coterie.[39] More 'popular'
ballads still revolved around cults of personality: William Elderton with
his red nose, Dick Tarlton the jester.[40] Broadside epitaphs sang the personal
praises of merchants and gentry. Respectable clergymen and educated laymen signed their names to ballads expounding religious doctrine and argument for reform. The Elizabethan 'ballad' was more often the wit, poetry
or polemic of an individual author than it was the anonymous story or
'folksong' transcribed from tradition.[41]

However, on the seventeenth-century broadsides, authors were never
named, with two sorts of exception. The first was for the very rare ballad
hacks whose names seem to have carried with them a popular following:
names such as Martin Parker, and Laurence Price (usually known just as
M.P. and L.P.). There are only two ballads which touch on religious issues
by these authors; godliness was not their speciality.[42] The second kind
of named author was the narrator and main character of the ballad; some

---

[36] Of the early seventeenth-century religious ballads, eight out of forty have no tune named
on the broadside. Half of these eight are to a 'pleasant' or 'excellent' tune, i.e. their own.
If anything, secular ballads without named tunes are even less common.

[37] Shakespeare, *The winter's tale*, IV, iv, 288–94.

[38] Forty-seven out of sixty-four ballads.

[39] There are thirteen surviving in the Society of Antiquaries (nos. 20–32).

[40] Hyder E. Rollins, 'William Elderton: Elizabethan actor and ballad writer', *Studies in Philology*, 17 (1920), pp. 214, 235–7, 239.

[41] There are only twenty extant broadsides of 'traditional folksongs' prior to 1640, according
to Thomson, 'Development of the broadside ballad trade', p. 57. However, Thomson does
not discuss the possibility that other ballads may have been 'folksong' in the sixteenth
and seventeenth centuries, even if they have not survived into the twentieth century.

[42] Martin Parker, 'A scourge for the pope' [1624], Pepys, I, 60–1; Laurence Price, 'Bee patient
in trouble' [1636], RB repr. III, p. 174.

of these personae were fabricated. In religious ballads of this category, we have three martyrs, two parish clerks, a saint and a prophesying Jew.[43] Criminals' last repentance ballads are the most common examples of the suppositious narrator–author.

With these exceptions, the standard ballad of the early seventeenth century went into the world authorless. The original names attached to the 'stock' ballads were simply dropped off the broadsides as the copyright changed hands.[44] What had once been an author's medium – a vehicle for propaganda and personal opinion, or for building a popular reputation as a story-teller – was now a publisher's medium, governed by time-tested commercial dictates. This authorlessness may signify an important change in attitude: the ballad was not an individual creation but a piece of public property, known to an increasingly broad public. Some of the oldest and best-loved ballads, like 'Guy of Warwicke' and 'Chevy Chase', may have reached this status long before they first appeared in broadside form.

The shift to timeless, authorless ballads was not total or permanent. During the Civil War and Interregnum the ballad was seized as a polemical weapon; outlawed in 1649, with flogging as punishment for sellers and singers.[45] But in 1655–6, when Cromwell reimposed effective licensing, the ballad publishers re-registered their copyrights to the favourite 'stock' ballads.[46] The standardized ballad – in two-part format, with familiar woodcuts, with the tune named but not the author – had become a publishing staple, and a constant, slowly shifting bottom layer in the popular culture.

FROM PROPAGANDA TO POPULAR STOCK

By the middle of Elizabeth's reign the ballad had been abandoned as a vehicle for Protestant reform. But this did not signal the demise of the godly ballad; as we have seen, a third of the 'ballad partners' stock was still religious. The popular titles moved from the ideological control of authors

[43] 'Rogers will', 'John Carelesse', 'Anne Askew', 'The clarke of Bodnam', 'St Bernard's vision' (App. A nos. 2, 3, 29, 31, 46); 'A godly song ... made by T. Byll, being the parish clerke of West-Felton'. 'Calebbe Shillocke, his prophesie' (App. B nos. 79, 68).

[44] Because the sixteenth-century copies do not survive, we do not, in most cases, know the authors. An exception is Thomas Deloney who included ballads like 'The Duchess of Suffolk' in his own printed collections (Strange histories, of kings, princes, dukes (1602); The garland of good will (1631), repr. in The works of Thomas Deloney, ed. F.O. Mann (Oxford, 1912)).

[45] Hyder E. Rollins, ed. Cavalier and puritan. Ballads and broadsides illustrating the period of the great rebellion, 1640–1660 (New York, 1923), pp. 48–51; Rollins, 'Black-letter broadside ballad', p. 321.

[46] The Protector's orders for regulation of the press on 28 August 1655 re-emphasized the requirement that works be reviewed before publication. Registration collapsed again in 1659. (Michael John Seymour, 'Pro-government propaganda in Interregnum England' (Cambridge PhD, 1986), p. 305, ch. 8 Table 1, p. 563 n. 26.)

to the commercial control of a group of specialist publishers. If religious ballads made up a smaller percentage of the trade as a whole, it is probable that for each title the output in real numbers was much higher than during the Elizabethan 'gospelling' period. The print runs were probably larger, distribution was better organized, and the greater emphasis on woodcuts and tunes meant that the ballads were reaching more people on the fringes of literacy. The seventeenth-century stock ballad tells us little about the situation at the cutting edge of Protestant reform, but perhaps much more about the impact of Protestantism on a wide public and about their religious tastes.

To explore these tastes we will concentrate on a group of forty-six ballads of long duration on the market. Of this 'stock', thirty-four comprise all those religious ballads in the 1624 entry which can be traced. Of these thirty-four ballads, at least twenty-nine lasted more than a quarter century, twenty-two were sold over a half century, and eight of these survived a full century or more. To them I have added all ballads not on this list which appear to have lasted twenty-five years or more in broadside form. [47]

This group of long-lived ballads can be compared against a background of 119 less successful ballads: that is, all those pre-1640 religious ballads whose texts have survived in some form or other, but which show no evidence of long-lasting popularity. [48] From the Stationers' Register (aided by Rollins Index) I have also identified registered ballads surviving, not on broadsides, but in contemporary manuscripts or printed collections of songs. This adds to the sample of extant broadsides some thirty-eight ballads which were once printed in black-letter form. [49]

This larger group of 'short-lived' ballads is composed of 103 ballads of Elizabethan origin, and only 16 ballads which could have been written after 1603 (consistent with the decline of godly-ballad entries in the Stationers' Registers). Of the 'stock' ballads, too, the majority (twenty-eight, or 60%) can be shown to be of sixteenth-century origin, while several more almost certainly date from earlier than their first appearance in manuscript form (1614–16) or in the 1624 Stationers' Register entry. Broadly speaking, the 'short-lived' ballads are the outpourings of the Protestant reformers (and imitative hacks) in the Elizabethan period, primarily before 1586. The 'stock' ballads are the select group of those ballads which found commercial success in the early decades of the seventeenth century, sometimes lasting right into the eighteenth century.

---

[47] See App. A.

[48] See App. B.

[49] See App. C. The manuscripts are commonplace books, some of which were apparently almost entirely copied from broadsides, like the volume in which Richard Sheale's songs were recorded (see pp. 16–17).

A straightforward equation of 'duration' with 'popularity' is not intended. Of the thousands of ballads written, accidents of publication history helped determine why the 'partners' acquired the copyrights to some and not to others. At our most cautious, we could interpret the 'partners' godly ballad stock simply as a list of what was available to the public over a number of years. If the ballads did not reflect popular opinion, at least their repeated publication may have helped to shape it.

At our boldest, we might infer from Thomson's findings (about the impact of broadsides on folksong) that many ballads in the 'stock' lists passed into wide oral currency for some generations, even if they are no longer known as 'folksong' today. In other words, that they came to be passed on by word of mouth, not just read or sung directly from the broadside. Thomson himself calculated that only some 15% of broadsides have been perpetuated within the folksong tradition, but we might question his assumption that folksong can be defined by nineteenth- and twentieth-century collections.[50]

Since a claim of seventeenth-century 'folksong' status is impossible to measure, here we will take a middle ground between caution and optimism. It seems reasonable to argue that the titles the 'partners' collected and kept in stock were the ones they expected to sell. If we compare the 'partners' entries of 1624, 1656 and 1675 we see not only continuity, but also flexibility in reaction to public demand, as new titles were added and unpopular titles dropped from the list (see Table 2). The ballad 'stock' should, then, provide a certain measure of success, and some illumination of popular religious tastes. As Eamon Duffy said in a recent study of godly chapbooks, 'they encapsulate the religion for which poor men ... were prepared to part with money'.[51]

The intention is not to overstress the importance of these religious stock ballads in themselves; by the late seventeenth century they were drops in a sea of 'irreligious' song. Their survival was very much against the odds: educated Protestants had lost interest in them as a vehicle for reform, and the circumstances in which broadside ballads were performed (the activities of alehouse, marketplace and village green discussed in chapter 1) were not normally the most conducive to 'godliness'. Those which did endure, against all probability, may yield some insight into the inarticulate beliefs of 'the multitude', most of whom conformed (whether with enthusiasm or reluctance) to the 'commonplace prayer-book religion'.[52]

Table 2 illustrates all those pre-1640 ballads which continued to appear

[50] Thomson, 'Development of the broadside ballad trade', p. 23.
[51] Eamon Duffy, 'The godly and the multitude in Stuart England', *Seventeenth Century Journal*, 1 (1986), p. 43.
[52] Patrick Collinson, *The religion of Protestants. The church in English society 1559–1625*, The Ford Lectures 1979 (Oxford, 1982), p. 192. On the problems of evaluating the degree of absenteeism from church, see *ibid.*, pp. 207–20.

Table 2. *Continuity of the 'partners' godly ballad stock*

Title[a]	by 1586	1624	1656	1675	1712	1754
Protestant martyrs/heroines						
'Duchesse of Suffolke'	–	x	–	x	–	x
'I am a poore woman and blinde' ('Anne Askew')	–	x	–	x	–	–
'Roger's will'	?	x	x	–	–	–
Social morality						
(a) Calls to reform						
'Christ's teares over Jerusalem'	–	x	–	x	–	–
'Bell-man for England'	x	–	–	x	–	–
(b) Godly aphorisms						
'Proverbs of Salomon' ('Solomon's sentences')	x	x	–	x	–	–
'100 godly lessons'	–	x	–	x	x	–
Death and salvation						
(a) Salvation through faith						
'Clarke of Bodnam'	–	x	–	x	–	–
(b) Medieval doom						
'St Bernard's vision'[b]	–	–	x	x	x	x
'sore sicke deare freinds' ('The deadmans song')	–	x	–	x	x	–
'Good people all repent' ('A warninge to worldlings')	–	x	–	x	–	–
Stories						
(a) Old Testament/Apocrypha						
'David and Bethsheba'	?	x	–	x	x	x
'Tobias of Ninive'	–	x	–	x	x	x
'Susannah'	x	x	–	x	–	–
(b) New Testament						
'When Jesus Christ was 12'	x	x	–	x	–	–
'Resurrection of Christ'	?	x	–	x	–	–
'Joseph and Marye' ('Joseph the carpenter')	–	x	–	x	–	–
'Prodigal child'	?	–	x	–	–	–
'The sinner's redemption'	–	–	x	–	x	–
(c) 'Christian legends'						
'Doctor Faustus'	–	x	–	x	–	x
'Wandering Jew'	–	–	x	x	–	–

in the 'partners' stock lists after 1640, and some titles which still survived
in the Norris–Brown entry of 1712, and in William Dicey's catalogue of
1754. It is not quite a list of 'greatest hits'. Our focus on the 'partners'
stock lists excludes a number of successful ballads whose lives spanned
the half-century leading up to the formation of that syndicate.[53] However,
the outstanding examples of continuity are here, including the most enduring
title in each category. Beginning with the short-lived ballads, we will narrow
in on the successful godly 'stock', and finally these eight archetypical ballads
will provide a still more concentrated focus for discussion.

The writers of the 'short-lived' Elizabethan ballads pursued Protestant
aims in roughly four areas. The first was religio-political: the galvanizing
of popular support for the Protestant nation, against the papists at home
and abroad. The second was the social reform which was meant to go
hand in hand with religious reform. Thirdly, in the sphere of individual
faith, was the teaching of the Protestant doctrine of salvation through Christ
alone. Finally, the popularization of Scripture would help effect transition
to a book-based religion. Table 3 gives the percentage of both the short-lived
and the stock ballads within these four categories, which provide the basis
for discussion in the rest of the chapter.

The godly ballad 'stock' gives us some measure of how far Protestant
goals were achieved in each of these areas. We must remember, of course,
that these ballads do not represent the whole range of popular religious
song. They occupy a section on the spectrum of belief between, on the
one hand, Protestant psalms and hymns never published in broadside form,
and, on the other hand, 'popish' carols which survived in oral tradition.
Nevertheless, within these four dozen stock ballads is reflected a religious
culture which is far from monolithic, showing a fragmentary reception of
Protestant doctrine.

Key to Table 2:
By 1586 = Stationers' Register entry to predecessors of 'partners'.
1624, 1656, 1675 = batch Register entries to 'partners' (Arber, IV, pp. 131–2;
 Eyre, II, pp. 36–7; Eyre, II, pp. 496–501).
1712 = entry to Thomas Norris and Charles Brown, 20 September 1712. (Reprinted
 in R. S. Thomson, 'The development of the broadside ballad trade and its influence
 upon the transmission of English folksongs' (Cambridge PhD, 1974), App. B.)
1754 = Dicey catalogue 1754. (Reprinted in *ibid.*, App. C.)
Titles in bold = ballad in each category with longest survival.
[a] Title given as in 1624, or first partners' entry. Alternative titles, if very different,
are given in brackets.
[b] Extant copy from *c.* 1640, John Wright, RB orig. I, 376–7.

[53] See Watt, 'Cheap print and religion', p. 115 n. 67.

The most striking feature of Table 3 is the failure of the 'religio-political' ballads in the long term: they make up 43% of the short-lived ballads and only 9% of the popular stock. Meanwhile, the survival of the Scripture stories is notable: 10% of the short-lived group and 30% of the stock. The successful ballads are evenly distributed between social concerns, death and salvation, and biblical tales, some 30% in each category. What is much more interesting than these bald figures, however, is the way these themes are portrayed in the stock ballads; the ingredients which account for their popularity.

For each of the four broad aims of early Elizabethan ballad writers, we can see Protestant legacies in the popular godly 'stock'. Some of the political element remained in the stories of Protestant martyrs. Many of the social concerns were incorporated into the sets of pithy aphorisms on practical morality. The doctrine of salvation through faith was dramatized in the 'last dying speeches' of repentant sinners. Stories from the Old Testament and Apocrypha took their place quite comfortably with songs of secular origin in the ballad tradition.

Yet, at the same time, there were strong elements of continuity with pre-Reformation piety. Medieval traditions of death and judgement persisted; the nativity was still a focus of devotion; saints and deadly sins remained part of the conceptual framework. The ballads used conflicting languages of religious discourse; possibly addressing a variety of audiences, possibly conflicting 'audiences' within the individual ballad buyer.

Religio-political ballads

The most notable feature of the sixteenth-century religious balladry is its politicized nature. The largest group, which accounts for over two-fifths of sixteenth-century 'short-lived' godly ballads surviving in print or manuscript, may be described as 'religio-political'. We have a few Catholic ballads from Mary's reign and three Family of Love broadsides published in Cologne.[54] However, the censorship restrictions (discussed in chapter 2) meant

[54] Catholic ballads: Leonard Stopes, 'An Ave Maria in commendation of our most vertuous queene' [1553?], SA no. 35; William Forrest, 'A new ballade of the marigolde' [1553?], SA no. 36; 'An exclamation upon the erronious and fantasticall spirite of heresy, troubling the unitie of the church' [1553?], SA no. 44. Family of Love broadsides: 'A new balade or songe, of the lambes feast' (Cologne, 1574), Collmann no. 80; STC 1858, Hendrik Niclas, 'A benedicitie or blessinge to be saide over the table' (Cologne, 1575); STC 18548.5, Hendrik Niclas, 'All the letters of the a.b.c.' [Cologne, 1575].

   The present study is restricted to the *printed* broadside ballad, and ballads from manuscript have only been included where there is evidence (from the Stationers' Register) that they appeared in printed form. This stipulation excludes Catholic ballads from the reigns of Elizabeth and James I, such as those preserved in BL Addit. MS 15,225, reprinted in Hyder E. Rollins, *Old English ballads 1553–1625* (Cambridge, 1920).

Table 3. *Short-lived ballads and godly 'stock' compared*

	Short-lived ballads		Popular stock		Total	
	No.	%	No.	%	No.	%
I Religio-political						
(a) Polemic						
Anti-papism	31	26	–	–	31	19
Patriotic Protestantism	9	8	–	–	9	5
Catholic	4	3	–	–	4	2
Refrain from controversy	3	3	–	–	3	2
Sectarian	2	2	–	–	2	1
(b) Protestant martyrs and hero(ine)s	2	2	4	9	6	4
Total	51	43	4	9	55	33
II Social morality						
(a) Calls to reform						
Wickedness of the age	8	7	2	4	10	6
Warning approach of Judgement day	6	5	1	2	7	4
Cities destroyed by sin	4	3	4	9	8	5
Lists of biblical sinners	5	4	–	–	5	3
Remember the poor	3	3	–	–	3	2
Misc. social sins	3	3	–	–	3	2
(b) Godly aphorisms	3	3	7	15	10	6
Total	32	27	14	30	46	28
III Death & individual salvation						
(a) Salvation through faith in Christ						
Exposition	3	3	–	–	3	2
Parody of secular song	4	3	–	–	4	2
God/Christ in dialogue with sinner	3	3	1	2	4	2
Personal confessions	4	3	5	11	9	5
(b) Medieval doom						
Remember death	8	7	3	7	11	7
Dramatizing events after death	2	2	5	11	7	4
Total	24	20	14	30	38	23
IV Scripture stories						
(a) Old Testament/Apocrypha	10	8	5	11	15	9
(b) Gospels	2	2	7	15	9	5
(c) Christian legends	–	–	2	4	2	1
Total	12	10	14	30	26	16
Total no. of ballads	119		46		165	

that the overwhelming majority of these polemical ballads were vehicles for a nationalistic Protestantism, and its corollary, anti-Catholicism.

The pope in his fury

The most imaginative of the anti-Catholic ballads drew upon literary devices which had become standard to Reformation polemic; used either to heap ridicule upon popish practices and sexual mores, or for the more sober creation of a patriotic Protestant mythology. In 1570–1, there appeared a series of mock epistles to and from the pope, set to the latest tune, 'Row well ye Mariners'.[55] The pope was shown to have particular concern for his rebellious Catholic 'friends' in England; thus the link was successfully made between the traitorous enemy within and the foreign enemy without. One Stephen Peele, probably the bookseller of that name, penned both a letter to Rome and its reply.[56] In 'The pope in his fury doth answer returne, To a letter ye which to Rome is late come', the pope canonizes John Felton, together with the northern rebels Christopher and Thomas Norton:

> But yf I could haue at once
> The paryng of his toe,
> His head, his quarters, or his bones,
> That with the wynde doe bloe
> Then should they be layde up by mee
> As reliques of great dignitie.

While such epistles were written and sold largely for their entertainment value, they contributed to an anti-Catholic climate whereby the mere mention of relics, saints, masses or Purgatory in other ballads seems to have been sufficient to conjure up ridiculous associations and an atmosphere of derision.[57]

---

[55] The first surviving ballad of this series was by the dramatist Thomas Preston: 'A lamentation from Rome, how the pope doth bewayle, That the rebelles in England can not prevayle' (1570), Collmann no. 75. These mock epistles were related to the 'pasquinade' tradition of anti-papal satire, which originated in Italy before the Reformation. (See John King, *English Reformation literature: the Tudor origins of the Protestant tradition* (Princeton, 1982), pp. 371–9.)

[56] 'A letter to Rome, to declare to ye pope, J. Felton his freend is hangd in a rope' [1571], Collmann no. 70; 'The pope in his fury doth answer returne, To a letter ye which to Rome is late come' [1571], Lilly, p. 33. Stephen Peele, bookseller, was free of the Stationers' Company in 1570, dealt in ballads, and made his last entry in 1593. (McKerrow, *Dictionary of printers 1557–1640*.)

[57] See, for example, ballads by William Elderton: 'A ballat intituled Northomberland newes' [1570], Collmann no. 41; 'A ballad intituled, A newe well a daye, as playne maister papist as Donstable waye' [1570], Lilly p. 1.

If laughter was one tool of Reformation literature, another was a patriotic religious zeal based on the mythology of the English as an elect people under a godly ruler.[58] Scripture provided the imagery of the nation as a fortress of faith, as for example in Isaiah 25–6: 'We have a strong city; salvation will God appoint for walls and bulwarks.' The siege of a fortress was used as an extended allegory for the religious struggles of Mary's reign in 'The cruel assault of Gods˙fort' [*c.* 1560], written by the godly ballad publisher John Awdeley. While Awdeley made use of biblical resonances, the immediate inspiration was in fact a ballad from 'Tottel's miscellany' (1557), 'Thassault of Cupide upon the fort where the louers hart lay wounded and how he was taken'.[59] Awdeley's moralization began with Edward VI building a fort to shield God's truth, continuing a myth of the pious young king which was carefully fostered in the press during his reign.[60] Then followed a catalogue of the papists who besieged the fort in the Marian period, led by 'general Gardner' and 'captain Boner'; and of the Protestants killed in defending the fort, the martyrs of 1555–6. The ballad ended, of course, with the Lord sending a new 'godly captaine', Elizabeth.

When the Protestant nation was not a fort it might be a temple, as in 'The reedifying of Salomons temple, and the laborers thereof' [1564?] based on 1 Kings 6.[61] Or it might be a field to be tilled, as in 'Prepare ye to the plowe' [1570] by William Elderton:

> The queene holdes the plowe, to continew good seede;
> Trustie subiectes, be readie to helpe, if she neede.[62]

But despite their clever use of biblical allegory or satire, these politicized ballads did not survive to be sung by a seventeenth-century public. Only three anti-Catholic ballads surviving in broadside form were written in the early seventeenth century, two of them apparently in reaction to James' 1624 decree expelling Jesuits and priests from the country.[63] There are no anti-Catholic ballads in the long-lived 'stock' collection, with the excep-

---

[58] John King charts the evolution of Protestant aspirations in a national context under Edward VI in *English Reformation literature*, pp. 161–206.

[59] Collmann no. 3. *Tottel's miscellany* (1557), ed. Edward Arber (1870), p. 172. (The original title was *Songes and sonettes, written by the ryght honorable Lorde Henry Haward late Earle of Surrey, and other.*) 'The Cruell assaulte of Cupydes forte' was entered as a broadside in 1565–6 to Thomas Purfoote (Arber, I, p. 303).

[60] See, for example, the broadside prayers issued during his sickness and after his death, STC 7508–9 in App. D.

[61] Collmann no. 85.

[62] Lilly, p. 174. This is listed on Table 3 as a 'patriotic Protestant' ballad: concern over the popish threat is secondary to the construction of a positive national image.

[63] 'The shamefull downefall of the popes kingdome. Contayning the life and death of Steven Garnet' [1606?], Manchester, I, 54; Martin Parker, 'A scourge for the pope' [1624]. Pepys, I, 60–1; 'A New-Yeeres-gift forthe [*sic*] pope' [*c.* 1625], Pepys, I, 62.

tion of the stories of martyrs discussed below. This religious propaganda appears to have been the most ephemeral side of the godly ballad trade.

Of course, we must take account of changed political circumstances. By the 1620s, anti-popery was no longer simply a patriotic emotion directed against an external enemy, but a focus for discontent with the foreign policies of the English monarch, and with the 'Armenian' innovations of the English church. Ballads containing anti-popery of this subversive nature were unlikely to be printed, but travelled round the country in oral or manuscript form. The diary of a Suffolk clergyman, John Rous, records numerous rhymes and songs which 'came abroade' during the 1620s and 30s, including attacks on the popish tendencies of the Laudian church, as well as many slanders on the Duke of Buckingham.[64] Rous may have heard some of these libels performed aloud, although in most cases he seems to have 'received' them in the form of written copies. They varied in sophistication, from Latin verses for an educated readership, to simple jogging rhymes written to common tunes, which may well have been popular at the alehouse.[65] Most of this polemic was short-lived by definition, appearing and disappearing rapidly in reaction to events. It was never integrated into the tradition of long-enduring ballads, whose survival was reinforced by wide dissemination in printed form over several generations.

The Duchess of Suffolk

However, the Elizabethan religio-political ballads did leave one notable legacy in the popular 'stock', a group of four ballads on Protestant martyrs and heroines. Their survival confirms the impression of popular piety given by the success of Foxe's 'Book of martyrs', which achieved a status close to that of a second Bible. The horrifying human image of the martyr was worth a thousand abstract arguments in the task of embedding anti-Catholic feeling in popular consciousness. The 1624 stock incorporated two ballads from Foxe, one from Coverdale and one story of a maid martyred in Paris. Foxe included forty-eight women on his list of 358 Henrician and Marian martyrs:[66] in the ballads they are overrepresented. Three of the four stories had a female protagonist, just as the Old Testament ballads (below) featured beautiful young women. These songs performed the function of replacing Catholic saints with Protestant ones at the level of those unable to afford

---

[64] Richard Cust, 'News and politics in England', *Past and Present*, 112 (1986), pp. 60–90. Mary Anne Everett Green, ed., *The diary of John Rous*, Camden Society, 1st ser., vol. 66 (1856), p. 14.

[65] Latin verses in *ibid.*, pp. 53, 86–7. For an example of a libel to a well-known tune, 'the cleane contrary way', see F.W. Fairholt, ed., *Poems and songs relating to George Villiers, Duke of Buckingham*, Percy Society, vol. 29 (1850), pp. 10–13.

[66] Patrick Collinson, *The birthpangs of Protestant England. Religious and cultural change in the sixteenth and seventeenth centuries* (1988), p. 75.

a set of Foxe themselves. Ballads on the Duchess of Suffolk and Anne Askew popularized the Foxeian view of history as the progressive Protestant struggle towards true religion.[67] They are the residue of the Elizabethan mythologizing of the recent past: the golden age of Edward's reign; the dark ages under Mary.[68]

The most successful ballad in this category was the story of the Duchess of Suffolk's exile during Mary's reign (Plate 1a).[69] It was adapted from Foxe by Thomas Deloney, who set it to the tune 'Queen Dido', and included it in his collection of *Strange histories, of kings, princes, dukes... With the great troubles of the dutches of Suffolke* (1602). The polemical stance is made explicit in the first stanza:

> When God had taken, for our sinne,
> that prudent Prince, King Edward, away,
> Then bloody Bonner did begin
> his raging malice to bewray
> All those that did God's Word professe
> he persecuted more or lesse.

Yet the appeal of the ballad, which was still for sale in 1754, must also have operated on another level, as an adventure story. Deloney simplified the complex details of the duchess's exile on the Continent to focus on the theme of disguise and revelation. Just as in secular ballads like 'King Edward the fourth and a tanner of Tamworth', there is the familiar story of lords and ladies disguised as ordinary folk.[70] The duchess and her husband Bertie flee with their baby to Flanders, accompanied by only one nurse (who later runs away), and dressed as 'people poor'.[71] Being refused shelter, and unable to speak the local language, they are forced to take refuge from the rain in a church porch.[72] Deloney invents an added detail about a sexton who tries to evict them and is struck on the head with the church keys by Bertie. Complete with a lurid woodcut of the sexton with blood

---

[67] 'The most rare and excellent history of the Dutchesse of Suffolkes calamity' [written by 1602], RB repr. I, p. 287; 'A ballad of Anne Askew, intituled: I am a woman poore and blind' [1624?], Manchester, I, 54.

[68] Discussed by King, *English Reformation literature*, pp. 443–4.

[69] Pepys, I, 544–5.

[70] On a hunting trip, King Edward has a humorous exchange with a tanner who takes him for a penniless highway thief. Eventually the king reveals his identity by blowing his bugle horn and summoning his 500 lords and knights. (Child no. 273.) A broadside of this song was registered to Edward White in 1586. (Arber, II, p. 451.)

[71] 'People poor' seems to imply a worse state of degradation than the description in Foxe: 'apparelled like a meane Marchantes wife' with a small retinue dressed 'like meane servantes'. John Foxe, *Actes and monuments of matters most speciall in the church*, 4th edn (1583), II, pp. 2078–81.

[72] This situation would be familiar to the ballad audience, since church porches were common lodging places for the vagrant poor. (Peter Clark, *The English alehouse: a social history 1200–1830* (1983), p. 136.)

The most Rare and excellent History,
Of the Dutchess of Suffolks Calamity,
To the Tune of, Queen Dido.

When God had taken for our sin,
 that prudent Prince K. Edward away,
Then bloody Bonner did begin
 his raging malice to bewray:
All those that did Gods Word profess,
He persecuted more or less.

Thus whilst the Lord on us did lowre,
 many in Prison he did throw,
Tormenting them in Lollards Tower,
 whereby they might the truth forego:
Then Cranmer, Ridley, and the rest,
Were burning in the fire, that Christ profest.

Smithfield was then with Faggots fill'd,
 and many places more beside,
At Coventry was Saunders kill'd,
 at Worster eke good Hooper dy'd:
And to escape this bloody day,
Beyond Sea many fled away.

Amongst the rest that sought relief,
 and for their Faith in danger stood,
Lady Elizabeth was chief,
 King Henries Daughter of Royal blood:
Which in the Tower did Prisoner lye,
Looking each day when she should dye.

The Dutchess of Suffolk seeing this,
 whose Life likewise the Tyrant sought:
Who in the hopes of heavenly bliss,
 within Gods word her comfort wrought:
For fear of Death was fain to flye,
And leave her house most secretly.

That for the love of God alone,
 her Land and Goods she left behind:
Seeking still for that precious Stone,
 the Word and Truth so rare to find:
She with her Nurse, Husband, and Child,
In poor array their sighs beguil'd.

Thus through London they passed along,
 each one did take a several street,
Thus all along escaping wrong,
at Billingsgate they all did meet,
Like people poor in Gravesend-Barge,
They simply went with all their charge.

And all along from Gravesend-Town,
 with Journeys short on foot they went,
Unto the Sea-coast came they down,
 to pass the Seas was their intent:
And God provided so that day,
That they took Ship and sail'd away.

And with a prosperous gale of wind,
 in Flanders they did safe arrive,
This was to their great ease of mind,
 and from their heavy hearts much woe did drive;
And so with thanks to God on high,
They took their way to Germany.

Thus as they travel'd still disguis'd,
 upon the High-way suddenly,
By cruel Thieves they were surpriz'd,
 assaying their small company:
And all their treasures and their store
They took away and beat them sore.

The Nurse in midst of their sight,
 laid down the Child upon the ground,
She ran away out of their sight,
 and never after that was found:
Then did the Dutchess make great moan
With her good Husband all alone.

The Thieves had there their Horses kill'd,
 and all their money quite had took,
The pritty Baby almost spoil'd,
 was by the Nurse likewise forsook:
And they far from their friends did stand,
and succourless in a strange Land.

The Sky likewise began to scowl,
 it Hail'd and Rain'd in piteous sort,
The way was long and wondrous foul,
 then may I now full well report,
Their grief and sorrow was not small,
When this unhappy chance did fall.

1(a) 'The Dutchess of Suffolk', pt 1.

1(b) 'The Dutchess of Suffolk', pt 2.

pouring from his head (Plate 1b), this event presumably emphasizes their inhospitable reception. The interest of the story is in the temporary inversion of hierarchy; in what happens when the nobility are stripped of the appearances which define their role:

> Loe! here a Princess of great blood
>   doth pray a peasant for reliefe,
> With teares bedewed, as she stood,
>   yet few or none regards her griefe!

The couple are taken before the magistrates, and when Bertie makes a speech in Latin they are recognized and their identity revealed by a learned doctor:

> Behold, within your sight, quoth he,
> A Princes[se] of most high degree.

The heroine is thus incorporated into traditional ballad themes and conventions.[73] At the same time as Protestant historiography is popularized, much of the specific Protestant content and motivation is lost.

If the ballad shows us little of the personality of Catherine Brandon,

---

[73] Revelation scenes like this occur in many of the long-enduring secular ballads. 'Hynd Horn', dressed in beggar's weeds, reveals himself to his love on her wedding day. (James Kinsley, ed., *The Oxford book of ballads* (Oxford, 1982 edn), no. 32.) In 'The famous flower of serving-men; or, the lady turn'd serving-man', the lady enters the king's service, and after revelation of her identity she is made queen. (*Ibid.*, no. 47.) This is one of a genre of ballads which turn both status and gender upside down, as high-born ladies disguise themselves as male servants. See, for example, 'Child Waters' and 'Rose the Red and White Lilly'. (*Ibid.*, nos. 40, 49.)

dowager duchess and great Protestant patroness, at least many of the idiosyncratic details of her story remain.[74] This is far less the case with Anne
Askew, who becomes a generic victim of popery, bearing little resemblance
to the strong, intelligent woman revealed in her 'examinacyons', edited by
John Bale in 1546–7.[75] The ballad in the 1624 stock, 'I am a woman
poor and blind', is a lament written in a tone of feminine weakness and
supplication to her oppressors, of whom Bishop Gardiner is the chief villain.
Askew warns her audience against the wicked gardener who sows 'feigned
seeds, with Popish Ceremonies', the allegorical figure of evil and popery.

Such a portrayal of the Protestant martyr in terms of one-sided victimiza-
tion seems to have fit the needs of later generations which saw 'popish
plots' lurking around every corner. While there was ample material in Anne
Askew's own testimony to provide a vibrant, rational defence of pure Protestant doctrine, instead she became known through the broadside press
only as the disembodied representation of a meek and pure Protestant faith.
Anne Askew's song is the musical equivalent of the woodcuts which illustrated the *Actes and monuments* itself: generic images of martyrs in flames,
which were repeated and used interchangeably, and which offered 'types
of martyrs' to the viewer.[76]

Some of the stubbornness and strength which was stripped from Anne
Askew remains in the persona of 'a vertuous maid in Paris, who was by
her own mother procured to be put in prison, thinking thereby to compel
her to popery: but she continued to the end, and finished her life in the
fire'.[77] When, in the ballad, the girl's mother commands her to go to mass,
she refuses to worship 'that filthy idol'. She is eventually led to her execution,
where she delivers a last exhortation to the ladies of Paris:

> 'You Ladies of this City
>   mark well my words', (quoth she)
> Although I shall be burned,
>   yet do not pitty me;
> Yourselves I rather pitty
>   and weep for your decay,
> Amend your time [*sic*] fair Ladies,
>   and do not time delay.

[74] For Catherine's patronage of Protestant literature in Edward's reign, see King, *English Reformation literature*, pp. 104–6.
[75] *The first examinacyon of Anne Askewe, latelye martyred in Smythfelde, with the elucydacyon
of J. Bale* (1546). *The lattre examinacyon of Anne Askewe, with the elucydacyon of J.
Bale* (1547). Both published in Wesel by D. van de Straten.
[76] There were two types of illustration in the 'Book of martyrs': the narrative scenes which
directly illustrated certain events in the text, and the interchangeable images of martyrs
in flames, which were repeated as many as seven times in one edition. (Ruth Samson
Luborsky, 'Connections and disconnections between images and texts: the case of secular
Tudor book illustration', *Word and Image*, 3 (1987), p. 82.)
[77] Ent. to Yarrath James, 1 August 1586, RB repr. I, p. 35.

This appeal to religious solidarity among women accords with the picture we have that in both France and England it was often the women who became fierce Protestant converts.[78] Presumably the relative vulnerability of women in society also made their courage in the face of evil seem even more heroic and song-worthy.

Nevertheless, once again we have little detail about the background and identity of the 'vertuous maid' in Paris: she has been transformed into the generic type of a martyr. The same is true of the one male martyr to be included in the 1624 stock, the famous John Careless.[79] The first lines of this ballad, 'Some men for sodayne joye do wepe, and some in sorrowe synge', were quoted in Shakespeare's *King Lear* and in Heywood's *Rape of Lucrece*.[80] Nashe referred to it as the typical religious ballad: 'such another device it is as the godly Ballet of John Carelesse, or the song of Green sleeves moralized'.[81] The ballad, which purports to be Careless' own words, is taken directly from Miles Coverdale's *Certain most godly, fruitful, and comfortable letters of such true Saintes and holy martyrs of God, as ... gave their lyves for the defence of Christes holy gospel* (1564).[82] The original readers would probably have known the background of this Coventry weaver who died in prison in Mary's reign. But the ballad which reached later audiences was again a disembodied expression of faith: a classic repentance and comfort tract like the 'penitent sinner' ballads (below), albeit of better quality than most.

It seems that the buyers of broadside ballads were not expected to be interested in the historical specificity of the martyrdoms, or in the martyrs' rational arguments about Protestant doctrine. Either the heroine became assimilated into traditional narrative themes, having little to do with Protestantism, as in the semi-fictional account of the Duchess of Suffolk's exile. Or else the details were pared away and we are left with only the emotional religious core of the ballad: not unlike what has been described as the 'lyric'

---

[78] Among many studies on this subject see W.J. Sheils, 'Oliver Heywood and his congregation', in W.J. Sheils and Diana Wood, eds., *Voluntary religion* (1986), pp. 268–70; Sherrin Marshall Wyntjes, 'Women in the Reformation era', in Renate Bridenthal and Claudia Koonz eds., *Becoming visible: women in European history* (1977), pp. 165–91.

[79] 'A godly and vertuous songe or ballade, made by the constant member of Christe, John Carelesse', in Miles Coverdale, *Certain most godly, fruitful, and comfortable letters* (1564), pp. 634–8.

[80] *King Lear*, I, iv, 168; *Rape of Lucrece*, in Heywood's *Dramatic works* (1874 edn), V, p. 179. (Information from Rollins, *Old English ballads*, p. 47.)

[81] Thomas Nashe, *Have with you to Saffron-Walden* (1596); repr. in R.B. McKerrow, ed., *The works of Thomas Nashe*, 2nd edn, revised by F.P. Wilson (5 vols., Oxford, 1958), III, p. 104. The work Nashe is comparing with these godly ballads is Barnaby Barnes' *Divine century of spiritual sonnets*.

[82] We do not have an extant broadside version, but there seems no reason to doubt that it was the same ballad as that found in BM Sloane MS 1896, taken from Coverdale. (Rollins Index no. 1303.)

core in secular folksong.[83] The martyrs become no more than cardboard cut-outs: the supreme representations of tenacious Protestant faith, and the residue of the Elizabethan anti-Catholic mythology.

Social morality

Christ's tears

Leaving the overtly anti-Catholic ballads, we are left with those Elizabethan ballads which are better described as 'edifying' than 'political'; ballads which addressed themselves directly to the morality and salvation of the people. Yet the polemical element was by no means absent: it expressed itself in the zeal of new reformers for the transformation of society and its morals. This reforming drive reflected Protestantism in its most youthful stage, when the true religion was expected to solve all social problems. Whether by the seventeenth century Protestant reform in general had hardened into 'middle age' is a question outside the scope of this study, but certainly the youthful reforming zeal was no longer expressed through the medium of the ballads.[84]

The largest group of ballads for social reform formed a diatribe against the wickedness of the age; a straightforward catalogue of social ills. 'Sin' and 'repentance' in most of the sixteenth-century ballads referred to the social sins of the community or nation.[85] The city of London, for example, was urged to take collective responsibility for its particular sins (including 'whoredom', gaming houses and drunkenness), and received collective punishment in the form of the plague, or lightning striking St Paul's Cathedral.[86] The ruling classes were held primarily responsible, and specific social vices were attacked, such as rent-racking, imprisonment for small matters, usury and bribery. As the ballad of 1562 claimed in its title, these were days when 'neybourhed, love and trew dealyng is gone'.[87] But despite the large number of these diatribes which poured out of the presses in the

[83] Tristram Potter Coffin, *The British traditional ballad in North America* (1977 edn), pp. 165–7 (discussed above pp. 37–8).
[84] Patrick Collinson, *From iconoclasm to iconophobia: the cultural impact of the second English Reformation* Stenton lecture 1985 (Reading, 1986), p. 4.
[85] The distinction between 'personal sin' and 'sins of society' was made by Eamon Duffy in the context of a discussion of Restoration chapbooks in 'The godly and the multitude', pp. 31–55.
[86] William Birch, 'A warning to England, let London begin: To repent their iniquitie, and flie from their sin' [1565], Collmann no. 9.
[87] John Barker, 'A balade declaryng how neybourhed, love and trew dealyng is gone' [1561], Lilly, p. 134.

1560s and 1570s, they had limited appeal in the long run. Only two such ballads survived in the popular seventeenth-century stock.[88]

The preoccupation with the sinfulness of the time was often linked with the conviction of many English Protestants that they were experiencing the last days before the prophecies in Revelations would be fulfilled. The apocalyptic tradition, an important strand of English Protestantism since John Bale's *Image of both churches* (Antwerp, [1545?]), produced a group of ballads warning that the general Judgement Day was imminent.[89] These alarums left one legacy to the popular stock, in the ballad of the 'Bell-man for England' ringing his metaphorical bell to wake the people for the Day of Judgement.[90]

Another version of the alarum theme looked, not forward to doomsday, but backward to the biblical examples of cities destroyed for their sin, a theme also developed in pamphlet literature.[91] The most potent of lessons was that of Jerusalem: here, not the heavenly Jerusalem, nor the new Jerusalem to be created from a reformed society, but the negative image of a great city-nation struck by God's wrath.[92] The account of Jerusalem's fall reached the English public in 1558 in the version by 'Joseph ben Gorion', much abridged from Josephus' original history.[93] The impact on English culture can be measured by the eleven editions which had appeared by 1615,

[88] 'A most excellent godly new ballad: shewing the manifold abuses of this wicked world' (ent. 1586), Manchester, I, 4; 'A proper new ballad ... wherein is shewed how men ought not to set their mindes on worldly pleasure' (1614), Shirburn, p. 50.

[89] Sixteenth-century alarums include 'A ballett of the last dayes' [ent. 1569–70?], Seng no. 30; 'A godly exhortacon of doomes daie is at hand' (ent. 1584), in Rollins, *Old English ballads*, p. 245; 'Aryse and wak, for Christes sake' [ent. 1557-8?], MS Ashmole 48 no. 52; 'A warning unto repentaunce and of Christes comming unto judgement' [pre-1576], in Rollins, *Old English ballads*, p. 240. Seventeenth-century examples: 'A prophesie of the judgment day. Being lately found in Saint Denis church in France, and wrapped in leade in the forme of an heart' [1620?], Pepys, I, pp. 36–7; 'Miraculous newes from the cittie of Holdt in Germany, where there were three dead bodyes seene to rise out of their graves' [1616], Shirburn, p. 76.

[90] 'A bell-man for England' (ent. 1586), beginning 'Awake! Awake! Oh Englande', survived some ninety-five years. (Shirburn, p. 36.) On the figure of the bell-man, see discussion of *memento mori* ballads, below.

[91] Lessons for England, and especially London, were drawn from the fate of Sodom and Gomorra; while the sparing of Nineveh was used to show the power of repentance. ('Of the horrible and wofull destruction of Sodome and Gomorra' [1570], Lilly, p. 125; 'The history of the prophet Jonas. The repentance of Ninivie that great Citie' [?ent. 1562–3], Pepys, I, 28–9.)

[92] 'Of the horyble and woful destrucion of Jerusalem' [1569?], Collmann no. 5; 'A warning or lanthorne to London. A dolefull destruction of faire Jerusalem' [?ent. 1586], Shirburn, p. 32; 'Christs teares over Jerusalem' [written c. 1593?], BL Cup.651.e(26).

[93] It was believed to be a lost manuscript by Josephus himself; a shorter version of his history written 'unto his countreymen the Jewes' (Joseph ben Gorion (pseud.), *A compendius and most marveilous history of the latter tymes of the Jewes commune weale*, trans. P. Morwyng, 3rd edn (1567), sig.A2–A2v. In fact it is from Abraham ben David's abstract in Book 3 of Sefer ha-Kabalah (see STC 14795).

and by the morbid fascination in the broadside ballads with the graphic detail of the Jews' famine and suffering. The ballad audience received little military or political information, but much in the way of 'human interest' details drawn directly from the Joseph Ben Gorion account:

> Their very dung they layd not wast
> but made therof their meate.
> And, through the famyne long begunne
> the mother was glad to eate her sonne.[94]

Whether such details performed the additional function, intended by their authors, of frightening the ballad buyers into repentance was a question irrelevant to the publishers as these titles passed into the seventeenth-century popular stock. This category of ballads did survive well, probably because they provided gripping and dramatic stories from which the warning to repent emerged secondarily as the moral.

The *pièce de résistance* of this genre was 'Christs teares over Jerusalem', an anonymous ballad based on Thomas Nashe's book of that name, and probably first printed soon after the book's appearance in 1593.[95] Both book and ballad combine Christ's prophecy of the destruction of Jerusalem in Matthew 23 and 24 with the description of the event itself forty years later. Interest in the theme was apparently at a high pitch in the early 1590s with the appearance of Thomas Lodge's folio translation of the works of Josephus, but Nashe used the more accessible octavo abridgement as his source.[96] From the 'Joseph ben Gorion' account he expanded the speech of the mother Miriam to her infant son before she kills him and roasts him for meat, exploring her dilemma through an impassioned monologue and warning to 'Mothers of London'.[97]

In the broadside version there is room only to highlight a few of the salient details:

> Yea, Dogs and Cats they eat, mice, rats and every thing,
> For want of food, 'their Infants young unto the Pot they bring'.

Yet the ballad is striking in its almost Aristotelian dramatic unity, whereby it succinctly combines a metrical paraphrase of Christ's own warning from the Gospels, a brief but emotive description of the crucifixion and of Jerusa-

---

[94] 'A warning or lanthorne to London. A dolefull destruction of faire Jerusalem'. These details are found in Joseph ben Gorion, *Compendius history*, sig.Bb4, Gg1v–Gg3; in turn drawn from passages in Josephus. See Flavius Josephus, *The famous and memorable workes of Josephus*, trans. by Thomas Lodge, 2nd edn (1609), pp. 717, 724, 734.

[95] Pepys, II, 6. It refers to the Armada which God sent against England 'of late' and to a recent plague, probably that of 1592.

[96] Lodge's translation ent. to R. Walley 7 March 1591. STC 14809.

[97] Thomas Nashe, *Christs teares over Jerusalem* (1593), sig.I2–4. Joseph ben Gorion, *Compendius history,* sig.Gg2–Gg5. In Josephus she speaks only a few lines to her son. (Josephus, *Workes*, p. 734.)

2 'Solomon's sentences'.

lem's fall, and an account of plagues and punishments sent to contemporary England. Its attribution to Thomas Deloney is questionable, but the unabashed borrowing from Nashe suggests the work of a fellow dramatist or semi-professional writer, rather than a reformer from outside the London literary world.[98] It is the capacity for narrative and dramatic structure which meant the survival of a ballad like 'Christs teares' for over eighty years, and the still birth of many attempts by ministers and other amateurs.[99]

Solomon's sentences

Some of the sixteenth-century social conscience did remain in the godly ballad 'stock'. However, concern with drunkenness or oppression of the poor appears to have had more appeal when presented in a set of handy rules, rather than as a sweeping call to reform. The aphoristic ballads have the effect of blunting any sense of immediacy, turning urgent responsibilities into eternal platitudes. Religion in these ballads is less a blueprint for collective salvation than a code for moral behaviour in everyday life, designed primarily to be implanted in the minds of the young.

The primary source of authority for these godly precepts was the wise king from Scripture (Plate 2). 'Solomon's sentences' was first registered in

---

[98] The ballad has been attributed to Thomas Deloney (RB repr. VII, p. 789; Mann, ed., *Works of Deloney*, p. 496) on the basis of its refrain 'Repent, fair England, now repent', mentioned in Nashe's caricature of Deloney: 'not one merrie Dittie will come from him, but The Thunderbolt against Swearers, Repent, England, Repent, and The Strange judgements of God'. (Nashe, *Have with you to Saffron-Walden*, in McKerrow, ed., *Works of Nashe*, III, p. 84.) However, this was a common type of refrain, and if Deloney had been copying Nashe's own title and theme, Nashe would surely have mentioned it.

[99] A number of unsuccessful ballad writers simply hammered their message across by accumulating biblical examples to illustrate a particular sin. For titles of these 'list' ballads see Watt, 'Cheap print and religion', p. 133 n. 115.

1586, and remained in the ballad stock until at least 1675.[100] Although it purports to be in Solomon's words, the ballad is in fact closely based on 'the booke of Jesus the sonne of Sirach whiche is called in latine Ecclesiasticus.'[101] This apocryphal book of the second century followed the literary example of Proverbs, and was included in the 'Books of Solomon' published separately in ten editions from 1537 to 1551.[102]

The gems of advice chosen by the ballad versifier as most applicable to his Elizabethan audience deal with financial matters, the raising of children, the running of a household. The advice is aimed at young males: the ballad preserves the formula 'My son . . .' which begins each chapter of Proverbs, and is copied in Ecclesiasticus:

> My sonne,' saith Solomon the wise
> If thou true wisdome wilt attaine . . .

The son in the ballad is warned in turn never to smile on his daughters, because they are prone to wantonness.[103] Budding young householders are advised not to go to law with the magistrate and to pay their labourers promptly, implying that at least in 1586 an audience of reasonably wealthy yeomen or tradesmen was expected. There is no contradiction between striving for personal wealth and giving to the poor; in fact, these aims appear to be complementary. The reader is exhorted to succour his poor neighbour; he is also warned to work for his old age while he is still young. There is an emphasis on good works which must have appealed to the Pelagian tendency which we are told lingered on, especially in rural England.[104]

This Elizabethan ballad appears to be the only successful attempt to base such aphorisms on Scripture. But the practical morality and literary format of Ecclesiasticus, and the other 'Books of Solomon', appear to have been a source of inspiration for the whole genre of aphoristic ballads. To give structure to this ballad wisdom, various narrative devices were employed, of which the most common was the 'last dying speech' of a parent, giving advice to his or her children. If the biblical Solomon was the archetypical wise father, the next best authority was a Protestant martyr. The earliest parental-advice ballad appears in Foxe: 'The exhortacion of Robert Smith,

---

[100] 'A most excellent new dittie, wherein is shewed the sage sayings, and wise sentences of Salomon' (1586), Collmann no. 84. Pepys, II, 64.

[101] *The holie bible* [Bishops' version] (1569). Passages which are directly versified in the ballad include 3:10. 5:1, 6:6, 7:20–1, 7:23–4, 8:12, 9:1, 9:6, 25:2.

[102] STC 2757 to 2759.

[103] Ecclesiasticus 7:24. 'If thou have daughters, keepe theyr body, and shewe not thy face cheereful towarde them.'

[104] Richard Baxter commented on this Pelagian element amongst his parishioners. (*Confirmation and restauration, the necessary means of reformation and reconciliation* (1658), pp. 157–65. Discussed in Duffy, 'The godly and the multitude', p. 39.)

unto his children, commonly set out in the name of maister Rogers'.[105] This was supposed to have been written in prison by the martyr Smith (d. August 1555), and brought to publication by Mathewe Rogers, with those whose name the ballad became firmly associated.[106] The text gained weight from its origin in such emotionally and spiritually significant circumstances:

> where I amonge myne Iron bands
> inclosed in the darke
> afewe dayes before my death
> did diddicate this warke.

The same text was also one of several godly pieces in a 'little booke' registered in 1577, although the first surviving copy in chapbook form dates from 1648.[107]

This death-bed advice became a convention of seventeenth-century popular literature, and the speaker became no longer a martyr, but just an ordinary parent. By the time Pepys was collecting chapbooks, 'penny godlinesses' for sale included *The father's last blessing, The mother's blessing* and *The young man's last legacy*.[108] The advice of these generic parental figures was presumably intended to help the individual parent in his or her job of inculcating the correct moral virtues and enforcing discipline in the household. One of the most popular ballads, registered in 1624 and still on the stock list in 1712 was 'An hundred godly lessons that a mother on her death-bed gave to her children whereby they may know how to guide themselves towards God and man, to the benefit of the commonwealth, joy of their parents, and good to themselves'.[109] While the role of a mother was appropriate as teacher and conveyer of semi-proverbial wisdom, the primary audience for the ballad was presumed to be male children: for example, several stanzas were devoted to the choice of a virtuous wife. These ballads of parental wisdom reinforced the centrality of the household as a unit for moral and religious education.[110] The woodcut illustrating a copy of 1686–8 shows seven children gathered around the death-bed, and a large hearth suggesting warmth and security (Plate 3).

Another organizing principle for the aphoristic ballad was the simple 'abc', each stanza beginning with a letter of the alphabet in order. 'Abc's were

---

[105] Foxe, *Actes and monuments* (1563 edn), sig. 3U$_2$–3U$_2$V
[106] 'Mastare Rogers to his childerne', in BM MS Stowe 958; 'Mathewe Rogers to his childrine', in Cambridge University MS Ff.5.14. Entered as 'Rogers will' in 1624.
[107] Arber, II, p. 319. *The exhortation that a father gave to his children, which he wrot a few days before his burning* (1648), discussed below, p. 318.
[108] Spufford, *Small books*, pp. 201–3.
[109] [Ent. 26 November 1590?], Pepys, II, 16–17.
[110] On the 'good household' see ch. 6.

3 'An hundred godly lessons'.

recorded from the first year of the Stationers' Register.[111] The abc genre
grew out of the method by which most readers would have learnt their
letters, using the 'ABC with the catechism' published officially from the
mid-sixteenth century (and by the Stationers' Company itself since 1616).[112]
The abc format was also used for religious songs on the Continent: the
Swedish psalm number 260 was known as 'The Golden ABC'.[113] Social
obligation is at the core of 'A right godly and Christian A,B,C / Shewing
the duty of every degree', which admonishes the reader to 'give almes',
'oppresse no man by usury' and 'minister justice, magistrates!'[114]

The last and most inventive way to present aphoristic wisdom was to
structure it around a metaphorical gimmick or pun. 'A dozen of poynts'
played on the double meaning of 'points' as not only particulars in a discourse, but also the thread 'points' which were the normal means of closing
a garment before the button became widespread: 'The gift is small, a Douzen
of Points, wherewith I'd wish you knit your joynts.'[115] The printed sheet

[111] Rollins Index nos. 2–4. An even earlier survival is Thomas Knell, 'An ABC to the christen
congregacion' (1549), Collmann no. 56.
[112] W.W. Greg, *A companion to Arber* (Oxford, 1967), pp. 21, 24. I am grateful to Helen
Weinstein for allowing me to read her unpublished paper on seventeenth-century English
primers.
[113] Egil Johansson, 'The history of literacy in Sweden', in Harvey J. Graff, ed., *Literacy and
social development in the West: a reader* (Cambridge, 1981), p. 162.
[114] [Ent. 19 August 1579?], RB repr. II, p. 160. Another successful ABC ballad, 'An excellent
song wherein you shall finde / Great consolation for a troubled minde' (known as 'Ayme
not too hie') is more concerned with the individual's preparation for 'Bridegroome Christ'
(RB repr. I, p. 325).
[115] 'A godly new ballad, intituled, A dozen of poynts' (ent. 1624), Euing no. 126.

is used as a paper representation of a material object familiar to the ballad buyers and probably available from the very same pedlars. Points were standard items in the inventories of late seventeenth-century chapmen, such as the foot pedlar Richard Riddings of Bury, Lancashire; and at 1d. per dozen they cost the same as the ballad in their name.[116] In *Bartholomew Fair*, Nightingale sells 'A dozen of poynts' and other godly ballads of this type:

> Night. Heare for your love, and buy for your money,
> A delicate ballad o'the Ferret and the Coney.
> A preservative again' the Punques evill.
> Another of goose-green-starch and the Devill.
> A dozen of divine points, and the Godly garters:
> The Fairing of good councell, of an ell and three-quarters.[117]

The chapmen's stock-in-trade was dominated by cheap linen cloths sold by the ell, so this too was an appropriate catchword for a book or ballad to be sold along the same network of distribution.[118]

The use of numerical or alphabetical devices like the 'Dozen points', '100 godly lessons' or 'Christians ABC' was meant to help the hearer or reader commit the advice to memory. This mnemonic function is emphasized by the dying 'mother':

> Consider daily in your minds
> the words which I shall tell.

> Print well in your Remembrance
> the Lessons I have shown.[119]

Two of the seven aphoristic ballads have no tune, and were perhaps meant to be stuck up on the wall.[120]

There is nothing specifically Protestant about most of these godly precepts ballads, yet the collective impact is that of moderation and industry, and other qualities we have come to associate with the 'Protestant work ethic'. Four of the seven specified a male audience, and four of the seven specifically

---

[116] Inventory of Richard Riddings, 1680, in Margaret Spufford, *The great reclothing of rural England: petty chapmen and their wares in the seventeenth century* (1984), p. 152.

[117] Ben Jonson, *Bartholomew Fair* (1614), II, iv, 9–16. A broadside entered to the ballad publisher John Charlewood in 1578 was 'A paire of garters for yonge menne to weare yat serve the Lord God and lyve in his feare'. See pp. 248–50 for a pair of 'gloves' in this genre.

[118] Spufford, *Great reclothing*, pp. 90, 158–9, 163, 165–6 and so on. Another metaphor ballad was 'A table of good nurture' which referred to 'table' as a broadside and 'table' as an eating place. (Ent. 1624, RB repr. II, p. 170.)

[119] '100 godly lessons', Pepys, II, 16–17.

[120] See chs. 4–6. The two were 'Dozen of poynts' and 'Rogers will'.

addressed children rather than adults.[121] The 'Table of good nurture' was subtitled: 'Wherin is contained a Schoole-masters admonition to his Schollers to learne good manners: the Father to his Children to learne virtue: and the Houshoulder to his servants to learne godlinesse.' Here is the concept of the ballad as a teaching aid, especially for children, to be used like a catechism within the household.

In what kind of 'household' would such a ballad be sung, or read, or stuck up on the wall? The advice was not entirely universal as to social class: as we have seen the reader was expected to be employer rather than labourer and oppressor rather than oppressed. Nevertheless, since some of these ballads survived over a period of a century, the hints about their intended Elizabethan audience may tell us nothing about who they reached as the market broadened. These godly aphorisms were apparently very popular and could take other forms than the ballad, such as the broadside without a tune or the 'penny chapbook'.[122]

Death and salvation

The clerk of Bodnam

The loudest voice of the early Elizabethan 'edifying' ballads was the call for collective repentance and social reform. But there were also ballads which presented the more personal side of the Protestant message: the saving power of faith. Their tone is positive, promising that the offer of grace is infinite and universal, if only the sinner will take the first step.[123] The central Protestant doctrine of justification by faith alone is made an encouraging proposition in these ballads.

Despite the positive message, there were some modes of expressing it which may have found some favour in the early Elizabethan years, but which were out of fashion by 1624. One technique often used for this theme was the moral parody of the secular song, most often a love song, of which Christ becomes the object:

> Thou art my saviour sweete,
> foode and delight to mee . . .
> To my tast, honnie sweete,

---

121 A male audience was specified in '100 godly lessons', 'Solomon's sentences', 'Table of good nurture', 'Christian ABC'. Children were addressed in '100 godly lessons', 'Solomon's sentences', 'Table of good nurture', 'Rogers will'.
122 See pp. 235, 300–3.
123 In 'A Christian conference betweene Christ and a sinner' (beginning 'I am a poore sinner') Christ promises he will receive the sinner 'If once I do see thee be sory in heart'. (Ent. 1586, RB repr. III, p. 164.)

to my eare, melodie.[124]

Sometimes this emotive relationship with Christ was extended by having him reply to the narrator, turning the empassioned monologue into a dialogue. In 'I am a poore sinner', the sinner claims he is too filthy and wicked to receive Christ's favour, but Christ offers rhyming words of comfort (to the tune of 'Goe to bed, sweet heart'):

> And turn away from thy sin, that's the way to begin –
> I that redeemed thee bids thee come to me.[125]

While several of these dialogue ballads were written in the sixteenth century, only this one continues into the seventeenth-century 'popular stock'. The invention of non-scriptural speeches for God or Christ was a dubious exercise for Protestants, with their emphasis on biblical authority and the clearing away of superfluous apocrypha. The reaction of a nineteenth-century editor to the ballad 'Glad tydings from heaven' indicates the continuity of this Protestant attitude: 'This is a strange religious ballad, in which Christ is made the speaker throughout in the narrative of his sufferings, and numberless things are put into his mouth that he never did say.'[126]

If love songs and dialogues with Christ did not endure, there was still a coherent group of seventeenth-century 'stock' ballads which dealt with the personal relationship between the sinner and his saviour. These were the last dying speeches addressed to God in the crucial dramatic moments when the speaker's eternal fate lay hanging in the balance. They still carry the 'emotional burden' of the late medieval iconography of death (as described by Phillipe Ariès), where the dying man's attitude in his 'last fleeting moment' had the power to save or damn him.[127] Unlike the aphoristic ballads which used the same death-bed fiction, these ballads were more concerned with the dying soul than the surviving kin, although the family was still present and gathered round the bedside. These ballads seem to have functioned as guides to the appropriate mental framework before death.

The inherited models for personal address to God had been the prayers and visions of a celibate, monastic tradition. These saints, monks and abbesses were replaced by lay people with strong involvement in the Prot-

---

[124] This song is based on 'Dainty come thou to me', rendered as 'Jesu come thou to me'. ('The sinner, despisinge the world and all earthly vanities ...' [ent. 1568-9?], Rollins, *Old English ballads*, p. 198.) Most godly ballads used popular tunes, but this group went beyond that to structure the text around a 'moralization' of the original words. Moralizations survive of Elderton's 'Gods of love' [1563], the popular 'Bonny broome', [c. 1635], and an early Elizabethan favourite 'I might have lived merelie' (ent. 1564–5). (Collmann no. 7; Pepys, I, 41; Rollins, *Old English ballads*, p. 216.)

[125] Ent. 1586, RB repr. III, p. 164.

[126] William Chappell in RB repr. I, p. 401.

[127] Philippe Ariès, *Western attitudes toward death: from the middle ages to the present*, trans. Patricia M. Ranum (Baltimore, 1974), pp 36–8.

estant church. The archetypical ballad of personal faith (surviving at least from 1624 to 1688) was attributed to a parish clerk: 'A very godly song, intituled, the earnest petition of a faithfull Christian, being clarke of Bodnam, made upon his death-bed, at the instant of his transmutation' (Plate 4).[128] Another ballad which lasted over sixty years was 'The zealous querister's songe of Yorke', addressed 'to all faithfull singers and godlye readers in the world' (acknowledging the double function of the ballad as song and printed text).[129]

The melody of 'The clarke of Bodnam' does not survive, but it was described as a 'sweet solemn tune' and may have imitated the toll of the passing-bell, as hinted in the text:

> Now my painful eyes lye rowling, and my passing-bell is towling,
> Towling sweetly, I lye dying, and my life is from me flying.

The bell was a recurring aural symbol of death (see below, p. 113); here it punctuates the text for dramatic effect: 'Now the bell doth cease to toul, sweet Jesus Christ receive my soul.' The development of a popular Protestant formula for one's final discourse with God may have filled a gap where the sacrament of the last rites once gave comfort. Ballads like the 'Clarke of Bodnam' took a standard form: confession of complete unworthiness and repentance of sins, followed by prayers for grace, expressions of faith and hope for reception in heaven. God, whether Father or Son, is a close and kindly figure: 'my loving Father sweet', 'blessed Son', 'sweet Jesus'.[130] They are thoroughly Protestant ballads, but there is little sense of a predestined elect. For the clerk, grace is a gift offered by Christ to all and available to the last minute:

> Yet though my sins like scarlet show, their whiteness may exceed the snow,
> If thou thy mercy do extend, that I my sinful life may mend.
> Which mercy, thy blest word doth say, at any time obtain I may.

This 'earnest petition' hovers on the brink of one of William Perkins' list of erroneous 'common opinions': 'That howsoever a man live, yet if hee call upon God on his death bedde, and say *Lord have mercy on me*, and so go away like a lambe, he is certainly saved.'[131] Here there is little of

---

128 Ent. 1624. RB repr. VII, p. 40. Pepys, I, 48–9.
129 In *The song of Mary the mother of Christ* (1601), repr. Rollins, *Old English ballads*, p. 163, entered in 1624 by its first line 'Jerusalem my happie home'. As a personal expression of faith it is similar to the other ballads discussed in this group, but it does not take place on the death-bed.
130 'The sorrowful lamentation of a penitent sinner' ('O Lord my God I come to Thee'), ent. 1624, RB repr. VIII, p. 99; 'Clarke of Bodnam'.
131 Quoted in Ian Green '"For children in yeeres and children in understanding": the emergence of the English catechism under Elizabeth and the early Stuarts', *Journal of Ecclesiastical History*, 37 (1986), p. 414.

A very godly Song, intituled, The earnest petition of a faithfull Christian, being Clarke of *Bodnam*, made vpon his Death-bed, at the instant of his Transmutation.

To a pleasant new tune.

NOw my painfull eyes are rowling,
And my passing Bell is towling:
Towling sweetly: I lye dying,
And my life is from me flying.

Grant me strength, O gracious God,
For to endure thy heauy rod:
Then shall I reioyce and sing,
With Psalmes vnto my heauenly King.

Simeon that blessed man,
Beleeued Christ when he was come,
And then he did desire to dye,
To liue with him eternally.

Christ wrought me a strong saluation,
By his death and bitter passion:
He hath washt and made me cleane,
That I should neuer sinne againe.

Grieuous paines doe call and cry,
O man, prepare thy selfe to dye.
All my sinnes I haue lamented,
And to dye I am contented.

Silly Soule, the Lord receiue thee,
Death is come, and life must leaue thee,
Death doth tarry no mans leasure,
Then farewell all earthly pleasure.

In this world I nothing craue,
But to bring me to my Graue,
In my Graue while I lye sleeping,
Angels haue my soule in keeping.

When the Bells are for me ringing,
Lord receiue my soule with singing:
Then shall I be free from paine,
To liue and neuer dye againe.

Whiles those wormes corruption breed on,
Wayte my noysome corpes to feed on,
My feruent loue (this prison loathing)
Craues a robe of Angels cloathing.

Farewell world and worldly glory,
Farewell all things transitory,
Sion hill my soule ascendeth,
And Gods Royall Throne attendeth.

Farewell wife and children small,
For I must goe now Christ doth call,
And for my death be ye content,
When I am gone, doe not lament.

Now the Bell doth cease to towle,
Sweet Iesus Christ receiue my soule.

4 'The clarke of Bodnam', pt 1.

the insistence on outward and life-long godliness found in many early seventeenth-century catechisms:

> Q. What if good workes be wanting?
> A. Then is iustifying Faith wanting whatsoever we professe.[132]

While faith could be presented through the exemplary godliness of the
clerk or chorister, it was also considered appropriate to represent the ordinary parishioner to himself more closely through the persona of the generic
'sinner'. 'The sorrowful lamentation of a penitent sinner' and 'The dying
teares of a penitent sinner' are two pre-1640 titles in a genre which continued
to spawn new imitations in the second half of the century.[133] Although
the titles present the speaker or singer as socially neutral, he invariably
turns out to be a head of household and a father.[134] There is the same
death-bed concern for the children's upbringing which was expanded in
the aphoristic ballads.

Did ordinary 'sinners' turn to such ballads in moments of sudden concern
for their souls, perhaps as death approached? Or did these ballads merely
present a self-image for a limited audience known to others as 'the godly
sort'? Some clue as to the appeal of these death-bed songs may be found
by looking at a class of broadsides on the fringes of 'religious' balladry:
the repentance speech of the criminal or murderer. Stories of crimes were
a source of gruesome entertainment and collective disapprobation; at the
same time the emphasis on last-minute conversion and salvation for even
the lowest dregs of society may have been comforting. Two of the 1624
stock, 'George Sandars' and 'Ned Smith' would be virtually indistinguishable
from the other 'penitent sinner' ballads if the title explaining the sensational
background of the repentance speech were removed:

> I am a prisoner poore,
> Opprest with miserie;
> O Lord, do thou restore
> That faith which wants in me.[135]

I have not included these criminals in the catalogue of 'godly ballads':
the public interest in macabre stories involved aspects of social psychology
from which it is difficult to separate the religious element. Nevertheless,
an examination of the popular 'George Sandars' is very suggestive about

---

[132] James Balmford, *A short catechisme, summarily comprizing the principall points of Christian faith* (1607), sig.A8v.

[133] 'The sorrowful lamentation', ent. 1624 (as 'O Lord my God I come to Thee'), RB repr.
VIII, p. 99. 'The dying teares', ent. 24 December 1638, RB repr. IV, p. 362.

[134] Penitent sinner ballads after the Restoration used a wider range of narrators: e.g. 'The
sorrowful mother, or the pious daughter's last farewell', RB repr. VIII, pp. 90–2; 'The
young-man's repentance, or, the sorrowful sinner's lamentation', RB repr. VIII, pp. 100–2.

[135] 'The wofull lamentation of Edward Smith, a poore penitent prisoner in the jayle of Bedford,
which he wrote a short time before his death' [*c*. 1625], Pepys, I, 59.

a wide public interest in themes of repentance.[136] The first part of the ballad is a straight narrative telling how Sandars killed his uncle, accused his own father of the murder, and confessed just as the hapless father was about to be hung. This dramatic moment is illustrated in a woodcut with speech bubbles (father: 'I am giltles'; Sandars: 'Save my Father I am giley [*sic*]').

The second part is a repentance song packed with biblical parallels and doctrinal teaching almost worthy of a catechism. First Sandars identifies himself with a list of Old Testament figures who suffered trials and tribulations:

> Mongst Lions fell in *Daniels* Den am I,
> In lowest prison cast with *Ieremy*
> Fed with *Elias* by the Ravens fell
> And plac'd with *Ionas* in the maw of hell.

Then follow, in appropriate order, the concepts of original sin, repentance and saving grace:

> I sinned have, for sinne did *Adam* die . . .
>
> Shall *Mary* weepe, and shall my eyes be dry?
>
> Oh let me now with holy *Abraham* spie
> A saving Ram that *Isaac* may not die . . .
>
> Make me now a sparrow in they house O King
> That Swallow-like I may there sit and sing.

The woodcut is unusually allegorical for a ballad illustration. A man is chained to the wall outside a prison, in the window of which we see a female figure. A speech bubble explains the emblem: 'Lord bring my soule out of prison. Psal.142.7.'

Ballads and pamphlets describing executions were numerous and immensely popular.[137] This ballad of Sandars, set, of course, to the tune of 'Fortune my foe', could have been sung to an absorbed crowd in the marketplace or even the alehouse. If the audience was interested in concepts of sin and the soul in this context, might they not listen to 'The dying teares of a penitent sinner' with the same morbid fascination? Perhaps we should not be too narrow-minded about the potential audience for these seemingly indigestible offerings.

---

[136] 'The confession and repentance of George Sandars gentleman late of Shugh in the County of Hereford, who unnaturally killed his Uncle, and accused his own father for the murder: but by Gods providence being discovered, he dyed for the same. Where he writ this song with his owne hand' [*c.* 1618], Manchester, II, 10.

[137] J.A. Sharpe, '"Last dying speeches": religion, ideology and public execution in seventeenth-century England', *Past and Present*, 107 (1985), pp. 147–65.

5   'St Bernard's vision', pt 1.

St Bernard's vision

The clerk of Bodnam was the incarnation of a seventeenth-century godliness, the exemplary Protestant on his death-bed. But he and his fellow 'penitent sinners' could not chase away the more traditional vision of damnation and salvation, descended from the art, drama and song of pre-Reformation Catholicism, with little sign of any break. In more than half the stock ballads dealing with death, a retributive God is less interested in repentance and faith than in the preparation for salvation with good works, and the promise of 'Jerusalem my happie home' is balanced (if not overshadowed) by the very real threat of hell-fire. If the ballad buyer found the Bodnam parish clerk too bland for his taste, he could choose a broadside of 'St Bernard's vision' [c. 1640], with a woodcut of demons prodding a naked body with pitchforks (Plates 5, 23).[138] Here was a tiny fragment of the great medieval painting of 'The Doom' which had stood over the chancel arch in the parish church, now transferred to the cottage wall.

The ballad of 'St Bernard's vision' is a dramatization of the after-life,

---

[138]   RB repr. II, p. 491. Pepys, II, 4.

using a narrator who experiences a death-like state, but is then revived to tell the tale. This device came from a long tradition of clerical vision literature, made familiar to a wide audience through its influence on the paintings of 'dooms', the most common narrative theme on church walls.[139] The specific source was the supposititious 'Visio Sancti Bernardi', translated into English metre by William Crashaw in 1613, and published in one 8vo and three 12mo editions between 1613 and 1632.[140] The ballad is a condensed version of Crashaw's metrical pamphlet, and follows it quite closely in sense, borrowing the occasional phrase word-for-word.[141]

'St Bernard's vision' is a powerful argument for the continuity of a medieval religious outlook well into the early modern period. The first extant copy dates from *c.* 1640, and the ballad was one of only half a dozen seventeenth-century religious titles still available in Dicey's catalogue of 1754. In addition to the song, the eighteenth-century chapmen also sold a woodcut picture on the theme: 'The Broad and Narrow Way to Heaven and Hell, or St Bernard's Vision, with descriptionary Verses'.[142]

The ballad version is subtitled 'A briefe discourse (dialogue-wise) betweene the soule and the body of a damned man newly deceased, laying open the faults of each other; with a speech of the divel's in hell'. The lugubrious tune 'Fortune my foe' is well suited to the wailing and groaning of the body and soul in their pain. The soul berates the body for its sins and pleasures which have brought them both to hell, 'where we in frying flames for aye must dwell'. The body disclaims the responsibility:

> I was your servant, form'd of durt and clay;
> You to command, and I for to obey.

The preoccupation with the relationship between body and soul in Greek philosophy and medieval Christian theology is here popularized for an early modern Protestant audience.

'The deadmans song' was another vision of the after-life, experienced by a narrator who lay apparently dead for five hours.[143] It was entered by its first line ('sore sicke deare freinds') in 1624 and was still part of the Norris–Brown ballad stock in 1712. The dead man's description of

---

[139] For example, the 'Vision of Tundal', 'St Patrick's Purgatory' and the 'Vision of the Monk of Eynsham'. (A. Caiger-Smith, *English medieval mural paintings* (Oxford, 1963), pp. 36, 31.) The individual image of St Christopher was the only subject painted more often than the Last Judgement.

[140] STC 1908.5 to 1909.7.

[141] Crashaw's verse rhymes abab, while the ballad is in the common rhyming couplet form. The ballad removes St Bernard's decision, after the vision, to renounce the world and follow a monastic life.

[142] Cluer Dicey and Richard Marshall, *A catalogue of maps, prints, copy books, drawing-books, histories, old ballads, patters, collections &c* (1764), p. 65.

[143] 'The deadmans song, whose dwelling was neere unto Basing Hall in London' (ent. 1624), Pepys, I, 55.

heaven and hell again follows the conventions of clerical vision literature and wall painting. Heaven is a great city made of diamonds, pearls and gold, surrounded by fields of flowers. Hell, where the 'deadman' himself is taken, is the real focus of the ballad, described in lurid imagery. As in the 'doom' paintings, the inhabitants are punished according to which of the seven deadly sins they have committed. The lecherous fry on hot beds with brimstone pillows: the gluttons are fed with 'dishes full of crawling Toades' and have their fat flesh plucked from the bone 'with red hot pincers'.[144]

This group of ballads passes on, almost unchanged, a centuries-old vision of the Last Judgement based on the individual's sins or merits in this life.[145] Only one of these after-life ballads presents the Protestant message of the sinner saved by faith alone. 'In slumbring sleepe I lay' has Satan appearing to claim the narrator after the last trumpet, bearing a list of sins.[146] But the narrator continues to have trust 'in the blood of Christ'. The saviour himself shows Satan the 'booke of life' where, sure enough, the sinner's name is written. The positive moral that Christ 'will save all such as truly see in mee' is matched by the up-beat dance tune 'Rogero'. Yet, while the medieval gloom and doom of 'St Bernard's vision' was popular for over a century, this ostensibly more comforting Protestant ballad does not seem to have lasted beyond the year 1624–5.

The distinction between these two approaches to death is useful for the purpose of discussion, and would have meant something to a seventeenth-century Protestant reformer. But the ballad buyers themselves did not necessarily perceive any contradiction between different schemes of salvation. It is quite possible that if a husbandman was of a mind to purchase a ballad about death, 'The clarke of Bodnam' might do just as well as 'St Bernards vision'; indeed he might have both of them up on the cottage wall.

The preoccupation with death was an area of shared culture spanning the doctrinal rift between Catholic and Protestant. Perhaps for this reason, the Reformation seems to have increased the prominence of various traditional but relatively non-religious allegories for mortality, such as the

---

[144] Similar details can be found in the story of the knight Owen's descent into the cave of 'St Patrick's Purgatory' (to name just one medieval example of the after-life legend). The gates of paradise are made of 'Jaspers, topaz and crystal / Margarites and corral / ... And diamonds for the nones.' Punishment is according to the individual's sins: 'On some sat toads black / Ewts, nadders and the snake / That fret them back and side / This is the pain of gluttony.' (From 'Owain Miles', an old English poem in the Auchinleck MS, Edinburgh, cited in Shane Leslie, *Saint Patrick's Purgatory* (1932), pp. 152, 155.)

[145] This group is distinct from the warnings of the imminent Judgement Day discussed above, p. 97. Here the judgement is not prophesied for the general populace within historical time; it is the timeless Judgement Day where the individual is brought to his reckoning.

[146] 'A comfortable new ballad of a dreame of a sinner, being very sore troubled with the assaults of Sathan' (ent. 1624), Pepys, I, 39.

personification of death itself as the omnipresent skeleton-figure. The 'dance of death' was updated in a seventeenth-century 'Death's dance' [*c.* 1625] which had the grim reaper appearing at the London docks, in St Pauls, at the Royal Exchange and in the city suburbs.[147] Other ballads bear refrains very like the burdens of earlier carols:

> O mortall man, behold and see,
> This world is but a vanitie.[148]

> Remember man both night and daye
> Thou must needs die, there is no nay.[149]

The message is that of the medieval morality play: what use are worldly riches when we must all die? 'Good people all repent with speed', one of the 'partners' ballads on the stock lists in both 1624 and 1675, is a warning of mortality in this simple and relatively secular vein.[150]

These ballads performed the same function as a visual *memento mori*. To keep the thought of death constantly in mind was the key to living virtuously in this life and preparing properly for the life-to-come.[151] The mnemonic tricks prescribed included turning the physical aspects of daily life into allegories or premonitions of death. 'A good exhortation to every man what he should doo when he goeth to bed and when he riseth' [1580?] advised thinking of one's bed as a grave, the waking cock as the last trumpet and the 'spendent sun' as the visage of God on Judgement Day. This ballad was later reworked as a plain broadside, with the tune removed, probably intended to be stuck up on the wall for daily reference.[152]

Possibly the most commonly recommended *memento mori* was an aural one: the recurring toll of bells which formed a background to daily life in every town. Inspiration for godly metaphors was found in both the passing-bell announcing a death, and the bell of the watchman on his nightly rounds. By 1580 it was commonplace to suggest an equation between these two sounds:

> The nightly Bell which I heare sound,
> as I am laid in bed:

---

147 RB repr. I, p. 283.

148 'A pretie dittie and a pithie intituled O mortall man' (ent. 1563–4), Rollins, *Old English ballads*, p. 265.

149 SA no. 43.

150 'A warninge to worldlings to learne them to dye' [pre-1616], Shirburn, p. 25. The ballad urges preparation for death while one still has health and understanding. There is no mention of Christ or the elect, nor any sense of reforming zeal.

151 This principle was central to the philosophy of the *Ars moriendi*, which went through multiple reprints across Europe in the late fifteenth and early sixteenth centuries. (Roger Chartier, *The cultural uses of print in early modern France*, trans. Lydia C. Cochrane (Princeton, 1987), pp. 52, 61.)

152 STC 10627, Huntington Library. STC 10626.5 'A godly exhortation, necessary for this present time' (1603).

6   'A bell-man for England', pt 1.

Foreshowes the Bell which me to ground,
    shall ring when I am dead.[153]

Two of the stock ballads, 'The bell-man's good morrow' and 'A bell-man
for England' took the metaphor a step further beyond death to describe
the bell-man as waking the hearers from sin by calling them to the Day
of Judgement.[154] The bell-man became a stock character of godly print,
portrayed in woodcuts with his lantern and bell, and his dog (Plate 6).[155]
    Emblems of mortality like the sound of the watchman's bell, the skeleton-
figure with his spear and the dance of death were intelligible and potent
for both the most backward recusant and the most committed Protestant.
Even the visions of the after-life were based on the shared belief in a tangible
heaven and hell, despite some disagreement over how to reach the right
place. The fear of death lay at the core of popular religion long before

[153] 'A good exhortation to every man what he should doo when he goeth to bed and when
      he riseth' [1580?].
[154] 'The bell-mans good morrow' (or, 'From sluggish sleepe', ent. 21 November 1580, Shirburn,
      p. 182) retains an emphasis on the individual's preparation for death, and has been categor-
      ized as a *memento mori* ballad. 'A bell-man for England' ([pre-1580], Shirburn, p. 36)
      has more in common with the alarums which warn the society as a whole of the coming
      Judgement Day (discussed above, p. 97).
[155] Pepys, I, 54. Thomas Dekker used the bell-man in his rogue pamphlets, as a figure of
      morality exposing the London underworld of crime. (Dekker, *The belman of London*
      (1608); *Villanies discovered by lanthorne and candle-light* (1616 edn.).) Samuel Rowlands
      continued in the godly ballad tradition of the *memento mori*, with a pamphlet entitled
      *Heavens glorie [etc]. The common cals, cryes and sounds of the bell-man or divers verses
      to put us in minde of our mortalitie* (1628).

and long after the Reformation, and on this theme the ballads testify to just how little had changed.[156]

Stories

The 'gospelling movement' of the 1550s and 60s has now been well chronicled.[157] The psalms were the major target for metrical paraphrase, while the 'Books of Solomon' (Song of Songs, Ecclesiastes and Proverbs) were also popular sources. But if some gospellers were inspired primarily by those parts of Scripture with the most obviously 'poetic' qualities, others had broader hopes for the metrical paraphrase as a pedagogical tool. William Samuel introduced his rhyming Pentateuch with these aspirations:

My mynd is that I wold have my contrey people able in a smale some to syng the hole contents of the byble, & where as in tymes past the musicians or mynstrells, were wont to syng fained myracles, saints lives, & Robin hode, in stede thereof to sing, undoutyd truthes, canonycall scryptures, and Gods doynges ... Also thys my doyngs I trust shall cause the scrypturs, to be often read, as the man that hearyth a parte of a story in the scryptures, & doth not knowe the hole: thys may move the hole to be red.[158]

This latter hope is not unlike the ballad seller's tactic of chanting out only half the song in order to sell his product! It is in this spirit that some gospellers published their paraphrases in the medium most accessible to a wide audience, the broadside ballad.

The Scripture paraphrases are the one genre of religious ballad for which we can use the Stationers' Register in a discussion of content. Many were recorded plainly by their book and chapter reference, probably indicative of a close, literalistic paraphrase: 'taken out of the 14 chapter of saynt Luke' (1568–9) or 'the xjth and xijth chapters of the ijde boke of kynges' (1569–70).[159] In the Register, there are three dozen titles of ballads from Scripture in the decade from 1560–1 and 1570–1.[160] In the next decade for which the Register survives, 1576–7 to 1586–7, there are less than half as many biblical titles (roughly sixteen); then only a dozen more for the rest of the period up to 1640. Old Testament and apocryphal subjects make up almost two-thirds of the Scripture ballads, both in the Stationers' Register and amongst surviving copies, while the other third are from the Gospels. How-

---

[156] See Spufford, *Small books*, pp. 204, 207.

[157] King, *English Reformation literature*. Rivkah Zim, *English metrical psalms: poetry as praise and prayer 1535–1601* (Cambridge, 1987).

[158] William Samuel, *The abridgements of Goddes statutes in myter* (1551), sig. A2–A2v. Cited in King, *English Reformation literature*, p. 212.

[159] Arber, I, pp. 384, 415.

[160] Of these, two dozen have vanished without leaving a copy. As the Stationers' Register only begins in 1557–8, we have no comparable record of the gospellers' use of broadsides in the 1550s.

ever, the balance was probably more even than would appear: I have not
counted unknown 'Christmas carols' as Scripture ballads, but those which
do survive are usually narratives of the nativity story taken directly from
the Gospels.[161]

David and Bethsheba

One of the aims of the Protestant ballad writers was to replace the saints'
lives and miracles of popish piety with characters and events from the Old
Testament. The ballads stayed fairly close to the scriptural text, sometimes
embroidering the settings and physical descriptions of the characters, but
avoiding the pure inventions and apocryphal trappings which had grown
up around Old Testament stories in the medieval drama: such as Noah's
wife who refuses to enter the Ark, or Cain's garrulous servant in the Wakefield cycle.[162] The increasingly restrictive reverence of seventeenth-century
Protestants towards biblical texts is illustrated by the report of Henry Gosson's visit to the High Commission in 1631–2. Gosson's song of how 'Jacob
came to Heaven gate and Adam kept the doore', was printed 'before he
was born' and it is quite likely that it was inoffensive to the Elizabethans.[163]
It may even have been properly licensed: a likely identification might be
'the complaynt of Adam our greate graunde ffayther &c' entered to John
Alde in 1563–4; or perhaps 'Adams fearfull fall' published by William Pickering in 1570–1.[164] Sixteenth-century audiences were used to biblical characters being treated with humour in the mystery plays, but for stricter seventeenth-century Calvinists such merriment was blasphemous.

Fidelity to biblical authority did not preclude captivating the audience
with a good story. Some of the ballad subjects recorded in the Stationers'
Register are obvious choices for their dramatic quality: Jonah and the whale,
Abraham offering Isaac, Daniel in the lion's den, David and Goliath.[165]
The public was familiar with these themes in Elizabethan wall paintings
and hangings of the same period.[166] Lesser-known episodes could be chosen
for their sensational value; such as the description of the famine in Samaria
(from what is now II Kings 6), where a woman is constrained to eat her

---

[161] There appear to be eight carols registered in broadside form (see below, p. 121).

[162] Martial Rose, ed., *The Wakefield mystery plays* (1961).

[163] Gardiner, ed., *Reports of cases in the courts of Star Chamber and High Commission*,
       p. 314 (discussed above, pp. 43, 74).

[164] Arber, I. pp. 362, 436. The latter was probably acquired by Edward White and registered
       on 1 August 1586: 'of the creation of the world and Adams fall'. (Arber, II, p. 451.)
       If it was in White's stock, it is likely to have been passed on to the 'partners'.

[165] Arber, I, p. 205 (1562–3); I, p. 378 (1568–9); II, p. 359 (1579–80); III, p. 486 (1611–12).

[166] Jonah and the Whale is depicted in an early seventeenth-century wall painting at Waltham
       Abbey Cross, Hertfordshire. Daniel in the Lion's Den was described in 1632 as a common
       theme for alehouse walls. (See pp. 211, 194.)

son for hunger.[167] But others were picked because their message was relevant to contemporary concerns. The history of 'Manasses kynge of Juda', who brought punishment upon Jerusalem with his graven images and false altars, was an obvious lesson against popish idolatry.[168] A ballad of the briber Gehazi, whose seed was punished with leprosy, ends with a plea to Elizabeth to expel bribers from the land.[169]

Yet the Old Testament ballads which endured in the godly 'stock' did not show the same breadth of themes and lessons. The most popular stories were those involving a beautiful young woman, shown to be either a paragon of virtue, or inconstant and deceitful, or unwittingly the cause of men's destruction. Ballads of 'Constant Susanna', Sampson and Delilah or David and Bethsheba came closest among the godly ballads to the narratives Child collected, and which we have come to think of as defining balladry.[170] The same ballad clichés were used: the 'maidens' are always 'fresh and gay', 'faire and bright'.[171] The opening of 'The story of David and Berseba' is similar in essence (if less satisfying as poetry) to those of 'traditional' ballads such as 'Little Mousgrove and the Lady Barnet' or 'Fair Margaret and Sweet William':[172]

> It chaunced so, upon a day,
>   the king went forth to take the ayre
> All in the pleasant moneth of May,
>   from whence he spide a Lady faire.
>
> Her beauty was more excellent
>   and brighter than the morning Sunne
> By which the king, incontinent,
>   was to her favour quickly wonne.
>
> She stood within a pleasant Bower,
>   all naked, for to wash her there;
> Her body, like a Lilly Flowere,
>   was covered with her golden haire.[173]

The scriptural version tells us only that David saw from the roof of the palace 'a woman washyng her selfe, and the woman was very beautiful to look upon'.[174] The incorporation of this story into the body of 'folksong'

---

[167] 'and taken out of the vjth chapeter of the iiijth boke of kynges &c', Arber, I, p. 379 (1568–9).

[168] Arber, I, p. 401 (1569–70).

[169] 'A proper new balad of the bryber Gehesie. Taken out of the fourth boke of kinges, the v chapter [1566], Lilly, p. 42.

[170] F. J. Child, *The English and Scottish popular ballads* (5 vols., 1882–98).

[171] Delilah in 'A most excellent and famous ditty of Sampson judge of Israell, how he wedded a Philistine's daughter' (?ent. 1563–4), Pepys, I, 32.

[172] Kinsley, ed., *Oxford book of ballads*, nos. 44, 58.

[173] 'The story of David and Berseba' [?ent. 1569–70?], RB repr. I, p. 270.

[174] *The holie bible* [Bishops' version] (1569), II Samuel 11.

was apparently successful, since the ballad, probably first registered in 1569–70, was still for sale in the Dicey catalogue of 1754.

These ballads were versifications of the same themes popular in other forms of contemporary literature, particularly the drama. Thomas Garter's *Commody of the moste vertuous and godlye Susanna* (1578) was published by Thomas Colwell who also registered the ballad.[175] George Peele's *The love of King David and fair Bathsabe* (registered 1594) was 'divers times plaied upon the stage' by 1599.[176] Both of these show the influence of Ovidian eroticism (there was a swell of translations of Ovid from 1560 to 1580) particularly of the scene of Actaeon gazing at Diana as she bathes naked in the spring.[177] 'When Jepha judge of Israell' tells of Jephthah's promise to God that in return for victory in battle he will sacrifice the 'first quick thing' he meets on his return, which turns out to be his own virtuous daughter. The story of Jephthah, used in university play and broadside ballad alike, was appealing to the educated Renaissance playwright and audience because of its closeness to Greek mythology.[178]

However, the appeal of 'pagan' themes was by no means confined to the elite: sacrifices, riddles, magic and miracles were the stuff of the 'traditional' ballads. 'Tobias of Ninive' paraphrases only the narrative chapters of the apocryphal Book of Tobit, making the magical content of the story dominant, and Old Tobias' relationship with God subsidiary.[179] The subtitle advertizes a story about a young woman guarded by an evil spirit: 'A pleasant new ballad of Tobias, wherein is shewed the wonderfull things which chanced to him in his youth: and how he wedded a young Damsell that had had seven husbands and never enjoyed their company: who were all slaine by a wicked spirit.'[180] There is little to distinguish this 'biblical' ballad from 'Lady Isabel and the elf-knight':

> Seven king's-daughters here hea I slain,
> And ye shall be the eight o them.[181]

Lady Isabel charms her wicked spirit to sleep, while Tobias chases his away by an object with miraculous powers: the smoke from the heart and liver of a fish. The final scene is the archetypical return home of the hero after

---

[175] Repr. Oxford, 1937. The ballad was registered in 1562–3 and the play written by 1568 (Murray Roston, *Biblical drama in England* (1968), p. 87); there does not appear to be any direct relationship in treatment of the story. The ballad is a close paraphrase of the apocryphal book. ('The ballad of constant Susanna' (ent. 1562–3), Pepys, I, 33. *The byble in English* [Great Bible version] (1553).)

[176] Roston, *Biblical drama*, p. 100.

[177] *Ibid.*, pp. 88, 102.

[178] *Ibid.*, p. 79. Manchester, II, 56, written by 1603

[179] Tobias' advice to his son, prayers and thanksgivings are omitted.

[180] Ent. 1624, RB repr. II, p. 621.

[181] Child no. 4.

a voyage: here Tobias now uses the fish's magic gall to restore his aged father's eyesight. The original process of apocryphal creation melded superstition with Christian themes: the success of ballads like 'Tobias' (on the stock lists from 1624 to 1754) shows that such a combination was still appealing to the early modern audience.

There was a tendency to add a moral tag at the end of these ballads. This is one of the standard features which often distinguishes broadside texts from versions of the same song collected orally.[182] The lesson of 'David and Berseba' is summarized in the last stanza:

> The scourge of sinne thus you may see
> for murther and adultery.
> Lord! grant that we may warned be
> such crying sinnes to shun and flie.

Susanna is a model to all young women:

> She feared God, she stood in awe,
> As in the storie we have read
> Was well brought up in Moses' law
> Her parents they were godly folke.

Yet one has to suspect that the real appeal of the ballad lay in the image of naked Susanna washing herself in the orchard, an object of fantasy which probably titillated the viewers of Renaissance paintings on the theme just as much as it did the wicked elders whose lechery was supposedly condemned.[183]

When Jesus Christ was twelve

Perhaps even more than the Old Testament ballads, the ballad titles from the Gospels in the Register of the 1560s show a great seriousness of didactic purpose. The early Elizabethan reformers tried to popularize the teachings of Christ, and especially the parables. Ballads were registered on the fig tree and the grain of mustard seed, the ten servants and ten talents, the rich man and the unjust steward.[184] The sermon on the mount was the source of two ballads: one versifying the beatitudes, the other drawing out the message 'that we shulde not be Carefull of wordly vanytes' by the example of the fowls of the air and the lilies of the field.[185] These excerpts were rich in poetry, allegory and edifying content. By setting them to popular tunes the reformers tried to give unlearned people direct access to the concepts of Christian faith and (if William Samuel's hopes were typical) to

---

[182] This feature is often remarked upon in discussion of 'traditional' versus broadside ballads. (E.g. Evelyn Kendrick Wells, *The ballad tree* (1950), pp. 214–215.)
[183] John Berger, *Ways of seeing* (Harmondsworth, 1972), p. 50.
[184] Arber, I, p. 414 (1569–70); II, p. 376 (1580–1); II, p. 376 (1580–1).
[185] Arber, I. p. 415 (1569–70); I, p. 416 (1569–70).

provoke further interest in the vernacular bible reading which was one of the main objects of Protestant Reformation.

We do not know what tunes the gospellers chose as settings, but apparently these passages were not appealing as songs. Only one parable remained in the popular 'stock': the story of the prodigal son.[186] This had a particularly strong plot line, and was also a frequent subject of prints, hangings and wall paintings.[187] The prodigal son theme was a staple of the Tudor moral interlude, although plays like *Nice Wanton* (1560) ignored the biblical ending and meted out due punishment to the erring youths.[188] The broadside belongs to this tradition. The allegorical message of God's forgiveness for sinners is brought out in the last stanza of the ballad, but the message functions mainly on a literal level:

> Young Men, remember! Delights are but vain,
> And after sweet pleasure comes sorrow and pain.[189]

The ballad belongs with the stories of ungrateful children and misspent youth which were a continuing strand in popular balladry; from the six-teenth-century 'example of an ungratious sonne, who in the pride of his hart denied his owne father: and how God for his offence turned his meate into loathsome toades' to the late seventeenth-century 'Good fellows resolu-tion' which became the well-known 'Wild rover'.[190] As with the biblical love stories above, the scriptural theme of the prodigal son was assimilated to popular archetypes of folksong.

With this exception, the seventeenth-century ballad stock contains nothing of Christ's teachings, but moves back to basic events of his life and death which had been the central themes of pre-Reformation piety: the virgin birth, the passion and resurrection. There was a continuing demand for the familiar nativity story which had been popularized more than any other religious theme through its celebration at Christmas and in carols. Although reformers aimed to curtail the excesses of Christmas-time festivities, books

---

[186] Child no. 56, a ballad based on the parable of 'Dives and Lazarus', may also date from the sixteenth century, but there is no record of printed copies in the seventeenth century. ([Ent. 1577–8?].)

[187] See pp. 202–5.

[188] Leonard Tennenhouse, ed., *The Tudor interludes Nice Wanton and Impacient Poverty* (1984 edn.). Other prodigal son plays were Thomas Ingeland's *The Disobedient Child* and George Gascoigne's *Glass of Government* (1577). (Roston, *Biblical drama*, pp. 58–9.)

[189] 'A new ballad; declaring the excellent parable of the prodigal child' [ent. 1570–1?], RB repr. II, p. 393.

[190] 'A most notable and worthy example of an ungratious sonne' (ent. 8 August 1586), Col-lmann no. 86. 'Good fellows resolution' discussed in Thomson, 'Development of the broad-side ballad trade', pp. 232–6.

of carols had continued to be published.[191] But there are only some eight entries for carols in broadside form, mostly from the 1630s.[192] During Elizabeth's reign the publication of carols seems to have been controversial. William Pickering's entry for 'a Dyaloge upon Christes byrth' in 1564–5 has an added note: 'a nombre muste Dysplease with'.[193] Richard Jones' ballad on 'the byrth of Christe' has been identified with a 'carroll' in a manuscript of Yorkshire Catholic provenance.[194]

Of the seven long-enduring ballads from the Gospels, four were about the nativity.[195] But none of these (nor any of the stock New Testament ballads) were registered during the prime 'gospelling' period before 1570, when the parable of the mustard seed was meant to replace the babe in the manger.[196] 'A Christmas caroll called the righteous Joseph' survived from 1639 until at least the 1670s.[197] The greater emphasis on 'righteous Joseph' may have been an attempt to counter any tendency toward the cult of the virgin Mary. In 'Joseph and Mary' the dramatic focus is on Joseph's bewilderment at Mary's pregnancy, his thoughts of casting her out and his reassurance by the angel Gabriel:

> And so to put her from him quite
> Who was his joy and heart's delight
> That blessed Virgin fair and bright
> Whom he did love so dear, so dear.

Joseph is also included in the ballad pictures: the only woodcut scene of the holy family surviving on a ballad before 1640 shows the flight into Egypt, with Joseph leading Mary and Jesus on a donkey (Plate 22).[198] The

---

[191] Books of Christmas carols were entered in 1562–3; 1569–70 (twice); 11 December 1587; 26 August 1617; 16 May 1621; 21 November 1633; 9 November 1638. (From Rollins Index no. 301.) Other 'godly Carolles', not specified for Christmas, were registered in 1562–3; 1580–1. (Arber, I, p. 294; II, p. 383.)

[192] Arber, I, p. 265 (1564–5); I, p. 402 (1569–70); II, p. 641 (12 December 1593); IV, p. 204 (15 November 1628); IV, p. 307 (1633–4); IV, p. 331 (1634–5); IV, p. 456 (1638–9); IV, p. 508 (1639–40).

[193] Arber, I. p. 265. This did not prevent Edward White from acquiring the title for his stock: Arber, II, p. 451 (1586-7).

[194] BL MS Cotton Vesp.A.XXV, fol. 151v; repr. Seng no. 33.

[195] 'A most excellent ballad of Joseph the carpenter and the sacred Virgin Mary' (ent. 1624), RB repr. VII, p. 781; 'The sinner's redemption. Wherein is described the blessed nativity of our lord Jesus Christ' (ent. 13 June 1634), RB repr. II, p. 486; 'An excellent ballad of the birth and passion of our saviour Christ' [pre-1616], Shirburn, p. 60; 'The Angel Gabriel: his salutation to the blessed Virgin Mary' [ent. 22 February 1639?], Pepys, II, 30.

[196] The 'stock' ballads from the Gospels were registered in 1578, 1588, 1624 (two), 1634, 1639.

[197] 'The Angel Gabriel: his salutation to the blessed Virgin Mary' (begins 'When righteous Joseph wedded was').

[198] 'Glad tydings from heaven: or Christs glorious invitation to sinners' [c. 1630], RB repr. I, p. 402.

woodcut on the earliest copy of 'Joseph and Marye' from 1678–80, shows a crude little virgin and child with two angels hovering in the air; it was full of wormholes by this time and may have been used on the pre-1640 editions.[199] Within the restrictions of Protestant censorship, the miracle of the virgin birth was still a powerful theme in popular religious print, if not as central as it once had been.

In this group of carol-like ballads from the Gospels, religion is still primarily the record of miracles and wonders. 'The glorious resurrection' features a woodcut of the Roman centurions leaping back in alarm as Christ rises from the tomb they are guarding (Plate 21).[200] The ballad challenges the hearers to accept the miracle:

> What faithless, froward, sinful man
> so far from grace is fled,
> That doth not in his heart believe
> the Rising of the Dead?

The single most successful ballad from the Gospels was 'A new ditty, shewing the wonderfull miracles of our lord' (known by its first line 'When Jesus Christ was 12'), which survived on the 'partners' stock list of 1675, a century after its first registration.[201] In a jogging rhythm it describes how Christ turned the water into wine, fed the multitude with the loaves, raised Lazarus from the dead, healed the lepers, the lame and the blind. This is a story to compete with any of the contemporary miracles described in the sensational new ballads:

> But yet for all these wonders great, the Jews were in a raging heat,
> Whom no persuasions could intreat, but cruelly did kill him.
> And when he left his life so good, the Moon was turned into blood,
> The earth and Temple shaking stood, the graves full wide did open.

'When Jesus Christ was 12' is a succinct paraphrase of the plot-line of Christ's life, and may have performed a mnemonic function for its singers, like a musical catechism. However, it is devoid of any of the parables and teachings which the early Elizabethan gospellers had hoped to spread; indeed, devoid of any message about how to behave towards God or one's neighbour in the 'Christian' way.

Doctor Faustus and other strange histories

With their emphasis on the miraculous, some of these gospel ballads approached the world of 'history – true & fabulous' which many of the

---

[199] Pepys, II, 27.
[200] 'A most godly and comfortable ballad of the glorious resurrection of our lord Jesus Christ' [ent. 1588?], RB repr. I, p. 388.
[201] Ent. 11 September 1578, Shirburn, p. 103.

broadside ballads inhabited.[202] The popular 'stock' included two last story ballads, both well known, which seem to belong in these borderlands between 'religion' and 'magic'. (In Tables 2 and 3 I have categorized these as 'Christian legends'.) The myth of the wandering Jew, known in England from at least the thirteenth century, enjoyed a revival of popularity in 1620, when Richard Shanne recorded in Addit. MS 38,599: 'The Historie of A wanderinge Jewe, much spoken of this yeare. This is drawne out of the printed storie worde for worde, there was allso his picture livelie drawne, and all the cuntrie was full of Ballades, expressinge the same.'[203] 1620 was the year in which Cuthbert Wright registered the ballad which became part of the 'partners' stock, although a version was already in print in 1612.[204] The ballad adopts the moralizing tone of the other 'godly' broadsides, with the refrain:

> Repent, therefore, O England! Repent while you have space;
> And do not (like the wicked Jews) despise God's proferred Grace.

The presentation of a detailed account of the hapless shoemaker's travels in the guise of 'news' presumably satisfied the demand for veracity.[205] The wandering Jew functions as a link between the received truth of the Bible and the tangible reality of contemporary Europe.

'Doctor Faustus', was first registered to Richard Jones in 1589, five years before the first recorded performance of Marlowe's play (Plate 7).[206] This condensed account of Faustus' pact with the devil in return for knowledge and magical powers is set firmly in a religious context, and sung to the dirge-like tune of 'Fortune my foe':

> All Christian men, give ear a while to me,
> How I am plung'd in pain but cannot die;
> I liv'd a life the like did none before,
> Forsaking Christ, and I am damn'd therefore.

---

[202] This is one of the headings under which Pepys arranged his ballads. (Pepys, I, p. 63.)

[203] BL Addit. MS 38,599, fol. 51v. Cited in RB repr. VI, p. 688.

[204] 'The wandering Jew; or, the shooemaker of Jerusalem' [ent. 21 August 1612?], Pepys, I, 524–5.

[205] The assertion of a ballad's truth frequently appeared in the title: 'A true and dreadfull testimonie of Gods wrathe shewed in the parishe of Llandrillo in the Countie of Merioneth in Wales', 'A true relacion of those wicked Murthers &c', 'A true Report happened in Germany at Melwing by A mayd of 14 yeres old'. (Arber, II, p. 407; IV, p. 508; II, p. 375. See also Rollins Index nos. 2711–42.)

[206] 'The judgment of God shewed upon John Faustus, Doctor of Divinitye' (ent. 1589), Shirburn, p. 72. RB orig. II, 235. Woodcut also used for 'The tragedy of Doctor Lambe', Pepys, I, 134. The German text of the Faustbook appeared in 1587. The first English adaptation (*The historie of the damnable life, and deserved death of doctor John Faustus*, trans. P.F.) was printed in 1592, but may have been available earlier in manuscript. (C.F. Tucker Smith and Nathanial Burton Paradise, eds., *English drama 1580–1642*, 2nd edn (Lexington, Mass., 1961), pp. 168–9.)

7   'Doctor Faustus'.

These legends, with their complicated literary histories, were presumably
no different to the ordinary buyer or listener from other ballads or pamphlets
involving witchcraft, devils and the supernatural.[207] There was a broad
cross-section of 'news' ballads: miraculous happenings, monstrous births,
floods and fires, which sometimes made use of religious judgements, but
which (like the criminals' last speeches) appealed to their audience primarily
on other grounds.

In a ballad published by Henry Gosson, a rich but barren lady hurls
insults at a poor beggar woman blessed with twins. The lady is 'by the
hand of God most strangely punished, by sending her as many children
at one birth, as there are daies in the yeare', each baby the size of a new-born
mouse (Plate 8).[208] In folk tales, similar phrases ('as many children as there
are holes in a sieve') express, through hyperbole, the problems of poor
households with too many mouths to feed.[209] In the ballad, the notion

---

[207] Although ballads of 'miracles' in the natural world were common, witchcraft appeared
    much less frequently. 'Damnable practises of three Lincolne-shire witches, Joane Flower,
    and her two daughters, Margret and Phillip Flower' was printed in 1619. (Pepys I, 132–3.)
    Other ballads of 'three witches' were registered: one trio were executed at Chelmsford
    in 1589, and another at Huntingdon in 1593. (Arber II, pp. 526, 641.)

[208] STC 15120. 'The lamenting lady, who for the wrongs done to her by a poore woman,
    for having two children at one burthen, was by the hand of God most strangely punished'
    [*c.* 1620?], Pepys, I, 44–5.

[209] Robert Darnton, *The great cat massacre and other episodes of French cultural history*
    (New York, 1984), p. 31.

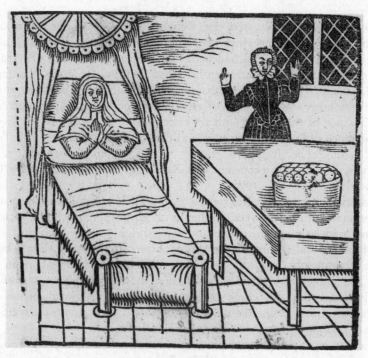

8 'The lamenting lady', pt 2.

of divine justice has been invoked in the service of social inversion: the rich lady is taught a lesson about what it is like when children become burdens rather than blessings.

Did people really believe in the 'heavie hand of heaven' inflicting justice, eye-for-an-eye? Did ballads like these affect, for example, the way a Wiltshire servant in 1635 interpreted her own misfortunes? Pregnant by her master, Anne Nightingale accepted £10 to name her fellow servant as the father, but afterwards repented for her perjury: 'she confesseth that God is a just and righteous God unto her and that he hath justly punished her for her foul and false accusation by taking from her the use of her limbs'.[210] An attempt to probe further into popular belief would have to look for oblique references to ideas like God, sin and death in a wide range of ballads, not only in those dealing directly and primarily with 'religion'.[211]

Meanwhile, the general picture of popular piety gleaned from the stock

---

[210] Martin Ingram, *Church courts, sex and marriage in England, 1570–1640* (Cambridge, 1987), p. 330.
[211] This is the approach taken by Helen Weinstein in her thesis on the later seventeenth-century ballads (Cambridge PhD, in progress).

godly ballads is a conservative one. Religion is about the same fear of death and personal judgement which preoccupied medieval Catholics; it is about practical lists of good and bad behaviour; and about stories of miracles, a virgin birth, heroism and even love and trickery. However, judging by the ballads, certain Protestant lessons had been absorbed by some of their buyers: notably the centrality of repentance and salvation through faith. The absence of the saints (with the exception of Bernard and his vision), the presence of Protestant martyrs and the emphasis on certain Old Testament lessons: collectively these choices created a popular broadside balladry we could describe as distinctively 'post-Reformation', if not thoroughly 'Protestant'.

Historians have drawn too rigid a dichotomy between Protestantism and 'traditional culture'; between a religion of 'serious doctrine' and 'a culture imbued with symbolism, magic and superstition'.[212] The theory of social 'polarization' underestimates the ability of the culture to absorb new beliefs while retaining old ones, to forge hybrid forms, to accommodate contradictions and ambiguities. There were situations in which the values of a reforming Protestantism did come into conflict with traditional beliefs and recreations, but sources like the godly ballads suggest that there were also areas of gradual and unconscious cultural integration.

The 'top eight' ballads, which we have used as exemplars, illustrate the successful fusion of new and traditional elements in popular piety. Ballads like 'The Duchess of Suffolk' and 'David and Bethsheba' were produced from the assimilation of Protestant goals (the creation of a martyrology, the spread of Scripture) to the themes of secular balladry (disguise and revelation, adulterous love). Some of the early zeal for the reform of society was distilled into the powerful image of the fallen city in 'Christs teares over Jerusalem', but the rhythmic platitudes of 'Solomon's sentences' are more typical of the practical morality which dominated much of seventeenth-century godly print. 'The clarke of Bodnam' and 'St Bernard's vision' show the co-existence of Protestant and traditional approaches to death. 'When Jesus Christ was 12' and 'Doctor Faustus', like the many 'news' ballads steeped in the language of providence and judgement, suggest that there was no clear line between 'religious' belief and a fascination with the magical and miraculous.

Some of the aims of early Protestant propaganda were encapsulated in this balladry, but simplified to black and white by the exigencies of song. The broadside ballad was not an appropriate medium for doctrinal or emotional complexity, if it was to be performed by travelling singers intent on catching the attention of an audience. Man's relationship to God was

[212] A.J. Fletcher and J. Stevenson, 'A polarised society?' in Fletcher and Stevenson, eds., *Order and disorder in early modern England* (Cambridge, 1985), pp. 3, 9.

reduced to 'the dying tears of a penitent sinner'; the problem of salvation to the fear of torments in hell. Stories of martyrdom and biblical lessons were pared down to their 'emotional core'.[213] The ballad heroes and heroines were archetypes: the poor, blind Anne Askew; the wise king Solomon; the constant Susanna; the righteous Joseph; the faithful clerk of Bodnam. Judging by their longevity, these new saints succeeded in populating the imagination of at least some of the readers and singers in seventeenth-century England.

[213] See the arguments of Tristram Potter Coffin on folksong, discussed above, pp. 37–8.

II

THE BROADSIDE PICTURE

4

Idols in the frontispiece

PRACTICAL ICONOPHOBIA

Broadside ballads were probably among the first printed texts to reach the cottages of artificers and husbandmen, some time in the late sixteenth or early seventeenth centuries. However, the cottage walls of a hundred years earlier may already have been decorated with another kind of printed object, which was more pictorial than textual. The devotional images of the church could be taken home in the form of cheap single-sheet woodcuts like Plate 9.[1] These pre-Reformation 'images of pity' contained few or no words, but spoke the complex language of saints' emblems and pictorial conventions (here, the instruments of the passion) which the medieval audience had learnt to 'read'. The twenty-seven examples of 'images of pity' known to survive may represent thousands of paper images of Christ, Our Lady and various saints, which were for sale at cathedrals and shrines.[2]

The 'images of pity' disappeared around 1535, burnt up in the first fires of the Reformation.[3] This pietà was lucky to escape with only defacement of the offending inscription: 'Who ever devoutly beholdeth these arms of Christ's passion hath [. . .] years of pardon.' From the Protestant point of view, these were pictures of the most dangerous sort: icons; objects of devotion, meditation and prayer.

Protestantism and religious images were by no means inherently incompatible. Robert Scribner has shown us how German woodcut artists turned the Catholic iconographical tradition to the service of the Lutheran Reformation.[4] However, if the English reformers followed the German lead in their attempt to create a body of Protestant balladry, they failed to exploit the potential of the woodcut picture. There is no evidence of a large-scale

[1] Bodleian Library, Oxford, MS Rawlinson D.403.f.1.v.
[2] A list of extant 'images of pity' can be found in STC 14077c.6–.23B
[3] The latest copy listed is STC 14077c.11B [1534?].
[4] Robert Scribner, *For the sake of simple folk* (Cambridge, 1981), chs. 2 and 7.

attempt to replace the 'images of pity' with cheap acceptable pictures which might disseminate Protestant ideas to a wide audience.

One factor behind this neglected opportunity was a practical one: English woodcut, as we will see later, was a relatively underdeveloped art.[5] But there were also growing ideological obstacles to the deployment of religious imagery. The position of images in English culture was far from clear-cut: Margaret Aston's comprehensive study of *England's iconoclasts* has revealed a complex interplay of theological, legal and practical forces. A controversy which was, at its most theoretical, a 'hair-line textual quibble' over the numbering of the Ten Commandments, would eventually crack into a 'deep ceremonial rift, separating Protestant from Catholic, reformed churches from Lutherans, Englishmen from Englishmen'. In Catholic teaching, the divine prohibition against graven images was subsumed under the first commandment. But the warning against idolatry became increasingly important for reformers of the 1520s and 30s, until, in the teachings of Bucer and Calvin (and contemporary English reformers), it was elevated to a position of prominence as a separate second commandment. Another textual problem was the interpretation of the Hebrew 'graven image': was it limited to three-dimensional imagery, and to idols of false gods? Or did it include all religious images, perhaps even human art of any kind?[6]

This controversy over what constituted a 'graven image' was reflected in the tangled web of legal policy constructed under Henry VIII, Edward VI and Elizabeth I. Elizabeth's Injunctions of 1559 harked back to a moderate position which had been worked out in the Edwardian Injunctions of 1547; however, the visitation articles framed by her leading clergy took up the more radical iconoclasm of 1548. This line between 'moderate' and 'radical' positions was constantly shifting, but we can identify certain crucial points of reference in demarcating the boundaries. Moderates tended to focus on the social function of an image: was it the object of pilgrimage, of offerings, of adoration? Radicals condemned not only 'abused' images, but images in themselves. Moderates were concerned primarily with images in churches, while thorough iconoclasts looked beyond the church to domestic decoration. The moderate Elizabethan homilist recognized a greater danger in three-dimensional sculpture than in flat painting, but the radical iconoclast was increasingly marked by a rejection of images less obviously

---

[5] It is difficult to find a satisfactory explanation for this. According to David Bland, England 'was one of the very few countries of Western Europe where printing was not pioneered by Germans and possibly as a consequence both typography and illustration were retarded'. (David Bland, *A history of book illustration* (2nd edn, 1969), p. 137.)

[6] Margaret Aston, *England's iconoclasts*, vol. I: *Laws against images* (Oxford, 1988), pp. 391, 379–82, 393.

9 An 'image of pity', with the pietà and instruments of the passion. From an early
sixteenth-century manuscript in the Bodleian Library, Oxford.

prone to idolatry, such as stained glass windows. Given the discrepancies in 'the network of ecclesiastical articles and injunctions, parliamentary statutes and royal proclamations', actual practice varied from church to church across the realm, and iconoclasm itself could become 'nine-tenths of the law'.[7]

How much did the 'reformation of images' change the visual culture of sixteenth-century England? Patrick Collinson has described a major cultural watershed, which he dates fairly precisely to the years around 1580. A decisive change in attitudes to the graphic arts took place at the same time as the reformers' disassociation from balladry and religious theatre. Collinson argues that the 'iconoclasm' of the first generation of Protestant reformers was transformed into the 'iconophobia' of their spiritual descendants. Iconoclasm, according to Collinson, 'may imply the substitution of other, acceptable images, or the refashioning of some images for an altered purpose'. Iconophobia is 'the total repudiation of all images'; hostility to art in general.[8]

This vision of a major cultural cleavage is a compelling one, but, I will argue, misleading in several important ways. Let us deal first with the chronology of iconoclasm, and then with the more crucial issue, the extent of its effect on ordinary English men and women.

According to the traditional view, the reformation of images was an event which occurred in the early sixteenth century, while the reigns of Mary and of Charles I were merely brief reincarnations of sacred imagery which had already suffered its fatal blow with the break from Rome.[9] However, recent work on household inventories supports Collinson's argument for cultural continuity right through the Edwardian years to the early part of Elizabeth's reign. Pictures of the passion, the virgin Mary and saints remained perfectly acceptable in private houses throughout this period.[10] But what of the supposed break with the past around 1580? How can we measure 'iconophobia', not only in the churches, but in private houses, cottages, inns and alehouses? Ideally we should have a comprehensive survey of surviving images in various media over a number of decades, including

[7] *Ibid.*, pp. 220–342, 337, 260.
[8] Patrick Collinson, *From iconoclasm to iconophobia: the cultural impact of the second English Reformation*, Stenton lecture 1985 (Reading, 1986), p. 8; re-stated in Patrick Collinson, *The birthpangs of Protestant England. Religious and cultural change in the sixteenth and seventeenth centuries* (1988), p. 117.
[9] John Phillips, *The reformation of images: destruction of art in England 1535–1660* (Berkeley, 1973), p. 208.
[10] Susan Foister, 'Paintings and other works of art in sixteenth-century English inventories', *The Burlington Magazine,* 123 (1981), pp. 273–82.

book illustration, wall painting and stained glass.[11] 'Cheap print' on its own is problematic as evidence for the chronology of iconoclasm, because of its patchy survival rate. For example, the ballad illustrations of the 1620s unabashedly depict scenes from the Gospels which one might expect to have been labelled popish.[12] But since we have very few godly ballads surviving for several decades beforehand, we cannot be sure if this is a constant tradition from Elizabethan days, or a revival of religious images made possible because of 'Arminian' trends in the church. We have a long list of prints sold by a woodcut publisher of the mid-sixteenth century, but almost nothing remains from the stock of the printsellers who carried on his business in late Elizabethan London.

Given these caveats, the evidence of the present study does suggest a tightening restriction on religious images dating from the middle of Elizabeth's reign, with an anti-Calvinist 'contrary cultural tide' in the 1620s and 30s.[13] However, there is nothing to indicate a sudden break, or a 'total repudiation' of images. Rather, there seems to have been a continuing process of substituting acceptable images for unacceptable, albeit within increasingly constrictive boundaries. Painters and printers continued to cater to the demand for religious figure subjects, but saints were replaced by Old Testament scenes; then by Apocrypha and parables; then by allegorical and classical figures. If we probe long enough in the 1580 cultural fault-line, we may find the crack opening wider to encompass a few more years on either side, then perhaps a decade or two, until several generations of English Protestants disappear down the abyss and the concept becomes meaningless.

More crucial than the dating of this reformation of images, however, are the claims Collinson, Aston and others make for its effect on the English *mentalité*. Iconoclasm was more than just the smashing of external images: taken to its logical conclusions it was a profound mental revolution, a reaction against the role of the visual and sensual in religious perception. The desire to purify the mind itself of its inner idols had an influential expression in Calvin's *Institutes*: 'Man's nature, so to speak, is a perpetual factory of idols ... the mind begets an idol; the hand gives it birth.'[14] This concept of 'idols of the mind' was inherited by William Perkins:

---

[11] Work towards a catalogue of book illustration before 1640 has been in progress for several years: Ruth Samson Luborsky and Elizabeth Morley Ingram, *English books with woodcuts: 1536–1603*. The Courtauld Institute for the Conservation of Wall Paintings has a new post-graduate programme and is collecting files from across the country. A forthcoming PhD thesis by Joseph Michel will survey wall paintings of the period 1550–1640. County studies in progress include Muriel Carrick on Essex and E.L. Rowse on Hertfordshire (for the RCHM).

[12] See below, pp 168–72.

[13] Collinson, *From iconoclasm to iconophobia*, p. 24.

[14] Quoted in Aston, *England's iconoclasts*, p. 437.

I answer, the right way to conceive God, is not to conceive any form, but to conceive in mind his properties and proper effects. So soon as the mind frames unto itself any form of God (as when he is popishly conceived to be like an old man sitting in heaven in a throne with a sceptre in his hand) an idol is set up in the mind.[15]

Similar concern about 'false imagining' can be found in English writings throughout the seventeenth century.[16] It would be foolish to deny the existence of this inward-looking iconoclasm as a strand in English Protestant theology, or to doubt the genuine preoccupation of the more 'hardline' Protestants with purification, even mortification, of the visual imagination.

However, Collinson is making far wider claims for the notion of 'iconophobia', and the mental shift he describes is applied not just to a minority of educated and committed Protestants, but to the nation as a whole:

Culturally speaking ... the Reformation was beyond all question a watershed of truly mountainous proportions. On the far, late medieval side of the range, the landscape consists of images, concrete symbols, mime, the ritualised acting out of religious stories and lessons, a certain artlessness. Religion was 'intensely visual' ... On this side of the divide we confront the invisible, abstract and didactic word: primarily the word of the printed page, on which depended the spoken words of sermon and catechism. In crossing this range we are making a journey from a culture of orality and image to one of print culture: from one mental and imaginative 'set' to another.[17]

This idea of a fundamental change in the *mentalité* of the nation is a more precise formulation of arguments put forward in the work of Frances Yates and Walter Ong, among others.[18] Ong's shift from 'orality to literacy' was an ongoing process over several centuries; here, the change has been compacted into a single generation, and the explanatory weight has shifted from the technological momentum of print to the ideological momentum of Protestantism. The result is an account which, although illuminating in many ways, underestimates the continued importance of the oral and the visual for the vast majority of English men and women in the seventeenth century. Collinson has exaggerated the 'visual anorexia' of English culture in this period, and overstated the extent to which people were cut off from traditional Christian imagery.[19] The present study will suggest some ways in which visual communication continued to play a role in mainstream Protestant culture; and, conversely, how post-Reformation religion continued to have a place in the mainstream visual culture.

---

[15] William Perkins, *Warning against the idolatry of the last times* (1601), quoted in Aston, *England's iconoclasts*, p. 453.

[16] *Ibid.*, pp. 458–60.

[17] Collinson, *Birthpangs of Protestant England*, p. 99.

[18] Walter J. Ong, *Orality and literacy: the technologizing of the word* (1982); Frances A. Yates, *The art of memory* (1966).

[19] Collinson, *Birthpangs of Protestant England*, p. 119.

When evaluating 'the real extent of practical iconophobia',[20] there are a number of biases which can too easily distort our impressions. The first is an anachronistic concept of a 'picture'. The Italianate notion of a framed, four-square, self-sufficient work of art was common currency in educated circles, but not universal. Framed pictures or prints may be absent from inventories, but the thriving arts of sixteenth-century England were the 'decorative arts' (not precluding narrative subjects) which must necessarily be recreated from fragmentary evidence. Craftsmen of all kinds copied elaborate designs from emblem books, or from pattern books like the 'Booke of sundry draughtes for glasiers, plasterers and gardiners' registered in 1627.[21] The ladies who used *A schole-house for the needle* embroidered not only unicorns, peacocks, flowers and abstract designs, but scenes of Adam and Eve, the pelican in her piety, and even the crucifixion.[22] At the humbler level which interests us here, we will see that even alehouse and cottage interiors were often rich with stained cloths and painted designs on the walls.

The second bias is to pay too much attention to the images created during our period, and not enough to what was left over from the medieval church. Late Elizabethan and Jacobean England was very far from being 'totally isolated from the christian iconographical tradition'.[23] In 1587, William Harrison described how the 'stories in glasse windowes' still remained in most parts of the realm, because of the high cost of replacing them.[24] The church walls may have been whitewashed, but according to William Dowsing's catalogue of destruction, many images of Christ, the virgin Mary, saints and even God the Father remained in such materials as stained glass and stone until the 1640s.[25] These images were seen weekly, and (for the most part) accepted, by the practitioners of the prayer-book religion. Dom-

[20] Collinson, *From iconoclasm to iconophobia*, p. 25.
[21] Rosemary Freeman, *English emblem books* (1948), pp. 90–2. Entry for Richard Shorleyker in R. B. McKerrow, *A dictionary of printers and booksellers in England, Scotland and Ireland, and of foreign printers of English books 1557–1640* (1910).
[22] *A schole-house for the needle* (1624 edn), sig.A2–4.
[23] Collinson asks, rhetorically, 'What do we know about the capacity to form mental pictures of someone who has almost never seen an actual picture? What would our minds eye conception of Christ consist of if we had been totally isolated from the christian iconographical tradition?' (*From iconoclasm to iconophobia*, p. 23.).
[24] The 'monuments of idolatrie are remooved ... onelie the stories in glasse windowes excepted, which for want of sufficient store of new stuffe, and by reason of extreame charge that should grow by the alteration of the same into white panes throughout the realme, are not altogither abolished in most places at once, but by little and little suffered to decaie, that white glasse may be provided and set up in their roomes.' (William Harrison, *A description of England, or a briefe rehersall of the nature and qualities of the people of England* (1587 edn), ed. Frederick J. Furnivall (2 vols., 1877), I, pp. 31–2.) The comments were made in the first edition of 1577, and repeated in the 1587 edition, which was much altered in other sections.
[25] *The journal of William Dowsing Parliamentary Visitor* (1844 edn).

estic wall paintings of biblical scenes, even if executed before the 'cultural watershed' of 1580, were visible throughout our period.[26] The visual environment should be seen as a whole, and it was not a blank slate in 1580.

The third danger is that of blurring the distinction between rejection of religious pictures, and hostility to art in general. The early seventeenth century saw the proliferation of print shops in London, and there is no evidence to exclude the 'godly sort' from among the buyers of portraits and allegorical themes, like the four virtues and the ages of man.[27] The rise of the emblem book, of which the first English version was published in 1586, shows the continued importance of the pictorial in the Protestant approach to spiritual and moral truths.[28] Although the emblem book, as such, was 'certainly no part of popular culture',[29] it shows an attempt to incorporate into the typographic world a sense of visual symbolism which was deep-rooted and widespread. Sermon writers used visual metaphors, while poets like George Herbert displayed 'a constant readiness to see a relation between simple, concrete, visible things and moral ideas'.[30] The *memento mori* ballads were based on the assumption that this habit of mind was common; that ordinary people could turn the objects of daily life into visual allegories for death and the world beyond. Dramatists alluded constantly to pictures: 'You never saw Pride pictured but in gay attire'; 'Death is ne'er pictured but with an upper chap only'; 'Your death has eyes in's head then. I have not seen him so pictured'. Thomas Dekker's readers needed no introduction to the figure of Justice in a triumphal arch: 'I hope you will not put me to describe what properties she held in her hand, since every painted cloth can inform you.'[31] Familiarity with the decorative arts, and a highly developed sense of visual allegory, is taken for granted in the audience.

In fact, contemporary aesthetic theory, primarily based on the doctrines of the Italian humanists, assumed an 'indissoluble bond' between word and image. Poetry was a 'speaking picture', as expressed in the Horatian phrase 'ut pictura poesis'. Ernest Gilman has described a continuous interplay in English poetry of this period between 'iconic' and 'iconoclastic' impulses; between a lively inherited visual tradition and a logo-centric Protestantism. Far from simple repression of the image by the word, Gilman sees an ongoing

[26] See pp. 200–11.
[27] On engraved prints, see pp. 141–3, 161–2.
[28] Geoffrey Whitney, *A choice of emblemes* (facs. edn, Amsterdam, 1969).
[29] Patrick Collinson, *The religion of Protestants. The church in English society 1559–1625*, The Ford Lectures 1979 (Oxford, 1982), p. 236.
[30] Freeman, *English emblem books* , pp. 87, 155.
[31] Robert Tailor, *The hogge hath lost his pearle* (1614); Thomas Nashe, *Christs teares over Jerusalem* (1593); William Shakespeare, *Cymbeline* (1609–10), V, iv, 178–9; Thomas Dekker, *The magnificent entertainment* (1604). All cited in Samuel C. Chew, *The pilgrimage of life* (New Haven, 1962), pp. 261–2.

and fruitful confrontation.[32] This tension is expressed most blatantly in the paradox of a Quarles emblem: the aim is to teach the eye to turn from flesh toward Divine Love, yet the emblem itself is an icon, and potentially a distraction from that very purpose.[33] Much of the power in the poetry of Spenser, Donne and Milton comes from their attempt to confront and correct the 'iconic power' of their own language; from the conflict between the impulse to 'plant eyes' in the mind, and the desire to move beyond visualization to hearing as the medium of revelation.[34] Collinson's account of 'iconophobia' would remove, or at least severely weaken, the 'iconic' force in this tug of war, as if the battle were already won by the word, and the image relegated to a position of impotence in English culture.

These metaphors of conflict and of replacement have limited explanatory value; we need to look, not only at the direct and deliberate displacement of images by words, but also at areas where texts slowly integrated into visual culture. As with the ballads, there was interaction between Protestant goals and the forces of tradition and continuity. On the one hand, the broadside picture was subject to the censorship of church and state, and affected by 'iconophobic' opinion in the capital. On the other hand, it was responsive to the demands of broadside buyers throughout the country, at least some of whom were still bowing down to pictures of God the Father as 'a little old Man in a blue and red Coat' in a painted window.[35]

Our approach in this chapter will be to look in turn at the two ends of the spectrum of religious pictures: first, at the development of imagery for iconophobic Protestants, and then at the continuity of traditional visual language. The labels 'Protestant' and 'traditional' are by no means hard and fast distinctions, but intended only to help make sense of attitudes which were usually unarticulated, and often ambiguous. In chapter 5 we will look for evidence of ways in which the gap between these positions could be bridged; in particular, by 'stories' for walls, which satisfied the demands of a wide audience for narrative religious themes, within boundaries acceptable to most thoroughgoing Protestants.

Before launching into a study of content, we will have to deal with the technical problems of assessing the extent of the trade in woodcut pictures. 'Cheap print' will at each stage be set in the context of other related media. Not only is the evidence too scanty on its own (from the historian's point

---

[32] Ernest B. Gilman, *Iconoclasm and poetry in the English Reformation. Down went Dagon* (Chicago 1986), pp. 14, 3, 11.

[33] *Ibid.*, pp. 99–102.

[34] *Ibid.*, pp. 83, 169, 125.

[35] Henry Sherfield case in Sollom Emlyn, ed., *A complete collection of state trials and proceedings for high-treason, and other crimes and misdemeanours* , 3rd edn (1742), pp. 399–400, 404. One Emma Browne was seen bowing down to the window, some time before Sherfield smashed it. When questioned she answered that God was 'in the window, is he not?'.

of view), but the appeal and meaning of these pictures for the audience itself can only be assessed in relationship to the wider visual environment in which they saw it.

THE WOODCUT PICTURE TRADE

The English single-sheet woodcut is an elusive artefact. Even for the eighteenth century, when catalogues show that thousands of cheap pictures were sold wholesale to chapmen, almost nothing of this trade remains.[36] The woodcut survivals from the sixteenth and early seventeenth centuries number a few dozen; a meagre collection compared with the thousands reproduced in numerous German catalogues.[37]

I have searched for all single-sheet prints in the revised STC, which now appears to be extremely reliable in its coverage of library holdings.[38] I have also searched in departments of prints and drawings, for which STC coverage is sporadic, and where cheap woodcut prints are likely to be lost amongst boxes of anonymous 'ephemera'.[39] The result is a provisional checklist of some fifty-five woodcut pictures, as well as ninety text-dominated broadsides, listed in Appendices D, E and F.[40]

A more thriving woodcut trade may have existed than is indicated by these survivals. By the 1660s, the ballad and chapbook publisher Charles Tias stocked 'pictures' by the ream. In the 1664 inventory of Tias' stock, an indecipherable number of reams (plural) were valued at £2.10s.; that is, at least 1,000 pictures worth .6d. each or less.[41] Tias' pre-1640 trade

---

[36] Morris Martin, 'The case of the missing woodcuts', *Print Quarterly* , 4 (1987), pp. 343–61. Cluer Dicey and Richard Marshall, *A catalogue of maps, prints, copy-books, drawing-books, histories, old ballads, patters, collections &c* (1764).

[37] There are over 3,000 woodcuts reproduced in two German catalogues alone: Max Geisberg, ed., *The German single-leaf woodcut: 1500–1550* (4 vols., New York, 1974), and Walter L. Strauss, ed., *The German single-leaf woodcut 1550–1600* (3 vols., New York, 1975).

[38] The compilers have, for example, caught such items as broadsides used as end papers for a manuscript (STC 10626.5 and 17770.7), or used as scrap paper for recording college accounts (2756.5). Items found independently which I have not been able to locate in the revised STC have been in departments of prints, rather than in libraries. All single-sheet prints with letterpress text are meant to be included, but I have found several items missed, primarily from BM Prints, Case 270*. (See Apps. E and F.) The inclusion of engravings from copper plate is by the compilers' admission 'sparse and somewhat arbitrary'. (STC, pp. xxv–vi.)

[39] For sources covered see Tessa Watt, 'Cheap print and religion c. 1550 to 1640,' (Cambridge PhD, 1988), p. 182 n. 38.

[40] In a 'woodcut picture' the image is dominant, and takes up the most space on the page; in a 'broadside' or 'table' the text is dominant, although there is obviously some overlap.

[41] PRO, Prerogative Court of Canterbury, Prob. 4. 8224. Discovered by Margaret Spufford, and discussed in *Small books and pleasant histories. Popular fiction and its readership in seventeenth-century England* (1981), pp. 91–101.

ancestors also sold woodcut pictures, as we will see, but no inventory survives to suggest the volume of their production.[42]

The German broadsheets were preserved within several large collections put together by sixteenth-century observers. French political woodcuts of the late sixteenth century were collected by Pierre de L'Estoile, while devotional prints produced in Paris were bound together in an album (which has survived) used by an agent as a sample book to take around to shopkeepers.[43] The survival of English woodcuts, on the other hand, seems to have been left to chance.

Single sheets of paper were obviously the most flimsy products of the press: the survival rate is so low that for sixteenth-century broadside ballads we have now only some 300 examples remaining out of an estimated 3,000 distinct titles, representing perhaps 3 million separate copies. This translates to a survival rate of 1 in 10,000.[44] For the slightly less flimsy newsbooks of 1620–42, a slightly better survival rate of 0.013% has been calculated.[45] It is certainly possible that the handful of extant woodcuts also represent a much larger trade, which was unfortunately not usually recorded in the Stationers' Register as the ballads were.[46]

Copper engravings have, with a few exceptions, been excluded from our catalogue of 'cheap prints' on the basis of price. Harrington commented in 1591 that engravings on 'brass' (that is, copper) were superior to woodcuts because 'the more cost, the more worship'.[47] Detailed copper engravings would yield only a few hundred copies, as opposed to several thousand for a woodblock, and the time taken for each impression was longer.[48] Woodblocks could be set up in the press together with the printer's type,

---

[42] My search for inventories in the Prerogative Court of Canterbury, Archdeaconry and Commissary Courts was unsuccessful.

[43] Pierre de L'Estoile's collection is entitled 'Les Plus Belles Figures et drôleries de la Ligue', Bibliothèque Nationale, Réserve des Imprimés, La.25.6. The sample book is in the Cabinet des Estampes, Ed.5g.réserve. Both are discussed in Jean Adhémar, 'La Rue Montorgueil et la formation d'un groupe d'imagiers parisiens au XVIe siècle', *Le Vieux Papier*, 21 (1954), pp. 25–34.

[44] See p. 11. If we take the extremely conservative estimate of 200 copies in a print run, this gives us 600,000 copies in total, or a survival rate of 1 in 2,000.

[45] Folke Dahl, *A bibliography of English corantos and periodical newsbooks 1620–1642* (1952), p. 22.

[46] Some of the pictures discussed below were registered, such as John Awdeley's 'Daunce and song of death (STC 6222, ent. 1568–9, App. F). But if we did not have the surviving picture, the title in the Stationers' Company Register would appear to be a ballad entry. (Arber, I, p. 387.) Perhaps there are other such 'ballads' which were, in fact, woodcut pictures.

[47] Cited in Freeman, *English emblem books* , pp. 54–5.

[48] The woodcut blocks used for German broadsides could yield perhaps 3,000 or 4,000 copies before deterioration. (Scribner, *For the sake of simple folk*, p. 5.) In Paris, a plate for confraternity images cut out of pear wood was in use for ninety years (until 1756), and had 5,000 or 6,000 copies pulled from it. (Roger Chartier, *The cultural uses of print in early modern France* , trans. Lydia C. Cochrane (Princeton, 1987), p. 235.)

and run off in one impression, while inscriptions on copper had to be engraved backwards, a special and laborious skill. In the craft of wood cutting there was not necessarily a connection between quality and price, but on copper plate, a fine etching would yield far fewer impressions than a coarse one. It was not until the mid-seventeenth century that profit-conscious engravers would develop a system of engraving to make deep, wide, regular gouges which would yield a larger number of copies.[49]

One of the earliest English printsellers to apply these commercial principles was Peter Stent (*c*. 1642–65), who bought plates from lesser artists, and even employed engravers as journeymen working at relatively low rates by the hour or the piece.[50] But there is little evidence of production on this scale before 1640. The cheapest engraved prints in the early seventeenth century would have cost around 6d. (except for small quarto portraits), which puts them at the top of our range of 'cheap print'.[51] Most copper engravings before 1640 were out of range. The pre-1640 religious prints in the British Museum Satires series are an example.[52] These are by known artists like Cornelis Danckertsz and Martin Droeshout.[53] Their fine detail and smatterings of Latin belie their recent billing as 'popular prints': such pictures would probably have cost 1s. or more, and were not generally for humble or rural buyers.[54]

The print shops which sold these engravings were a new phenomenon in the early seventeenth century. In 1599, George Humble and John Sudbury were the first specialists in the trade, selling mostly portraits.[55] Similar

---

[49] The first competent book on the subject was published in 1645 by Alexander Bosse, who described how 'to make hatchings that swing, big, fat and thin, as needed, as the engraver's tool does, and with which the plates may be printed for a long time'. (W.M. Ivins, jnr, *Prints and visual communication* (1969 edn), pp. 16, 76.)

[50] Alexander Globe, *Peter Stent, London printseller c. 1642–65* (Vancouver, 1985), p. 31. Globe claims that Stent's main clientèle were the 'urban working and middle classes'.

[51] Peter Stent's prices have been estimated at 6d. to 1s. for portraits on royal paper, under 6d. for pot paper, and 1d. to 3d. for quartos. His small, crude portraits of Civil War leaders may have cost less than a penny. (*Ibid.*, p. 28.)

[52] Recently reprinted in John Miller, ed., *Religion in the popular prints 1600–1832* (Cambridge, 1986).

[53] Hind, II, p. 341. Droeshout is famous for his portrait of Shakespeare, although it was not his best effort.

[54] A copy of BM Satires no. 41, designed by Samuel Ward in 1621, cost 1s. in 1740. (BM Satires no. 1233.) This was exorbitant compared with the copper prints sold wholesale by Cluer Dicey and Richard Marshall in 1764. 'Copper Royal Sheet Prints' were almost twice the price of 'Wood Royals', but this still worked out at just under a 1d. each. (Dicey and Marshall, *A catalogue of maps, prints, copy-books*.) John Miller does comment in his introduction to the religious 'satires' that typical prints in the 1750s would have cost 6d. plain and 1s. coloured, which put them 'beyond the means of most wage-earners and craftsmen'. (Miller, ed., *Religion in the popular prints*, p. 14.)

[55] Leona Rostenberg, *English publishers in the graphic arts 1599–1700* (New York, 1963), p. 3.

shops soon proliferated, with the major upsurge in the 1620s and 30s.[56] The new interest in prints was part of the aesthetic movement which had been growing gradually since the beginning of James' reign, encouraged by the writings of Henry Peacham, Richard Haydocke and other popularizers of artistic theory for the gentry and prosperous urban classes.[57]

Did this movement have any effect at the lower levels of the social scale? There is some evidence of a growing trade in cheap woodcut pictures from the second decade of the century, parallel to the rise in copper prints, but aimed at less wealthy urban buyers, and at a wider rural audience. From 1613 onwards, the pages of the Society of Antiquaries collection of broadsides, previously dominated by text, suddenly explode with both engravings and cruder woodcut pictures of poster-size proportions (mostly 19–20 in × 14–15 in). We are, of course, at the mercy of the collectors' habits. A graphic warning is provided by the survival pattern of broadsides depicting deformed babies and monstrous animals. The Huth broadside collection, now split between the British Library and Huntington, preserves fifteen such prints, of which fourteen are suspiciously from the decade 1561–71.[58] These broadsides, which luckily caught a collector's interest for a few years, were probably a staple product of the press throughout our period.

Nevertheless, it is interesting to see the imprint of the leading ballad publishers, including Henry Gosson, John Wright and John Trundle, on the large poster-portraits of royalty which survive from the early seventeenth century. Pictures of the marriage of Frederick and Elizabeth, Charles I as a young prince, his marriage to Henrietta Maria and the royal line from Henry VII (Plate 10) may have been distributed to a rural market along with the ballads.[59] The publishers also offered satirical prints, like 'Fill gut, & pinch belly' (Plate 11, printed by Edward Allde for Henry Gosson in 1620) which brought a popular theme from France to an English audience,

[56] In Cornhill, shops were set up by Thomas Jenner (active 1622–73), John Hinde (*c*. 1630–41) and Thomas Booth (1630s). Engravings could be bought in Lombard Street from Roger Daniel (1621–66) and Thomas Geele (*c*. 1630); in 'Brittaynes Burse' from Thomas Johnson (1625–30); in Blackfriars from Thomas Banks (1637–49). (Globe, *Peter Stent*, pp. 212–16.)

[57] Karl Josef Höltgen, 'The reformation of images and some Jacobean writers on art', in Ulrich Broich, Theo Stemmler and Gerd Stratmann, eds., *Functions of literature: essays presented to Erwin Wolff on his sixtieth birthday* (Tübingen, 1984). Michael Leslie, 'The dialogue between bodies and souls: pictures and poesy in the English renaissance', *Word and Image*, 1 (1985), pp. 16–30. F.J. Levy, 'Henry Peacham and the art of drawing', *Journal of the Warburg and Courtauld Institutes*, 37 (1974), pp. 174–90.

[58] App. F.

[59] STC 17699.5 (Frederick and Elizabeth). STC 5024.3 and STC 13541.7 (Charles I as Prince of Wales). SA no. 232 (marriage of Charles and Henrietta Maria). SA no. 132 (The royal line ... [imprint missing]).

10 'The royall line of kings, queenes, and princes, from the uniting of the two
royall houses, Yorke, and Lancaster' [1613?].

11 'Fill gut, & pinch belly: one being fat with eating good men, the other leane for want of good women' 1620.

via the intermediary of a copper engraving by Renold Elstrack.[60] During this period the ballad partnership was forming, and the cheap end of the printing trade was becoming more specialized. These portraits and satires may represent an attempt to translate the themes of the rising trade in copper engravings into the lowlier medium of woodcut, with an eye to the unexploited commercial possibilities of a wider public.

The ballad publishers dabbled in woodcut pictures as a sideline, but there were others who made them their bread and butter. In 1630, a list of printers to contribute to the repair of St Paul's mentioned 'Widow Sherleaker who lives by printing of pictures.'[61] Her husband, Richard Shorleyker, worked from 1619 to 1630 publishing woodcut pattern books acquired from his master Walter Dight, as well as single-sheet woodcuts. A surviving print of 1623 translates into visual terms the brand of humour found in jest-books and proverbial collections.[62] The viewer is asked to decide 'Which of these fower (four), that here you see / In greatest daunger you thinke to be.' The four scenes depict a client between two lawyers, a goose between two foxes, a maid between two friars and a rat between two cats. The parable in which lawyers are likened to foxes, ready to devour a poor goose, appeared in Samuel Rowlands' *Doctor Merrie-man: or, nothing but mirth.* [63] Friars, too, were a popular butt of satire long after their extinction in England, as we know from the chapbook tradition.[64] In 1624, Abraham Holland suggested that a taste for similar pictures (if more scatalogical) had reached as far as 'North-Villages':

> So if upon the wall
> They see, an Antique in base postures fall:
> As, a Frier blowing wind into the taile
> Of a Babboone, or an Ape drinking Ale,

[60] STC 23757, App. F, 19 in × 14 in. The story derives from a French oral tradition which can be traced to a version of the *Roman de Renart* called *Renard le Contrefait*, written by an ex-cleric of Troyes between 1328 and 1342. (See Jean Adhémar, *Imagerie populaire française* (Milan, 1968), p. 50; Hind, II, pp. 210–13; Justin Fanil, 'L'Origine de la facétie "Bigorne et Chicheface"', *Aesculape* , 35, no. 5 (May 1954), pp. 115–19, especially German engraving p. 117.)

[61] McKerrow, *Dictionary of printers 1557–1640*. Richard Shorleyker died in that year, and his widow continued to print under his name. (STC 21826.4. *A schole-house for the needle* (1632 edn).) In chapter 5, I will also look at a line of woodcut printers working in the Blackfriars from the late 1540s to at least 1616.

[62] STC 11211.5, App. F. On 4 June 1627 Shorleyker acquired copies formerly owned by Dight: W. Gedde's 'Booke of sundry draughtes for glasiers, plasterers and gardiners', Peacham's 'Emblems' and 'A scholehouse for the needle'. (McKerrow, *Dictionary of printers 1557–1640*.) The only other single sheets surviving with the Shorleyker imprint are 'The armes of the tobachonists' (1630) and 'The popes pyramides' (below).

[63] Samuel Rowlands, *Doctor Merrie-man: or, nothing but mirth* , 2nd edn (1616), sig.A4–A4v. First registered in 1607.

[64] Such tales as 'Friar Bacon' and 'The friar and the boy' survived in the 1689 trade list of William Thackeray. (Spufford, *Small books*, pp. 259, 265.)

> They admire that, when to their view perhaps
> If ye should set one of Mercators Mapps
> Or a rare Piece of Albert Durer, they
> Would hardly sticke to throw the toy away,
> And curse the botching painter.[65]

The impression of a Jacobean upsurge in the woodcut trade is supported by the inclusion of pictures in the Wood–Symcocke patent for the printing of broadsides (1619): it is the first time they are mentioned in the licensing instructions concerning ballads and pamphlets.[66] Our impression is also reinforced by the improved state of book illustration, indicating the presence of the necessary craftsmen. Illustration had never been a strong tradition in England: although Caxton and his successors used woodcuts in abundance, they relied heavily on imported blocks from the Low Countries, and on inferior English copies of these blocks.[67] After 1535, illustrations became less and less the norm.[68] Works commissioned from foreign craftsmen by a few scholar-publishers like John Day (including Foxe's 'Book of martyrs') are striking exceptions to prove the rule. Day had to ask the Stationers' Company for leave to employ more than the permitted maximum of four foreigners, probably to make room for his woodcut artists.[69] The added expense involved was reflected in a doubling of the normal prices when a book was illustrated; a practice sanctioned by a Stationers' Company ordinance of 1598.[70]

However, in the first third of the seventeenth century the situation apparently changed, provoking these comments in 1638:

> Books, gaudy, like themselves, most do now buy,
> Fine, trim, adorned Bookes, where they may spy

[65] A[braham] H[olland], 'A continued inquisition', against paper-persecutors, in John Davies. *A scourge for paper-persecutors, or papers complaint, compil'd in ruthfull rimes, against the paper-spoylers of these times* (1624), sig. A2v of the section by Holland. This passage carries on from that quoted on p. 39.

[66] The 1619 patent was to include 'all Portraictures and pictures whatsoever, with or without their severall inscriptions (Except such as shall be bound in Bookes.)'. (W.W. Greg, *A companion to Arber* (Oxford, 1967), p. 166.)

[67] Edward Hodnett, *Francis Barlow, First master of English book illustration* (1978), pp. 35–9.

[68] Henry VIII's ban on old religious books in 1535 had apparently rendered useless much of the printers' stock of devotional wood-blocks. (Edward Hodnett, *English woodcuts 1480–1535*, 2nd edn. (Oxford, 1973), p. vi.) The woodcuts were used again in Mary's reign in the Catholic primers which came off the presses in great numbers. (Luborsky and Ingram, *English books with woodcuts: 1536–1603*, work in progress.)

[69] Alfred Pollard, *Fine Books* (East Ardsley, 1973 edn), p. 263. Others who used Continental craftsmen in the service of Reformation iconography were Robert Crowley, John Bale and Walter Lynne. (John King, *English Reformation literature: the Tudor origins of the Protestant tradition* (Princeton, 1982), pp. 462–4.)

[70] Francis R. Johnson, 'Notes on English retail book-prices, 1550–1640', *The Library*, 5th ser., 5 (1950), pp. 84, 90. The average illustrated book was priced 75–100% higher than other books of the same number of sheets. (See p. 262.)

> More of the Carvers than th'Authors skill,
> And more admire the Pencill, than the Quill:
> Pamphlets, whose Outsides promise, they may finde
> What may their Eyes feed, rather than their minde:
> Nay nowadayes who almost doth behold,
> One booke without a gaudy Liv'ry sold?[71]

Quantifiable evidence of a rise in book illustration is beyond the scope of this study, but the impressions of our satirist have been confirmed in a recent study of pamphlets (which were usually adorned with woodcuts, rather than the engravings increasingly used for more substantial works).[72] Few of the illustrations used on Elizabethan pamphlets were original, but in the early seventeenth century a trend toward a closer relationship between image and text meant that woodcuts were now commissioned for each occasion. The crude title-pages of news pamphlets on snowstorms and strange murders indicate the presence of woodcut craftsmen in England, however amateurish, who could produce pictures to order while the news was still fresh.

This presence is confirmed by the hundreds of woodcuts used on the broadside ballads; some from old blocks, but the majority newly cut. The involvement of the cheap-print publishers in large decorative woodcuts was a natural extension of their activities obtaining illustrations for their ballads. As we noted in chapter 3, it was only during the careers of the 'ballad partners' that illustrations became standard fare. Until now we have concentrated on the ballad as an oral medium, but there is evidence that their visual dimension accounted for a large part of their appeal.

Contemporary accounts suggest that ballads were the most common form of 'cheap print' to be used as decoration in humble households. Nicholas Bownde wrote in 1595 that they were set up in the cottages of illiterate 'Artificers' and 'poore husbandmen'.[73] In 1624 Abraham Holland mocked the habit in northern villages of sticking up ballads of 'Chevy Chase' or the latest execution over the chimney.[74] In houses of more exalted social status the ballads might be found in the nursery, as we hear from Bartholomew Cokes, 'an esquire of Harrow' in Ben Jonson's *Bartholomew Fair* (1614): ' *Cokes:* O, sister, do you remember the ballads over the nursery

---

[71] John Hooper, in Robert Farlie, *Lychnocausia* (1638), cited in Freeman, *English emblem books*, p. 126.
[72] Marie-Hélène Davies, *Reflections of Renaissance England: life, thought and religion mirrored in illustrated pamphlets 1535–1640*, Princeton theological monograph series, vol. 1 (Allison Park, Pennsylvania, 1986).
[73] Nicholas Bownde, *The doctrine of the sabbath* (1595), pp. 241–2.
[74] A[braham] H[olland], in Davies, *A scourge for paper-persecutors, or papers complaint* (1624), sig.A2v of section by H[olland]. See p. 39.

chimney at home o' my own pasting up? there be brave pictures, other manner of pictures than these, friend'.[75]

The increasing importance of the ballad's visual function is indicated not only by the inclusion of woodcuts as a standard feature, but also by a change in how these woodcuts were used. Art historians have distinguished tal), general (or typical) and direct. '"General" means that the image is appropriate to but not specific to the whole text or to its parts; "direct" means that the image depicts a particular textual reference, whether by visual translation or by commentary.'[76] The Elizabethan ballad publishers, when they used pictures, applied them 'decoratively': figure subjects were just part of their stock of ornaments, along with border blocks and initial letters.[77] In the early seventeenth century, woodcuts on broadsides and pamphlets became more closely related to the subject of the text. Most of the ballad illustration was now 'general' (which for the godly ballads meant keeping a stock of religious pictures), although woodcuts were sometimes commissioned for a specific ballad.[78] The ballad publishers did continue to three ways in which an image can illustrate a text: decorative (or ornamenuse generic figures of ladies with fans, gentlemen in cloaks and kings with sceptres (the descendants of the 'factotums' sprinkled over the pages of early sixteenth-century books), but even these were applied with care to fit the ballad.[79] There were also godly 'factotums', such as the men and women kneeling in prayer, which acted as familiar trademarks, by which the buyer could recognize the religious ballad as a genre.[80]

The distribution of cheap woodcut pictures appears to have been closely linked to the development and specialization of the ballad trade in the early seventeenth century. We find the imprint of the leading ballad publishers on the large woodcut sheets, and apparently the ballads themselves were a more common form of decoration than broadsides in which the picture

---

[75] Ben Jonson, *Bartholomew Fair*, III, v. 43–5. On ballads as the standard alehouse decoration, see p. 194.

[76] Ruth Samson Luborsky, 'Connections and disconnections between images and texts: the case of secular Tudor book illustration', *Word and Image*, 3 (1987), p. 74.

[77] For example, 'In praise of my Ladie Marques' (1569), BL Huth.50.(2). 'The plagues of Northumberland', Huth.50.(20). 'A newe ballade of a lover extollinge his Ladye', Huth. 50.(27).

[78] For example, 'The most rare and excellent history of the Dutchess of Suffolk's calamity' (Edward Wright [c. 1635]); 'A pleasant new Ballad of Tobias' (Francis Coules [c. 1640]). On pamphlets: Davies, *Reflections of Renaissance England*, pp. 38, 43, 46–8.

[79] For example, 'The story of David and Berseba' (John Wright, c. 1635); 'The constancy of Susanna' (Henry Gosson, c. 1625). On 'factotum' blocks: Hodnett, *English woodcuts*, p. vii.

[80] 'An excellent song wherein you shall finde / Great consolation for a troubled minde' (assignes of Thomas Symcocke, [1628–9]). 'The sinner's supplication' (Henry Gosson, [c. 1630]). 'An Askew, intituled, I am a woman poore and blind' (Alex Milbourne, [after 1692]).

was dominant. The demand for woodcuts may also have been stimulated by the rise of copper engraving, creating a taste for prints which was imitated down the social scale. However, novelty should not be overemphasized, as we do have a few dozen extant woodcut pictures spread throughout the second half of the sixteenth century. Although we lack the evidence to assess their importance in a trade context, they do give us some indication of the development of iconography in post-Reformation England.

PICTURES FOR PROTESTANTS

In chapter 3 we discussed four aspects of religion to which Protestant propaganda addressed itself in the ballads: anti-popery, social morality, individual salvation and Scripture stories. Which of these were most suitable for pictorial expression? In England there were obstacles to the popularization of the Bible through the direct portrayal of scriptural characters and events.[81] Meanwhile, the doctrine of salvation and the rules of 'Christian' conduct were not easily expressed through simple pictures. Medieval concern for social behaviour developed into a pictorial tradition of the 'moralities', using schemes like the 'seven deadly sins' and 'the living and the dead'; an iconography which continued into the seventeenth century. English reformers' attempts at teaching positive doctrine were expressed primarily through broadside texts, sometimes combined with images: the 'godly tables' to be discussed in chapter 6. Even in Lutheran Germany, it was difficult for Reformation propaganda to find theological images which were different from those of medieval Catholicism. Bob Scribner argues that 'pedagogic propaganda produced so little that was positive, compared to the undeniable success of its anti-papal features'.[82]

However, the German anti-papal satire did show the success of a visual approach to the first goal discussed in chapter 3, that of political reform. We will begin by looking at the evidence for the deployment of cheap printed images in the war against Catholicism in England, following the German model.

This poisonous tree: images politicized

A handful of English anti-papal woodcut prints survive from the sixteenth century. A few may have been made in Germany or the Netherlands; others copied from Continental prints. All borrowed the imagery of the Continental Reformation, and especially the strategy of associating the pope and the Catholic church with corrupt worldly wealth and with evil omens manifested

---

[81] But see the development of acceptable scripture 'stories' in ch. 5.
[82] Scribner, *For the sake of simple folk*, p. 228.

12   'The husbandman. Doctor Martin Luther. The pope. The cardinall'. Woodcut from a ballad [*c.* 1550?].

in nature. The German tradition of Lutheran hagiography is represented in a broadside of Luther, the pope, a cardinal and a husbandman in the Pepys collection, dating from around 1550 (Plate 12).[83] Luther fights the pope with a pen, using God's word to defend the husbandman from his clerical oppressors. The pope is armed with a sword, or worldly power, and supported by the cardinal bearing a pardon, the false offer of salvation. Below the picture, verses in the mouth of each character form a short dramatic interlude, or perhaps a ballad (although no tune is named). In the true spirit of the early Reformation, the plain, humble husbandman is on the side of God's 'swete word', and his liberation is the central focus of the struggle.[84] In a possible appeal to real husbandmen, this broadside addresses all levels of literacy, through both visual and (potentially) oral channels.

Plate 13 was probably printed some thirty years later, and seems to support the view that the common man had by this time lost his status as champion of the Reformation, and was now portrayed as an ignorant opponent of the Gospel.[85] Here he is portrayed as a devil, raking a dung of coins over

[83]   Pepys, I, pp. 16–17, App. B no. 2. Scribner, *For the sake of simple folk*, ch. 2.
[84]   See, for example, discussion of Protestant adaptations of the Piers Plowman theme in King, *English Reformation literature*, pp. 319–39.
[85]   BM Prints, Case 270. Probably printed after 1579 (see below, p. 154). Collinson, *From iconoclasm to iconophobia*, p. 5.

13 'From Simons ambition and Judas covetise/This poysonous tree planted in Rome doth rise . . .'. Woodcut representing the Catholic church.

the roots of the Catholic church, while Ignorance waters the soil. However, the identification of the demon-figure with 'the husbandman' comes purely from the small white-letter caption, since the woodcut artist has given us no visual clues of such an intention. This makes it unlikely that the publisher and craftsmen were working together, and suggests that the woodblock may have been obtained from abroad; the publisher then manipulating the meaning of the image with his choice of English captions.

While the woodcut of Luther fighting the pope is self-sufficient as an image (within certain iconographical conventions), the Catholic tree requires a degree of literacy for its full appreciation. The roots of the tree spring up from 'Simon Magus' and especially 'Judas' whose speech scrolls betray their ambition and covetousness; the base is bolstered up by 'Gratian' and 'Peter Lombard'; the trunk filled with a chronological list of popes; and the leaves with varieties of Catholicism. The genealogical tree was a familiar visual scheme, particularly as used in depictions of the biblical tree of Jesse. The standard pose used for Jesse, reclining with head in hand, and with the tree growing from his body, is echoed in the broadsheet's depictions of Simon Magus and Judas.[86] The 'poysonous tree planted in Rome' may have been juxtaposed in the viewer's mind with this holy genealogical tree. But the evil tree also descended from the tree of the seven deadly sins, which was the most common representation of the sins in wall painting from the late fourteenth century. In this tradition, too, the trunk or 'root' sometimes took the form of a man.[87] In the *Kalender of shepardes*, each branch of the 'tree of vyces' was broken down into smaller branches representing related evils, from which it was a short step to the leaves of the evil sects on the Catholic tree.[88]

The print combines other types of symbolism used in Lutheran propaganda. Simon Magus wallows in crucifixes, bells, pardons, chalices and popish trinkets scattered on him by a figure representing worldly wealth and secular power. The creature sprouting from the head of the tree (in the place held by pride in traditional depictions of the seven sins) is a legendary animal embodying the wickedness of the pope. The tradition of the 'papal ass' drew on the ubiquitous belief in the supernatural significance of misbirths and natural portents. The creature was supposed to have been found in the Tiber at Rome in 1496: part-ass, part-female, part-dragon. It was used for anti-papal polemic in Italy, transmitted to Germany via engravings, and used by Luther and Melanchthon in a pamphlet called *The*

---

[86] See the title-page of *A booke of Christian prayers* (John Day, 1578).

[87] A. Caiger-Smith, *English medieval mural paintings* (Oxford, 1963), pp. 49–53.

[88] *Here begynneth the kalender of shepardes, Newely augmented and corrected* (1556 edn), sig. H1v.

papal ass of Rome and the monk calf of Freyberg (1523).[89] An English version did not appear until 1579, which sets a probable earliest date for our woodcut.[90]

The other image from the pamphlet, the 'monk calf' was an actual misbirth: a calf born near Freiberg with a large flap of skin on the back like a cowl, and a bald spot on the head similar to a tonsure. This was used by Luther to discredit the religious orders, but Plate 14 turns this around, associating it with Luther himself (who was, of course, also a monk).[91] This is a tree of the Protestants' genealogy from the Catholic point of view, with Protestant sects branching off from the original 'arch heretics' Luther and Katherine, Zwingli, Melanchthon and Rotman. Both the anti-Catholic and the anti-Protestant prints aim to discredit the opposition by picturing it splitting up into a mass of sects, and by associating it with creatures evil and grotesque.

'The popes pyramides' [1624] develops both the tree motif and the association with the grotesque in a new direction (Plate 15).[92] The tree or 'pyramid' is formed of serpents: Antichrist in animal form. The smaller snakes wear monks' tonsures and cardinals' hats; the entire hierarchical structure supports the triple crown of the pope, who has set himself up in the Temple of God. The prototype was an engraving printed in the Netherlands in 1599, with French and Dutch verses.[93] The English version borrows from the seven deadly sins tradition again, which often depicted dragons' heads sprouting from the tree-man with pageants of the sins enacted in their mouths.[94]

Another Continental theme depicts the pope on a horse, giving the two-finger blessing (Plate 16): on the left a verse attacks the pope's 'trappings fine'. This fragment is one half of a standard image contrasting the pope in his finery on an expensive horse, with Christ in rags on a donkey.[95]

[89] Christiane Andersson, 'Popular imagery in German Reformation broadsheets', in Gerald P. Tyson and Sylvia Wagonheim, eds., *Print and culture in the Renaissance: essays on the advent of printing in Europe* (1986), pp. 122–7.

[90] *Of two woonderful popish monsters, to wyt, of a popish asse and of a moonkish calfe*, trans. 'out of French' by J. Brooke, 1579.

[91] Ashmolean Museum, Department of Prints, file of 'anonymous English woodcuts'. Although found as a separate sheet, it was apparently not originally a broadside. The text invites the reader to discover further monstrous images of Protestantism 'in this booke'.

[92] STC 20113.5. App. E. The printer, Richard Shorleyker, may have had a line in cheap prints, as we have another woodcut picture from his shop dated 1623 (see above, p. 146).

[93] Wolfgang Harms, ed., *Deutsche illustrierte flugblätter des 16. und 17. jahrhunderts. Wolfenbuttel II.* (Munich, 1980), p. 115. The reference to 2 Thessalonians 2:4 is explicit in the Dutch copy, and alluded to in the English text: 'He can do much, nay more then God can doe ...'.

[94] Caiger-Smith, *English medieval mural painting*, pp. 51–2.

[95] BM Prints, Case 270*. Harms, *Deutsche illustrierte flugblätter*, pp. 40, 41, 42. Dating 1560–5 and later, from a source of 1523.

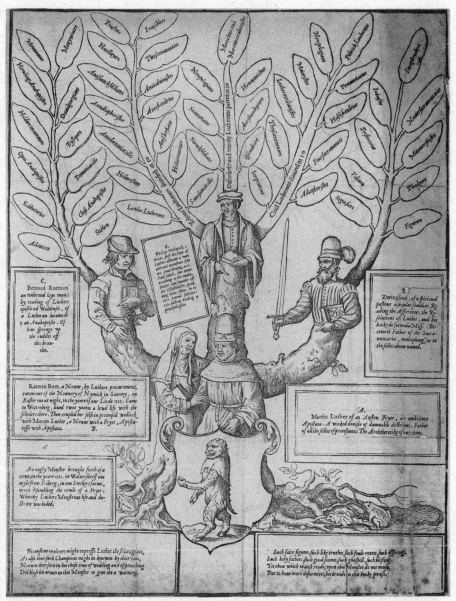

14 'A showe of the Protestants petigrew'. Woodcut depicting the genealogy of Protestantism.

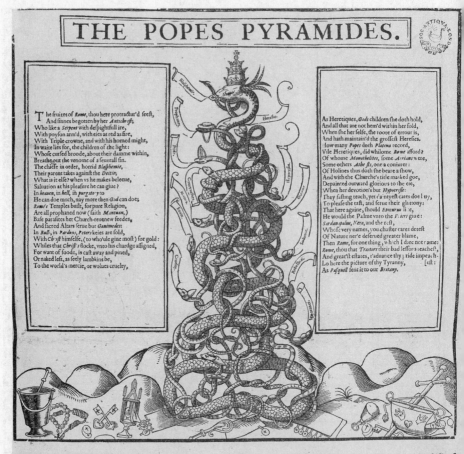

15 'The popes pyramides' [1624?].

16   The pope on a horse. The missing left half of the woodcut probably depicted Christ on a donkey.

The fact that Christ is missing from the English copy may not be purely an accident of survival, given Calvinist qualms about the depiction of sacred subjects.

Satirical pictures of the pope were a feature of book illustration from the mid-sixteenth century.[96] As the papal image continued to appear on broadsheets as late as the 1640s, it presumably had some meaning in 'popular' culture.[97] But it is difficult to assess how other themes used in the Continental Reformation may have survived the channel crossing. In theory the broadside of Luther and the pope should have been the perfect piece of propaganda, with its use of both the self-sufficient image and the dramatic dialogue or song. In practice it seems uncertain that the figure of Luther had the same impact in the England of 1550 as it did in the Germany of 1520, beyond a limited educated audience.

The anti-Catholic ballads were, as we saw, generally set within a national context. Fears of the popish threat from within the country (the northern rebellion) or from the foreign enemy without (the Spanish Armada) apparently had greater emotional impact than distant, dead European theologians. When an indigenous tradition of anti-Catholic prints did develop, the heroes were the English Protestant martyrs and the godly English monarch, the villains were the perpetrators of the 'popish plots'.

This iconography had its most influential expression in the woodcuts of Foxe's 'Book of martyrs'; images of burning and torture which were a powerful, emotional message against popery, intelligible even to those who could not read a word of the text. Although long and expensive, a copy was placed in every cathedral, and the 'Book of martyrs' appeared as a prized possession in rural wills of the seventeenth century.[98] The fold-out 'Table of the 10 Persecutions of the primitive church' was apparently hung up as a print.[99] Five copies of the 1610 and 1632 versions have survived separately in libraries and print rooms; either detached from their books, or more probably sold separately in the first place. In the Cambridge copy of 1570, the gruesome scenes of torture are brightly coloured.[100] While it seems an unpleasant picture for the parlour, the '10 Persecutions' is listed in printsellers' catalogues a century later; probably referring to engraved copies of the original woodcut.[101] (The first engraved version was sold by W. Riddiard around 1625.)[102] This seems to have been one of the few

[96] For example, *The beginning and ending of all Poperie* (*c.* 1548), trans. Walter Lynne (2nd edn, 1588); *A nunnes prophesie, or, The fall of friars* (1615).

[97] For example, Martin Parker, 'A scourge for the pope' [1624]), Pepys, I, 60–1.

[98] Adam Eyre of Yorkshire left one in the 1640s; so did Edward Hammond of Cambridgeshire in the 1660s, both yeomen. (Spufford, *Small books* , p. 46; Margaret Spufford, *Contrasting communities English villagers in the sixteenth and seventeenth centuries* (Cambridge, 1974), pp. 331–2.)

[99] John Foxe, *Actes and monuments* (edns of 1570, 1583, 1610, 1632, etc.), page location varies.

[100] STC. 11227.5 and 11228.3. Foxe, *Actes and monuments* (1570 edn).

[101] Peter Stent, *A catalogue of some plates* (1658). Robert Walton, *A catalogue of divers maps, pictures &c* (1666). I was directed to these by Anthony Griffiths, 'A checklist of catalogues of British print publishers c. 1650–1830', *Print Quarterly*, 1 (1984), pp. 4–22.

[102] STC 11227.5

religious themes acceptable amongst the mid- to late seventeenth-century 'godly sort': a 1666 catalogue described it 'as a convenient Table for Ornament of every good Christian House, to stir them up to stand to the Faith'.[103]

This kind of scene does not seem to have been produced specially in single-sheet form until the early seventeenth century. The British Museum has a dozen anti-Catholic 'satires' surviving from before 1640.[104] They are set firmly in the English political scene, focussing on key events in the nation's Protestant struggle against Rome: the martyrdom of the Marian reformers, the destruction of the Spanish Armada, the gunpowder plot, the collapse of a secret recusant chapel in Blackfriars in 1623. Most of these incidents already played an accepted role in the national ideology, but sometimes the prints were more controversial, urging Protestant alliance as the major factor in international politics.[105]

These prints have been discussed elsewhere.[106] For the period before 1640 they are all copper engravings of reasonably good quality, which were too expensive to be considered truly 'cheap print'.[107] While their iconography is interesting to the historian, they do not represent a wide attempt to mobilize popular support for Protestantism as the German broadsheets did. This may have had much to do with the character of the English Reformation 'from above', which did not rely on support from 'the people' for its political survival. English visual propaganda on a larger scale came with the breakdown of authority during and after the Civil War.[108] But if there is limited evidence for the positive deployment of cheap religio-political images before 1640, anti-Catholicism had a greater influence in another form, as a force restricting the use of sacred images.

This marvellous strange fish: images secularized

The attitude to religious images in print was possibly even more ambiguous, throughout our period, than the regulations on ecclesiastical decoration. Luther once remarked on the inconsistency of iconoclasts who destroyed

---

[103] Walton, *A catalogue of divers maps, pictures &c* (1666). Walton advertised 'very neat ornaments for houses, Gentlemens studies and closets', which suggests a clientèle of gentry, professionals, and substantial tradesmen. (Robert Walton, *A catalogue of some pleasant and usefull maps and pictures* (1659).)

[104] BM Satires, nos. 10, 11, 13, 41, 42, 63, 67, 69, 81, 87, 95, 101.

[105] *Ibid.*, nos. 81, 101.

[106] *Catalogue of prints and drawings in the British Museum, Division 1, Satires, Vol. 1. 1320–1689*, ed. Frederic G. Stephens (1870). Miller, ed., *Religion in the popular prints*.

[107] See above, pp. 141–2.

[108] Using the British Museum catalogue of *Satires*, Dagmar Freist found 430 prints for the period 1640–6 (including both broadsides and pamphlet illustrations), of which some 200 related to religious and political disputes. (Dagmar Freist, 'Popular pamphlets, tracts and broadsides of the 1640s. Modes of thought and expression in propaganda' (Freiburg, unpublished dissertation, 1987), p. i.)

the pictures on walls while treating bible illustrations with reverence. Pictures 'do no more harm on walls than in books', he wrote; but 'I must cease lest I give occasion to image breakers never to read the Bible or to burn it.'[109]

The fact that reading required some education as a prerequisite could be used as an argument for allowing religious illustration in print. When Archbishop Laud was charged with permitting bibles with superstitious pictures to be sold, he claimed that 'they were not to be sold to all comers, because they may be abused, and become evil; and yet might be sold to learned and discreet men, who might turn them to good.'[110] This was a neat reversal of the view held a century earlier that pictures were 'laymen's books' especially for the unlearned and the illiterate.[111]

For some of Laud's 'iconophobic' contemporaries, it made no difference whether the images were meant for scholars or simple folk. The illustrated bibles provoked the indignation of 1,000 Londoners in the 1640 'Root and Branch Petition', which protested against 'Popish pictures both engraved and printed, and the placing of such in Bibles.'[112] Such images were a focal point in the confrontation between the two movements historians have labelled 'Arminianism' and 'Puritanism'. The prosecutors at Laud's trial apparently objected to any image of Christ, and even to the portrayal of the Holy Ghost in the symbolic form of the dove.[113] William Dowsing tore down hundreds of seemingly innocuous ornaments, such as the angels or cherubim together with the word 'Jesus' repeated many times over, which was the standard vault decoration in the parish churches of Suffolk.[114]

The force of this iconophobia seems to have had an effect on the policies

---

[109] Cited in Elizabeth L. Eisenstein, *The printing press as an agent of change* (2 vols. in 1, Cambridge, 1980 edn), p. 68.

[110] *The works of the most reverend father in God William Laud, D.D.*, vol. IV, ed. James Bliss (Oxford, 1854), p. 240. The offending bibles were registered by Laud's printer Richard Badger in 1637 as 'the whole story of the Bible cutt in brasse peeces [i.e. copper plate] with sentences of Scripture and certaine verses graven underneath them'. (Arber, IV, p. 371.)

[111] This metaphor of the picture as a book had a long history in medieval thought, descended from its first formulation by Gregory the Great. (*Sancti Gregorii Magni*, vol. 3, Patrologiae Cursus Completus, ed. Jacques Paul Migne, vol. 77 (Paris, 1849), cols. 1027–8.) Gregory argued that 'a picture is introduced into a church so that those who are ignorant of letters may at least read by looking at the walls what they cannot read in books'. The Ten Articles in 1536 prohibited idolatrous worship of images, but condoned their use in the proper way 'as laymen's books to remind us of heavenly things'. (Phillips, *Reformation of images*, p. 54.)

[112] J. P. Kenyon, ed., *The Stuart constitution 1603–1688* (Cambridge, 1966), doc. no. 49.

[113] *Works of Laud* , IV, pp. 204–5.

[114] *The journal of William Dowsing*, pp. 1, 21, 23–4 (entries for Sudbury, Cochie, Dunwich, Bramfield and Benacre). A surviving example of a similar kind of vault decoration, dated *c.* 1600, is in Muchelney Abbey. (Edward Croft-Murray, *Decorative painting in England 1537–1837* (2 vols., 1962), I, p. 30 and pl. 46.)

of publishers and craftsmen. How did they respond to restrictions in the range of acceptable images? The development of what we might call 'iconography for iconophobes' could take several directions.

One response was the use of biblical figures which were not associated with cults of devotion; generally, a shift from saints, and the central characters of the Gospels, to Old Testament figures. Printers used woodcut border compartments which bore a panoply of generic holy men and women from the Old Testament, helpfully labelled.[115] The same figures which dominated the frontispieces of the Bible and other official religious books were acceptable on church walls: especially the tribes of Israel, and Moses and Aaron flanking the Tables of the Law on the reredos.[116] Old Testament and apocryphal episodes were developed in narrative woodcut prints and wall paintings (a topic reserved for chapter 5). When the human figure of Christ was shown, potentially devotional scenes like the crucifixion or virgin and child were generally avoided, at least until the influence of the anti-Calvinist movement in the 1620s.[117] Printers' devices portrayed Christ in emblematic roles which illustrated the central doctrines of Protestantism: Christ as the Good Shepherd (from John 10:11–14), and Christ triumphing over death, emerging from a grave with one foot on a skeleton.[118]

A second reaction of publishers and craftsmen was to sidestep direct depictions of the sacred by developing allegorical or emblematic themes instead. The most frequent image of the deity from the 1570s to the 1630s was the abstract Hebrew Tetragrammaton; although popular pamphlets on natural disasters or plagues often used the hand emerging from the clouds holding a rod or sword.[119] Certain safe religious emblems were used and re-used on title-pages: the female personifications of 'Faith', 'Hope' and 'Justice';

---

[115] R. B. McKerrow and F.S. Ferguson, *Title-page borders used in England and Scotland 1485–1640* (1932), nos. 151, 176, 178.

[116] Tribes of Israel (late sixteenth-century) in Buton Latimer, Northamptonshire (Croft-Murray, *Decorative painting*, I, pp. 31, 187), and in Eyam, Derbyshire (*Eyam Parish Church: notes for visitors*). On Moses and Aaron see below, p. 246.

[117] Under the influence of 'Arminianism', the boundaries of iconography began to stretch again. See, for example, George Yates, *The miraculous week of our blessed saviours pilgrimage. Containinge his (Birth. Circumcision. Baptisme. Temptation. Passion. Resurrection. Ascention)* [c. 1620]; Samuel Rowlands, *A sacred memorie of the miracles wrought by our lord and saviour Jesus Christ* (1618); John Taylor, *The life and death of the virgin Mary* (1620).

[118] R. B. McKerrow, *Printers' and publishers' devices in England and Scotland 1485–1640* (1913), no. 153; McKerrow and Ferguson, *Title-page borders*, no. 32. The Good Shepherd complemented the self-image of English Protestants as God's flock persecuted by the Romish wolves. It also appeared frequently in German broadsides. (Scribner, *For the sake of simple folk*, p. 50.)

[119] Davies, *Reflections of Renaissance England*, pls. 55, 77.

the pelican in her piety; the Paschal lamb.[120] Engraved prints of quasi-spiritual themes like the four virtues took their place among other numerical series such as the four ages of man, the four continents, the five senses, the twelve months, the prophecies of the twelve sibyls.[121] Woodcut prints in the emblematic tradition were also available, although 'the figure of True Religion' seems unconvincing as a picture for the alehouse or cottage wall.[122]

A final response to the problems surrounding religious imagery was simply avoidance. Apart from the anti-Catholic 'satires', the bulk of the copper engravings were secular, with a predominance of maps and portraits of the royalty and nobility.[123] The earliest printseller's stock of which we have a full reconstruction, that of Peter Stent (*c*. 1642–65), contained just 34 religious prints out of a total of 623 items.[124] The large woodcut pictures distributed by the leading Jacobean ballad publishers were also dominated by portraits and satires (as we saw above), with not a biblical picture among them.

Some of the most common woodcut images did treat subjects which were largely 'religious' in implication, but the Christian context was no longer present in the picture itself. Death is the primary example of what we might describe as a sacred theme which was visually 'secularized'. The fear of death was central to the piety of the broadside ballads, and it was expressed equally well as a pictorial theme in the woodcuts. But the vision of death was shorn of the spiritual dimension which had been present in medieval wall paintings and in the woodcuts of the *Ars moriendi*: the angels and demons at the bedside, the weighing of souls, the intercession of the virgin, the divine judge.[125] Instead, craftsmen relied almost entirely on the more earth-bound image of Death personified as a skeleton, lurking with his poi-

---

[120] For the female personifications see McKerrow and Ferguson, *Title-page borders*, nos. 127, 129, 150, 165, 174. For pelican see McKerrow, *Printers' devices*, nos. 125, 137, 181. For lamb see *ibid.*, no. 194; McKerrow and Ferguson, *Title-page borders*, no. 148.

[121] STC 197.7, 25907.5, 1497.5, 12561.4, 22527a.5. Other themes include the four complexions and elements; the seven passions and seven liberal arts and sciences; the nine women worthies. See entries for engravers George Glover and William Marshall in Arthur M. Hind, *List of the works of native and foreign line-engravers in England. From Henry VIII to the commonwealth* (1905).

[122] See p. 183.

[123] This conclusion is based on a study of single-sheet prints in the STC, and in Hind, *List of the works of native and foreign line-engravers*; Arthur M. Hind, *Engraving in England in the sixteenth and seventeenth centuries* (3 vols., vol. III compiled by M. Corbett and M. Norton, Cambridge, 1952–64).

[124] Globe, *Peter Stent* , nos. 387–420. There were seven Old Testament scenes (such as 'Abraham offering Isaac'), only four New Testament scenes ('Peter receives a key from Christ'), the ubiquitous 'Ten Persecutions', and several versions of the 'memento mori'. Untraced titles like the 'Ten Commandments' and the 'Lord's Prayer, &c' would have referred to the kind of text-dominated prints discussed in chapter 6.

[125] On woodcut depictions of death in the *Ars moriendi*, see Chartier, *The cultural uses of print*, pp. 32–70.

soned arrow around every corner. This omnipresent figure was not a Protestant invention, but seems to have increased in prominence as 'saints and dooms' became taboo.

Plate 17 was printed in 1568–9 by the ballad publisher John Awdeley, and is the visual equivalent of ballads like 'Death's dance' and the 'Shakeing of the sheets'.[126] In English wall painting, the dance of death theme first became common in the early sixteenth century, as a development from earlier iconography like the 'three living and three dead'.[127] The use of the skeletal figure of death is here combined with the image of the choral round or 'branle'. Versions of this basic folk dance were performed in every stratum of society. When danced at the Elizabethan court, its levelling effect contrasted with hierarchical dances like the pavan, done in a strict procession of couples. The ring dance provided an appropriate allegory for the egalitarianism of death.

The same basic theme that 'Death sparest not the chiefest high degree' was developed in the tradition of the 'Four Alls' (or Five, or more), known in France as 'Les Quatre Vérités'.[128] An English example of *c.* 1580 depicts a bishop, king, harlot, lawyer and 'country clowne', each with verses proclaiming their importance and power over the others.[129] Of course, Death arrives with his spear to win the contest. The Continental form usually depicts bishop, king, soldier and farmer, but in litigious England no opportunity is lost for satirizing the lawyer, while the harlot adds a touch of bawdry. The woodcut is sloppily coloured in bright hues of blue, purple, orange and brown, and with its large format (20 in × 14 in) it makes a striking wall ornament. The print (or a copy of it) was still available in 1656, when among his 'portratures cutt in wood' Thomas Warren registered 'A Divine, a Soldier, a Lady, a Lawyer, a Labourer and Death. 1 large sh.'.[130]

The removal of any specifically Christian iconography from the visual image of death does not seem to have weakened its power. In a Samuel Rowlands pamphlet of *c.* 1606, Time says to Death:

> Thy picture stands upon the Ale-house wall,
> Not in the credit of an ancient story,
> But when the old wives guests begin to braule,

---

[126] STC 6222; RB repr. I, 283; III, p. 184. This print was copied for a copper engraving a century later. (Printed by R. Walton (worked 1647–60). Bodleian, Francis Douce Prints, N.6. (59).)

[127] Caiger-Smith, *English medieval mural paintings*, pp. 45–9. Fifteenth-century versions of this theme showed three skeletons with staves suddenly appearing before three kings on horseback, making their horses rear.

[128] M. Dorothy George, *English political caricature to 1792. A study of opinion and propaganda* (Oxford, 1959), p. 9.

[129] STC 6223.

[130] Eyre, I, p. 48.

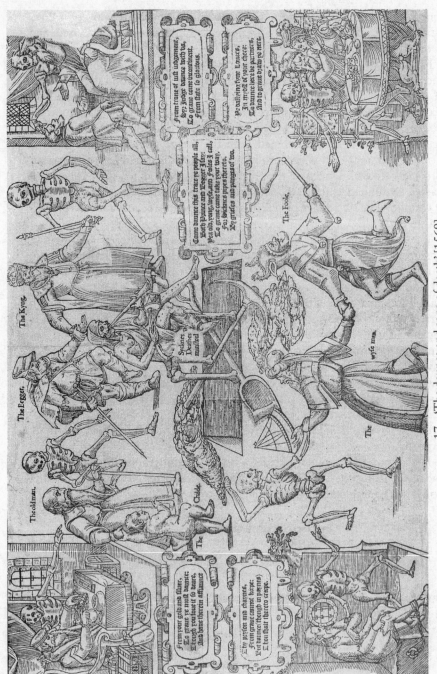

17 'The daunce and song of death' [1569].

> She points, and bids them read *Memento mori*:
> Looke, looke (saies she) what fellow standeth there,
> As women do, when crying Babes they feare.[131]

The characters of both Time and Death, familiar from broadside woodcuts, made the leap from paper to walls (and vice versa); pictured not only in the alehouse, but painted on the walls of the parish church.[132]

Possibly the most common form of woodcut picture was the half-text half-picture genre providing a 'true description' of marvellous creatures and deformed children. These were comparable to the French *canards* which proliferated in the sixteenth and early seventeenth centuries.[133] In England some fifteen examples survive in broadside form, virtually all from the 1560s.[134] The broadside of 'this marveilous straunge fishe' (Plate 18) is of better quality than most, but even the crudest woodcuts show care to match the physical details given in the description. These attempts at 'illustration' are interesting in a period when the correlation between text and image in books and ballads was often tenuous.[135] The texts, in prose or verse, were often by the same 'hacks' who produced broadside ballads, and usually emphasized the significance of these natural portents as signs of God's wrath.[136] These images may have satisfied some of the demand for the supernatural and the miraculous in the absence of religious prints.[137]

The 'secularization' of imagery cannot be explained in terms of 'secularization' of society as a whole, or mere lack of interest in religious art.[138] A catalogue of the cheap prints sold to chapmen in 1764 shows that eighteenth-century buyers were still very much interested in religious pictures,

---

[131] Samuel Rowlands, *A terrible batell betweene the two consumers of the whole world: time and death* [1606?], sig.E4v.

[132] Time and Death appear in churches at Yaxley in Huntingdonshire and at Westborough, Lincolnshire. (E. Clive Rouse, 'Post-Reformation mural paintings in parish churches', *The Lincolnshire Historian*, 1 (1947), p. 11.)

[133] In France the *canards* were produced most frequently as short octavo pamphlets, but also as broadsides. (Jean-Pierre Séguin, 'L'Information en France avant le périodique. 500 canards imprimés entre 1529 et 1631', *Arts et Traditions Populaires*, 11 (1963), pp. 20–32.)

[134] See App. F. Their survival appears to be thanks to the interest of one collector.

[135] STC 20570. Luborsky, 'Connections and disconnections between images and texts'. Davies, *Reflections of Renaissance England*, pp. 38, 43.

[136] For broadsides of this type by ballad writers John Barker and William Elderton see STC 1422 and 7565.

[137] Of course, it would be crude to think of monstrous creatures directly 'replacing' saints and pietàs; indeed, in France the *canards* existed side by side with devotional images.

[138] 'As a Protestant nation, the English have had a predilection for representations of themselves and their surroundings and an almost total lack of interest in religious art and very little more in mythological subjects.' ('English portraiture in the 17th century', *Encyclopaedia Britannica*, 15th edn (1985), vol XIX, p. 429.)

18 'The true discripcion of this marveilous straunge fishe' [1569].

now that the danger of popery had subsided.[139] Altogether, 200 different

[139] About one fifth of the prints advertised by Dicey and Marshall (excluding maps and perspective views) were religious. In the cheapest category of 'wooden prints' (just over 1/2d. each wholesale) the godlies made up one quarter. (Dicey and Marshall, *A catalogue of maps, prints, copy-books*, pp. 15–18, 62–6.)

religious prints were offered, covering every possible aspect of Christian devotion: 'Adam and Eve drove out of Paradise', 'Lord's Supper, neatly done', 'Christ crown'd with Thorns', 'Christ Crucify'd', 'Christ's Ascension', 'St. Laurence broiling on a Gridiron', 'Spiritual Combat, or War with the Devil'. These were pictures Thomas Bewick might have known as a boy, when he 'saw in every farm house, cottage and hovel, the walls hung around with large Wood cut prints'.[140] Most of these 'Scripture and other godly stories' would have been dangerous possessions in any farmhouse or cottage 150 years earlier: a picture of 'Christ crown'd with Thorns' would be grounds for reporting one's neighbour as a recusant.[141]

But what did post-Reformation farmhouses have to replace the former pictures of saints? The 'ballad partners' may have avoided religious themes in their large poster-size prints, but the woodcuts they used on their ballads tell quite a different story, testifying to a continued demand for religious images. Here, we find scenes of the holy family, the resurrection, and Christ in glory which one might expect to be considered idolatrous.

It may be that the physical size of the pictures was a crucial factor. A Christ of the dimensions of 'Fill gut, & pinch belly' (19 in × 14 in) would suggest the act of adoration, but these small woodcuts of several inches square would be more difficult to worship. The ratio of text to picture may have established the status of the woodcuts as illustrations, rather than meditational objects in themselves. Not all critics were fooled, however, and a Quaker tract of 1655 singled out ballad makers for special attack on account of the woodcuts: 'the Lord God of glory is arising, who saith, Thou shalt not make any Image of Male or Female, which you do amongst you, and are found upon your ballets, and so out of Gods councell, are amongst the heathen making Images'.[142] In William Cartwright's *The ordinary* (*c.* 1635), the puritan curate Sir Kit insults his companion, Rimewell the poet:

> Thou art a Lopaz; when
> One of thy legs rots off (which will be shortly)
> Thou'lt beare about a Quire of wicked Paper,

[140] Memoirs of Thomas Bewick (b. 1753), cited in Martin, 'The case of the missing woodcuts', p. 343.

[141] The 1584 inventory of Mrs Hampden of Stoke in Buckinghamshire included 'a picture of Christe' and 'a picture of (as it is termed) the Judgement daye', which were assumed to be incriminating. (Collinson, *From iconoclasm to iconophobia*, p. 37 n. 109, where two similar examples are noted.)

[142] This tract represents an extreme position against *any* images, not just religious images. However, it does illustrate the point that ballad woodcuts could give offence despite their relatively innocuous proportions, and that they were an ubiquitous form of image, worthy of attack. (*A declaration from the Children of Light*, cited in Hyder E. Rollins, ed., *Cavalier and puritan. Ballads and broadsides illustrating the period of the great rebellion, 1640–1660* (New York, 1923), p. 68.)

19 Woodcut of 1506, re-used on ballad of mid-seventeenth century. The cartouche
originally held the Lord's Prayer.

> Defil'd with sanctified Rithmes,
> And Idols in the frontisepiece: that I
> May speak to thy capacity, thou'lt be
> A Balladmonger.[143]

As the reference to 'Idols in the frontisepiece' suggests, even the crude little
woodcuts, which ran like a frieze along the top of the ballad sheets, were
the subject of criticism and controversy.

A QUIRE OF WICKED PAPER

The continued use of traditional iconography on the ballads may have been
partly a result of the economic advantages of using old sixteenth-century
woodblocks, at least in the beginning. The discarded blocks acquired by
the publishers were sometimes survivals from the pre-Reformation printing
houses, like the cut of Christ and his disciples used by Richard Harper
in the 1640s (Plate 19).[144] The scroll above their heads stands empty, but
it once held the Lord's Prayer, when it was used on Wynkyn de Worde's
Arte to lyve well of 1506.[145] Other woodcuts had belonged to Elizabethan

---

[143] William Cartwright, *The ordinary, a comedy* (written *c.* 1635), III, v, in *The plays and
poems of William Cartwright* , ed. G. Blakemore Evans (Madison, 1951), p. 317. Evans
has followed an earlier editor, W.D. Hazlitt, in changing 'sanctified' to '[un]sanctified'
in this passage. However, as he comments in a note, 'it is possible that to the zealous
Puritan, Sir Kit, the word "sanctified" had a Popish and unhallowed flavor'. (*Ibid.*, p.
643.)

[144] 'Friendly counsaile, or, Here's an answer to all demanders ...', RB orig. I, 16. Harper
was active 1633–52.

[145] Hodnett, *English woodcuts 1480–1535*, no. 477, figure 46. Late fifteenth- to early sixteenth-century costumes suggest similar origins for many other cuts used by Harper: RB
orig. I, 76, 77, 97, 124, 125, 166, 167, 265, 396. Other examples of early Tudor blocks
can be seen in Euing, pp. xiii, nos. 102, 235, 256, 257.

20 Generic Old Testament battle scenes.

ballad publishers: a dance of death series which appeared on Richard Hardy's ballads around 1681 was used by Alexander Lacy over a century earlier.[146] Still others may have been purchased from abroad, worn and mutilated from their original use on prayer books and bibles.[147] There are Old Testament scenes, often of battles, with no direct link to the text. Several 1620s ballads used a block which depicted, in one frame: the Gibeonites' slaughter of the sons of Saul, the four lepers bringing their report of the vacant camp after the siege and famine at Samaria, and several other episodes. The precise significance of the illustration was presumably lost on ordinary ballad buyers, but they may have liked the vaguely biblical atmosphere which it conveyed. (Plate 20).[148]

When the old blocks wore out and the publishers had scenes newly cut, they continued to cater to the demand for story-telling images, rather than emblems or abstractions. There were a number of new woodcuts depicting simple and familiar scenes from the Gospel. 'The sinner's redemption' carries a woodcut of Christ between two labourers with hoes; 'The glorious resurrection' shows him rising from the grave with the centurions leaping back in alarm (Plate 21).[149] Another ballad, in which Christ describes his life

[146] RB repr. IV, p. 75. BL Huth.50. (21)
[147] J.W. Ebsworth states in his notes to the Roxburghe Ballads, without giving evidence, that Richard Harper (working 1633–52) and other printers purchased worn blocks from abroad.
[148] From 'A prophesie of the judgment day' (for John Wright, [1620?]), Pepys, I, 36. Also used on 'The earnest petition of the faithfull Christian, being clerk of Bodnam' (for Henry Gosson, [1624?]). Pepys, I, 49; 'Glad tydings from heaven' (for Cuthbert Wright, [*c*. 1630]), RB repr. I, p. 404. J.W. Ebsworth deciphers the scene in RB repr. VII, p. 774.
[149] 'The sinner's redemption' [for John Wright?, 1634?], RB repr. II, p. 486; Pepys, II, 20 (post-Restoration). An earlier copy is 'A most godly and comfortable ballad of the glorious resurrection' (for Francis Coules, [1640?]), RB repr. I, p. 388. The cut of the resurrection was also used on 'Two pleasant ditties, one of the birth, the other of the passion of Christ' (assignes of T. Symcocke, [1628–9]), RB repr. II, p. 549.

21 'The glorious resurrection'.

22 The holy family's flight into Egypt.

and mission, depicts the holy family on their flight into Egypt (Plate 22);
while the earliest surviving copies of ballads on the birth of Christ (post-

23   Hell, from 'St Bernard's vision', pt 2.

Restoration) use woodcuts of the virgin and child which appear to be old stock.[150] 'The deadmans song' and 'St Bernard's vision' carry remnants of the medieval 'doom' paintings in their woodcuts of hell, where black demons prod the burning sinners with pitchforks (Plate 23).[151]

The most frequently used godly woodcut descended from a standard pre-Reformation image. On 'The sinner's supplication' Christ blesses the ballad buyer from the starry vault, with palms raised in benediction and rays emanating from the clouds.[152] It is a cheery, comforting image compared with the harsh vision of the deity used on contemporary plague sheets and news pamphlets: the hand of God descending from the clouds holding a rod or

---

[150] 'Glad tydings from heaven' (for Cuthbert Wright, [*c*. 1630]), RB orig. I, 134. Pepys, II, 27, 30.

[151] 'The deadmans song, whose dwelling was neere unto Basing Hall in London' (for Francis Coules, [*c*. 1640]), RB repr. I, p. 223. This later copy from Pepys, II, p. 8. 'St Bernard's vision' (for John Wright, [*c*. 1640]), RB repr. II, p. 491.

[152] 'The sinner's supplication' (for Henry Gosson, [*c*. 1630]), RB repr. II, p. 498. For similar images see Hodnett, *English woodcuts*, figures 66, 117.

24   Christ in glory, from 'The sorrowful lamentation of a penitent sinner'.

sword.[153] This Christ in glory was a copy of an earlier woodcut used on the pamphlet *Fire from heaven* printed by John Trundle in 1613, when it already contained several wormholes.[154] The 'partners' may have inherited this block when they acquired Trundle's stock in 1629, and the original appears on one of John Wright junior's ballads in 1636.[155] The 'partners' imitation, with the two little cherubs added, appears on over a dozen ballads from the 1650s to 80s, from the 'Clarke of Bodnam' to 'A letter for a Christian family' (Plate 24).[156] Like the more puritanical images of godly figures kneeling in prayer, it became a trademark recognizable to the godly ballad buyer.

The cottager who pasted 'The sinners supplication' on his wall apparently liked to have a figure of Christ to look at, even if only an awkward little woodcut Christ like this. The image might seem anachronistic in the context of art produced under the influence of Protestant aesthetics in the same period, but there is a strong likelihood that the ballad buyer was still familiar with just this sort of image in his local parish church. The diminutive scale of the woodcuts almost seems to mimic the experience of peering up at stained glass windows to make out the pictures of Christ and the saints, now banished from the walls down below.

As Laud argued at his trial, 'contemporary practice (which is one of the

[153] Davies, *Reflections of Renaissance England* , pls. 55, 77.
[154] *Ibid.*, pl. 78.
[155] 'Bee patient in trouble' (for John Wright (2), 1636), RB repr. III, p. 174.
[156] This copy from Pepys, II, 13. Others are in Pepys, II, 28, 29, 47, 63; Bodleian Library, Wood Ballads, Wood. 401.(66),(160); RB orig. II, 141, 248, 422; III, 371, 344.

best expounders of the meaning of any law) did neither destroy all coloured windows, though images were in them in the Queen's time, nor abstain from setting up of new, both in her and King James his time'.[157] Of course the period of Laud's influence did see a resurgence of sacred images like this. The 'Arminian' emphasis on church ritual and 'the beauty of holiness' led to a revival of stained glass in the 1620s. The crucifixion in Lord Maynard's private chapel at Little Easton (1621) was 'among the first of its kind in an English Protestant context'.[158] A painted glass scene of the deposition at Hampton Court, Herefordshire, spoke its own defence in an inscription below: 'The truth hereof is historicall devine and not superstissious.'[159] The new ecclesiastical art extended to parish churches, sometimes in the form of wall painting. Figures of St Matthew and St Luke were painted life-size in the chancel of Passenham Church, Northampton (1626–8), the adoration of the magi and the deposition in Newnham Regis Church, Warwickshire (*c.* 1630) and scenes from the creation to Pentecost in Exeter Cathedral.[160]

It is worth noting the quantity and variety of images which William Dowsing recorded in his destructive tour of Suffolk and Cambridgeshire in 1643–4. The following entry is not unusual: 'Sudbury, Suffolk. Peter's Parish. Jan. the 9th 1643 [1644] We brake down a Picture of God the Father, 2 Crucifix's, and Pictures of Christ, about an hundred in all; and gave order to take down a Cross off the Steeple; and diverse Angels, 20 at least, on the Roof of the Church.'[161] The large number of images ('an hundred in all') and the term 'brake down' suggest that most of these pictures were in glass windows. There were still pictures of the virgin Mary and of various saints, like Catherine with her wheel, or Laurence and his gridiron; and even 'one Pope with divers Cardinals'.[162] When paintings were specified, they were of subjects which might have been executed since the 1620s: Abraham offering up Isaac, the four Evangelists 'on the walls', the twelve Apostles 'painted in wood'.[163] Themes like 'the Pictures of the 7 deadly Sins' and 'seven Fryars

---

[157] *Works of Archbishop Laud*, IV, pp. 199–200. Not only stained glass was tolerated throughout these reigns: the paintings in the gallery at Lambeth, which had been there for at least the last forty years, included 'the *Ecce Homo*, as Pilate brought Christ forth, and showed Him to the Jews', described by Laud as a 'common' picture. (*Ibid.*, IV, pp. 204–5.)

[158] Nicholas Tyacke, *Anti-Calvinists: the rise of English Arminianism c. 1590–1640* (Oxford, 1987), p. 193, plate 3.

[159] *Ibid.*, p. 219, plate 4.

[160] Croft-Murray, *Decorative painting*, I, pp. 48, 211–12.

[161] *The journal of William Dowsing*, p. 1.

[162] *Ibid* ., pp. 11, 20, 17, 31, 21.

[163] Apostles in Brightwell, Suffolk. (*Ibid.*, p. 25.) Evangelists, Abraham and angels in Upper Papworth, Cambridgeshire. (*The Cambridge journal of William Dowsing 1643*, ed. A.C. Moule, repr. from the History Teachers' Miscellany (1926), p. 9.)

hugging a Nunn' indicate that the early seventeenth-century church still had much to stimulate the visual imagination of the parishioners.[164]

With the remnants of the medieval iconographical tradition still visible in the churches, it is not surprising that there was a market for a woodcut print of a traditional nativity scene like Plate 25.[165] The continuing popular attachment to images of the nativity is illustrated in an account of an image-breaking episode in Canterbury Cathedral. In December 1643, the iconoclast Richard Culmer

took a whole pike in his hand, and went up a ladder fifty-six steps high, and did full execution upon the idolatrous monuments there: whereupon some stirs began; a prebend[ary]'s wife cried out, 'Save the child', meaning, save the Christ lying in the manger pictured there. And Mr. Culmer's blood was then threatened by some that stood without the iron gates, in the body of the church.[166]

The woodcut 'Christus natus est' was published in 1631 and was apparently successful, since it was necessary to register it with the Stationers' Company six years later.[167] In fact, the title appears in an entry of broadsides some eighty years on, in 1712.[168] The same sort of piety was reflected in the ballad woodcuts, but this seems to be unique as a poster-sized print. Unless there were similar pictures which went unrecorded, one can only assume that large images depicting Christ and the virgin Mary were still uncommon as humble domestic decoration, even in the Laudian years.

The broadside combines various traditions of English popular print. Around the border of the nativity scene are the arms of the passion, which were a common feature of the pre-Reformation 'images of pity' (Plate 9). These were still familiar images in the 1640s, when William Dowsing found them carved in stone on the porch, in at least five parish churches in Suffolk: 'on the Porch, the Crown of Thorns, the Spunge and Nails, and the Trinity in Stone'; 'the Whip, and Pincers, and Nails, that was at Christ's Crucifying, and the Trinity, all in Stone'.[169] The instruments remained in post-Reformation iconography as an acceptable substitution for direct depictions of the

---

[164] *The journal of William Dowsing* , pp. 6, 2.
[165] STC 5209.5.
[166] Richard Culmer (jnr), *A parish looking-glasse for persecutors of ministers* (1657), pp. 5–6, quoted in Aston, *England's iconoclasts*, pp. 85–6.
[167] 'A Table called Christus Natus est with a picture in the middle of it.' Entered to John Stafford in 1637 (Arber, IV, p. 399).
[168] Norris and Brown 1712. Arthur Ponsonby describes a sheet of carols of 1701 which apparently used the nativity woodcut and the same 'explanation' down the side. This carol sheet was reproduced again in the early twentieth century by F. Sidgwick. (Arthur Ponsonby, *The priory and manor of Lynchmere and Shulbrede* (Taunton, 1920), pp. 13–15.)
[169] *The journal of William Dowsing* , pp. 7–8, 18, 23, 32.

CHRISTVS NATVS EST;

CHRIST is Borne.

Angels clap Hands; Let men forbeare to Mourne:
Their sauing-Health is come; For CHRIST is Borne.

London, Printed for IOHN STAFFORD, 1631.

O See! Mans Sauiour is in *Bethlem* borne,
His lodging base, he himselfe held in scorne,
The Cribbe at which the Oxe and Asse were fedde,
Mary (Chrifts Mother) makes her young Sonnes bed;
Yet see how Shepherds fall downe flat before him,
And how the Wife-men doe with guifts adore him,
Harke, what a heauenly Qurre of Angells sing
Sweet Carrols, at the birth of this new King;
O happy man! when thus, (thy Soule to saue)
Chrift comes from Heauen, and makes himselfe a Slaue.

See else that Pillar, where being naked bound,
Thy *Chrift* had his flesh tore with many a wound;
When a Cocke crowes, let it this griefe afford,
To thinke how *Peter* (thrice) denyed his Lord;
See *Iudas* Lanthorne, and see *Iudas* Pence,
See the Dice throwne, to vncloath Innocence;
See Pincers, Nailes, and Hammers, how they meete,
To naile to th' Croffe, Chrifts blessed Hands and Feet:
O Wretched Man! where Chrift for thee thus dyed,
Let him not ftill by thee be Crucified.

An Epitaph vpon Chrift, who was Buried in a new
Tombe, cut out of a Rocke, in which no
Man but he was euer inclosed.

Within this Rocke the Rocke himselfe is layd,
Who both the Tombe, and the Tomb-maker made,
A Man he was, no such man beside,
None liu'd so iuft, none fo vniuftly dyed:
He was in debt for nothing, yet did pay
The debts of all the World: at a fet day.
Neuer of Woman could fo much be faid,
When he was borne his Mother was a Mayd.
He many wonders wrought, and this a chiefe,
A very bad Man, made be a Good Theefe.
is happened well, he fo by Iewes was Croff'd,
For all the Soules i'th World had els bin loft.
Thirty three yeares he liu'd: Had not he bene,
No Chriftian vpon Earth had ere bin feene:
He dyed a King, yet was a Begger borne,
And wore (which no King doe) a Crowne of Thorne,
Firft went he to his Graue, from whence, to Hell,
Then vp to Heauen: And there this King doth dwell

FINIS.

The History of Chrift
his Life and Death.

The Explanation of this Picture.

A Religious Man inuenting the Conceits both from the Birdes and Beasts drawne in this picture of our Sauiours Birth, doth thus expresse them.

viz.

The Cocke croweth,
Chriftus Natus eft.
Chrift is borne.

The Rauen asked,
Quando?
When?

The Crow replyed,
Hac Nocte,
This night.

The Oxe cryed out,
Vbi? Vbi?
Where? where?

The Sheepe bleated out,
Bethlem.

A voyce from Heauen founded,
Gloria in Excelfis,
Glory be on high.

Whilft Armies of Angels fung,
Hallelujah,
Saluation, and Glory, and Honor, and power be to the great our God. Apoc. 19.1.

25   'Christus natus est' 1631.

passion, and were also used on title-pages, engravings and in a pamphlet by Samuel Rowlands.[170]

On the right of the woodcut is the 'explanation' of the so-called conceits: the Latin comic-strip speech bubbles. This is very much a down-market version of the emblem, where the viewer is not expected to decipher the meaning of the animal symbols on his own, and is helpfully given a translation of the simple Latin. There is a very simple wall painting of the same animals and their Latin calls in Shulbrede Priory, Sussex: an Augustinian priory, which was suppressed in 1537. The paintings in the Prior's Chamber date from the later sixteenth century, when customary courts and courts baron were held there, and they would have been seen regularly by all the tenants.[171] The theme of the animals announcing the nativity came from the legend that animals became articulate on Christmas Day.[172] This was one medieval apocryphal legend which did not embellish the lives of sacred biblical figures, but remained safely in the animal world, and thus survived for Protestant broadside buyers right into the eighteenth century.

In the 1631 broadside, the pre-Reformation traditions of the animals of the nativity, and the instruments of the passion, are combined with more contemporary elements. At the bottom right is an Epitaph of Christ, following the style of the broadside epitaphs produced by the London press. The left column is taken up with a history of Christ, which reads like a news-sheet narrative. The creator of the broadside has purposefully drawn on popular tabloid conventions, announcing the saviour's birth in the same way that one would announce the sighting of a monstrous fish between Dover and Calais.

'Christus natus est' is an artefact of the word-based information culture, yet at its centre is an image in the centuries-old tradition of Christian visual piety. This image might seem out of place in the context of Protestant 'iconophobia', yet it reflected an iconography which was still visible in village

---

[170] McKerrow and Ferguson, *Title-page borders*, no. 222. STC 22636.5. 'A type of the trew nobilitye, or, ye armes of a Christian emblazoned' (*c.* 1635), engraved by Jacob Florensz van Langeren after W. Slatyer. Samuel Rowlands, *The betraying of Christ* (1598).

[171] The priory was owned by Sir Anthony Browne and his heirs, the Viscounts Montague of Cowdray. (Shulbrede Priory 'notes for visitors'.)

[172] Versions are known in Italian and Portuguese, and in a French carol which is closest to the English version:

> Commes les bestes autrefois
> Parloient mieux Latin que François,
> Le cocq de loin voyant ce faict
> S'écria 'Christus Natus est.'
> Le boeuf d'un air lent ebauhi
> Demande 'Ubi, ubi, ubi?'.

('Joie des Bestes', quoted in Child, I, p. 233.) The ballad of 'St Stephen and Herod' preserves the related legend of the roasted cock which comes to life in its dish and cries 'Christus natus est'. (See also Ponsonby, *The priory of Lynchmere and Shulbrede*, pp. 13–15.)

churches across the country. Although much of the statuary and wall painting had been removed or covered up, the whole panoply of sacred subjects was still represented in stained glass, roof ornaments, stone work and other objects not generally considered to provoke idolatry. For every iconoclast there were many parishioners with a deep, even 'proprietorial' attachment to the images in their church.[173] And if some types of religious picture might cause suspicion of popery in a domestic setting, it was apparently an acceptable and widespread practice to paste up ballads adorned with little woodcuts of Christ in judgement and the holy family. The early seventeenth-century village still contained many images to help its inhabitants in converting the words of the Protestant religion into visualized experience.

[173] Aston, *England's iconoclasts*, p. 92.

5

Stories for walls

In 1638, Richard Brock of Bunbury had his alehouse suppressed. The Cheshire justices were petitioned by diverse inhabitants of the town, who complained that Brock and 'Joane his wife a recusant convict do keepe in their Alehouse (which is not fully five roodes distant from the chancell doore of the parish church) diverse pictures and other popish reliques.'[1]

Where did they obtain these pictures and relics? They might have bought them from the same wandering jacks-of-all-trades who carried broadside ballads. A Derbyshire piper was caught selling beads, crucifixes and books in Nottinghamshire in 1616.[2] In 1618 James I addressed the problem of popish peddling in his licensing order for petty chapmen: 'many of them being of no Religion, or infected with Poperie, carry abroad and disperse superstitious Trumperies, unknowne and unsuspected'.[3] When these trumperies included pictures, which had to be both easily transported and affordable, they were probably single-sheet woodcuts. They may even have been run off on a secret press not far from Bunbury: a satirical pamphlet of 1624 had Count Godomar advising the Jesuits and priests to 'be sure to have going in the North or West part of England, two Printers Presses at worke, which let be well stocked; also a small rolling presse for little Pictures of Saints, Veronica's heads, Crucifixes and the like'.[4] Pictures like this were also imported from the Continent. In 1579 Bernard Garter, self-styled 'citizen of London' published *A new yeares gifte, dedicted to the pope's holiness, and all catholikes addicted to the sea of Rome*. In it he exposed the trade

---

[1] S. Nantwich, 10 July 1638. J.H.E. Bennett and J.C. Dewhurst, eds., *Quarter sessions records with other records of the justices of the peace for the county palatine of Chester 1559–1760*, Record Society of Lancashire and Cheshire, vol. 94 (1940), p. 93.

[2] A.L. Beier, *Masterless men: the vagrancy problem in England 1560–1640* (1985), p. 97.

[3] Proclamation of 6 July 1618. STC 8571. Reprinted in P.L. Hughes and J.F. Larkin, eds., *Stuart royal proclamations*, vol. I (Oxford, 1973), p. 393.

[4] Thomas Scott, *The second part of vox populi, or Gondomar appearing in the likenes of Matchiavell in a Spanish parliament* (1624), p. 57. Gondomar also gave advice on the distribution of such items: 'You may doe it by some one poore yet trustie Catholique or two, to goe up and downe the Countrie in the habit and nature of Pedlers.' (*Ibid.* p. 56.)

in Catholic devotional objects smuggled into England: 'Our English fugitive, runnagate Papistes, which are beyond the Seas, sende into this Realme of Englande, Bulles, Pardons, Beades . . . and Pictures of Sainctes' among other things.[5]

The printer of the *New yeares gifte* obtained a large fold-out diagram depicting all of these objects, to help the good Protestant recognize a recusant when he saw one (Plate 26).[6] The central object in this diagram was a picture of St Nicholas, with Christ crucified and the virgin and child hovering above amidst clouds and cherubim. This image, with its emblematic function, may not be a direct copy of a real print. The composition has been arranged so as to make a point against Catholic belief in the intercession of the virgin Mary: 'The figure discloseth it selfe: For he knoweth not whether Christ or Mary be of greater power, and therefore standeth in doubt whiche way to turne himselfe.'[7] Nevertheless, such 'Pictures of Sainctes' were apparently widely available to the recusant community, and could be purchased in Cheshire at a price affordable to an alehouse-keeper.

Some devotional prints may have been run off the Jesuit Press at St Omers in the Spanish Netherlands. We know that in the early seventeenth century, crucifixes, beads and pictures of saints were often included with the Jesuits' shipments of books.[8] Another possible source was the rue Montorgueil in Paris, the centre of a thriving trade in religious woodcuts throughout the second half of the sixteenth century until the mid-seventeenth century.[9] (Plate 27 is typical of the Parisian output in this period.)[10] The rue Montorgueil woodcut artists were influenced by the Fontainebleau school of painting, and did much to popularize this school.[11] The Bibliothèque Nationale has surviving copies of woodcuts which were made for export, with blank cartouches ready to receive inscriptions in different languages. Among these are series on the lives of St Peter and St Augustine; and scenes from the

---

[5] B[ernar]d G[arter], *A new yeares gifte*, preface 3v.

[6] The printer was Henry Bynneman. Fold-out located between sigs.F4v and G1 in BL copy 3932.dd.15.

[7] *Ibid.*, sig.H2.

[8] Leona Rostenberg, *The minority press and the English crown 1558–1625* (Nieuwkoop, 1971), ch. 9.

[9] In the early seventeenth century the centre of gravity shifted to the rue St Jean de Latran and the rue St Jacques, and the medium to copper engraving. Jean Adhémar, *Imagerie populaire française* (Milan, 1968), p. 51. Marianne Grivel, 'Le Commerce de l'estampe à Paris au XVIIe siècle' (Sorbonne, Thèse de IIIe cycle, 1982), p. 90.

[10] 'Sanctus Petrus Apostolus. Sanctus Paulus Apostolus', by Jean de Gourmont (working 1562–96), Bibliothèque Nationale, Cabinet des Estampes, Ed.5g.rés., fol. 84. Jean Adhémar, *Inventaire du fonds français: graveurs du XVI siècle* (2 vols., Paris, 1938).

[11] Adhémar, *Imagerie populaire*, p. 53; Jean Adhémar, 'La Rue Montorgueil et la formation d'un groupe d'imagiers parisiens au XVIe siècle', *Le Vieux Papier*, 21 (1954), p. 30. Some of their woodcuts were copied directly from specific paintings.

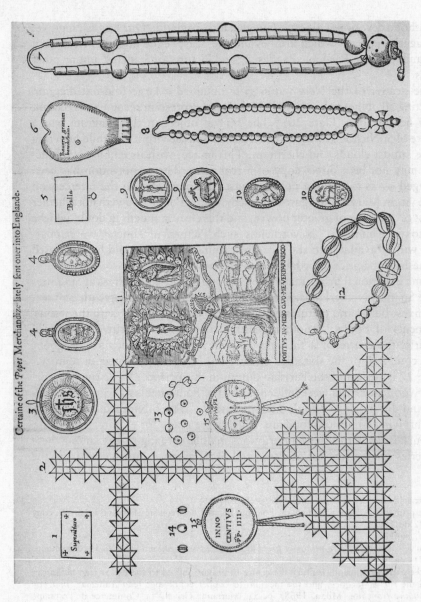

Certaine of the *Popes* Merchandiz lately sent ouer into Englande.

26 'Certaine of the popes merchandize lately sent over into Englande'. Fold-out diagram from B[ernard] G[arter]. *A new yeares gifte, dedicated to the pope's holiness* (1579).

27 'Sanctus Petrus Apostolus. Sanctus Paulus Apostolus'. Late sixteenth-century
woodcut from the shop of Jean de Gourmont in Paris.

life of Christ including the last supper, the road to Calvary and the crucifixion.[12] The export of thousands of such 'pictures of saints' to Spain has
already been documented.[13]

The author of the 1579 *New yeares gifte*, Bernard Garter, was apparently
confident about what constituted a popish picture. But in the early years
of Elizabeth's reign the rue Montorgueil publishers had a London outpost,
in the person of the French printer and craftsman Gyles Godet. Godet was

---

[12] Bibliothèque Nationale, Cabinet des Estampes, Ea.25.a.rés. The St Augustine series was
designed and cut by Nicolas Prévost (active 1571–99, d. before 1610). The lives of St
Peter and of Christ were designed by Marin Boussy (active *c.* 1570, d. 1578). (Adhémar,
Graveurs du XVI siècle, II, entries for 'Prévost', 'Boussy'.)

[13] Spanish trade discussed in Grivel, 'Le Commerce de l'estampe', p. 402. I have looked in
printed transcripts of port books, without success, for any mention of pictures imported
to England. (Brian Dietz, *The port and trade of early Elizabethan London: documents*,
London Record Society (1972); R.W.K. Hinton, *The port books of Boston, 1601–1640*,
Lincoln Record Society Publications (1956).) A search through the much larger volume
of unpublished port books could be a worthy project.

a *bona fide* member of the Stationer's Company, who openly registered and published a variety of religious woodcuts in the Paris style.

Gyles Godet immigrated to England in the late 1540s, and worked in Blackfriars until his death around 1571.[14] He belonged to the French reformed church in London, and according to the Returns of Aliens he left France because of religion.[15] However, he was not so zealous as to move again during the reign of Mary, and his religion did not prevent him from having intimate business connections with the woodcut designers in Paris, who were by all accounts staunchly Catholic.[16]

Godet's blocks were designed in Paris by François Gence, who was an 'imagier en papier': that is, he drew the lines on the woodblocks, but did not cut them himself.[17] It seems that Godet performed all the other roles involved in the production of his woodcuts: that is, he was the publisher who commissioned the themes, the craftsman who carved between the lines of the drawing, the printer who ran them off the press and probably the printseller too.[18] Luckily, Godet's Paris connections meant that some woodcuts with his imprint were included in an album of samples for retailers, which survives in the Bibliothèque Nationale.[19] Most of the prints in the album are biblical stories told in a series of six pictures of 36 × 47 cm, or roughly folio size. The three series by Godet are the history of Joseph, the history of St Paul and the prodigal son (Plates 29, 32).[20]

Godet's press in the Blackfriars, as we will see, represents a compromise position, bridging the gap between the demands of a public not yet weaned from devotional images and the boundaries of Protestant iconography. Until now we have emphasized the conflict between 'traditional' and 'Protestant' attitudes; between the Bunbury alehouse-keeper and the 'citizen of London' on his anti-papist crusade. In this chapter we will look at the development of a core of narrative pictorial themes, which appear to have satisfied the demands of the majority; all but the most extreme iconophobes and the

[14] Ernest James Worman, *Alien members of the book trade during the Tudor period* (1960), p. 25. Godet's will is in the Public Record Office, Commissary Court of London, Reg. 16, fol. 48.

[15] Elsie Johnston, ed., *Actes due Consistoire de l'Eglise Française de Threadneedle Street, Londres*, Vol I: *1560–1565*, Publications of the Huguenot Society of London, vol. 38 (1937), pp. 15, 16, 90. *Returns of Aliens dwelling in London, Henry VIII to James I*, ed. R.E.G. Kirk and Ernest F. Kirk, 3 vols., Publications of the Huguenot Society of London, vol. 10 (in 3) (1900–8), pt 3, p. 408.

[16] Johnston, ed., *Actes du Consistoire de l'Eglise Française*, I, p. 15. Adhémar, 'La Rue Montorgueil', pp. 25–34.

[17] Adhémar, 'La Rue Montorgueil', p. 31. Adhémar, 'François Gence', *Graveurs du XVI siècle*, II.

[18] Sometimes these were all separate people, but it was not uncommon for various functions to be combined in this way.

[19] Cabinet des Estampes, Ed.5g.rés.

[20] *Ibid.*, fols. 10–12v, 80–2v, 92–4v.

practising recusants. First we will look at Godet and his trade descendants in the Blackfriars, who have apparently not been known to historians of print selling in England until now.[21] Then we will trace how similar themes, primarily from the Old Testament and Apocrypha, were copied from print into other media like wall painting and painted cloth. We will try to set these 'stories' in a physical context, on the walls of private houses and cottages, and especially in the public inns and alehouses, nodal points of communication throughout our period.

IN THE BLACKFRIARS

In 1562–3, a list of twenty-seven items was entered to Gyles Godet in the Stationers' Company Register, from which we can construct a picture of his woodcut stock (App. G). Over half the titles are religious, but if we compare Godet's themes with the overall production of the Paris woodcut artists, we see that his choices were carefully pruned for the English market. Rather than virgin and child or passion scenes, he chose safer religious allegories like 'The fygure of True Religion', 'The pycture of True Sobryete' and 'The pycture of Charyte'. Other scenes which presumably used uncontroversial iconography were those delivering moral injunctions: 'The instruction of a very faythfull man', 'The Tenne Commandementes' and 'The Rememberaunce to Dye'.

When Godet published portraits of religious figures, he avoided the saints offered by his rue Montorgueil counterparts, opting for characters from the Old Testament: 'The pycture of Saloman the wyse'; 'The geneolige or lyne of our savyour Christe as touchynge his humanyte from Noee to Davyd'. The latter was probably much like his 24-sheet 'genealogie of all the kynges of England' which survives in the British Library, substituting biblical drapery for coats of armour.[22] One surprise on the list is 'The Creation of the Worlde', which is hard to imagine in the Fontainebleau style without an anthropomorphic God the Father. If it was anything like the Creation scene in Plate 28, done by two rue Montorgueil craftsmen, it is interesting to find it printed in England of the 1560s without censure.[23] Perhaps Godet would have answered as Laud did, when defending a glass window which was said to contravene the article of 1571 against 'pictures of false and

---

[21] Leona Rostenberg claimed that prints were not a speciality trade until 1599, when George Humble and John Sudbury set up their partnership selling engravings. (Leona Rostenberg, *English publishers in the graphic arts 1599–1700* (New York, 1963), p. 3.)

[22] Gyles Godet, *To the reader. Beholde here a brief abstract of the genealogie of all the kynges of England* [1562?].

[23] Germain Hoyau and Mathurin Nicolas, 'La Genèse' [1565–74], Bibliothèque Nationale, Cabinet des Estampes, Ed.5g.rés. fol. 1.

28 'La Genêse' [1565–74]. Version by Germain Hoyau and Mathurin Nicolas, rue Montorgueil, Paris.

feigned Miracles': 'I do not think that the Story of the Creation was a Picture of false Miracles'.[24]

The Creation is an anomaly amidst the emblematic and Old Testament titles, and may not have survived beyond the 1560s. Murray Roston has commented that in biblical drama there was from the mid-sixteenth century 'a gradual move down the ladder of sanctity'. First the depiction of central figures from the Gospels was considered irreverent, then slowly the Old Testament became sacrosanct too. The playwrights moved a rung down to the Apocrypha, and finally to the histories of Josephus. The traditional mystery cycle was replaced in Lincoln in 1564 by the story of Tobias, while in 1584 Coventry commissioned a play on the destruction of Jerusalem.[25]

A parallel 'ladder of sanctity' seems to exist in pictorial art, although Old Testament figures were never completely driven off the stage as they were in plays. Godet's selection of themes in the 1560s represented a first step down this ladder, in tune with the subjects which inventories show to have been common in paintings and cloths of the same period.[26] Godet's 'histories' or 'stories' told in six pictures, which survive in the Paris sample book, illustrate a tradition of religious narrative which would be popular in English decorative arts for some years to come, even when the specific episodes were chosen from further down the 'ladder of sanctity'.

The tradition of visual 'stories' from the Scriptures had immaculate Protestant credentials. Luther expressed a wish for 'the whole Bible to be painted on houses, on the outside and inside, so that all can see it. That would be a Christian work.'[27] While Calvin was less sympathetic than Luther to most religious imagery, he allowed that biblical scenes, shown in their historical function, could be of 'use in teaching or admonition'.[28] The Elizabethan homily against idolatry made a careful distinction between narrative pictures and static icons: 'And a process of a story, painted with the gestures and actions of many persons, and commonly the sum of the story written withal, hath another use in it, than one dumb idol or image standing by itself'.[29]

William Perkins was against biblical painting in churches, but not in dom-

---

[24] The exchange took place during the trial of Henry Sherfield, 1633. (Sollom Emlyn, ed., *A complete collection of state trials and proceedings for high-treason, and other crimes and misdemeanours*, 3rd edn. (1742), p. 405.)

[25] Murray Roston, *Biblical drama in England* (1968), pp. 118, 120.

[26] See below, pp. 201–2.

[27] Quoted in Ernest B. Gilman, *Iconoclasm and poetry in the English Reformation. Down went Dagon* (Chicago, 1986), p. 35.

[28] Jean Calvin, *Institutes of the Christian religion* (1536), trans. Ford Lewis Battles, ed. John T. McNeill (2 vols., Library of Christian Classics, vol. XX, 1961), Book I, ch. 11, section 12.

[29] Quoted in Margaret Aston, *England's iconoclasts*, vol. I: *Laws against images* (Oxford, 1988), p. 405.

estic settings: 'We hold the historical use of images to be good and lawful: and that is, to represent to the eye the acts of histories, whether they be human or divine: and thus we think the histories of the Bible may be painted in private places.'[30]

The biblical series published by Gyles Godet fulfil the Calvinist conditions of historical characters taking part in historical events. Some of the Parisian woodcuts were large frontal portraits of saints with their symbols, suggesting a devotional purpose (Plate 27). Godet's St Paul is only a small character in a complex narrative scene (Plate 29). The style is a naturalistic one, typical of the Fontainebleau influence. The rounded hatchings give an impression of movement which was absent from the more static woodcuts familiar in sixteenth-century English books; the use of the lines to reveal muscles and the folds of clothing creates a new three-dimensional quality. The scenes have a life of their own beyond the border frame: the viewer is more safely distanced from these scenes than with the flat, iconic 'images of pity' in the pre-Reformation period. Here the lines of relationship happen between characters within the picture, rather than between the picture (of saint or virgin) and the viewer outside.

In the St Paul series there is an attempt to obtain the sense of chronological sequence and of dialogue which is possible in books and not so easy in pictures. Godet's designer tried some complex narrative techniques, with up to seven events per frame. In the scene of Paul's conversion, a ray of black-letter type emerges from Christ's figure in the clouds, much like a comic-strip speech bubble. Another scene uses the interesting temporal arrangement of Eutychus falling and being raised at one and the same time. These narrative devices again make the picture more like a book to be read than an icon to be worshipped.

These prints would have been coloured before being sold to the customer, usually by young children working in the shop (as we know from the practices of other rue Montorgueil publishers; and from some of Godet's own pictures of English royalty, which survive in their full coloured splendour in the British Museum).[31] Although the pictures could be read flat like a book, they were also suitable to be hung or pasted on the wall; decorative and entertaining, as well as instructive.[32]

---

[30] William Perkins, *A reformed Catholike* (Cambridge, 1598), quoted in *ibid.*, p. 451.

[31] Adhémar, *Imagerie populaire*, p. 6. Coloured pictures and fragments by rue Montorgueil publishers are found in Bibliothèque Nationale, Cabinet des Estampes, Ea.17.rés. Godet, *Abstract of the genealogie of all the kynges of England*, copy in BL G.6456. STC 7588, 'Loe here the pearle, whom God and man doth love' [woodcut portrait of Queen Elizabeth, w. verse, 1563].

[32] In France, religious woodcuts were mounted on mantelpieces or bedsteads in frieze-like series called *tours de cheminées*, or *tours de lit*. (Roger Chartier, *The cultural uses of print in early modern France*, trans. Lydia C. Cochrane (Princeton, 1987), p. 236.)

Paule, Paule, Why persecutest thou me?

Paule preacheth Iesus with in Damask

Heere Christ did say this persecuting Saule   So thus of vexer Christians by the Word   2
And from his rage full straightly did him call.   He made him preach to Christias by his Word.

29 'The historie of S. Paule'. Second in series of six scenes, printed by Gyles Godet in the Blackfriars,
London [1563?].

Godet's Paris connection helps us to estimate the price of his woodcuts. We have a 1598 inventory of one of the rue Montorgueil woodcut designers, Denis de Mathonière.[33] The uniformity of style throughout these woodcuts means that we can extrapolate Godet's probable prices from this inventory. De Mathonière's woodcut prints were valued in bulk at about 0.17d. Even with a retail mark-up of four times that amount, they would still be under 1d. each; 4d. for a series of six.[34]

For Godet we should allow some added expense in importing the designed blocks from France, and perhaps a further mark-up because there was less competition in the market. There is a possible clue in the 1578 inventory of a Cambridge bookseller, John Denys. At the end of the list of goods in the shop are several items which were apparently pictorial: 'Tipus orbis pictae' (12d.), 'Tabule cebetis pictae' (6d.), 'v other small pictures' (6d.), 'a Rolle of the kynges' (6d.), 'the storye of David' (6d.), 'helias' (6d.), 'the storye of Joseph' (7d.).[35] A 'story' is a term normally used to describe a picture, or a series of pictures.[36] The 'stories' of David and of Joseph were surely series of biblical pictures in the rue Montorgueil tradition; perhaps even Godet's own, since we know Joseph was one of his themes.[37]

A series of six might be expensive for the ordinary husbandman or craftsman; but the single woodcuts, at roughly 1d. each ('v other small pictures' at 6d.), would be within reach of even the bottom levels of the social scale. The fact that the Cambridge bookseller had so few pictures in stock does not seem to indicate a booming trade.[38] In 1585 Roger Ward had a few more prints in his Shrewsbury bookshop: '20 pictures not colored', '3 pictures in collers' and 'i picture of London'. In 1616 John Foster of York had thirteen

[33] Jean Adhémar and George Wildenstein, 'Les Images de Denis de Mathonière d'apres son inventaire', *Arts et Traditions Populaires* (1958), pp. 150–7.

[34] Marianne Grivel gives one instance of an inventory evaluation of a print which was one quarter of the price later charged to a customer. ('Le Commerce de l'estampe', p. 352.) It seems unlikely that inventories as a rule undervalued prints by such a high factor; however, to avoid overoptimism about the accessibility of prints, I have accepted this mark-up in the discussion which follows. I have used an exchange rate of 10d. tournoise = 1d. sterling. (Information from Dr Peter Spufford.) De Mathonière's woodcuts were valued on average at 1.7d. tournois = 0.17d. sterling × 4 = 0.672d. i.e. about 4d. for a series of six.

[35] Reproduced in E.S. Leedham-Green, ed., *Books in Cambridge inventories* (Cambridge, 1986).

[36] Susan Foister found that in the inventories of the prosperous classes a 'story' usually referred to a framed painting. (Susan Foister, 'Paintings and other works of art in sixteenth-century English inventories', *The Burlington Magazine*, 123 (1981), p. 275.) The term 'story' was also used for the biblical series in Godet's Stationers' Register entry.

[37] Godet died *c*. 1571 but his woodblocks continued to be used (see below, pp. 190–1).

[38] Compare Charles Tias' 1664 stock, which contained pictures in 'reams' (see p. 140). On the rise in ownership of pictures by the period 1675–1725, see Lorna Weatherill, *Consumer behaviour and material culture, 1660–1760* (1988), pp. 44, 46 (Tables 3.1, 3.2).

pictures ready for sale, valued at 2s., or under 2d. each.[39] It may be that despite their reasonable price, prints at 2d. were not as good value for humbler households as sturdier decorations like painted cloths, which would better survive the ravages of smoke from the hearth (as well as serving the practical purpose of insulation). But as we will note later, the woodcut pictures may have reached a wider public through use as patterns by craftsmen in other media.

There are clues that the French community in London continued to support a tradition of printing woodcut pictures, but we know little of the character of their stock. Jean 'de Horse' was admitted to the Stationers' Company in 1580 'as a brother'; that is, without serving an apprenticeship.[40] He was described in the 1582–3 Returns of Aliens as one who 'useth selling of pictures and making of brushes, and now dwelleth in the Black-friars'.[41] In the same year, he was reported in the Stationers' Company Register as having one printing press, so the pictures he sold must have been woodcuts rather than paintings.[42] In 1581, he paid the Stationers' Company a lump sum of 10s. for some unspecified copies which, if they were single-sheet woodcuts, would represent thirty separate titles. Dehors may have imported his woodblocks from France; the records of the French church show that he did make a journey to Rouen on at least one occasion.[43]

Jean Dehors may have been the Frenchman of that name who arrived in England in the 1540s and was made a denizen in 1550. He may also have been a feltmaker by training.[44] In 1582 he had two 'servants', Anthonie Vernell and Giles Bullenger, the latter only recently arrived from France. This Bullenger apparently inherited his master's press and materials, as in 1593 he was recorded as a 'Printer of Storyes'. Bullenger also lived in St

---

[39] Alexander Rodger, ed., 'Roger Ward's Shrewsbury stock: an inventory of 1585', *The Library*, 5th ser., 13 (1958), p. 262. Robert Davies, ed., *A memoir of the York press* (1868), p. 370.

[40] Arber, II, p. 683.

[41] Worman, *Alien members of the book trade*, pp. 32–3.

[42] Arber, I, p. 248. In December 1582 Christopher Barker wrote to Lord Burghley that there were twenty-two printing houses in London. (Arber, I, p. 248.) The 1583 list had one more added, probably that of Dehors. (Worman, *Alien members of the book trade*, p. 33.)

[43] Arber, II, p. 309. Johnston, ed., *Actes du Consistoire de l'Eglise Française*, I, p. 76, mentions a trip to Rouen in the early 1560s.

[44] *Returns of Aliens*, I, p. 413. *Letters of Denization and Acts of Naturalization for Aliens in England 1509–1603*, ed. W. Page, Publications of the Huguenot Society of London, vol. 8 (1893), p. 68. These records may belong to either of two John Dehors in London in this period: 'Jehan dehors dit la Brebis' (our Blackfriars printer), and 'Jehan dehors dit Justice' (a hatmaker in St Katherines). (See, for example, Johnston, ed., *Actes du Consistoire de l'eglise Française*, I, p. 76.)

Anne, Blackfriars and belonged to the French church. He married an English woman and had six children.[45]

We have no pictures surviving with the imprint of Jean Dehors, nor of Giles Bullenger. However, a Paul Boulenger, probably one of Giles' children, has left us four woodcut pictures printed between 1607 and 1616. Only one of them bears his imprint: 'The picture of the unfortunate gentleman, Sir Gervis Elvies Knight', printed 'at London in the Black-Friers, by Paul Boulenger. 1615'.[46] Another picture of 'Mistres Turners farewell to all women', printed for John Trundle in the same year, is set within the same classical border, with a similar typographical arrangement of title and verses.[47] The two broadsides deal with topical scandals, but the woodcuts themselves do nothing to illustrate the crimes: they were no doubt generic figures which Boulenger kept in stock. The costumes indicate that they were cut in the early seventeenth century, and probably by the same craftsman.

However, two other broadsides which have been credited to Boulenger have a longer history. In 1607 a woodcut called 'The good hows-holder' was printed 'at London in the Blackefriers' (Plate 38).[48] This picture was registered in 1564–5 to none other than Giles Godet, under the title of 'a christian exortation of the good husholder to his chyldren'.[49] The verses on the seventeenth-century copy, recommending the good Protestant virtues of thriftiness, charity and foresight, were probably new.[50] A final woodcut with the Blackfriars imprint, 'The historie of the life of man' has a letterpress text dated 1616, but the block itself appears to be older.[51] It is a visualization of the 'ages of man' from infancy to old age by means of a rising and declining stairway, a popular image from the sixteenth to the nineteenth centuries.[52] The border compartments, which bear the woodcut initials E[lizabeth] R[egina], are similar to those used by Godet in his biblical series. As they

[45] *Returns of Aliens*, II, p. 253. In 1593, Bullenger was described as '12 yeares resident', no denizen'. (*Returns of Aliens*, III, p. 445.) Another Giles Bullinger, an apothecary, had already been in England ten years in 1583 and had a French wife. (*Returns of Aliens*, II, p. 356.) Worman confuses the two in *Alien members of the book trade*, p. 8.

[46] The STC entry (7627.5.) claims that this item was printed *for* Boulenger, discounting the claim of the imprint '*by* Paul Boulenger'. However, it seems likely that Boulenger had inherited the press owned by Jean Dehors in the 1580s, and that because it was used only for woodcut pictures it was not normally counted in the list of printing presses.

[47] STC 24341.5.

[48] STC 13851. STC suggests Paul Boulenger as the printer. Another possibility might be his father Giles, who does not appear to be known to bibliographers.

[49] Arber, I, p. 272.

[50] As STC comments, the verses are about the householder, rather than an exhortation in his own words.

[51] STC 13526.5. The Pepys catalogue suggests *c.* 1600 as an estimate for the woodcut.

[52] Samuel C. Chew, *The pilgrimage of life* (New Haven, 1962), p. 148. There is a crude woodcut version on a ballad of 'The age and life of man' [1674–9], Pepys, II, 32.

were chipped and worn by 1616, they may well have been printing stock handed down for several generations.

We can now see a possible line of inheritance: Paul Boulenger received these old woodblocks from his father Giles, who inherited them from his master Jean Dehors, who acquired them from Godet. Godet and Dehors both lived in Blackfriars for over twenty years and attended the same church. Dehors may have taken over Godet's business and materials after his death in *c.* 1571, which would explain the entrance to the Stationers' Company 'as a brother' in 1580 and the ownership of a press in 1583. We do not know what else he printed besides Godet's worn stock, and whether he kept up the rue Montorgueil connection. Some of Godet's woodcuts ended up in other hands: the English kings from the 'genealogie' were used by Roger Ward in 1584. They were converted to the 'nine worthies', with a text explicating a moral lesson from each story.[53]

In April 1656, a bookseller and printer named Thomas Warren entered thirty-six 'portraictures cutt in wood' in the Stationers' Register (App. G).[54] This was the year in which Cromwell's orders for printing reinstated effective licensing, and the 'ballad partners' registered their old and successful titles. Like the ballads, Thomas Warren's woodcuts appear to be old blocks stock-piled from various sources.[55] The titles show a surprising degree of continuity with Godet's list almost a century earlier. In fact several of Warren's blocks were probably from Godet's shop (or copies of Godet's prints): 'The good hous-holder', 'The anatomy of man and woman'; perhaps the portrait of Henry VIII and 'A roll of all the kings of England since the conquest'.[56] Warren's print of 'The rich man in ye Gospell' was a parable comparable to Godet's story of the prodigal son, and 'True wisdome throwing ye world behind her' was probably similar to Godet's figures of Chastity and True Religion. The core of Godet's religious stock, made up of Old Testament portraits and narrative scenes acceptable to his Protestant market, was echoed in like spirit in Warren's list: 'The generation from Adam to Noah' (Godet registered Noah to David), 'A roll of all the kings of Israell', 'Jephtha offering his daughter', 'The historicall parts of the Bible in 42 sheets'.[57]

A 42-sheet series of biblical scenes would not have been affordable to

---

[53] Richard Lloyd, *A briefe discourse of the ... actes and conquests of the nine worthies* (1584).

[54] Eyre, II, pp. 46–7, 48, 50.

[55] 'The image of the life of man, by Apelles, in 9 large sheets' survives in the British Museum and probably dates from the late sixteenth century (BM Prints, Case 270). 'Six portratures, viz', A Divine, a Soldier, a Lady, a Lawyer, a Labourer and Death' is almost certainly the picture (or a copy) of the '5 Alls' we saw above, p. 163.

[56] Godet's woodcut 'The anatomie of the inward partes of man' [1559?] survives in Cambridge University Library (K.7.15.). Godet's roll of kings went right back into the mythical past, as far as 'the floude of Noe and Brute'.

[57] Warren offered only one New Testament scene involving the figure of Christ: 'Christ brought before Pontius Pilate and the elders. 4 large sh.'.

the same wide audience who bought ballads. However, it may have had a greater impact if it was used by other craftsmen as a pattern book. At all levels of skill, the major source copied by painters was the printed picture. Prints were the standard medium for passing visual information and artistic themes across geographical distances.[58] The influence of devotional wood-cuts has often been used to explain the late fifteenth-century 'decline' of wall painting into a style of stiff figures and harsh black outlines.[59] At the other end of the scale, the best surviving examples of Elizabethan decora-tive figure painting, the Cupid and Psyche murals of the 1570s at Hill Hall in Essex, were closely copied from engravings.[60] The artist at Stodmarsh Court near Canterbury, who copied four classical deities from engravings by Virgil Solis, faithfully copied the monogram too.[61] Other Elizabethan wall paintings have been traced to the emblem books of Alciati.[62]

Even when no direct source can be found, the close relationship between printed pictures and wall paintings is everywhere apparent. Painted texts were enclosed within borders of strap-work pattern or Renaissance orna-ment, borrowing the conventions of woodcut borders used in books and on broadsides.[63] The texts themselves were painted in the same black-letter style as the standard typographical font.[64] Paintings from the story of the prodigal son, the book of Tobit, and Dives and Lazarus look tantalizingly similar to the crude little pictures found on ballads, with their use of black lines suggesting an attempt to copy the hatchings of woodcuts.[65]

This same close relationship must have existed between prints and the ubiquitous 'painted cloths' which have not survived. Weekly searches by the Painter-Stainers' Company in 1632 uncovered several stationers involved in their trade. A stationer in Smithfield, Thomas Andrewes, was found to be hanging unlawful paintings out to sale. One Sherman, a bookseller by the Tower Ditch, had beeen making 'defective woorke' which was com-

[58] W. M. Ivins, jnr, *Prints and visual communication* (1969 edn).

[59] A. Caiger-Smith, *English medieval mural paintings* (Oxford, 1963), pp. 24–5. Edward Croft-Murray, *Decorative painting in England 1537–1837* (2 vols., 1962), I, p. 14. E. Clive Rouse, 'A wall-painting of St Christopher in St Mary's Church, Wyken, Coventry', *Transactions of the Birmingham Archaeological Society*, 75 (1957), pp. 36–42.

[60] Richard Simpson, 'Sir Thomas Smith and the wall paintings at Hill Hall Essex: scholarly theory and design in the Sixteenth Century', *Journal of the British Archaelogical Association*, 130 (1977), pp. 1–20.

[61] Francis W. Reader, 'Tudor domestic wall-paintings, Part II', *Archaeological Journal*, 93 (1936), p. 246.

[62] M. Carrick, P.M. Ryan and M.C. Wadhams, 'Wall paintings at Creswells Farm, Sible Hedingham, Essex', *Archaeological Journal*, 144 (1988), pp. 328–39.

[63] See Francis W. Reader, 'Tudor domestic wall-paintings', *Archaeological Journal*, 92 (1935), pp. 262, 270, for just two examples.

[64] Both painted and printed 'black letter' developed from hand-written forms of the manuscript period. (Philip Gaskell, *A new introduction to bibliography* (Oxford, 1972), p. 17.)

[65] See below, pp. 209–10.

monly sold in many booksellers' shops about the city.[66] It is not clear whether these painted wares were on cloth or wood or perhaps paper, but their sale at bookshops suggests that there was no firm line between 'prints' and 'paintings'.

These media of paper, cloths and walls must be seen together. Not only did they decorate the same rooms, they shared the same themes. Prints give us some idea about the painted cloths and walls which have fallen apart or been destroyed. At the same time, wall painting may preserve in stone the paper pictures we have lost.

THE VISUAL CONTEXT

In 1564, William Bullein wrote *A dialogue . . . wherein is a goodly regimente against the fever pestilence*, in which he used the journey of a London citizen and his wife into the countryside as an excuse for a literary rag-bag of fables, jests, allegories and word-emblems. 'Civis' and 'Uxor' arrive in a town several hours' ride past Barnet, where they find an inn for the night. It has 'a comlie parlour, verie netlie and trimlie apparelled, London like, the windowes are well glased, & faire clothes with pleasaunte borders aboute the same, with many wise saiynges painted upon them'.[67] Painted on these cloths, on the walls, on the chimney and on individual 'pictures' or 'tables' are both proverbial inscriptions (in Latin) and pictorial emblems. Civis reads and interprets the paintings at his wife's request:

UXOR. I pray you housband what is that writyng in those golden letters.
CIVIS. Meius est claudus in via quam cursor preter viam. That is, better an halting ma[n] whiche kepeth the right waie, then ye swift ronner besides, that wandereth a straie.[68]

UXOR. What beaste is that, havyng many colours, one bodie, and seven horrible heddes.
CIVIS. The bodie of sinne, with many infernall heddes: Wickednesse in every place under the Sonne.[69]

We would not for a moment want to suggest that Bullein was describing a real inn, or even a realistic one. He was creating a literary version of the new emblem books which had arrived from Italy and France.[70] Bullein

---

[66] Search of 26 April 1632. (Records of the Painter-Stainers' Company, Guildhall Library, L.37 MS 5667A.)

[67] William Bullein, *A dialogue bothe pleasaunte and pietifull, wherein is a goodly regimente against the fever pestilence* (1564), sig.H6.

[68] *Ibid.*

[69] Bullein, *A dialogue .. wherein is a goodly regimente against the fever pestilence*, 2nd edn. (1573), sig. K1v.

[70] The British Library has at least twenty-three editions of Andrea Alciati, *Emblemata* (Paris, 1542 etc.). The first English emblem book was Geoffrey Whitney, *Choice of emblemes* (1586).

has retained the medieval confidence in the didactic power of images, but here the pictures are mental ones, conjured up with words.[71]

The imaginary room Bullein creates owes something to the 'memory theatre', which involved thinking of the interior of a building, and placing components of a list to be memorized in the different niches of the building.[72] Each alcove was often permanently equipped with a symbolic figure: such as a sign of the zodiac or goddess. But if an Italian or Frenchman might imagine a large church-like hall full of statues, it is very English of Bullein to choose the more homely village inn decorated with wall paintings and cloths. Now that the churches were whitewashed, their visual richness had been transferred to secular interiors.

An ordinary inn may not have had painted Latin inscriptions and grand religio-political emblems as Civis described them, but wall paintings with moral sayings or figure subjects were a common feature of inns and taverns. Even mean alehouses were expected to provide decoration for their customers as Wye Saltonstall commented in 1631: 'A Country Alehouse. Is the center of the Towns good fellowship, or some humble roof't cottage licens'd to sell Ale. The inward hangings is a painted cloath, with a row of Balletts pasted on it'.[73] This standard decor is confirmed by Izaak Walton, who in 1653 described a visit to 'an honest Alehouse, where we shall find a cleanly room, Lavender in the windowes, and twenty Ballads stuck about the walls'.[74] According to Donald Lupton's account of 1632, the more substantial country alehouse-keepers arranged for a more permanent form of decoration:

If these houses have a Boxe-Bush, or an old Post, it is enough to show their Profession. But if they bee graced with a Signe compleat, it is a signe of good custome: In these houses you shall see the History of Iudeth, Susanna, Daniel in the Lyons Den, or Dives & Lazarus painted upon the Wall.[75]

Wall paintings of biblical stories, some illustrating the very episodes Lupton mentions, have been found in former victualling houses of this period.[76]

---

[71] Patrick Collinson has noted a similar case in Richard Bernard, *Contemplative pictures with wholesome precepts* (1610). (Patrick Collinson, *From iconoclasm to iconophobia: the cultural impact of the second English Reformation*, Stenton lecture 1985 (Reading, 1986), p. 23.) Bullein did at least entitle his work a 'dialogue' rather than 'pictures'.

[72] John Willis, *The art of memory so far forth as it dependeth upon places and idees* (1621), sig.B2v–B3.; Frances A. Yates, *The art of memory* (1966), pp. 135–74, 310–29.

[73] Wye Saltonstall, *Picturae loquentes. Or pictures drawne forth in characters. With a poeme of a maid*, sig.E10v.

[74] Izaak Walton, *The complete angler; or, the contemplative man's recreation* (1635), facs. edn (1876), p. 49.

[75] Donald Lupton, *London and the countrey carbonadoed and quartred into severall characters* (1632), p. 127. Peter Clark uses the same quotation as if it referred only to 'certain London alehouses', but in fact this passage comes in the section devoted specifically to the countryside. (Peter Clark, *The English alehouse: a social history 1200–1830* (1983), p. 67.)

[76] See below, esp. pp. 209–11.

Although the chances of survival have favoured the larger establishments we would call inns, contemporary descriptions suggest that these 'histories' were found in one medium or another (wall painting, cloth or paper) right through the victualling hierarchy.

This victualling hierarchy formed a national network of communications: in a census of 1577, over 14,000 alehouses, 2,000 inns and 300 taverns were listed in 27 counties, with 3,700 alehouses and 239 inns in Yorkshire alone.[77] With the growth of private marketing in the early seventeenth century, the inn became the most important meeting place for a 'community of wayfaring merchants'; it functioned as 'the hotel, the bank, the warehouse, the exchange, the scrivener's office, and the market-place'.[78] Bargains were drawn up here, grain bought and sold, carriers hired; some of the larger inns provided facilities for drovers or were used as wool marts, operating outside the regulations of the official market.[79] Lesser wayfarers stayed at the ubiquitous alehouses, located along all the main trading routes, in woodland hamlets, and in all but the smallest villages. A Hertfordshire tippler lodged 'all baggage people such as rogues, tinkers, pedlars and such like'; in 1640 an Essex alehouse harboured petty chapmen from Norfolk, Ely and Sherborne in Yorkshire.[80] Ballad sellers sold their wares at the alehouse; minstrels like Richard Sheale sang their songs of Chevy Chase, Bevis and Sir Guy; companies like the Yorkshire weavers and shoemakers performed their interludes.[81] Printed texts, oral songs and stories, and (as we see in this chapter) visual imagery were disseminated here.

The victualling house was the point of intersection between this nation-wide network of communications and the local community, of which it was also an important focus. The increasingly grand 'county inns' were used by the gentry, merchant and professional classes for administrative and political business; the small village alehouse was a social centre for husbandmen, labourers, poor craftsmen and servants.[82] Peter Clark has suggested that an upsurge of victualling in the century before the Civil War was partly a result of the alehouse taking over much of the 'communal

---

[77] Alan Everitt, 'The English urban inn', in Alan Everitt, ed., *Perspectives in English urban history*, (1973), p. 93. These figures seem to vary from county to county in their reliability, and should only be used with caution.

[78] Alan Everitt, 'The marketing of agricultural produce', in Joan Thirsk, ed., *The agrarian history of England and Wales*, vol. IV: *1560–1640* (Cambridge, 1967), pp. 562, 559.

[79] Ibid., pp. 559–62. John Taylor's *The carriers cosmographie; or a briefe relation of the innes in and neere London* (1637) gave the names of the specific inns where carriers could be found in and around London.

[80] Clark, *The English alehouse*, pp. 72, 70, 129.

[81] References to minstrels, interlude players, fiddlers, pipers and dancing in alehouses are common (see ch. 1 and Clark, *The English alehouse*, pp. 152–3).

[82] Everitt, 'The English urban inn', pp. 110–13. Clark, *The English alehouse*, pp. 125–7.

and ritual life' which had formerly centred on the parish church.[83] Such
a transfer may also have been reflected in the visual environment, as inns
and alehouses were decorated with the narrative wall paintings formerly
found in churches.

During Mary's reign, Protestant activists used alehouses for their conven-
ticles. In 1553, one Thomas Cundale of Orwell, Cambridgeshire, spent
an evening in the alehouse offering to show his friends an anti-Catholic
ballad entitled 'maistres masse'. A group of puritan farmers who marketed
in Royston in the 1630s used to meet afterwards at a local victualling house
to 'talk freely of the things of God'.[84] Some tipplers were proselytizers
for the opposite cause, like the bold Richard Brock of Bunbury in the 1630s,
who brought out 'one great Crucifix of brasse' and set it up in front of
the drinkers.[85] Even if alehouses were more often centres for 'popular irreligion', encouraging rowdiness and drinking during Sunday service time,
the news of political events and religious change was transmitted and discussed here.[86] The country alehouse described by Lupton in 1632 included
'tinkers and poor souldiers' among the drinkers, but at the same time 'either
the Parson, Churchwarden, or Clark, or all; are doing some Church or
Court-businesse usually in this place'.[87] The evidence of ballads and wall
paintings suggests that 'religious' song and imagery had a place in the victualling houses, belying any simple polarity between a godless 'alternative society'
and the church-going 'elite'.[88]

Even the labourer who lived in a flimsy shack that 'blew away', if he
could not afford ballads to decorate his own walls, was likely to come
into some contact with printed or painted 'stories' at the local alehouse.[89]
However, painting on cloths and even walls was also surprisingly common
in humble domestic interiors. Before looking at specific 'stories' we need
to examine the general evidence for the use of decorative painting.

[83] We would not want to exaggerate the image of the alehouse as a centre of culture in opposition
    to the church; as Clark himself says, 'the picture is more complex than a simple transfer
    of functions from church to alehouse might imply'. (*The English alehouse*, pp. 33, 50,
    152, 160.) Another important factor in the rise of the alehouse may have been the trend
    away from residential service, forcing wage labourers to purchase their own refreshment.
    (*Ibid.*, p. 111.)
[84] Margaret Spufford, *Contrasting communities. English villagers in the sixteenth and seven-
    teenth centuries* (Cambridge, 1974), pp. 245, 231–2.
[85] Bennett and Dewhurst, eds., *Quarter sessions records for Chester 1559–1760*, p. 93.
[86] Clark, *The English alehouse*, pp. 157–8.
[87] Lupton, *London and the countrey carbonadoed*, pp. 128-9.
[88] The 'alternative society' is Clark's terminology, although he is careful to present a more
    complex picture than a simple elite–popular divide. (*Ibid.*, pp. 159–60.) Possibly more
    emphasis could have been given to aspects of culture shared by the customers of both
    inns and alehouses (and, indeed, churches).
[89] In 1664 the Hearth Tax for Cambridgeshire noted in the case of a dwelling taxed in 1662,
    'the house blowne away'. (Margaret Spufford, *The great reclothing of rural England: petty
    chapmen and their wares in the seventeenth century* (1984), p. 3 n. 11.)

The real poor man's picture was the painted cloth. Almost none survive: like the clothing of the lower orders, they fell apart through use. They served a practical purpose of keeping out the draughts in the walls of timber frame houses, as the fillings of wattle and daub were prone to shrink.[90] For the second half of the sixteenth century, 56% of inventories in Nott-inghamshire (to pick a county at random) mentioned painted cloths or hang-ings.[91] Husbandmen worth only £20 in total might own 3s. worth of painted cloths.[92] Nicholas Chapman was worth just over £5 after his debts were paid, but still had 'wolle and paynted clothes' worth 4s. A 'halling' (painted cloth for the hall) could be worth as little as 4d.; while four 'queschens [cushions] with pentyd clothes' were valued at 4d. in total.[93] The wealthy John Bagaley who left an estate of £232 owned twenty-two painted cloths valued at £1.10s. or an average of 16d. each.[94] Unfortunately subjects are rarely listed.

Susan Foister has looked at inventories from 1417 to 1588 in class Prob. 2 of the Prerogative Court of Canterbury, which record the possessions of the wealthy classes, including many London merchants. Foister's conclu-sion that 'the majority of even the most prosperous class in Tudor England did not own any paintings or sculpture at all' should not be taken without its qualifying clause that 'they did frequently own painted hangings'.[95] Fois-ter's statistic that only 63 of 613 inventories listed works of art is highly misleading: although she carefully discusses the use of painted cloths, she does not include them in this count unless their subjects are named.[96] Many of the 'costryngs', 'hangings', 'pageants' and 'steyned cloths' may have been plain and functional, or purely ornamental, but we cannot assume this just because the subjects are not recorded. There was generally no reason for the assessor to list the subject of each cloth when 'painted clothes in the

---

[90] F.E. Matley Moore, 'Painted cloths', *Transactions of the Worcestershire Archaeological Society*, 3rd ser., 8 (1982), p. 74.

[91] 37 of 66 inventories. For the century as a whole the figure is 49 of 114 or 43%. (P.A. Kennedy, ed., *Nottingham household inventories*, Thoroton Society Record Series, vol. 22 (Nottingham, 1963).)

[92] Robert Albyn, husbandman, had 'hangynges' worth 3s.4d. in a total estate of £23. (1565–6) William Buller had 'One paynted clothe one bedd hanging with other 2 paynted clothes' worth 3s. in an estate of £20. (*Ibid.*, nos. 72, 74.)

[93] Nicholas Chapman (1563) in *ibid.*, no. 63. 'Halling' owned by Alexander Garthe, worth a total of £8.5s.3d. in 1544; 'queschens' by Agnes Peachie worth £1.17s.6d. after debts in 1558–9. (*Ibid.*, nos. 36, 52.)

[94] John Bageley (1563), *ibid.*, no. 61.

[95] Foister, 'Paintings and other works of art in sixteenth-century English inventories', p. 279. The first part of this conclusion is quoted in Collinson, *From iconoclasm to icono-phobia*, p. 27.

[96] Foister, 'Paintings and other works of art in sixteenth-century English inventories', App. 1, p. 280.

parlar' would do as well, just as '100 small & old bookes' was often considered adequate.[97]

While hand-painted cloths might seem a labour-intensive luxury product, there is evidence of mass production in the complaints made by the Painter-Stainers' Company about the use of stencils. The Company's Charter of 1581 declared it forbidden to make false or deceitful work 'wrought with stencil pattern or otherwise as painted and printed sleight upon cloth, silk, leather or other things ... with work of sundry colours or with gold foil or silver foil that is deceitful'.[98] Stencilling was still a problem in 1626 when the company's petition to the Lord Chamberlain called it 'a great hindern of ingenuity and a cherisher of idleness and laziness in all beginners in the said art'.[99]

The main point of this petition was that other crafts were encroaching on the painter-stainers' territory, including 'Bricklayers, Carpenters, Wyermakers, Boxmakers, Imbroydermakers, Turners, Joyners, Drummakers, Coachmakers, Virginall makers, Plummers, Glaziers, Armorers, Hottpressers' and especially 'Plaisterers' or 'Daubers'. If this was true, it would appear that painting, on a variety of surfaces, was in wide demand. The 1581 Charter required wares to be approved before they were conveyed 'to any fair or market' and forbade the selling of portraits and other work 'in and about the street', suggesting the involvement of travelling chapmen in the trade.[100] Painters were also based outside London, such as Thomas Gammige (d. 1578) of Walden, Essex. His widow's will of 1581 mentions 'all my frames with painted pictures or stories in them, together with all my stones, colours and frames, and all other things belonging to the said art, mystery, science or occupation of a painter'.[101]

Painted cloths were mentioned as the standard household decoration by Harrison in 1577: 'The wals of our houses on the inner sides be either hanged with tapesterie, arras worke or painted cloths, wherein either diverse histories or hearbes, beasts, knots and such like are stained, or else they

---

[97] Kennedy, ed., *Nottingham household inventories*, no. 54. Thomas Bound (1586) in Leedham-Green, ed., *Books in Cambridge inventories*. It was very common to list books in nameless batches. Painted cloths might be tattered from use and black with smoke by the time their owners died, which might be another reason for lumping them together in inventories.

[98] W.A.D. Englefield, *The history of the Painter-Stainers Company of London*, 2nd edn (1936), p. 68.

[99] *Ibid.*, p. 95.

[100] *Ibid.*, pp. 71, 68. 'The King's or Queen's Majesty's pictures' were specifically mentioned.

[101] James Ayres, *The Shell book of the home in Britain* (1981), p. 165. According to Ayres, the frames probably meant straining frames on which to paint the cloths (rather than frames to hang them in). The stones would have been for grinding paints.

are seeled with oke of our owne, or wainescot'.[102] In 1598 John Stow tells us 'now the workmanship of staining is departed out of use in England'. But in the late seventeenth century chapmen were still selling brown osna-brucks and brown hemp roles for 'painting' and for 'ordinary painting'.[103] Stow may have been referring to higher quality cloths for the wealthy mer-chants and yeomanry, who were increasingly building timber frame houses filled by lath and plaster or brick nogging rather than the draughty wattle and daub.[104]

Another commentator of 1601 said that the stainers were being put out of business by imported 'painted Flanders pieces' and that painters now had 'nothing to live on but laying of Oyl-Colours on Posts, Windows, &c.'.[105] The Elizabethans regarded every part of the interior of a room, including timber beams and supports, as an appropriate surface for painting. When wall painting did begin to die out in the second quarter of the seven-teenth century, it was partly because painting on timber frame was no longer considered acceptable: a smooth surface was desired. The extant examples are often found behind wainscot, or covered over with a continuous lath and plaster skin.[106] Perhaps the growing ownership of paintings and prints as we now know them changed ideas about what 'art' should be, and made the use of every odd surface for painting seem old-fashioned and inferior.

For the half-century before this, wall painting has been found in every size and standard of house still standing. Of course the chances of survival have favoured larger houses rather than cottages, especially for dwellings built before the late seventeenth century. Margaret Spufford describes the latter as the crucial period of 'rebuilding' for agricultural labourers and cottagers, when they 'might expect to move into a house which had at least a chance of standing up for more than a generation'.[107] Surviving wall paintings are most typically found in a yeoman's house, consisting of hall,

---

[102] This passage was included in Harrison's prefix to Holinshed's Chronicle (1577), but absent when the text was revised and published on its own in 1587. (Furnivall reprints the passage in his edition: William Harrison, *A description of England, or a briefe rehersall of the nature and qualities of the people of England* (1587) edn.), ed. Frederick J. Furnivall (2 vols., 1877), I, p. 235.) This removal appears to confirm Stow's comments below.

[103] Matley Moore, 'Painted cloths', p. 74. Spufford, *Great reclothing*, p. 112.

[104] Change in house-building techniques pointed out in Matley Moore, 'Painted cloths', p. 74.

[105] Complaint of 1601 recorded in Sir William and Heywood Townsend, *Megalopsychy* (1682), cited in Croft-Murray, *Decorative painting*, I, p. 30.

[106] Information from Joseph Michel (research student of the Courtauld Institute). Panelling was quite usual in early seventeenth-century farmhouses, and was often painted. (Ayres, *Shell book of the home*, p. 70.)

[107] Three-roomed cottages are the most common form of seventeenth-century house still stand-ing in West Cambridgeshire, and they survive in eleven counties of eastern England and parts of Oxfordshire. Unfortunately it seems to be impossible to determine how many are of pre-1640 origin. (Spufford, *Great reclothing*, pp. 2–3; Spufford, *Contrasting commu-nities*, pp. 25–6.)

parlour and service-end, with three chambers above; but paintings are some-times uncovered in dwellings of less than four rooms.[108] In a modest cottage in Chalfont St Peter, Buckinghamshire, there is a panel framed in strap-work with a black-letter text: 'When any thinge thou takest in hand to do or Enterpryse fyrst markewell the fynall end there of that may Aryse. Feare God.'[109] Another cottage at North Warnborough, Hampshire has some very crude stick-men which may represent the journey of the Magi to Bethle-hem.[110] Paintings in 'farmhouses' include a series on the prodigal son (see below) and a crude Adam and Eve (Plate 30, [c. 1627?]) with a black-letter placard: 'As by the disobedience of one mane many weare made sinners so by the obedience of one shall many be made righteous.'[111]

The greater number of wall paintings are to be found in manor houses, in substantial town houses once belonging to tradesmen and in former inns – which are, of course, the dwellings most likely to survive intact.[112] But paintings like the Adam and Eve suggest that the themes executed by pro-fessional painter-stainers in inns and manor houses might have been copied at a lower social level by unskilled locals. Even the simplest Adam and Eve were not created from a blank slate, but took up the conventional pose used in the woodcuts of the 'Biblia Pauperum', illustrating again the importance of printed pictures as a medium for dissemination of visual themes.[113]

The most common form of domestic wall painting was the ornamental pattern; sometimes imitating panelling or textile hangings; sometimes incor-

---

[108] Information from Joseph Michel. A small decorated cottage in Saffron Walden is described by Miller Christie and Guy Maynard in 'Some early decorative domestic wall paintings recently found in 'Essex', *Transactions of the Essex Archaeological Society*, 12 (1922), p. 23. Green Street Cottage, Little Hadham, Hertfordshire is a small four-roomed house painted in geometrical patterns. The smallest houses tend to have patterns (and sometimes texts) without figures, while the 'histories' have more commonly survived in manor houses and inns (see below).

[109] Francis W. Reader, 'Tudor mural paintings in the lesser houses in Bucks', *Archaeological Journal*, 89 (1932), p. 171, pl. XXV. I have been unable to ascertain the precise size of Reader's 'cottages'.

[110] Reader, 'Tudor domestic wall-paintings', p. 263 and pl. IX b (drawing).

[111] The Spring, Meadle, near Monks Risborough, in Reader, 'Tudor mural paintings in the lesser houses in Bucks', p. 170 and pl. XXIII c. The date 1627 is carved on a beam over the fireplace.

[112] Reader, 'Tudor domestic wall-paintings'; Reader, 'Tudor domestic wall-paintings. Part II'; Reader, 'Tudor mural paintings in the lesser houses in Bucks'. Philip Mainwaring John-ston, 'Mural paintings in houses: with special reference to recent discoveries at Stratford-on-Avon and Oxford', *Journal of the British Archaeological Association*, new ser., 37 (1931), pp. 75–100.

[113] Reader, 'Tudor mural paintings in the lesser houses in Bucks', pl. XXIII b.

30 Wall painting of Adam and Eve [*c.* 1627?], in a farmhouse near Monks Risborough, Buckinghamshire.

porating animals, mythical figures, flowers and texts.[114] But of figure subjects, biblical themes were possibly more frequent than any other. Although the survivals do not lend themselves to precise dating, we can roughly trace a slide of decorative painting, during the second half of the sixteenth century, down the 'ladder of sanctity', on the same route taken by biblical drama and printed pictures.

The evidence of inventories suggests that the balance shifted from New Testament to Old in the years soon after Elizabeth came to the throne. The iconoclasm of the later Henrician and Edwardian years did not prevent

[114] Reader, 'Tudor domestic wall-paintings, Part II', p. 245. This has been confirmed by Dr E. Clive Rouse, and by Joseph Michel.

people from having on their walls 'a clothe of christ', 'a table of s. barbara
& ecce homo', 'a story of saynt mathewe in bords' and even 'a story of
ower lady in bords oylled'.[115] But from the mid-sixteenth century, the narrative Old Testament picture was also becoming common. In the 1560s and
70s the old devotional images were almost entirely replaced by items like
a picture of 'Solomon', another of 'Barsaba', 'one painted storie of Adam
and Eva framed', and 'a table of pictures of thold testament'.[116] Towards
the end of Elizabeth's reign, in painting as in prints, allegorical subjects
and portraits became more common than religious themes.[117] By the end
of the century, gospel scenes in domestic wall painting seem to have been
genuine grounds for suspicion. When figures of the Evangelists have been
found from the late Elizabethan period, they turn out to be from the house
of a recusant, in an attic chamber reached by a ladder and trap-door, which
was probably used as a secret chapel.[118]

The four most popular biblical subjects of the late sixteenth century (based
on surviving wall painting and contemporary remarks) come below the Old
Testament on the bottom 'rungs' of the ladder of sanctity. Two were from
the Apocrypha: the stories of Susanna and of Tobias. The other two were
parables: Dives and Lazarus, and the prodigal son. Although these latter
were from the Gospels, they were apparently safe to depict because they
were only stories, containing no historical holy figures.

These four themes appeared on walls, on cloths and on paper. The prodigal son was one of Godet's series of six prints; the other episodes were
illustrated in the woodcuts on the broadside ballads. Thus, not only did
they cross over various visual media, but into oral culture as well. Susanna,
Tobias and the prodigal son were all among the long-enduring 'stock' of
godly ballads, and Dives and Lazarus was one of the 'traditional' songs

---

[115] Inventories of William Buckmaster, fellow of Peterhouse (1546); Robert Pickering, fellow
of King's (1551), in Leedham-Green, ed., *Books in Cambridge inventories*. Inventory of
Laurence Castell, draper (1559), in Foister, 'Paintings and other works of art in sixteenth-
century English inventories', p. 282.

[116] Inventories of Geoffrey Saunders, merchant taylor (1573); unnamed merchant (1562); Wassell Wessells (1575) in Foister, 'Paintings and other works of art in sixteenth-century English
inventories', p. 276. Inventory of Henry Cockcroft, chaplain of Trinity (1567) in Leedham-
Green, ed., *Books in Cambridge inventories*.

[117] Foister, 'Paintings and other works of art in sixteenth-century English inventories', pp.
277, 280. See inventories such as those of William Aunger (1589) and Thomas Lorkin
(1591), in Leedham-Green, ed., *Books in Cambridge inventories*. Aunger owned the Queen's
portrait and the Trinity College arms. Lorkin had maps, 'a picture of veritie', 'a table
of moses'; and portraits of 'doctor Hatcher', Sir Francis Drake and himself.

[118] Quendon Hall, Essex, late sixteenth century. (Croft-Murray, *Decorative painting*, p. 188.)
The estate (then called Newman Hall) was inhabited in the late sixteenth to early seventeenth
centuries by James Wilford, who forfeited two-thirds of his property for recusancy. (G.
Montague Benton, 'Wall-paintings at Quendon Hall', *Transactions of the Essex Archaeological Society*, 18 (1928), pp. 290–2.)

collected by Francis Child.[119] These stories, which are mentioned more frequently than any others, illustrate the fusion of various cultural strands: the Protestant impetus for popularization of the Scriptures, the iconophobic tendency to avoid the more sacred figures of Christianity and the traditional demand for narrative pictures.

The story of the prodigal son was a particularly popular one in taverns and inns during the 1590s, if Shakespeare is to be believed, and a favourite theme of Falstaff's. At the Boar's Head Tavern, Eastcheap, Hostess Quickly fears she will have to pawn 'both my plate and the tapestry of my dining-chambers' because of Prince Harry's visit. Falstaff suggests that her tapestries are out of fashion: 'Glasses, glasses, is the only drinking, and for thy walls, a pretty slight drollery, or the story of the Prodigal, or the German hunting in waterwork, is worth a thousand of these bed-hangers and these fly-bitten tapestries.'[120] A few years later, Falstaff's bedroom at the Garter Inn, Windsor, has been decorated to his taste: 'There's his chamber, his house, his castle, his standing-bed and truckle-bed; 'tis painted about with the story of the Prodigal, fresh and new.'[121]

Pictorial fashions like this may have spread along the network of inns and alehouses, and from these nodal points outward to the manor houses and cottages of the local communities. The story of the prodigal son is painted at Knightsland Farm, near South Mimms, Hertfordshire, in a frieze of five panels dated *c.* 1600 (Plate 31).[122] We can see the influence of Gyles Godet's woodcuts (Plate 32) or a similar series on the same theme, even though the two-dimensional, stunted figures in the paintings have more in common with ballad illustrations than with the classical, sculpted forms of the rue Montorgueil.[123] The closest relationship is in the scene with the harlots, set out of doors, playing gambling games at a table, under the grape-laden arches of an arbour (Plate 32a). The general organization of the paintings follows the same six scenes used in Godet's series, with the compression of Godet's scenes 2 and 3 into one panel. The gracefully mock-

---

119 'Stock' ballads in App. A (nos. 1, 26, 38). 'Dives and Lazarus' is not included in the stock list because there is no record of printed copies in the seventeenth century. However, it was registered in 1557–8 (App. C no. 2), and was included in Child's collection of ballads (Child no. 56).

120 William Shakespeare, *2 Henry IV* [written 1590–1?], II, i, 143–7. The mention of 'waterwork' (water colour) suggests that Falstaff had painted cloth in mind, as painting on plaster was done with oil and varnish. (Reader, 'Tudor mural paintings in the lesser houses in Bucks', p. 125.)

121 Shakespeare, *Merry Wives of Windsor* [written 1597?], IV, v, 6–8. It is not clear whether wall paintings or painted hangings are referred to here.

122 Photographs from RCHM. See also Croft-Murray, *Decorative painting*, p. 29 and pl. 38; Reader, 'Tudor domestic wall-paintings. Part II', p. 248 and pl. XXIII. Knightsland Farm is a two-storey house with attics and a cross-wing, built in the sixteenth century. (*RCHM Middlesex*, pp. 95–6.)

123 Bibliothèque Nationale, Cabinet des Estampes, Ed.5g.rés., fols. 92–4v.

31　Wall painting of the prodigal son story [*c.* 1600], Knightsland Farm, near
South Mimms, Hertfordshire.

ing harlot of Plate 32a is transformed into two irate women with a broom
and a pitchfork in the wall painting; but since there is nothing in the Lucan
parable about the prodigal being driven off when his money is spent, this
appears to be a contemporary pictorial convention.[124] (An edition of the
prodigal child ballad from 1663–74 also depicts an out-of-doors feasting
scene and an irate harlot with a broom.)[125] The painted columns dividing
the Knightsland Farm panels are additional evidence to suggest that prints
in the classical style like Godet's were being copied (Plate 32b).

The Knightsland Farm wall paintings preserve a subject commonly
depicted on other materials which have disintegrated. The prodigal theme
was told in painted cloths, such as the ones owned by a butcher of St.
Helen's, Worcester. The 1605 inventory of Christopher Coxe records a
series of hangings 'in the hall about the said rome conteininge the storye
of the progigall childe'. At Owlpen Manor in Gloucestershire, the prodigal
son appears on a rare extant painted cloth: an imitation tapestry, probably
much more expensive than our butcher's hangings, and apparently imported
'from some unknown foreign source'.[126]

This popular story appears to have been flexible in the purposes it served.
Like the broadside ballad on the theme, the painting could be taken as
a warning to youth not to waste away their money with riotous living.
As a lesson on the vanity of worldly pleasures and the importance of filial
piety, it was an appropriate accompaniment to the moral texts which were

[124] Luke 15:11–32. Perhaps satirical woodcuts like 'Fill gut & pinch belly' (Plate 11) influenced
the portrayal of these man-beating women.

considered suitable for domestic walls. The godly viewer might read the picture on another level, according to the original meaning, as a parable of God's mercy. But for a hardened sinner like Falstaff, the forgiveness extended to the returned prodigal might be taken as a good excuse for debauchery in the meantime. Visually, the tale could be a pretext for a lively scene of loose women, feasting and merry-making.

The parable of 'Dives and Lazarus' offered a similar pictorial opportunity to portray the rich man in his fine clothes at his sumptuous table. At Pittleworth Manor, Hampshire, the story was painted in 1580 in two panels: one of Dives and three other figures banqueting (Plate 33), the other of Lazarus outside the house with the dogs licking his sores.[127] Above is a black-letter inscription:

of Dives and poore Lazarus the Scripture telleth us playne the one lived in wealth the other ... payne. Dyves was well clothed and fared of the best but Lazarus for hunger lying at [hy]s [g]ate/coulde have no rest. Lazarus dyed for lacke of foode: so did the rich glutton for all his worldly good: in hell fyer for ever shall burne because his [remainder of text destroyed].

Depicted in contemporary Elizabethan costume, the banqueting scene must

---

[125] 'A new ballad; declaring the excellent parable of the prodigal child' (f. F. Coles, T. Vere and J. Wright, [1663–74]), Pepys, II, 84–5.

[126] Matley Moore, 'Painted cloths', pp. 73, 75.

[127] Photograph from Victoria and Albert Museum. See also Reader, 'Tudor domestic wall-paintings', p. 277 and pl. XVII.

Howe the prodigall childe, hauing trough his misgouernement spent all that euer he had, is lefte naked, & then being mocked of his yonkers & playe felowes, is turned a praye shamefullye. 3

32(a) The history of the prodigal son, scene 3. From a series of six woodcuts published by Gyles Godet in the Blackfriars, London [1566].

The history of the prodigal son, scene 6.

32(b)

33 'Dives and Lazarus'. Left panel of a wall painting, dated 1580, at Pittleworth Manor, Hampshire.

have presented a self-image to the manor house inhabitants, reminding them in their relative luxury of their duty to the poor. The image of the poor beggar functioned much like a skull on the desk, which warned one in the fullness of life to be thinking of death. In fact, such a *memento mori* appears as a moral text on another wall in the same room, amidst a brocade pattern of pomegranates: 'Thus lyving all waye dred wee death and diing life wee doughte.'[128]

The 'Dives and Lazarus' parable was also a standard theme of painted cloth. Again Falstaff is our informant, describing his soldiers as 'slaves as ragged as Lazarus in the painted cloth, where the glutton's dogs lick'd his sores'.[129] If the viewers at Pittleworth Manor identified with Dives, perhaps there were some who saw the story painted on rough brown hemp in an alehouse, for whom the meaning was rather different: a message of encouragement that the poor would go to heaven and the rich would get their just deserts.

The popular stories of Susanna and Tobias were probably (like their ballad versions) more entertaining than didactic in purpose. Painted cloths of the Susanna story once hung at Vaston Manor, Wootton Bassett, Wiltshire, but have now been lost.[130] At Little Moreton Hall in Cheshire, a frieze of Susanna and the Elders (*c.* 1575?) consists of six panels of black-letter inscription, each followed by a pictorial scene.[131] The inscriptions are a prose *précis* of verses 15–46 of the apocryphal biblical story. The pictorial panels were mostly painted on paper and pasted up afterwards, suggesting 'an artist working from a pattern-book in his workshop'.[132] This 'pattern book' may very well have been a series of six woodcut prints like the ones published by Godet in the Blackfriars, and his compatriots on the rue Montorgueil.

The schemes of story-painting on late Elizabethan walls seem to follow a common pattern: they are told in a horizontal series of panels (sometimes in the frieze), accompanied by black-letter texts; they use bold black outlines, with bright colouring, and their biblical characters are always dressed in contemporary costume. The custom of reinforcing the story in a text may have arisen partly from the need to establish good Protestant credentials: the Elizabethan homily distinguishes an idol from 'a process of a story, painted with the gestures and actions of many persons, and commonly the sum of the story written withal'.[133] At the White Swan Hotel in Stratford-on-Avon, formerly a tavern, are painted scenes from the story of Tobit dated *c.* 1570–80.[134] The scenes are separated and framed by classical columns,

---

[128] *Ibid.*, pl. XVI.

[129] Shakespeare, *1 Henry IV* [written 1590–1?], IV, ii, 25–6.

[130] Matley Moore, 'Painted cloths', p. 75.

[131] E. Clive Rouse, 'Elizabethan wall paintings at Little Moreton Hall', in Gervase Jackson-Stops, ed., *National Trust Studies 1980* (1979), pp. 113–18. Rouse says the paintings probably date from 'late in the third quarter or early in the last quarter of the sixteenth century'. Only fragments of the pictures survive intact.

[132] *Ibid.*, p. 114.

[133] Quoted in Aston, *England's iconoclasts*, p. 405.

[134] From Reader, 'Tudor domestic wall-paintings. Part II', pl. XXI. See also Johnston, 'Mural paintings in houses', pp. 90–3, pls. II, III.

A Pleaſant new Ballad of *Tobias*, wherein is ſhewed what
wonderful things chanced to him in his youth, and how he wedded a young Damoſel that
had ſeven Husbands, never enjoyed their company, who re all ſlain by an evil Spirit.
1030.   To a pleaſant new Tune.

34 'A pleasant new ballad of Tobias', pt 1.

as in the prodigal son scheme at Knightsland Farm. Scrolls with black-letter texts summarize the story: 'Heare tobit tobyas sent to ye sitte of rages for mone that was [lent]', and so on. A less prosperous alehouse-keeper might have stuck the same story on the wall in broadside ballad form (Plate 34).[135] With the strong black lines and stunted figures, the effect of these woodcuts is not unlike that of the painted series at the White Swan. Once again, the same theme spread to private houses: a 1575 inventory of Wassell Wessells (in the Prerogative Court of Canterbury) included 'a storie of Tobias'; while in Essex a mercer who died in 1584 owned 'a little story of Tobias' with other stained cloths.[136]

While these parables and Apocrypha were most common, a few Old Testament themes do survive. At the Black Lion Inn, Hereford, a series of biblical

---

[135] 'A pleasant new ballad of Tobias' (for J. Clarke, W. Thackeray and T. Passinger, [1684–6]), Pepys, I, 488–9. The same woodcuts were already in use on the version printed for Francis Coules [c. 1640], RB repr. II, p. 621.

[136] Foister, 'Paintings and other works of art in sixteenth-century English inventories', p. 276. F.G. Emmison, *Elizabethan life: home, work and land*, Essex Record Office Publications, No. 69 (Chelmsford, 1976), p. 22. Tobias is also one of the subjects of the painted cloths at Owlpen Manor.

scenes illustrated the breaking of the Ten Commandments.[137] This is a post-Reformation adaptation of the medieval 'morality' paintings, where the warning against ungodly behaviour had usually been presented in the format of the seven deadly sins.[138] Jonah and the whale, a popular story in the pamphlet and ballad press, had obvious pictorial possibilities; as did 'Daniel in the Lyons Den', mentioned by Lupton as a popular alehouse theme.[139] The story of Joseph (one of Godet's woodcut series) was depicted on painted cloths, and on a mural in Hadleigh, Suffolk. The elaborate architectural setting may indicate the influence of prints, like Godet's, from the Fontainebleau tradition.[140] Sometime during the reign of James I the Turners' Company paid £28 for five pieces of tapestry with the story of Joseph for the hall.[141]

A number of factors must have encouraged the repetition of the same stories in various different media. On the practical side was the availability of prints as models, and (one suspects) the habits of travelling painters who found it easiest to repeat the same themes. Meanwhile, the more a subject occurred in ballads and plays, and on the walls of inns and alehouses, the more fashionable it became. This recurrence presumably acted as insurance that a given theme was safe from criticism.

The need for a post-Reformation iconography was met partly by the 'safe' narrative biblical paintings we have been looking at, and also by secular and allegorical themes based on the new developments in printed pictures. The wall paintings at Knole in Kent (*c.* 1605) followed the lead of the up-market copper engravings: they depicted figures in elaborate feigned architectural settings, such as the six virtues, and the four ages of man after engravings by Crispin Van de Passe.[142] A tantalizing reference to 'A painted cloth of Robin Hood that hangeth in the hall' in an Essex inventory

---

[137] The paintings date from the middle to second half of the sixteenth century. The scenes, all Old Testament, include Joab slaying Amasa (6th commandment); the sin of Hophni and Phinehas before the tabernacle (7th); King David with a battle in the background, presumably that in which Uriah is slain (10th). *RCHM Herefordshire*, III (1934), p. 227.

[138] In wall painting the seven sins were usually contrasted with the seven works of mercy (Caiger-Smith, *English medieval mural paintings*, p. 54).

[139] Jonah and the whale is depicted on an early seventeenth-century wall painting from a substantial house at Waltham Abbey Cross, Hertfordshire. (Reader, 'Tudor domestic wall-paintings', pp. 255–6 and pl. V.) Croft-Murray (*Decorative painting*, I, p. 187) suggests the early seventeenth-century dating. For Lupton's reference to Daniel, see above, p. 194.

[140] A cloth of Joseph and his brothers survives at Owlpen Manor, Gloucestershire. (Matley Moore, 'Painted cloths', p. 75.) The wall paintings were found at a corn and seed merchant's shop, once a private dwelling built by Viscount Bayning in the early seventeenth century, to which period the paintings date. (Joyce Rushen, inset accompanying David Park, 'Picture books on walls', *Traditional Homes* (February 1987), p. 76.) Another of Godet's themes, the history of St Paul, is the subject of the painted hangings at Hardwick Hall, Derbyshire [*c.* 1600?]. (Matley Moore, 'Painted cloths', p. 74.)

[141] A.C. Stanley-Stone, *The worshipful Company of Turners of London* (1925), p. 136.

[142] Croft-Murray, *Decorative painting*, I, p. 184.

of 1589 suggests that stories from popular ballads, chapbooks and jest-books may have been transmitted visually on the painted cloths.[143]

One theme which did cut across many forms of oral and visual culture was 'the nine worthies', of medieval French origin. Traditionally this pantheon was made up of three pagans (Hector of Troye, Alexander the Great, Julius Caesar), three Jews (Joshua, King David, Judas Maccabeus) and three Christians (Charlemagne, King Arthur and Godfrey of Boulogne).[144] In England the lesser-known of these figures were sometimes deposed by more popular heroes like Guy of Warwicke, Pompey and Hercules. The worthies may have been popularized, like St George, by way of mummers' plays and pageantry. The homely performance Shakespeare gives us in *Love's Labours Lost* also contains a clue about the familiarity of the heroes as a visual theme. Costard chastises Sir Nathaniel after his faulty performance as Alexander the Great: 'O sir, you have overthrown Alisander the conqueror! You will be scraped out of the painted cloth for this. Your lion, that holds his poll-axe sitting on a close-stool, will be given to Ajax; he will be the ninth Worthy.'[145] One of the worthies, Hercules, is in fact the subject of a rare surviving painted cloth, now hanging in the Ipswich Museum.[146] Late sixteenth-century wall paintings of the entire nine worthies theme have been found in Amersham, Buckinghamshire, in a timber frame house which probably belonged to a prosperous tradesman at the time. The heroes, who stand about 4 feet high on nine panels around the room, have idiosyncratic faces which suggest the possibility that they commemorate a local pageant of townsmen.[147] A life-size version was painted at Harvington Hall, Worcestershire (*c.* 1576–8), while the lone figure of Hercules in another substantial Amersham house (early seventeenth century) may once have been part of the series.[148]

The great appeal of the worthies can be explained by the way they integrated various cultural strands of the period: the medieval chivalry of the popular printed romances, the 'Renaissance' interest in classical mythology and the Protestant focus on the historical figures of the Old Testament and

---

[143] Inventory of Thomas Shouncke of Pyrgo Street in Havering, in Emmison, *Elizabethan life*, p. 22.

[144] As listed in Caxton's introduction to 'Morte d'Arthur', cited in Reader, 'Tudor mural paintings in the lesser houses in Bucks', p. 142.

[145] Shakespeare, *Love's Labours Lost* [written 1594-5?], V, ii, 574–8.

[146] An unpublished report by Sally Legg on the painted cloth of Hercules can be consulted at the Textile Conservation Centre, Apt 22, Hampton Court Palace.

[147] Reader, 'Tudor mural paintings in the lesser houses in Bucks', p. 145, pl. X.

[148] Croft-Murray, *Decorative painting*, I, p. 185. Former Church House, Amersham, in Reader, 'Tudor mural paintings in the lesser houses in Bucks', pp. 129–31. Hercules apparently had a life of his own, independent of the other worthies. He appears with the lion in an early seventeenth-century wall painting in Hulcott Manor House, Buckinghamshire (*ibid.*, p. 172), as well as in the Ipswich painted cloth mentioned above.

35 'A brave warlike song', pt 2.

Judaic history. They were entertaining and heroic, while at the same time permeated with a nationalistic sort of religiosity. The moralizing possibilities were brought out in a woodcut book printed in 1584 (from Godet's English kings) which was structured in the emblem-book formula of picture, explanation or history of each character, and 'motto' or moral.[149] An account of the worthies' adventures could be obtained more cheaply in a broadside ballad of *c.* 1626: 'A brave warlike song ...' to the tune of 'List Lusty Gallants' (Plate 35).[150] Here the nine worthies mingle with 'other brave Warriours' including recent explorers like Drake and Frobisher, and the 'seaven champions of Christendome' whose names are repeated in the refrain:

> Saint George for England
> Saint Denis for France
> Saint Patricke for Ireland,
> whome Irishmen advance,

[149] Richard Lloyd, *A briefe discourse of the ... actes and conquests of the nine worthies* (1584).

[150] 'A brave warlike song. Containing a briefe rehearsall of the deeds of chivalry, performed by the nine worthies of the world, the seaven champions of Christendome, with many other remarkable warriours' (f. Francis Coules, [1626?]), Pepys, I, 88–9.

Saint Anthonie for Italie
Saint Iames was borne in Cales
Saint Andrew is for Scotland
and Saint David is for Wales.

These 'saints' have been secularized through their assimilation to the military
spirit of chivalric romance. They were reproduced with stereotyped heroic
physiognomies in an octavo book of copper engravings published in 1623.[151]
However, unlike the worthies, they do not appear in wall paintings: apparently the early seventeenth-century public was not ready for saints on the
walls, even when stripped of most of their miraculous and talismanic power.

One of the results of Protestant constraints on the presentation of sacred
figures seems to have been to elevate classical and English heroes, which
then became confused with Old Testament figures and medieval saints in
the popular imagination. The nine worthies theme in balladry, pageantry,
painted cloth, wall painting and woodcut presents a striking instance of
wide familiarity with classical legends. The influence of 'Renaissance' classical tastes can also be seen in the ornamental schemes which were one of
the most common forms of wall painting, found even in modest farmhouses.[152] 'Antique work', incorporating armorini, mythical creatures,
flowers and so on, was the English interpretation of the Renaissance grotesque.[153] It was also used for the borders of printed books and broadsides,
and for hangings: an Essex inventory of 1589 lists a painted cloth 'of antique
work'.[154]

Iconoclasm was only one factor encouraging the dominance of ornamental
painting. Another may have been the practicality of a simple repetitive pattern for covering large spaces of wall. And the more positive demand for
Italianate fashion, which began at the upper social echelons, could trickle
down as it translated into the desire for a house that looked like that of
one's wealthier neighbours. Were the mythical creatures and foliage only
background decoration, or did they actually mean something to the inhabitants? The appearance of florid antique work together on the same wall
with religious inscriptions indicates that classical aesthetics and Protestant

---

[151] *The seaven champions of christendome* (sold by R. Daniel, 1623).

[152] An example of a painted beam found at 'Slaughters Farm' in Aston Clinton, Buckinghamshire, is given in Reader, 'Tudor domestic wall-paintings, Part II', p. 223. The use of
ornamental painting in houses of the lower social levels has been confirmed by Joseph
Michel, research student of the Courtauld Institute.

[153] Reader, 'Tudor domestic wall-paintings. Part II', p. 223. Croft-Murray, *Decorative painting*, I, p. 26.

[154] Emmison, *Elizabethan life*, p. 22.

36   Printer's device of Christ as the Good Shepherd. Cut for Henry Wykes in 1567.

piety were considered to be compatible.[155] However, some qualms over
the juxtaposition of pagan and sacred images in this period are apparent
in the alterations made by the printer Henry Middleton to his woodblock
device of Christ as the Good Shepherd. Originally cut in 1567 for Henry
Wykes, the image of Christ was framed by an oval border with several
tiny faces, a rampant lion and an elephant (Plate 36). In 1579 Middleton
had these creatures carefully cut out of the block and replaced with inanimate

[155] For example, wall paintings of the late sixteenth century at Vernon House, Farnham,
Surrey, and Loughton Manor House, Buckinghamshire. (Reader, 'Tudor domestic wall-
paintings', pp. 278–9 and pls. XVIII–XIX. Croft-Murray, *Decorative painting*, I, p. 184.)
The Vernon House text consists of the injunction 'SARVE GOD AL [THY?] LYFE LONGE'
and verses likening God's mercy to the 'pity parentes, unto their children beare'.

scroll-like decorations.[156] Here the pagan images were removed; but in the decoration of contemporary houses, Protestant opinion ensured that it was Christ who had no place on the walls, while the faces of the grotesque reigned triumphant.

A house decorated with 'antique work' could happily be inhabited by a mainstream English Protestant of 1600, who might equally happily purchase prints of the Ages of Man and books adorned with figures of Justice and Charity. Yet unless he were an extremely 'iconophobic' ancestor of William Dowsing, he would probably also approve of the wall painting of the prodigal son or Jonah and the Whale at his local inn. This tradition of biblical 'stories', found in inns and even alehouses (the supposed centres of 'irreligion'), seems to represent an aspect of shared culture between the more Protestantized and more traditional groups in society. The same stories recurred on the walls of the manor houses owned by the gentry and yeomanry, in the town houses of substantial tradesmen, and in the lowly broadside ballad. The same iconographical universe was inhabited by 'elite' and 'popular' classes, both rural and urban. The medium of print may have been an instrument of this shared visual culture, as ballads, woodcut prints and engravings influenced the themes portrayed in other crafts, from the mural paintings at Hill Hall to the roughest painted cloth.

So far we have looked primarily at the response of publishers and craftsmen to the post-Reformation cultural climate; at those who used religious themes largely for entertainment or in response to the devotional demands of their public. In the next chapter we will concentrate on the more active promotion of doctrine by committed Protestants, in the form of 'tables' which were partly pictorial, but relied very heavily on the use of texts.

[156] There were blocks of three sizes, two of which were owned and altered by Middleton (Plate 36 is the larger block). R.B. McKerrow comments that the alteration 'was very neatly done and must have cost a good deal of trouble' and marvels that such effort was made 'apparently for aesthetic reasons'. (R.B. McKerrow, *Printers' and publishers' devices in England and Scotland 1485–1640* (1913), nos. 153, 202, 207, and pp. xxxvi–xxxviii.)

6

Godly tables for good householders

At Feering House in Essex, a text from the Geneva Bible (Deuteronomy 6:4–10) is inscribed in black letters on a chimney breast:

> Hear, O Israel, The Lord our God is Lord onely,
> And thou shalt love the Lord thy God with al thine heart . . .
> And these wordes, which I commande thee this day, shalbe in thine heart.
> And thou shalt rehearse them continually unto thy children, and shalt talke of them when thou tariest in thine house . . .
> Also thou shalt write them upon the postes of thine house, and upon thy gates . . .[1]

These commands may have been intended metaphorically at first, but later the Jews wrote this passage on scrolls which were hidden in small containers (mezuzahs) attached to the doorposts and gates as directed.[2] In Elizabethan England, such texts were literally painted on the walls and timber 'posts' of the house: not only this passage, but by extension other biblical verses and moral inscriptions.

This practice had the weight of biblical authority behind it, but there was a more contemporary impetus. Texts which survive in houses date especially from the period c. 1560–80, and can be seen as echoes of the texts being inscribed in churches across the land.[3] Not only the prescribed Ten Commandments, but a variety of biblical passages or 'sentences' were

---

[1] *The bible and holy scriptures* [Geneva version] (1576 edn). Text mentioned in Muriel Carrick, 'Wall paintings in Feering and Kelvedon', *Historic buildings in Essex*, Publications of the Essex Historic Buildings Group, 2 (Sept. 1985), p. 6. The whole of Deuteronomy 6:4–10 is inscribed.

[2] A similar passage, Deuteronomy 11:13–21, is also written. *Encyclopaedia Judaica* (16 vols., Jerusalem, 1971), XI, cols. 1474–7.

[3] Early Elizabethan texts dominate the examples found in Edward Croft-Murray, *Decorative painting in England 1537–1837* (2 vols., 1962); Philip Mainwaring Johnston, 'Mural paintings in houses: with special reference to recent discoveries at Stratford-on-Avon and Oxford', *Journal of the British Archaeological Association*, new ser., 37 (1931), pp. 75–100; Francis W. Reader, 'Tudor domestic wall-paintings', *The Archaeological Journal*, 92 (1935), pp. 243–79.

inscribed in many parish churches.[4] The acknowledged purpose was not only didactic, but aesthetic, to fill the whitewashed spaces under which the idolatrous wall paintings now lay. In the absence of pictures, words themselves could take over a decorative function. In 1561 Elizabeth ordered that the Ten Commandments be painted on church walls 'not only [for] edification, but also to give some comlye ornament and demonstration, that the same is a place of religion and prayer'.[5] The new text-based aesthetic of the church was transferred to domestic interiors.

There were two basic schemes for incorporating texts into the design of a painted room. Brief phrases or aphorisms could be placed in cartouches around the room in a frieze. Alternatively, a longer biblical text or stanza of verse could be inscribed in a panel on the wall or over the chimney breast, framed in an ornamental border. The inscribing of black-letter texts was a special skill, and the preserve of the Painter-Stainers' Company, like any other painting. As usual, there were imposters from other trades. When the company began their weekly searches in 1632 they found a Walter Fenton of Grayes Inn Lane who 'hath panted a Roome with script woorke in Fetter Layne, if not more at Mr. Dewes at the 3 brod arross [broad arrows].'[6]

Excerpts from the psalms were favourite biblical texts, judiciously chosen for a domestic setting, such as Psalm 112:1–4, 'Riches and treasure shall be in his house, and his righteousness endureth for ever.'[7] *Memento mori* inscriptions were common; in three manor houses in Sussex and Surrey are black-letter verses on the brevity and vanity of life, whose similarity and common date [*c.* 1580] suggests the work of the same travelling

---

[4] In 1603, Canon no. 82 prescribed 'that the ten Commandements be set upon the East ende of every Church and Chappell where the people may best see and reade the same, and other chosen sentences written upon the walles of the said Churches and Chappels in places convenient'. (*Constitutions and canons ecclesiasticall agreed upon with the kings maiesties licence in their synode begun at London Anno Dom. 1603* (1604), sig.Oiv.) Visitations often referred to the necessity for repainting the Commandments and other texts. (E.g. *Articles to be enquired of within the diocese of London* (1640), sig.A3–A3v.) Specific examples of this 'sentencing' are given in E. Clive Rouse, 'Post-Reformation mural paintings in parish churces', *The Lincolnshire Historian*, 1 (1947), pp. 11–12.

[5] John Phillips, *The reformation of images: destruction of art in England 1535–1660* (Berkeley, 1973), p. 129.

[6] 31 May 1632. Painter-Stainers' Company Records, Guildhall L.37.MS 5667A.

[7] Excerpts from the Geneva Bible on chimney breast at Bridgefoot in Essex. Another chimney breast in the same house bears Psalm 14:1–2, (Carrick, 'Wall paintings in Feering and Kelvedon', pp. 5–6.) At the old rectory-house at Cocking, Sussex, were texts from the Bishops' Bible: Deuteronomy 6:3 and Psalm 51:17. (Johnston, 'Mural paintings in houses', p. 78.)

limner.[8] A variety of moral exhortations have survived, urging charity or remembrance of God, such as in the guest chamber at the former Crown Tavern, Oxford.[9] The room is painted in a striking pattern of linked arabesques and floral posies, above which are texts in a frieze: 'First of thi risyng / And last of thi rest be thou / gods servante for that hold i best . . .'. This was a wine tavern run by the vintner John Davenant, where (according to John Aubrey) Shakespeare himself used to stay once a year on his way into Warwickshire.[10]

Most of these inscriptions have survived, like other wall paintings, in the houses of the gentry, prosperous yeomanry and substantial tradesmen. However, once again they provide a record of the kind of texts which were common on the ubiquitous painted cloths. These were apparently the chief repositories of proverbial and moralistic wisdom:

> Who fears a sentence or an old man's saw
> Shall by a painted cloth be kept in awe.[11]

In *As You Like It*, Jaques questions Orlando about his love Rosalind:

JAQ: What stature is she of?
ORL: Just as high as my heart.
JAQ: You are full of pretty answers; have you not been acquainted with goldsmiths' wives and conn'd them out of rings?
ORL: Not so; but I answer you right painted cloth, from whence you have studied your questions.[12]

Sir William Cornwallis tells us of moral inscriptions in a small town alehouse: 'not a Poste, nor a painted cloth in the house, but cryes out *Feare God*, and yet the Parson of the Towne scarce keeps this instruction'.[13] This comment might be taken as purely metaphorical, were it not that both painted posts and painted cloths were common features of alehouse deco-

---

[8] Pekes farmhouse, Chiddingly, East Sussex; old Court House or Manor House, Bramley East, Surrey; White House, Balcombe, Sussex. (In Johnston, 'Mural paintings in houses', pp. 79–82.) The text at Chiddingly is typical:

> In lyfe theare ys no suer staye
> For fleashe as flower dothe vade awaye
> this carcas made of slyme and claye
> muste taste of deathe theare ys no waye.
> while we have tyme then lett us praye
> to god for grace bothe nighte and daye.

[9] Johnston, 'Mural paintings in houses', pl. VII. (Now no. 3 Cornmarket, Oxford.)
[10] *Ibid.*, pp. 93–100.
[11] William Shakespeare, *The Rape of Lucrece* (1594), lines 244–5.
[12] William Shakespeare, *As You Like It* (written *c.* 1599), III.ii.268–75.
[13] William Cornwallis, *The first part of Essayes* (1600), 1606 edn, sig.L3v.

ration, and that the painted cloth was almost a synonym for a moralistic saying. The very words 'Feare God' were inscribed in a rectangular panel forming part of an arabesque frieze at Loughton Manor in Buckinghamshire. A similar frieze at Stokes Poges Manor included 'Feare the Lorde' among other such precepts as 'Love thi neighbour', 'Beware of Pride', 'Obey the Prince'.[14] The exhortation to 'Feare God' appeared in the frieze at the Crown Tavern, Oxford, and at the end of the text in a modest 'cottage' in Chalfont St Peter, Buckinghamshire.[15]

The evidence suggests that exhortations like this were widespread, and that even the 'illiterate' would have had contact with large black-letter texts on the walls, not only in church, but also in drinking places, neighbours' dwellings, and even their own. The non-reader's familiarity with these texts must have constituted a form of secondary literacy, like that of the immigrant or tourist who can recognize certain shop and street signs in a foreign language. The ubiquitous phrase 'Feare God' might have had the same mysterious authority for an 'illiterate' viewer that the sacred Hebrew Tetragrammaton had for the more educated Englishman. Perhaps he attributed to it a talismanic power to protect the inn or household from harm. As the text became more familiar, it might (as Cornwallis seems to suggest) simply have faded into the background like 'Home Sweet Home' on a nineteenth-century American sampler.

The categories used by historians of communications do not quite fit these painted texts-for-walls: they are not 'print', but neither are they really 'script'. In some ways they may be seen as extensions of the printing press: they share the same style of lettering, and their widespread domestic use is a reflection of the growing literacy made possible by print.[16] Probably representing the first and most common form in which an 'illiterate' would encounter the written word, these painted texts were an important element in the process of 'typographic acculturation' in England.[17]

If wall paintings and hangings could take over some of the didactic functions we usually associate with print, print could be appropriated for walls.

---

[14] Francis W. Reader, 'Tudor mural paintings in the lesser houses in Bucks', *Archaeological Journal*, 89 (1932), pp. 167, 172.

[15] Johnston, 'Mural paintings in houses', p. 98. Reader 'Tudor mural paintings in the lesser houses in Bucks', p. 171.

[16] Both the typographical font and the painted scripts were based on hand-written forms from the manuscript period. English 'black-letter' type face developed from a late fifteenth-century French 'textura' script. (Philip Gaskell, *A new introduction to bibliography* (Oxford, 1972), p. 17.) However, by the late sixteenth century its association with print was firmly established.

[17] Term used by Roger Chartier in a discussion of the *images volantes, placards,* and other ephemeral print which was circulated and posted up in French cities. (Roger Chartier, *The cultural uses of print in early modern France*, trans. Lydia C. Cochrane (Princeton, 1987), p. 159.)

Not only printed pictures, but printed texts had a potential function in domestic decoration. We have already seen that broadside ballads were a widespread, lowly form of ornament, used in cottages, nurseries and ale-houses. Further evidence of the variety of items, both pictorial and textual, which were attached to seventeenth-century English walls, can be found in a little tract of 1621 on *The art of memory*, written by John Willis, Stenographer. Willis instructs his reader on the creation of 'Repositories': that is, imaginary buildings of specified dimensions, in which 'Ideas' (or visual representations) can be placed for later recovery. The placement of these images within the rooms must be as realistic as possible:

Let the position or situation of every Idea be such as is most agreeable to the thing signified thereby. For those things which we commonly hang upon a wall, or fasten thereunto, are here also in like manner to be used. As if the Idea be some picture of a man; because it is the use of a picture to be hung upon a wal, we must therefore suppose it to hang upon the opposite wall: if it be a Proclamation or Title page of a booke, that it is pasted unto the wall; if it is a new Pamphlet, that it is fastened to the wall with nailes.[18]

Sheets of paper might be pasted or nailed to the wall; they might also be attached to the painted cloths. A Cambridge inventory of 1547–8 lists 'v papers pynned apon the hangynges'; normally such 'papers' were not considered worthy of inclusion in an inventory.[19] Papers pinned or nailed up could not have lasted very long before they became black with smoke from the hearth, or fell apart. But there was a way to make them more durable. In the British Library survives a unique object: a folio sheet (283 × 328 mm) pasted on a wooden board about 10 mm thick.[20] It is not varnished in any way, and is very brown from smoke, with patches stained a darker brown and others burnt. The concept is not unlike that of a horn-book, but the solidity of the wood and the ravages of smoke suggest that this plaque was mounted on the wall of somebody's hall. Printed with woodblocks, it depicts rows of crude little devices (a cock, the lamb of God, a mermaid, etc.) alternating with biblical verses made roughly into couplets: 'The painefull hand: shall rule the lande', 'A vertuous wife gives husband life', 'An evil woman is like a scorpion'.

The origins of this rare xylographic print would be a complete mystery, were it not that several sheets of the same design survive in another form:

[18] John Willis, *The art of memory so far forth as it dependeth upon places and idees* (1621), sig. B2v–B3.

[19] William Robinson, Fellow of Pembroke (1547–8); his 'papers' were valued at 6d. together. Thomas Greenwood of Clare Hall (1546–7) had 'iiij mappes & iij papers [upon the same]' i.e. fastened to the painted cloths in his 'high chamber'. (E.S. Leedham-Green, ed., *Books in Cambridge inventories* (Cambridge, 1986).) The fact that single sheets of paper were not normally considered worthy of listing is illustrated by the complete absence of broadside ballads in seventeenth-century inventories.

[20] STC 12743, 'The painefull hand: shall rule the lande'.

37   'The painefull hand: shall rule the lande'. Xylographic lining paper for an oak
box [*c.* 1630?]

as lining papers for an oak box owned by the Victoria and Albert Museum
(Plate 37). Here we can make out the detail which dates the papers to
the 1630s : the feathers of the Prince of Wales flanked by CP for Carolus
Princeps (b. 1630).[21] Lining and binding papers provided a practical use
for stationers' waste paper, already printed on one side, and they were
sometimes interchangeable with wallpapers. An example bearing Tudor
Roses and the Arms of England (dated *c.*1550–75) has been found both
lining an old box at Longwitton Hall, Morpeth, and adhering to the lath
and plaster at Besford Court in Worcestershire. A wallpaper of *c.*1509
in Christ's College master's lodge was printed on the verso of a proclamation
of Henry VIII, an epitaph on Henry VII, an indulgence, a poem and other
assorted documents.[22] To cover a whole wall with a paper design would
have been a luxury in our period, and impractical on the wattle and daub

---

[21] Department of Furniture and Woodwork (W.51–1926). Photograph from Victoria and
Albert Museum. STC, without this information, suggested a date of [*c.* 1620?].

[22] Charles C. Oman and Jean Hamilton, *Wallpapers: a history and illustrated catalogue
of the collection of the Victoria and Albert Museum* (1982), pp. 12, 10.

surface of cruder homes.[23] But the wooden plaque in the British Library is suggestive about the variety of uses to which such printed sheets could be put. It would have been very cheap to buy a sheet or two of this printed waste paper and paste it to a piece of wood, to a timber post, or directly onto the wall.

The xylographic wallpaper illustrates particularly well the involvement of the printing press in domestic decoration. But any single sheet of print, even if purely textual, could be used as a fixture for the wall. The titles of some of the religious broadsides explicitly state their purpose to be stuck up on the wall: 'The Christians jewell [fit] to adorne the hearte *and decke the house* of every Protestant' (my emphasis), 'Christian admonitions, against the two fearefull sinnes of cursing and swearing, most fit *to be set up* in every house' (my emphasis). Other broadside titles imply that they should be put somewhere where they are permanently accessible: 'A godly meditation day and night to be exercised'.[24]

Another indication that a decorative function is intended can be the use of the term 'table': 'A lokinge [glass] . . . or a worthy table to be had in every good Christian [house]', 'In this table is set forth three principall things . . .'.[25] Tables listed in inventories were at first pictorial: 'j table of Imagerye' (1549), 'two tables, one with the college arms, and the other with Christ' (1550–1).[26] But later we also see tables of words: 'a table with certeyne texts of Scripture olde' (1573), or 'a table of moses' (1591).[27] In Willis' *Art of memory* he describes the use of 'Scriptile ideas', whereby sentences or quotations to be remembered are 'supposed to be written in a plaine white table hanged up in the midst of the opposite wall . . . the frame or border whereof is oake, very broad and chamfered'.[28] The term 'table' was used primarily for paintings in our period, but increasingly for paper images, like Foxe's 'Table of the ten persecutions' or the broadside registered with the Stationers' Company as 'A Table called Christus Natus est with

---

[23] It is generally accepted that wallpaper was a luxury in Britain until the mid-nineteenth century. (James Ayres, *The Shell book of the home* (1986), p. 165.) Oman and Hamilton (*Wallpapers*, pp. 9–12) suggest it might have been common in the sixteenth century, but the evidence comes primarily from sources like Christ's College master's lodge and the halls of the gentry.

[24] STC 23499, 23741.5, 17773.5. Broadsides mentioned in this chapter are listed in App. D.

[25] STC 16802.7, 6170.5.

[26] Inventory of Agnes Cheke (1549); John Erlyche, former fellow of King's (1550–1), in Leedham-Green, ed., *Books in Cambridge inventories*.

[27] Inventory for William Mace of Bishopsgate, London and Royston (1573) in Susan Foister, 'Paintings and other works of art in sixteenth-century English inventories', *The Burlington Magazine*, 123 (1981), p. 277. Thomas Lorkin, Regius Professor of Physic (1591) in Leedham-Green, ed., *Books in Cambridge inventories*.

[28] Willis, *Art of memory*, sig.B10.

a picture in the middle of it'.[29] By the early seventeenth century 'table' was also used in the sense of a systematic list of facts, arranged in columns: 'A table briefly pointing out such places of Scripture as condemne the principall points of popery' (1625).[30] The flexible term 'table' provides an appropriate label for the broadsides to be discussed in this chapter, caught somewhere between decorative 'imagerye' and the schematic arrangement of printed words.

These godly tables do not form a distinct genre in the usual sense of the term. They encompass a variety of categories: pictures, poems, prayers, catechisms, mementos of death, devotional guides and so on. However, these disparate items are linked by a similar physical function. Looked at as texts-for-walls the godly broadsides can usefully be seen as a coherent group despite the fact that examples may be in prose or verse, illustrated or plain, and preserved in the library or in the department of prints and drawings. We have seen how the range of acceptable images narrowed during the century after the Reformation. These 'godly tables' help to fill in a gap in the English visual tradition: they show how the seventeenth-century English Protestant tried to give his religion visual expression using the printing press and the vocabulary of texts and images available and acceptable to him.

A checklist of tables has been drawn up in Appendix D. From searching through the larger collections, and through all single sheets in the pre-1640 STC, I have gathered seven dozen broadsides on religious themes, of which some four dozen have the characteristics of 'tables' for reference, as described in this chapter.[31] Like the woodcut pictures, it is hard to know what volume of trade these survivals indicate. The broadsides are not always distinguishable in the Stationers' Register, or even registered. They have had little chance of survival except by inclusion in haphazard volumes of broadsides like the Society of Antiquaries, Crawford and Bute collections. A few others have been bound up with books, used as end papers for manuscripts, or had their blank side used for account keeping, by no less a clerk than Matthew Parker who recorded the Corpus Christi accounts of 1551

---

[29] Entered to John Stafford in 1637 (Arber, IV, p. 399). Foister's examples of 'tables' in glass, alabaster and sculpture come from the early sixteenth century. (Foister, 'Paintings and other works of art in sixteenth-century English inventories', p. 275.) The Elizabethan inventories in Leedham-Green (*Books in Cambridge inventories*) appear to use the term only for flat pictures, presumably on panel: 'a table of succession of kynges', 'a calendre table', 'A table with verses and all the Colledges Armes' (Christopher Brown 1558–9, Miles Buckley 1559, William Aunger, 1589).

[30] STC 24953.3

[31] Characteristics of 'tables' may include arrangement according to a visual scheme; reference to 'household' use; rules, prayers or advice to be followed 'daily'. Broadsides less likely to be used as 'tables' include propaganda and satire.

on the back of a sheet of excerpts from the 'Books of Solomon'.[32] There were neither publishers nor authors who specialized in 'godly tables' the way they specialized in ballads, yet their *ad hoc* publication may have added up to a significant aspect of the printing trade.

'The good hows-holder' (Plate 38) is one of Godet's woodcuts which was reprinted by Paul Boulenger in 1607.[33] It bridges the gap between the woodcut 'pictures' of the early Elizabethan period, and the godly 'tables' of a later Protestantism. Not only was 'The good hows-holder' a safe, acceptable, image for the early seventeenth-century Protestant, but its moral tone is typical of the era's approach to religion through an appeal to practical, mercantile virtues like thriftiness, and foresight. This is an old and familiar stereotype, laid out in classic works such as Louis Wright's *Middle-class culture in Elizabethan England* (1935) and Christopher Hill's *Society and puritanism in pre-revolutionary England* (1964), but although we now question their anachronistic use of a class framework, there is more than a grain of truth in their analysis of early Protestant tastes and values. The good Protestant was in theory responsible for the education and religious upbringing of his entire household, whether it consisted of just one family or a bevy of apprentices, servants and journeymen. This print is a self-portrait for these new patriarchs, searching for guides and models to help them in their role as spiritual leaders within the home.

Much of the recent research on family history suggests that the Reformation did little to change the structure of the patriarchal nuclear unit, or the principles (such as that of companionship and mutual responsibility in marriage) which governed domestic affairs.[34] However, Patrick Collinson has argued that Protestant doctrine presents 'an ideal type of certain significant features of the Western European family'; that '(in England at least) it was in the form of the Protestant Family that these features became elevated to a high point of explicit consciousness'.[35] Like the many 'conduct books' which appeared in the late sixteenth and early seventeenth centuries, the picture of the 'good householder' was part of the process by which this consciousness was formed.

The good householder was not only the product, but the market for the product. It is the concept of the good household which created a demand for these 'tables', to assert and reinforce the godliness of a household by sanctifying its walls. For some, this must have been a matter of public image and of fashion, like 'Feare God' on the alehouse cloths. But this public

[32] STC 2756.5.
[33] STC 13851. BM Prints (c.2.E.6–38).
[34] Patrick Collinson, *The birthpangs of Protestant England. Religious and cultural change in the sixteenth and seventeenth centuries* (1988), pp. 60–93.
[35] *Ibid.*, p. 93.

The good   Howſ-hol-
                                der.

The good Howſ-holder, that his Howle may hold,
  Firſt builds it on the Rock, not on the Sand,
  Then, with a warie head and charie hand
  Prouides (in tyme) for Hunger and for Cold:
Not daintie Fare and Furniture of Gold,
  But handſom-holſom (as with Health dooth ſtand),
  Not for the Rich that can as much command
  But the poor Stranger, th'Orfan & the Old.

And (thus) to theſe to ſtand full open wide,   For, Theſts right Fuel of Magnificence;
  Hee neither wrings with Wrongs, nor racks his Rents;   As Protean Faſhions of new Prodigalitie
  But ſaues the charge of wanton Waſte & Pride;   Hane quight worn-out all ancient Hoſpitalitie.

PRINTED AT LON-
DON IN THE
BLACKE
FRIERS.

1607.

38 'The good hows-holder'. Woodcut registered to Gyles Godet, 1564–5.
Reprinted [by Paul Boulenger?] in the Blackfriars, 1607.

function was better accomplished by large painted texts, with their permanent platitudes visible from across the room. Printed tables had to be read
from close up; they were more private, and usually longer and more complex.

Many of these broadsides were for householders who took seriously the injunction 'thou shalt rehearse them [these commandments] continually unto thy children, and shalt talke of them when thou tariest in thine house'.

The use of these tables required literacy from only one member of the household. John Taylor's table against swearing 'necessary to be set up and read in every house' was addressed to 'thou that these Lines dost eyther heare or reade'.[36] This suggests that the householder was expected to read the broadside aloud to his family, and to his servants or apprentices if he had any. Bullein's dialogue between Civis and Uxor at the inn depicts the husband in the role of mediator, reading and interpreting the texts for his illiterate wife.[37]

For full-time 'good householders', a printed text on the wall was not meant to be just a piece of information to be read, digested and folded away in a book. It could be consulted, memorized, recited, meditated upon, pointed to for authority. The meaning of the printed object on the wall lay in taking the activities of the household (such as prayer, song, instruction and discipline of children) and freezing them into permanent visual form. This, at least, was the ideal purpose envisaged in such titles as 'A godly meditation day and night to be exercised'.[38]

A prayer is perhaps the example of a broadside whose function was most clearly defined: it was to be read aloud, or memorized and recited aloud; its meaning was in the oral performance. In this it was no different from a prayer to be found in a book, but if pasted on the wall it would presumably achieve a special status. Several of the prayers I have found in broadside form are for protection from the plague: this was a theme of particular concern to the household as a whole, demanding collective attention. This motive of household prayer is reflected in the titles: 'A praier very comfortable and necessary to be used of all Christians every morning and evening, amongst their families' [c. 1603], 'In the time of Gods visitation by sicknesse, or mortality especially, may be used by governours of families' [1607?].[39]

At first these prayers were printed very plainly, but later the genre was taken over by the publishers of ballads and pamphlets, like John Trundle, Henry Gosson and Thomas Lambert, who adorned them with images of death: corpses, skulls and kneeling figures in prayer. 'Lord have mercy upon us' (Plate 39) belongs to a group of five broadsides of that title, of which the first appeared in 1625, and the rest during the plague of 1636.[40] The woodcut showing the city of London as the inhabitants flee, with the angel

---

[36] STC 23812.7.
[37] See pp. 193–4.
[38] STC 17773.5.
[39] STC 20192.5, 20197.7.
[40] STC 19251.3. Others in the series are STC 4273, 20206, 20823–4, 20875. Another plague broadside is STC 19598.2 'The cities comfort'.

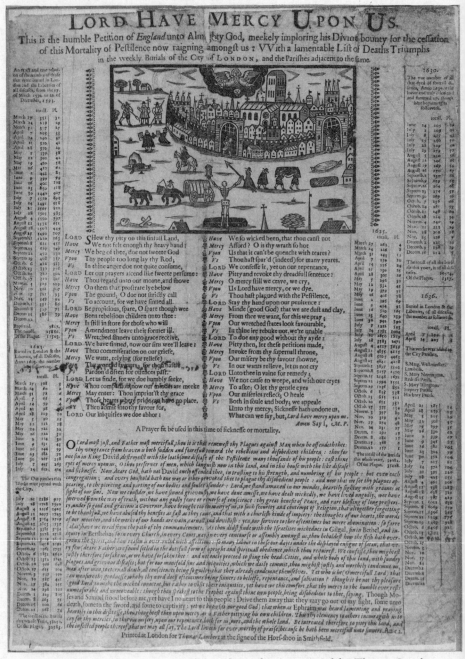

39 'Lord have mercy upon us'. Plague sheet of 1636, printed for Thomas Lambert, with verses by Martin Parker.

of death above and the skeletal figure of death brandishing his spear and hourglass, is typical of broadside ballad iconography; and the verse prayer is signed by Martin Parker, the most popular of seventeenth-century ballad hacks. In the margins are the weekly burial statistics for 1636, with figures from other plague years for the purpose of comparison. The title came, of course, from the method of marking infected houses with a painted red cross and a large sheet of paper printed with the words 'Lord have mercy upon us' and fastened on the door.[41] Hence these broadsides for the interior of the house echoed and expanded upon the paper messages (or pleas) to be seen on the exterior of doomed houses around the city.

Other broadsides in the series included recipes for cures, so that the purchaser's various needs for spiritual aid, medical advice and news or information were all catered for within the one sheet. In another example from 1636, remedies based on walnut kernels, treacle or endive water are complemented with a metaphorical recipe: 'First, fast and pray, and then take a quart of Repentance of *Ninive*, and put in two hand-fuls of Faith in the blood of Christ, with as much Hope and Charity as you can get, and put it into the vessell of a clean Conscience.'[42] The remedy is an excerpt from *Crumms of comfort*, by the publisher of the broadside Michael Sparke, who takes the opportunity to advertise his book in the bottom right corner of the broadside.[43] This kind of medical allegory is the basis of another plain little table (only 1/2 sheet folio), 'The seven soveraigne medicines and salves, to be diligently applied to the seven deadly wounds and sores' (1603). One black-letter stanza is devoted to each pair of opposite sins and virtues :

> Lechery is the seventh sore,
>   that worketh shame eche where:
> Chastity is a salve therefore,
>   but oft this salve is deare.[44]

The medieval morality of the seven deadly sins survived long after the Reformation as an iconographical framework, despite its lack of scriptural authority, and can also be found in woodcuts and engravings of the period. The continued vigour of the sins, which, unlike the decalogue 'made little of obligations of God, as compared with obligations to one's neighbour'

---

[41] F. P. Wilson, *The plague in Shakespeare's London* (Oxford, 1927), pp. 61–4.

[42] STC 20875.

[43] Michael Sparke, *Crumms of comfort, the valley of teares, and the hill of joy* (1627 edn), sig.A11–12v. Ent. 7 October 1623, but no copies survive before the 1627 edn, labelled the 'sixt'. Sparke's remedy may have been inspired by *The kings medicines for the plague. Prescribed for the yeare 1604. by the whole colledge of physitians* (1630), discussed below, p. 291.

[44] STC 17770.7.

confirms the impression given by aphoristic ballads like the 'Christians ABC': the provision of a code of conduct was, for many buyers of cheap print, one of the main functions of religion.[45]

Looking more closely at Plate 39 again, Martin Parker's verse prayer is a word-game incorporating the phrase 'Lord have mercy upon us', repeated vertically down the left margin to provide the first word of each line. Some prayers without pictorial adornment made this arrangement of the text the visual focus of the broadside, as in 'A divine descant' [*c*. 1620?] (Plate 40).[46] The Elizabethans and Jacobeans enjoyed acrostic poems and other word-games allowing the text to be read vertically as well as horizontally. The use of two different fonts, and the decorative border, shows a concern for visual effect, for the text as an image. Yet the title 'A divine descant' comes from the world of song. The expansive couplets form a treble accompaniment to the main prayer, a pleasant diversion. But there is also a pedagogical logic to the piece. The writers of catechisms often experimented with techniques to avoid mindless rote-learning by their pupils; using poetry, or tabular layout, or reversing the natural order so that the catechumen gave the questions rather than the replies.[47] The author of this little piece might have intended the same effect: to jolt his readers out of a parrot-like repetition of the Lord's Prayer, and make them see possible layers of meaning contained within the words.

Broadsides which play with variations on the Lord's Prayer or the Creed seem to have been popular. In 1627 John Okes printed 'A short interpretation of the Lords Praier: necessary for all householders to learne, and to teach their children and servants'.[48] The prayer is in a white-letter column on the left, with black-letter points expanding on each phrase by means of a system of brackets. A preacher from Wolborrow in Devon created a rhyming dialogue between Satan and a Christian, with each of the Christian's lines ending in a successive portion of the Creed.[49] Similar tricks have a history as old as print: under Mary I, there were *Ave Marias* printed

---

[45] John Bossy, 'Moral arithmetic: seven sins into ten commandments', unpublished paper, p. 2. The transition from the moral code of the sins to that of the commandments should not be exaggerated, since the seven sins made frequent appearances in popular print at least until the mid-seventeenth century.

[46] STC 6766.5.

[47] Ian Green, '"For children in yeeres and children in understanding": the emergence of the English catechism under Elizabeth and the early Stuarts', *Journal of Ecclesiastical History*, 37 (1986), p. 423.

[48] STC 16823.

[49] STC 14706. Thomas Johnson, 'Stand up to your beliefe, or, a combat betweene Satan tempting, and a Christian triumphing' (sold by T. Hunt, Exeter, [1640]). Another broadside published in 1641 uses the tactic, printing the Lord's Prayer and Creed in two vertical columns, with expansive couplets to the left of each phrase. R[ichard?] B[raithwaite], 'A paraphrase upon the Lords prayer, and the Creed'.

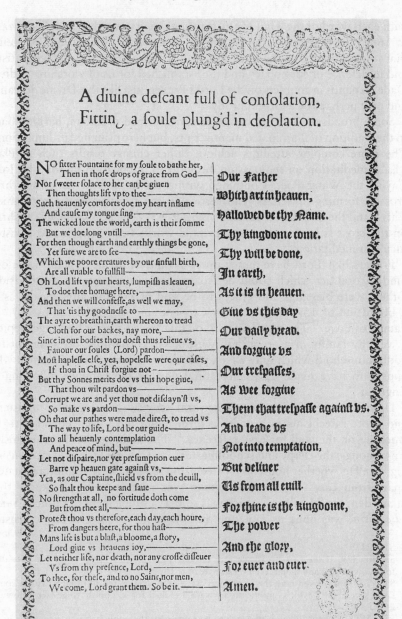

A diuine deſcant full of conſolation,
Fittin a ſoule plung'd in deſolation.

NO fitter Fountaine for my ſoule to bathe her, — **Our Father**
  Then in thoſe drops of grace from God——
Nor ſweeter ſolace to her can be giuen — **Which art in heauen,**
  Then thoughts lift vp to thee——
Such heauenly comforts doe my heart inflame — **Hallowed be thy Name.**
  And cauſe my tongue ſing——
The wicked loue the world, earth is their ſomme — **Thy kingdome come.**
  But we doe long vntill——
For then though earth and earthly things be gone, — **Thy will be done,**
  Yet ſure we are to ſee——
Which we poore creatures by our ſinfull birth, — **In earth,**
  Are all vnable to fullfill——
Oh Lord lift vp our hearts, lumpiſh as leauen, — **As it is in heauen.**
  To doe thee homage heere,——
And then we will confeſſe, as well we may, — **Giue vs this day**
  That 'tis thy goodneſſe to——
The ayre to breath in, earth whereon to tread — **Our daily bread.**
  Cloth for our backes, nay more,——
Since in our bodies thou doeſt thus relieue vs, — **And forgiue vs**
  Fauour our ſoules (Lord) pardon——
Moſt hapleſſe elſe, yea, hopeleſſe were our caſes, — **Our treſpaſſes,**
  If thou in Chriſt forgiue not——
But thy Sonnes merits doe vs this hope giue, — **As wee forgiue**
  That thou wilt pardon vs——
Corrupt we are and yet thou not diſdayn'ſt vs, — **Them that treſpaſſe againſt vs.**
  So make vs pardon——
Oh that our pathes were made direct, to tread vs — **And leade vs**
  The way to life, Lord be our guide——
Into all heauenly contemplation — **Not into temptation,**
  And peace of mind, but——
Let not diſpaire, nor yet preſumption euer — **But deliuer**
  Barre vp heauen gate againſt vs,——
Yea, as our Captaine, ſhield vs from the deuill, — **Us from all euill.**
  So ſhalt thou keepe and ſaue——
No ſtrength at all, no fortitude doth come — **For thine is the kingdome,**
  But from thee all,——
Protect thou vs therefore, each day, each houre, — **The power**
  From dangers heere, for thou haſt——
Mans life is but a blaſt, a bloome, a ſtory, — **And the glory,**
  Lord giue vs heauens ioy,——
Let neither life, nor death, nor any croſſe diſſeuer — **For euer and euer.**
  Vs from thy preſence, Lord,——
To thee, for theſe, and to no Saint, nor men, — **Amen.**
  We come, Lord grant them. So be it.——

40 'A divine descant full of consolation' [*c.* 1620?].

with each word of the 'Hail Mary' forming the first word of a verse stanza.[50] In 1641, the religious variation on the acrostic was such a familiar genre that it was adopted as the form for a satirical broadside against separatists, and in defence of episcopacy and the established forms of worship. 'A divin Oade' expands in couplets on the Lord's Prayer, just like the 'Divine descant', and may perhaps be a direct parody.[51]

Some broadsides tried to create pictures formed of letters, harking back to the tradition of illuminated manuscripts, but here print had its limitations. The more complex attempts achieve rather clumsy results such as Plate 41, 'A meditation on the passion' brought to publication in 1630 by John Taylor the Water Poet. Contained within the horizontal verses are three crosses, forming (in letters read vertically) the speeches of the good thief, Christ and the bad thief from Luke (23.39–43). The popish image of Christ on the cross is here replaced by printed words from Scripture as a visual focus for meditation.[52]

Prayers like 'Lord have mercy upon us' and 'A divine descant' were one kind of oral act which could be frozen into visual form on a broadside. Others were blessings and graces to be said before and after meals, as in a broadside of 1575 produced in Cologne and imported for use by the Family of Love.[53] The woodcut used on this 'benedicitie or blessinge' depicts a wealthy family in a grand hall with classical columns, an image of the godly household which may have appealed to the prosperous yeomen who appear to have made up a substantial part of the Family's following in England.[54]

Domestic catechizing was another oral activity encouraged by ministers, and short catechisms in broadside form might have been intended to be stuck up on the wall for easy reference.[55] The main market for catechisms was amongst the clergy and schoolmasters, and there is little evidence surviving to tell us whether household catechizing sessions were common practice, apart from cases where a clergyman was present.[56] We do know that in Sweden, the 'Hustlava', which was sold as a supplement to Luther's *Small catechism*, was hung as a plaque on household walls. The text consisted

---

[50] STC 23292.

[51] SA no. 329. If the two broadsides are directly related, this might suggest a later date for 'A divine descant' than the STC estimate of *c.* 1620.

[52] STC 23772a.5. Even here the result may have been considered too suggestive for some, since several of Taylor's publication's were attacked for a 'popish' tinge (see below, p. 292).

[53] STC 1858, 'A benedictie or blessinge to be saide over the table before meate and a grace or thankesgeevinge to be saide after meate'.

[54] Christopher Marsh, 'The Family of Love in England 1560–1630' (Cambridge PhD in progress).

[55] SA no. 253. STC 16824, STC 25109.5.

[56] Green, '"For children in yeeres and children in understanding"', p. 420.

A MEDITATION ON
THE PASSION.

This is the day where **I. N. R. I.** ght well content,
Our blessed SAVIOVR did himselfe present,
A LIVING SACRIFICE our soules to free
From sinne, death, hell, to liue eternally.

Awake my soule   *THIS DAY SHAL*   sacred be

With Hymnes and Songs   T o his deare memory;
Whose dolorous   Dea   T H our angry God appeas'd,

And   Lord remember   n o w   If thou bee   pleas'd,

For who	me	he suffered th	V	s, for whom	The	se woundes
By	wh	ich his goary	B	loud so mu	CH	abounds,
For m	en,	vile mé, hartr	E	nding st	RI	pes he bore
With	th	orns his head,	W	ith nailes hi	S	flesh was tore.
His I	ou	elie, Lill		e hands were f	T	retched wide,
To well	co	me death	I	hat entred at hi	ſ	side.
As strea	me	s of bloud guſ	H	t foorth	a	nd thus did dure.
The wor	ſt	that wrath or	M	alice co	u	ld procure.
LORD,	in	to pity turn	E	thine angri	e	brow,
Say	to	my soule	I	am conten	t	ed now.
His death,	th	y life, his wou	N	des,	t	hy balme, shall be;
His pa	y	nefull passion	P	leades	ſ	o powerfully.
O	K	ing, ô Chriſt, th	A	t didſt thy lif	e	bestow
For ſ	in	ful wretches, g	R	ant my	l	ife may show
Such liuin	g	fruites of ze	A	le, of	f	aith, of loue,
To GO	D,	to goo	D	nesse,	an	d the life aboue;
Then I	o	uing, seru	I	ng,	lau	d ing thee at laſt,
I	m	ay of Paradi	CE	ſweet IESVS	VS	taſte.

This moſt excellent inuention was done by an vnknowne Author, and for the worthines of it, *I thought it pity to let it be concealed or ſmothered in ſilence; for which cauſe it is Printed, and I* haue annexed to it theſe following Verſes.

Vpon the good Thiefe.	Vpon our bleſſed Sauiour.	Vpon the bad Thiefe.
Let no man deſpaire, for, one was ſaued.	Death brings life:	Let no man preſume, for, but one was ſaued.

Vpon the good Thiefe.

HE that had long beene a nſtorious Thiefe,
Was in Repentance and in Faith ſo briefe,
That at the point of Death, in little ſpace
He gaind forgiueneſſe by our Sauiours grace:
In death he kept Chriſt Ieſus company,
Expreſſing Loue, Faith, Hope, and Charity.
By Loue and Faith, he zealouſly belieu'd
His ſinnes were pardon'd, and his ſoule repriev'd:
And his fixt Hope did full aſſurance gaine
Of free remiſſion from eternall paine.
He praid, Lord I thy Kingdome haue forgot,
Yet when thou thither comſt forget me not:
But though I ſtil haue ran aſtray from thee,
Yet (in thy mercy) Lord remember me.

Vpon our bleſſed Sauiour.

HE that (of nothing) euery thing did frame,
Was pleas'd to change his glory for our ſhame;
He ſinleſſe was, yet, ſinne for vs was made,
And our three foes, Sin, Death, and Hell inuade,
Ther'i nothing dearer ſince the world began
To God, then is the ſoule and corps of man;
When leproſie of ſinne had vs ore ſpread,
That all were vnto Satan forfeited,
Then Gods bleſt Son came downe, and on the Croſſe
He payd our ranſomes, and redeem'd our loſſe.
And as vnto the bleſſed Thiefe he ſaid,
(When he to him with true contrition praid)
He ſayes to all that doe repent their vice
That they ſhall be with him in Paradice.

Vpon the bad Thiefe.

HE that would liue accurſt, accurſt would die,
Through want of faith his Sauiour to apply:
It was the bodies death he fear'd to die,
Not ſoule and bodies death eternally.
A longer, not a better life to haue
He wiſh'd, when he bade Chriſt his life to ſaue:
This wicked Thiefe did as the Iewes bad done,
Who ſaid (if he be Gods eternall Sonne)
Let him come downe, now from the Croſſe, and w.
Will ſtrait beleeue in him, that is it He.
Eu'n ſo this Thiefe, with damned doubt ſaid thus
If thou beeſt Chriſt, then ſaue thy ſelfe and vs.
But ten times happy had he beene I ſay,
If that ſame doubtfull I F had beene away.

IO. TAILOR.

Printed at London *by* THOMAS HARPER. 1630.

41 'A meditation on the passion'. With verses by John Taylor, 1630.

of Bible verses outlining Christian duties within the hierarchy of church, state and household.[57]

In England, there does appear to have been a demand for tables which helped with the moral and disciplinarian aspects of the householder's job. In 1626 the ballad publisher Francis Coules printed a broadside taken from a pamphlet about the 1625 plague by the popular 'Water Poet' John Taylor (who was always aware of his market): 'A warning for swearers and blasphemers. Shewing Gods fearfull iudgements against divers for profaning his holy name by swearing. Necessary to be set up and read in every house, for the avoiding of oaths.'[58] The broadside enumerates ancient and recent examples of swearers punished, such as a mariner of Ragusa who drowned overboard, 'and nothing but his tongue was only lost'. Presumably it was felt to have the desired sobering effect on the household, since another broadside against swearing was borrowed from the same pamphlet around 1630.[59] Distributed by 'ballad partner' Henry Gosson, it bore the same direction 'to be set up in every house'.

Other broadsides dealt more generally with social behaviour and etiquette. 'Table observations' [*c.* 1615] was a list of rules such as 'Pick no quarrels', 'Tell no long tales' and 'Use no long meals'.[60] This was the prototype for 'King Charles's Twelve Good Rules' which were to be posted in many an eighteenth-century farmhouse.[61] Similar advice was to be found in a table of metrical aphorisms based on the 'Books of Solomon' [*c.* 1550]:

> Use not at borde
> To rayle in worde
> Of them that be absent,
> Flee depravyng
> And backebytyng
> No tyme to that consent.[62]

The pithy moral advice accredited to the wise sage was particularly appealing in this period, and was later made into the popular ballad 'Solomon's sentences'.[63] Other ballad devices, such as the parental persona of 'An hundred godly lessons that a mother on her death-bed gave to her children', were

---

[57] Egil Johansson, 'The history of literacy in Sweden', in Harvey J. Graff, ed., *Literacy and social development in the West: a reader* (Cambridge, 1981), p. 157.

[58] STC 23812.7. Reprinted from STC 23754, *The fearefull summer: or Londons calamity, the countries courtesy, and both their misery* (Oxford, 1625).

[59] STC 23741.5. 'Christian admonitions, against the two fearfull sinnes of cursing and swearing'.

[60] STC 23634.7.

[61] Morris Martin, 'The case of the missing woodcuts', *Print Quarterly*, 4 (1987), pp. 353–5.

[62] STC 2756.5. Excerpts are based on Proverbs, Ecclesiastes and Wisdom.

[63] 'Solomons sentences' [*c.* 1615], Collmann no. 84. Ent. to Edward White 1 August 1586.

also used in tables like 'The counsell of a father to his sonne, in ten severall precepts. Left as a legacy at his death'.[64]

Of course, the ballads themselves could also function as 'tables': the line between these two genres was very fine. Sometimes only the direction 'to the tune of –' distinguishes a ballad, and even then this did not preclude its use as a decorative reference text. The ballad was the most common form of godly table, and the aphoristic ballad was particularly suited for this role. Plate 42 is a ballad which, although printed very plainly without woodcuts or adornment, is organized along fundamentally visual lines: that is, alphabetically. 'A right godly and Christian A,B,C' was one of the aphoristic stock ballads published in 1625 for 'partner' Henry Gosson. It was a short step from the 'Christian ABC' to 'Finch his alphabet' (Plate 43), published by another 'partner' John Wright.[65] This broadside uses the same idea, but strips the ABC of its tune and takes it one more step in visualization by adding a picture of the godly in prayer. The primary purpose is no longer musical but visual. This intent is expressed in the subtitle 'A godly direction, fit to be *perused* of each true Christian'. It has lost some of the rigour of the song : the Christians' ABC had a consistent voice, using a fierce imperative ('Arise!' 'Beware!' 'Confesse!'). Finch's alphabet, on the other hand, is a hodgepodge of godly sayings; some addressed to the reader, some appealing to God, some making objectified moral statements. It has been divorced from the coherent voice of an oral performance. However, it still draws from the oral tendency to encapsulate wisdom in proverbs and clichés.

The ABC format was also used by Hendrik Niclas on another Family of Love broadside from Cologne.[66] There is one pithy sentence for each letter, and an introduction addressed to the Family's children:

O Yee Youngones, have a good regarde unto these Sentences, and take the Instruction of those-same effectually to Heart. Enterprise not, nor-yet take; in any-wyse; upon you, to reade many or great Bookes, er-ever yee have well exercised you in the A.B.C., and can perfectly spell all Woordes, to an apt Sentence.

There is a woodcut of school children in a classroom, and Niclas refers to the broadside as 'this Crosse-rowe', suggesting that it could be used like a hornbook, perhaps even mounted on horn or wood.

The practical rules and values and ABCs were predicated on a larger religious framework, the teaching of which was also the job of the good

---

[64] STC 4900.5, William Cecil, Baron Burghley, 'The counsell of a father' (1611).

[65] RB orig. I, 492. STC 10869.5

[66] STC 18548.5, 'All the letters of the a.b.c. by every sondrye letter whereof, ther is a good document set-fourth and taught, in ryme' ([N. Bohmberg, Cologne], 1575). Reprint from Euing no. 1.

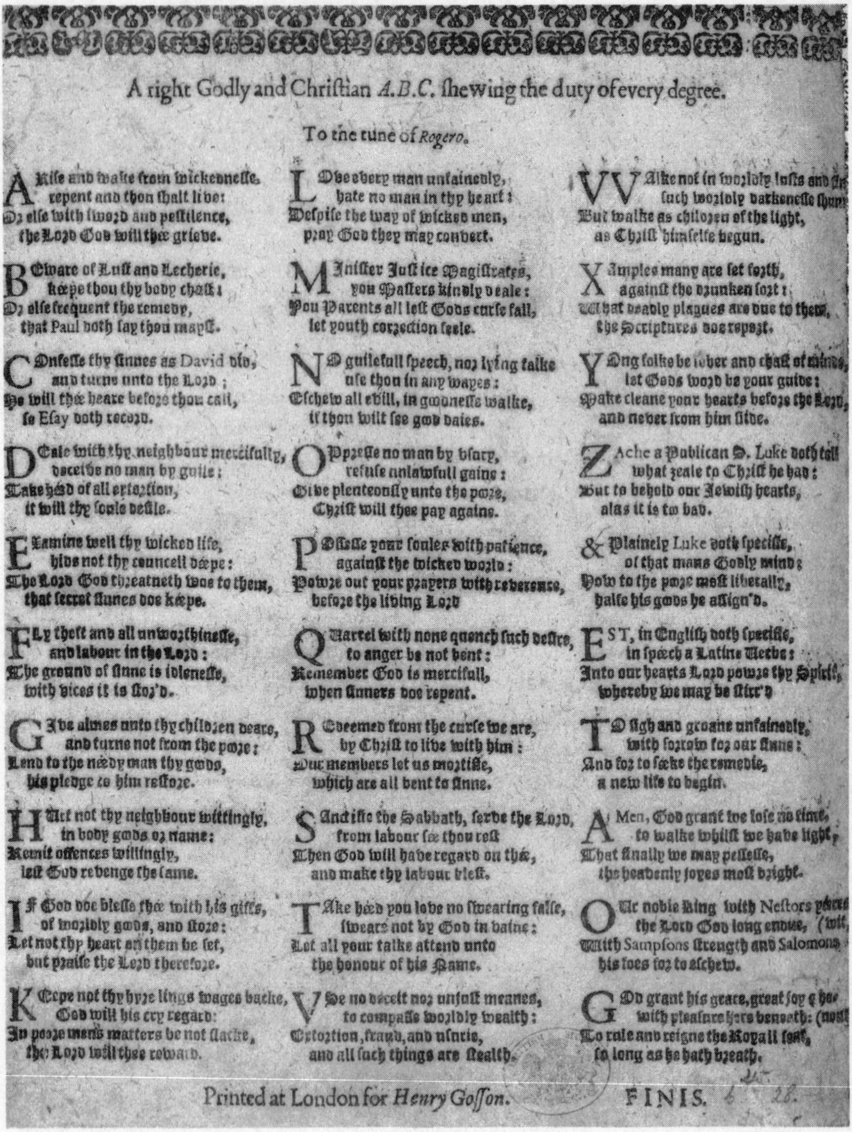

A right Godly and Chriſtian *A.B.C.* ſhewing the duty of every degree.

To the tune of *Rogero*.

ARiſe and wake from wickedneſſe,
repent and thou ſhalt live:
Or elſe with ſword and peſtilence,
the Lord God will thee grieve.

BEware of Luſt and Lecherie,
keepe thou thy body chaſt:
Or elſe frequent the remedy,
that Paul doth ſay thou mayſt.

COnfeſſe thy ſinnes as David did,
and turne unto the Lord;
He will thee heare before thou call,
ſo Eſay doth record.

DEale with thy neighbour mercifully,
deceive no man by guile:
Take heed of all extortion,
it will thy ſoule defile.

EXamine well thy wicked life,
hide not thy councell deepe:
The Lord God threatneth woe to them,
that ſecret ſinnes doe keepe.

FLy theft and all unworthineſſe,
and labour in the Lord:
The ground of ſinne is idleneſſe,
with vices it is ſtor'd.

GIve almes unto thy children deare,
and turne not from the poore:
Lend to the needy man thy goods,
his pledge to him reſtore.

HUrt not thy neighbour wittingly,
in body goods or name:
Remit offences willingly,
leſt God revenge the ſame.

IF God doe bleſſe thee with his gifts,
of worldly goods, and ſtore:
Let not thy heart on them be ſet,
but praiſe the Lord therefore.

KEepe not thy hirelings wages backe,
God will his cry regard:
In poore mens matters be not ſlacke,
the Lord will thee reward.

LOve every man unfainedly,
hate no man in thy heart:
Deſpiſe the way of wicked men,
pray God they may convert.

MIniſter Juſtice Magiſtrates,
you Maſters kindly deale:
You Parents all leſt Gods curſe fall,
let youth correction feele.

NO guilefull ſpeech, nor lying talke
uſe thou in any wayes:
Eſchew all evill, in goodneſſe walke,
if thou wilt ſee good daies.

OPpreſſe no man by uſury,
refuſe unlawfull gains:
Give plenteouſly unto the poore,
Chriſt will thee pay againe.

POſſeſſe your ſoules with patience,
againſt the wicked world:
Powre out your prayers with reverence,
before the living Lord

QUarrel with none quench ſuch deſire,
to anger be not bent:
Remember God is mercifull,
when ſinners doe repent.

REdeemed from the curſe we are,
by Chriſt to live with him:
Our members let us mortifie,
which are all bent to ſinne.

SAnctifie the Sabbath, ſerve the Lord,
from labour ſee thou reſt
Then God will have regard on thee,
and make thy labour bleſt.

TAke heed you love no ſwearing falſe,
ſweare not by God in vaine:
Let all your talke attend unto
the honour of his Name.

VSe no deceit nor unjuſt meanes,
to compaſſe worldly wealth:
Extortion, fraud, and uſurie,
and all ſuch things are ſtealth.

VVAlke not in worldly luſts and ſin
ſuch worldly darkeneſſe ſhun:
But walke as children of the light,
as Chriſt himſelfe begun.

XAmples many are ſet forth,
againſt the drunken ſort:
What deadly plagues are due to them,
the Scriptures doe report.

YOng folke be ſober and chaſt of minde,
let Gods word be your guide:
Make cleane your hearts before the Lord,
and never from him ſlide.

ZAche a Publican S. Luke doth tell
what zeale to Chriſt he had:
But to behold our Jewiſh hearts,
alas it is too bad.

& Plainely Luke doth ſpecifie,
of that mans Godly mind:
How to the poore moſt liberally,
halfe his goods he aſſign'd.

EST, in Engliſh doth ſpecifie,
in ſpeech a Latine Verbe:
Into our hearts Lord powre thy Spirit,
whereby we may be ſtirr'd

TO ſigh and groane unfainedly,
with ſorrow for our ſinnes:
And for to ſeeke the remedie,
a new life to begin.

AMen, God grant we loſe no time,
to walke whilſt we have light,
That finally we may poſſeſſe,
the heavenly joyes moſt bright.

OUr noble King with Neſtors yeeres
the Lord God long endue, (wit,
With Sampſons ſtrength and Salomons
his foes for to eſchew.

GOd grant his grace, great joy & hea-
with pleaſure here beneath: (lth
To rule and reigne the Royall ſeat,
ſo long as he hath breath.

Printed at London for *Henry Goſſon*. FINIS.

42 The 'Christians ABC'. Printed for Henry Gosson [1625].

householder. Many of the godly tables tried to give visual expression to the more abstract structure of salvation and damnation. In these broadsides

Finch his Alphabet, or,

A Godly direction, fit to be perused of each true Christian.

ADAM our Father being the first man,
Through EVE his wife the which vile sinne began:
But God of his mercie thought it very good,
We should be sau'd through Christ our Sauiours blood.

BEtimes in morning when thou do'st awake,
Vnto the Lord see thou thy prayers make:
And after that then goe to thy Vocation,
This is a way that leadeth to saluation.

COmfort of comforts, none that I doe finde,
So great as for to haue a constant minde:
Trusting in God, and in his onely Sonne,
Comfort of comforts like to this is none.

DEath as a Sergeant commeth vnto all,
Prepare thy selfe therefore against he call:
For he that is prepared well to dye,
Shall liue with Christ in heauen eternally.

ENuie thou not to see thy friend doe well,
Enuie is a fiend that leadeth soules to hell:
Through enuie Cain did slay Abell his brother,
When on the earth there was not found another.

FLie thou from sinne, and eke from fond delight,
And feare the Lord of heauen both day and night:
For he that onely God the Lord doth feare,
No euill euer to him may appeare.

GIue laud vnto the Lord of heauen on high,
Which made the earth, the sea, and eke the skie:
And men he made him onely for to serue,
Then from his statutes see thou doe not swerue.

HAue mercy Lord on me I doe thee pray,
And eke conduct me in thy holy way:
And let thy precepts alwayes be to mee,
As sweet as euer hony from the Bee.

IN thee, O Lord, I onely put my trust,
For thou, O Christ, art onely true and iust:
There is no other God I know but thee,
In whom I onely trust saued to be.

KNowledge a vertue is most excellent,
If to know Christ the mind be onely bent:
But not to know him, and know all beside,
No goodnesse to the soule there can betide.

LOue God, in him put all thy trust and stay,
Both day and night vnto him doe thou pray:
And be not idle either day or night,
So shalt thou please the Lord of heauen aright.

MArke well my words, and ponder in your minde,
And then no doubt but you shall comfort finde:
Put trust in Christ who for mankinde did die,
So may'st thou liue with him continuallie.

NO man there is that two Masters can serue,
To one he cleaues, from other he will swerue:
He that on Mammon setteth his delight,
He cannot serue the Lord of heauen aright.

OMnipotent Lord, send to me thy grace,
Here in this life, in heauen a dwelling place:
And when my soule depart from body is,
Grant me sweet Christ to liue with thee in blisse.

PVt all thy trust and confidence in God,
And he will guide thee with his holy rod:
For he that trusts in him, and to him pray,
Shall liue in blisse with him another day.

QVit thou thy selfe alwayes from worldly care,
And see that thou the Lord of heauen doe feare:
For he that feares the Lord of heauen aright,
Shall liue eternall with the Lord of might.

REmember man that thou art borne to die,
And not to liue on earth eternallie:
Then liue on earth while here thou doe remaine,
Though being dead, to liue with Christ againe.

SInne not, but stand in awe of God the Lord,
Who made the heauen, the earth, and sea by word:
The skie, the Sunne, the Moone, the Starres also,
And euery creature that on earth doe goe.

TRust thou in God the Father of all might,
And pray vnto his Sonne both day and night:
Intreat his Spirit may thee alwayes guide,
So from his statutes thou shalt neuer slide.

VNto the Lord see that thou call and crie,
So mayest thou liue with him eternallie:
He is the Iudge that Widowes cause doth take,
And fatherlesse, when moane to him they make.

VVIsedome in man is a most precious thing,
When God did say to Solomon the King,
Aske what thou wilt, and I will giue to thee,
Wisedome (good Lord) grant wisedome vnto me.

X Erxes for his beastlinesse he had great blame,
Galba for his vertue he did get much fame:
affirmes that nothing is more pure
In man, then for in vertue to endure.

YOuth in it selfe vaine glory oft doth showe,
But age experience brings, whereby men know,
The idle follies that wilde youth doth bring,
Which makes them sigh when they may sit and sing.

ZEale mixt with faith, and in one heart combind,
Doth please the Lord, and comforteth mans mind.
So to conclude (with zeale) I make an end,
Zeale ioyn'd with Faith vnto the Soule is friend.

FINIS.

Printed at London for *Iohn Wright*, and are to be sold at his Shop in Gilt-spur-street.

43 'Finch his alphabet'. Printed for John Wright [*c.* 1635?].

one can sense a drive to encompass as much of Christian wisdom as possible within the boundaries of the page; to package it neatly into lists, diagrams, memorizable sayings, polarities of good and bad.

This sort of schematizing was by no means new; medieval man had the seven deadly sins, the fourteen holy helpers, the seven penitential psalms and numerous other aids to the memory. But with the advent of print this schematizing could now be frozen into a permanent visual form which was infinitely reproducible, and with the spread of literacy the schematizer had access to a potentially vast audience.[67] Some of these tables are less 'popular' than others, demanding quite a high level of religious education before they can be deciphered. However, by looking at these together with the simpler broadsides, one gains a sense of the mental habits from which they both spring. A metaphor used from Gregory the Great onwards had implied that pictures were only good if they could be read like books.[68] Now some Protestants tried to make pictures become books: one-page books, filled primarily with spatial arrangements of words; which were, after all, superior to images.

At the simplest level, 'Come ye blessed, &c. Goe ye cursed, &c'. [1628?] (Plate 44) represents the opposition of good and evil using the framework of the seven deadly sins.[69] Down the right border, cameo scenes illustrating the sins form (as the subtitle tells us) 'seaven dangerous steps descendant to destruction'. On the left, the opposite virtues make up 'the seavenfold ladder ascending to everlasting Felicitie'. Across the top, a woodcut depicts the Day of Judgement when these sins and virtues will be measured, with the chosen saints clustered in the clouds around the central figure of Christ, and the wicked souls fleeing into the mouth of hell at the right. Across the bottom, two armies do battle carrying banners representing the virtues and sins: the wicked army is being chased into the mouth of hell. In the bottom left corner under 'chastitie' we see a tiny portrait of the good household whose walls might be graced with this broadside: 'One spotlesse couple with your tender young' on their way to church. Perhaps the broadside was commissioned by the publisher, William Wilson, whose later almanacs and chapbooks show contact with the popular end of publishing.[70] In any case, he entrusted its sale to Francis Grove, a ballad and chapbook publisher

---

[67] David Cressy has demonstrated marked improvements in the ability to sign amongst the generation schooled between 1560 and 1580, with a 'second phase' of progress beginning in James' reign. (David Cressy, *Literacy and the social order. Reading and writing in Tudor and Stuart England* (Cambridge, 1980), pp. 168–71.)

[68] *Sancti Gregorii Magni*, vol. 3, Patrologiae Cursus Completus, ed. Jacques Paul Migne, vol. 77 (Paris, 1849), cols. 1027–8.

[69] STC 6798.7. The STC date [*c.* 1635?] will be corrected to [1628?] in vol. 3 Addenda. (Information from Katherine Pantzer.)

[70] Wing A3119, A2181, B874, A1554.

44 'Come ye blessed, &c. Goe ye cursed, &c.' [1628?]. Sold by Francis Grove.

with access to a wide popular audience via the pedlars' network centring
on the market at West Smithfield outside Newgate.[71]

'A godly meditation day and night to be exercised' (Plate 45) is a more
expensive copper engraving. But its artist, William Rogers, seems to have
been an unknown; and it is described by Hind, the expert on English engraving, as 'a second-rate production, probably done for a poorer clientele
of puritan caste'.[72] After 1640 it was sold by Peter Stent, who normally
charged between 6d. and 1s. for an oblong royal sheet.[73] This would have
made it accessible to the middling merchants and craftsmen in the city,
but it is unlikely it was peddled in the countryside. Like the 'Come ye blessed'
broadside, it expresses the polarity of good and evil, together with a related
theme, the passage of time. The basic arrangement is not unlike the other
broadside. The forces of good and evil in this world are represented by
the just and wicked merchants (on the left and right) who present possible
reflections of the viewer. Good and evil of the next world is visualized
as heaven and hell (at the top and bottom). The text is also organized
within this time framework: the viewer is exhorted to know things past,
understand things present, foresee things future. He is, more specifically,
to ponder over 'tyme lost', 'the shortness of lyfe' and 'the day of death
drawing neer'. If he exercises this meditation 'day and night' as he is
instructed, he will become hypersensitive to the movement of time. The
'meditation' gains its meaning as a measure of the acts he has performed
in the hours since it last was viewed.

When it was first engraved around 1600, this plate (like the last broadside)
had an image of Christ in glory at the top.[74] However, at some stage
this must have been considered too idolatrous, for it was removed by the
time John Overton printed this impression after the Restoration. It was
replaced by the safer triangle for the Trinity with the word 'eternity' inscribed
on it. Apart from this original slip, the whole production has avoided any
overt representations of biblical figures, depicting instead abstract religious
concepts in harmless emblematic form. At the four corners are female
personifications of the cardinal virtues; on the right, the 'wicked man' is
shown surrounded by emblems of sin: the peacock for pride; the goat for
lechery; the dog, ass and boar for folly, sloth, gluttony and other undesirable
qualities.

The text is organized by the peculiar use of the bracket, very much in
vogue at the time this was published. This habit was particularly influenced

[71] The Smithfield market was well placed for carriers going west or north-west from the
city. (Margaret Spufford, *Small books and pleasant histories. Popular fiction and its readership in seventeenth-century England* (1981), map 1 on p. 114.)

[72] STC 17773.5. Hind, I, p. 259.

[73] Alexander Globe, *Peter Stent, London printseller c. 1642–65* (Vancouver, 1985), p. 28.

[74] *Ibid.*, p. 117.

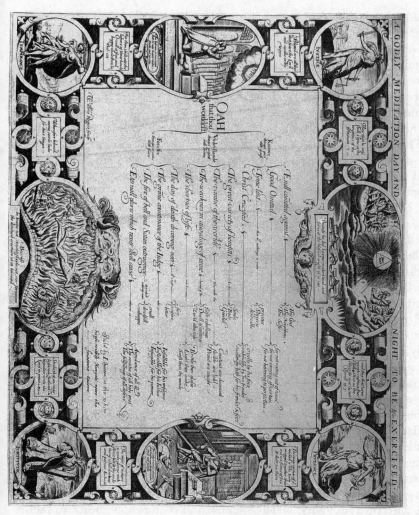

45 'A godly meditation day and night to be exercised'. Engraving by William Rogers [c. 1600]. This impression sold by John Overton, late seventeenth century.

by Ramism; the logical system invented by Peter Ramus in Paris using the method of bracketed tables of dichotomies, moving in stages from the most universal concept to the most particular.[75] The table reproduced here is certainly not Ramism; the brackets are merely used to break up the sentences into easily memorized chunks, and to make possible the movement of a given statement into various different channels, rather than in a simple straight line. However, it does indicate the widespread pedagogical appeal of these tidy bracketed tables.

The English were known for being particularly unsophisticated in their use of Ramism, already a rather unsophisticated method in itself. We are told that Richard Mather read Ramus at Brasenose, Oxford, for a few months 'with great relish and satisfaction, and thereupon quit the university for good to carry his knowledge of "logic" into his ministerial work'.[76] The result of similar enthusiasm can be seen in a number of complex, convoluted tables like 'A synopsis of theology or divinity' produced by Francis Roberts MA in 1645 'for the benefit of his flock'.[77] Some of these dealt with specialized and esoteric theological questions, but as we can see in the 'Godly meditation', the habit of using these bracketed flow-charts percolated down into simpler broadsides for an audience of 'middling' wealth and 'middling' education.

It seems unlikely that those at the bottom of the educational ladder, with only basic literacy, would make much of these schematic tables. Yet when Charles Gybbon put together 'A premonition for every disposition' (1588) (Plate 46), he envisaged it would be 'a comfort for poore-men' and 'for the profit of all if it be well applied'.[78] These comments may be suggestive about the misdirection of didactic zeal when reformers no longer wrote ballads or theatrical interludes. There are no woodcuts to attract a popular audience, although the table seems to be conceived of as a picture. Pictorial terms are used for some of the sections: 'A Mappe of man's miserie', 'A Mirror of Gods justice'. All of the author's or publisher's visual creativity has gone into arranging the brackets and exploiting the possibilities of some ten different type fonts, which organization is somehow meant to render the scriptural precepts more accessible.

According to the work of Walter Ong, Ramism (and its precursors and imitations) were particularly telling symptoms of the gradual formation of literate mental habits in the West, which reduced words and concepts to

---

[75] Walter Ong, *Ramus, method and the decay of dialogue* (Cambridge, Mass., 1958), p. 302.

[76] *Ibid.*, p. 303.

[77] Harvard, Bute Broadsides, A33.

[78] STC 11819.5. Charles Gybbon (fl. 1589–1604) was a miscellaneous writer whose works dealt with religious doctrine, marriage and inheritance, taxation. (STC 11816 to 11821.)

A premonition for euery diſpoſition:

Publiſhed for the profit of all if it be well applied.
By *Charles Gybbon.*

TO THE READER.

Art thou { Inſolent or ignorant of thy eſtate. / Intiſed, or enclined to euill. / Intangled, or ouercome of euill. } beholde { Thy apparant miſerie. / Gods pronounced iudgement. / Gods promiſed mercie. } And it may { Humble thee in preſuming. / Terrifie thee in attempting. / Comfort thee in diſpayring.

A Mappe of mans miſerie.	*A Mirror of Gods iuſtice.*	*A mention of his mercie.*
I know mine owne wickednes, and my ſinne is euer before me. *Pſal. 51. 3.*	If thou ò Lorde ſtraightly markeſt iniquities who ſhalbe ſaued. *Pſal. 130. 3.*	According to the multitude of thy mercies put away mine iniquities. *Pſal. 51. 1.*

| Our life we leade Gods lawes to learne, with will to do the ſame: | We read to know, and know to liue, and liue to prayſe Gods name. |

A caueat for Rich-men:
Be rich in Faith.

¶ To the ende you may vſe and beſtowe your goods to your owne good, and thy glory that gaue them, conſider of theſe ſentences pronounced againſt ſuch as abuſe them. And

¶ Speciall cauſes to dehort you from ſuch greedines in gathering, and gripleneſs in keeping your goods.

1. The deſire of money is the rote of all euill. 1. Tim. 6. 10.
2. A mans life ſtandeth not in his gods though he haue abundaunce. Luk. 12. 15
3. When he dieth he ſhall carrie nothing awaie with him. Pſalm. 49. 14. 17
4. His gods will not auaile him in the day of wrath. Prou. 11. 4.

A comfort for Poore-men:
Be poore in Spyrite.

¶ To the ende thou maiſt beare thy poouerty more patientlie, enter into this conſideration.

1. Haſt thou not a houſe { Our Sauiour Chriſt himſelfe had not whereon to reſt to hold thy head in. / his head. *Math. 8. 20.*

AT LONDON,
Printed by I. C. for Thomas Gubbin.
Anno. Dom. 1588.

46   'A premonition for every disposition'. By Charles Gybbon, 1588.

space on the page.[79] Ramism is very different from another type of sixteenth-century mental process, the 'memory theatre'. This technique depended on the visual imagination, with symbolic figures placed around an invented building.[80] Frances Yates claimed that Ramism (which substituted a mnemonic system based on the layout of a page) was successful partly because it 'provided a kind of inner iconoclasm, corresponding to the outer iconoclasm'.[81] That is, it smashed the figures in the niches of the memory theatre.

The plain, silent, spatialized universe of the printed word may have appealed to English Protestants.[82] And yet the beginning of the seventeenth century was also the time when emblem books and emblematic engraved title-pages were *gaining* in popularity: the old iconographic tradition in a new form. Like the arts of memory, the emblem books built up concepts from sets of related images, and gave the sense of vision a central role in the acquisition of moral and spiritual knowledge.[83] In many of the broadside tables we are not witnessing the word ousting the pictorial symbol, but rather a co-existence and tension between the two.

This multiplicity of approaches can be seen in 'The map of mortalitie' (1604) (Plate 47), which looks as though it may have been put together somewhat at random by the publisher, using woodblocks he had to hand.[84] The broadside takes up a theme of the 'Godly meditation', the passage of time, making the skull symbolizing death as the central image. Various simple emblems around it represent the path to the overcoming of death in eternal life: the cock (an awakening from sin); the swan (a pure conscience); the book (God's word); and in pride of place, Christ, who reverses Adam's fall and brings victory over death. The image of Christ as the Good Shepherd seems to have been relatively acceptable in a period when the crucified or resurrected Christ was not; it is one of the few pictures of Christ to be found on title-pages of the period.[85] There is verbal schematizing too, in the diagrammatic half-word half-pictures, of the Trinity, and the star of David filled with inscriptions on the theme of God as Love. This was a type of diagram popularized on the Continent in the first half of the sixteenth century by people like the Franciscan, Thomas Murner of Strasbourg. Such diagrams existed before print, but were not easily copied

---

[79] Ong, *Ramus, method and the decay of dialogue*, pp. 89–91.
[80] The 'repositories' could take other forms, such as the figure of a lion, or of Jonah's whale. Rosemary Freeman, *English emblem books* (1948), pp. 201–2.
[81] Frances A. Yates, *The art of memory* (1966), p. 231.
[82] Ong, *Ramus, method and the decay of dialogue*, pp. 4, 318.
[83] Sometimes there was a direct relationship between the arts of memory and the emblems. For example, John Willis (discussed above) derived some of his examples of 'repositories' from emblem books. (Freeman, *English emblem books*, p. 203.)
[84] STC 17294.
[85] See above, p. 215. The Good Shepherd also appeared frequently on German broadsides. (Robert Scribner, *For the sake of simple folk* (Cambridge, 1981), p. 50.)

❧ THE MAP OF MORTALITIE.

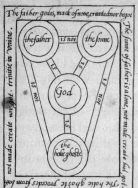

The father gods, made of none, created nor begot

the father — is not — the sonne

God

the holie ghoste

The sonne of father is a sonne, not made create but got

trinitie in Vnitie

not made create nor got

The holie ghost proceeds from both

As by first Adam all doe die
So in me all are made aliue,
Death's swallowed vp in victory,
And I æternall life do giue.

In god dwelleth he, that in loue doth dwell

where god alone, in all his glorie is

True loue it is, the euerlasting blisse

Earth
goes to
treades on
as to
shall to
vpon
goes to
though on
shall from

as moulde to moulde,
glittering in goulde,
returne nere should.
goe ere he would.
Consider may,
naked away.
be stout and gay,
passe poore away.

Awake from sinne,
that sleepe therin.

EARTHE

Prepare — for death, but — feare not — death

REMEMBER — THINE — END

A Conscience pure,
singes to last howre.

PRoude earth behold, as thou art we shall bee.
Against the graue, can no defence be made.
Dust will to dust, as thou art once were wee:
Worldes vainglorie doth thus to nothing fade.
Man doth consume as water spilt on sande.
Like lightnings flash, his life is seene and gone:
Our part is plaide, your part is now in hand,
Death strikes vnwares, and striking spareth none.
Life is a debt to death, all men must die:
But when, where, how, the Lord alone doth knowe.
As death leaues thee, euen so vndoubtedlie
Iudgement shall find thee when last trump shall blowe.
Consider this ô man whil'st it is day,
Thine owne Christes death, for thee (if thou be his)
Vile worldes deceites, helles torments, heauens ioy.
Prouide to day: in night no comfort is,
In season calme, with Noah build an arke:
With Ioseph lay vp store in plenties tyme:
How to be sau'd, let be thy chiefest cark,
Returne to God, repent thee of thy cryme.
That come death late, earlie, or when he list,
It be birth day of thine eternitie.
Of righteous men liueth ou the life in Christ:
Then sure the death of righteous shalt thou die.
Die to the world, the pompes thereof forsake,
That Christ may come and liue with thee in loue:
So in the world, when thou shalt farewell take
Thou maist goe dwell with Christ in heauen aboue.
Youth well to liue, age well to die should care:
In life, for death: in death for life prepare.

All flesh
as grasse
awaye
doth passe
and come
to naught

Gods word
most pure
aye doth
endure
not chang'd
in ought

A SHROVDE TO GRAVE

MEN ONLY HAVE

Sithe Adams fall did fill the world with sinne,
Whereby mans dayes (few) dayes of sorrow bin,
His life, no life, rather calamitie,
And worldes best pleasures, but meere vanitie:
Sith beautie, strength and wit, flowers fading bee,
Man made of dust, to dust must turne againe:
Sith all must die, by gods most iust decree,
And death no torment is, but rest from paine:
Why should fraile flesh feare death, that ends all woes,
That salues all sores, and takes man from his foes?
His shape though ougly 'tis, he bringeth peace,
Stints strife, ends cares, giues life, and wisht-for ease,
Men dying, sleepe: sleeping, from trauell rest,
To liue in ioy for euer with the blest.
Rather embrace, then feare so good a friend:
Yet wish not for him, that in sinne doth end:
But greater sinne, to feare him sure it is,
That troubles ends, and brings eternall blisse.
To faithfull soule, death's full of comfortes sweete,
That longeth with his Christ in Cloudes to meete.
In earth nought sweeter is to wisedomes sense,
Then to prepare for peace-full passage hence.
For, wise man all his life should meditate
On death: that come he sodaine, soone, or late,
He is prepared to entertaine him so,
As Captiues do, redeeming friends from woe.
Liue well thou maist: but can'st not liue long. Euen
So liue, that death may leaue thee fit for heauen:
And feare not death; pale, ouglie though he be,
Thou art in thrall, he comes to set thee free.

Imprinted at London by R. B. for *William Leggett*, and are to be sould at his shop in Holborne, ouer against S. Andrewes Church.

47 'The map of mortalitie' 1604.

like a text. Now even the most complicated designs could be cut on wood-block, like this, and reproduced for mass consumption.[86]

'The Christians jewell [fit] to adorne the hearte and decke the house of every Protestant' (Plate 48) is an anonymous copper engraving (with verses signed by William Grant) and was probably commissioned from a lesser artist like William Rogers of the 'Godly meditation' (putting the likely cost at around 6d.).[87] It was sold in 1624 by Thomas Jenner, who has been labelled as the first English printseller to specialize in pictures for 'puritans' of the 'middle class'.[88] Apart from the cost, the complexity of the design does suggest that it would be bought by committed and educated Protestants. It was 'taken out of' the church of St Mary Overy in Southwark, London, and appears to be a copy of a painted screen, probably of the reredos. The engraving preserves a three-dimensional quality, with its text inscribed on scrolls and tablets, particularly appropriate for the Ten Commandments imitating Moses' God-given tables.

The inscription of the Creed and Lord's Prayer together with the Ten Commandments was a common response to the Canons of 1604, while the use of Moses and Aaron above is an early version of the reredos which developed in later seventeenth-century churches. Moses and Aaron flanked the Tables of the Law in an altarpiece designed for Exeter Cathedral in 1639; and this became the standard form for many parish churches, includ-ing some of Wren's built after the Fire of London. This design originated with engravings, and the figures of Moses and Aaron in an architectural setting like an altarpiece were widely visible on the Cornelis Boel's title-page for the Authorized Version of 1611.[89] Here is an example of the fluid relationship between print and painting, and between decoration for churches and (like the 'Christians jewell') for homes. Designs from engravings were copied onto screens like the one in St Mary Overy, which was then copied back onto copper plate and sold for domestic decoration.

This 'Christians jewell' served both ornamental and didactic purposes: the standard central panel has been complemented with two side panels, forming a design which cogently teaches the basic principles of Protestant worship. The choice of images is shaped by the concepts of 'sacrament' and 'covenant'. While the illustrations are simple, these fairly complex theo-logical ideas are expressed through the symmetry of the design. The left

[86] Ong, *Ramus, method and the decay of dialogue*, pp. 85, 79.
[87] STC 23499.
[88] Leona Rostenberg, *English publishers in the graphic arts 1599–1700* (New York, 1963), p. 27.
[89] Croft-Murray, *Decorative painting*, I, p. 48. Margery Corbett and Ronald Lightbown, *The comely frontispiece: the emblematic title-page in England 1550–1660* (1979), pp. 94–5.

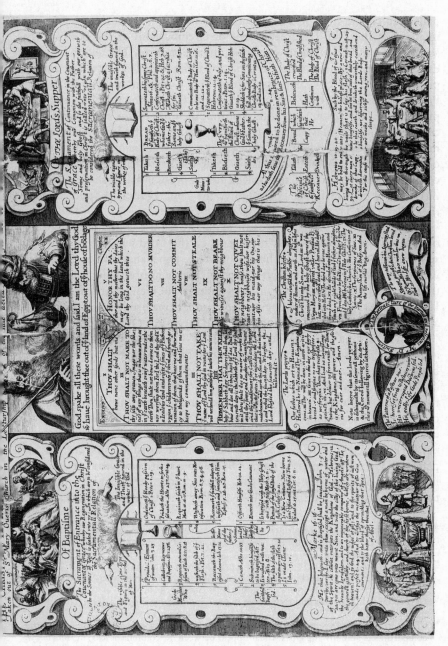

48 'The Christians jewell [fit] to adorne the hearte and decke the house of every Protestant'. Copper engraving, sold by Thomas Jenner [1624].

panel depicts the rites of entrance into God's covenant: at the top, the rite required in the Old Testament, that of circumcision; at the bottom, the sacrament required in the new religion, that of baptism. The text in between explains the sacrament in detail, using the ubiquitous brackets. The central panel depicts the covenant itself: the Ten Commandments, the Lord's Prayer and Creed. At the top are Moses and Aaron, the lawgiver and high priest of the Old Testament; at the bottom, the protector of the seventeenth-century flock, Thomas Sutton, who was lecturer in St Mary Overy before his death in 1623.[90] The right panel shows the sacraments of continuance of the covenant: at the top, passover; at the bottom, holy communion, celebrated kneeling around the table in proper pre-Laudian fashion. Christianity in this picture is the community, the congregation, bound through the covenant and reinforced through the sacraments.

While the 'Christians jewell' came explicitly from a church, many of the other godly broadsides, with their texts of the Lord's Prayer, Creed and scriptural passages, must also have looked like paper shadows of the church wall to the contemporary viewer. A popular title in printsellers' catalogues through to the eighteenth century was simply 'The Ten Commandments'.[91] Here are the visual surroundings of the church being brought into the home: a true 'spiritualization of the household', in the words of Christopher Hill.[92]

The idea of making a paper imitation of a physical object, in this case a church tablet, seems to be symptomatic of the early phases of print, when books were never just books, but 'looking glasses', 'maps', 'posies' and so on. If these titles were only metaphors, there were broadsides which took the image one step further by creating physical copies of these household objects. The best example is a broadside of the 1560s, '[Some f]yne gloves devised for newyeres gyftes to teche yonge peo[ple to] knowe good from evyll' (Plate 49).[93] The two gloved hands bear a list of sins on the left palm and virtues on the right palm. On the fingers are new year's resolutions in the form of short injunctions, such as 'to change carnal and worldly love to spiritual and godly love'; above are the Ten Commandments. Hands

---

[90] According to *DNB*, Sutton drowned when returning to London by sea from a visit to Newcastle. This unexpected death could have occasioned the engraving as a form of memorial, perhaps commissioned by the parishioners of St Mary Overy.

[91] Peter Stent, catalogues of 1653, 1662. Henry Overton, catalogues of 1673, 1717. From Anthony Griffiths, 'A checklist of catalogues of British print publishers c. 1650–1830', *Print Quarterly*, 1 (1984), pp. 4–22; Globe, *Peter Stent*, p. 116.

[92] Christopher Hill, *Society and puritanism in pre-revolutionary England* (New York, 1979), title of ch. 13.

[93] STC 23628.5. The printer, William Powell, used some of the same blocks (the border compartments and flower shapes which appear between the columns of text) in *Here begynneth the kalender of shepardes* (1559 edn). Since the impressions are brighter than those on the broadside, the 'fyne gloves' can be dated to between 1559 and 1567, when Powell ceased business. (Collmann, p. 264.)

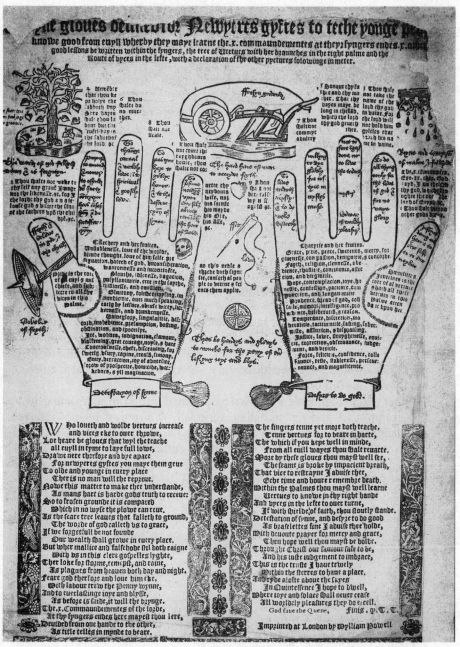

49 '[Some f]yne gloves devised for newyeres gyftes to teche yonge peo[ple to] knowe good from evyll'. Printed by William Powell [1559–67].

and diagrams of hands had long been used as mnemonic aids (by the Jesuits, among others) and for the teaching of music.[94] But these are gloves, not just hands, and the broadside gains added meaning if we know the social function of gloves in early modern England. They were, according to Margaret Spufford, cheap and common courtship gifts, costing (in the late seventeenth century) as little as 2d. to 4d. a pair.[95] These gloves were sold in the country by petty chapmen, just as the broadside gloves would have been sold. The sales patter of the pedlar or ballad seller is preserved in the verses at the bottom:

> Who loveth and wolde vertues increase
>   and vices eke to over throwe,
> Loe heare be gloves that wyl the teache
>   all evyll in tyme to laye full lowe,
> Drawe nere therfore and bye apace
>   for newyeres gyftes you maye them geve
> To olde and younge in every place.

It was common to give small tokens or gifts at new year: the broadside is presented as an alternative gift appealing to the giver to place spiritual values above the material. In other words, he or she had a choice of real gloves, providing warmth or fashion; or paper gloves, providing edification and the knowledge necessary for salvation. In the Stationers' Register there are at least nine other titles of single-sheet 'new year's gifts' listed from the 1560s into the seventeenth century – perhaps these were also edifying broadsides like this one.[96]

Other petty chapmen's wares were translated into print in a similar way. For example, 'A godly new ballad, intituled, A dozen of poynts' referred not only to the 'points' in an argument or list, but to the thread 'points' which sold for a penny a dozen in the late seventeenth century.[97] A broadside entered to the ballad publisher John Charlewood in 1578 was 'A paire of garters for yonge menne to weare yat serve the Lord God and lyve in his feare'.[98] Sadly this has not survived, but it may have taken some kind

---

[94] Alain Guillermou, *St. Ignace de Loyola et la compagnie de Jesus* (Paris, 1960), pp. 68–9. *The Oxford companion to music*, ed. Percy Scholes, 10th edn, revised by John Owen Ward (Oxford, 1970), pl. 161.

[95] Margaret Spufford, *The great reclothing of rural England: petty chapmen and their wares in the seventeenth century* (1984), p. 100. The inspiration for the broadside may have derived partly from the custom (at a more genteel level) of presenting a courtship gift of gloves, embroidered with hearts or phoenixes, together with a set of verses. (Freeman, *English emblem books*, p. 94.)

[96] Rollins Index nos. 1912–20.

[97] Spufford, *Great reclothing*, pp. 88, 152.

[98] 'A dozen of divine points and godly garters' were the object of Ben Jonson's satire in *Bartholomew Fair* (1614). See above, p. 103.

of diagrammatic form like the 'fyne gloves'.[99] John Rastall's description of a book peddlar in a town marketplace names '*Pinnes, Pointes, Laces and Whistles*' as one of the titles for sale.[100] It seems that in a society adjusting to literacy, print was not just print, but was incorporated into daily life by allying itself with other methods of communication – be it the tactile language of gloves and garters, or the oral activities of prayer, proverb and song discussed earlier.

One thing all of the godly tables have in common is their use of print for primarily mnemonic rather than narrative purposes: that is, they do not so much communicate new information to their readers, as remind them of information already known but repeatedly forgotten. This information may be in the form of specific concepts like 'sacrament' and 'covenant', the seven sins and virtues, the Lord's Prayer, Ten Commandments and Creed, or more general codes of moral and spiritual conduct. The necessity of constantly exercising one's memory was a central feature of Tudor–Stuart preaching. At the highest level, thinkers like Donne and Andrewes inherited the Augustinian concept of memory as an almost mystical faculty whereby each individual could rediscover the image of God imprinted on his soul. 'The art of salvation' said Donne 'is but the art of Memory.'[101] In the ballads and broadsides, memory was understood in the usual, common-sense way, yet the exhortation to 'remember' was extremely pervasive, most often coupled with the word 'death'.

The very simplest of godly tables was the *memento mori*: Plate 50 [*c.* 1640] is a quarto sheet bearing woodcuts of Time with his scythe and hourglass, Death with his spear, shrouded figures in coffins, skulls, cross-bones, spades and pick-axes.[102] The couplet 'And as I am, so must you be / Therefore prepare to follow me' was a standard inscription on funeral monuments, deriving from the medieval wall paintings of the 'three living and three dead': 'As you are, so once were we. As we were, so shall you be'.[103] After the Restoration, very similar engravings were used as funeral invi-

---

[99] If a text could be shaped around garters, garters could also bear a text. A silk pair bears the woven love mottoes, 'I like my choice to well to change 1717' and 'My (heart) is fixt I cannot range 1717'. (Spufford, *Great reclothing*, p. 101, illustration 12.)

[100] J. Rastall, *The third booke, declaring by examples ... that it is time to beware of M. Jewel* (1566), sig.A3. Cited in H.S. Bennett, *English books and readers 1558 to 1603* (Cambridge, 1965), p. 267.

[101] A. M. Guite, 'The art of memory and the art of salvation: the centrality of memory in the sermons of John Donne and Lancelot Andrewes', paper delivered at the 1987 conference, Centre for Seventeenth-Century Studies, Durham.

[102] STC 17816.5 A similar *memento mori*, now lost, is STC 26038.2, reproduced in Wilson, *Plague in Shakespeare's London*, p. 128.

[103] A. Caiger-Smith, *English medieval mural paintings* (Oxford, 1963), p. 45.

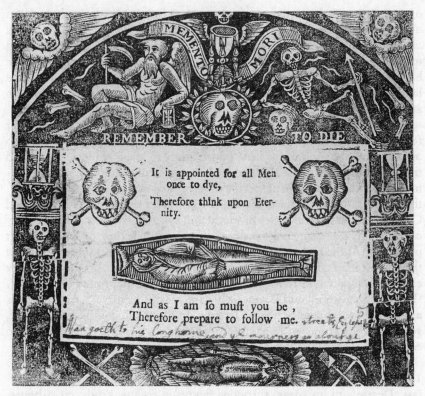

It is appointed for all Men
once to dye,

Therefore think upon Eternity.

And as I am fo muſt you be ,
Therefore prepare to follow me.

50 'Memento mori. Remember to die' [*c.* 1640].

tations: Pepys collected three examples with blanks for the name and date.[104]
Such mementos may have been quite widespread, just the simple xylographic
'wallpaper' pasted on wood may preserve a common form of print of which
we have lost almost all trace. These paper mementos performed the same
function as a skull on the desk, a gruesome corpse on the back of a mirror,
or the effigy of a cadaver carved on a tomb.

Of course, paper was a less enduring medium than stone, and the broadsides had their more ephemeral uses: they could be carried in the pocket,
passed around, used for writing paper or for waste paper. By emphasizing
one possible physical situation for the broadside, that is, as a fixture on
the wall, I have tried to underline one function of print: not so much as
a vehicle for conveying information, but as an object for display, to be
read over and over again as a daily exercise reinforcing essential truths.

[104] Pepys 2973/510 a, b, c.

Many of the 'tables' discussed in this chapter were 'patterns of printed words'[105] composed by ministers and zealous laymen for educated, pious householders who can only have been a minority. But I have also suggested ways in which the culture of word-patterns for walls could have much wider effects : in the 'sentences' painted in churches; in the cloth proclaiming 'Feare God' in the alehouse; in moralizing sayings like 'A vertuous wife gives housband life', interspersed with pelicans and mermaids, and pasted on a wooden board. By the 1750s, a woodcut print called 'King Charles's Twelve Good Rules' was described by Thomas Bewick as a 'constant' feature of 'every farmhouse, cottage and hovel'.[106] With its maxims like 'Pick no quarrels', 'Maintain no ill opinions' and 'Encourage no vice' (laid out neatly using brackets), it was a descendant of the moralizing, aphoristic broadsides of the present study.[107]

Popular Protestantism in table form, expressed through a bond of text and picture, became a hardy and time-tested product of the English printing press. When the mid-eighteenth-century publishers advertised over 200 'Scripture and other Godly Pieces ... printed from off wooden prints', they came 'with verses applicable to each Print'. A number of them appear to be directly within our 'godly table' tradition: 'the Lord's Prayer, finely ornamented in an emblematical and hieroglyphical Manner, in nine curious Descriptions', 'The Ten Commandments, with Moses and Aaron at full length', 'The Looking Glass which flatters not, adorned with suitable Figures and Verses', 'The Christian's Dial, or a cheap Watch for a Poor Man, with a fine Description of all the Hours of the Day'.[108] These were the pictures available to chapmen at a bulk price of a halfpenny; perhaps a penny or twopence to the customer. Obviously there was still a large demand for godly broadsides, with which the good eighteenth-century householder could sanctify the walls of his home.

[105] Patrick Collinson, *The religion of Protestants. The church in English society 1559–1625.* The Ford Lectures 1979 (Oxford, 1982), p. 234. Here, Collinson is referring to the oral patterns of catechisms and sermons.

[106] From British Library, Miss Banks' Collection, reproduced in Martin, 'The case of the missing woodcuts', p. 351. In the top corner of this print is a small 'No. 88', referring to the catalogue of William and Cluer Dicey, 1754. Bewick's comments are confirmed by Oliver Goldsmith, who mentions 'the twelve good rules' in both *The citizen of the world* (letter of 1759) and *The deserted village* (1770). (*Ibid.*, pp. 343–4.) There is no certain explanation for the eighteenth-century association of these rules with Charles I; Martin speculates that they may originally have been written by *James* I to regulate the behaviour of his courtiers and servants. (*Ibid.*, pp. 355–8.)

[107] An early version of this print was 'Table observations' [*c.* 1615], mentioned above, p. 234.

[108] Cluer Dicey and Richard Marshall, *A catalogue of maps, prints, copy-books, drawing-books, histories, old ballads, patters, collections &c* (1764), pp. 62, 17, 63, 64.

III

THE CHAPBOOK

The development of the chapbook trade

POPULAR PRINT

The broadside reflected the needs of a partially literate society. It was print for singing or print for looking at; a song or a picture or a 'table'. Now we will look at print primarily for reading, in book form. But books were still far from divorced from oral culture. A close relationship existed between ballads and books, as the favourite stories floated from one medium to the other. In 1615 Henry Parrot described the various types of customer who would peruse his new work at the book stall. The titles are familiar:

> Next after him, your Countrey-Farmer viewes it,
> It may be good (saith hee) for those can use it.
> Shewe mee King *Arthur*, *Bevis*, or *Syr Guye*,
> Those are the Bookes he onely loves to buye.[1]

These are the same stories which Puttenham tells us were sung as ballads by 'blind harpers or such like tavern minstrels'.[2] Medieval chivalric romances like Guy of Warwicke and King Arthur first appeared in manuscript form from 1200 to 1400, and were printed for a gentry audience in the first decades of the sixteenth century.[3] Excerpts must have continued to be sung by professional musicians, but in the late sixteenth century they were abridged into cheap and accessible broadside versions (see Table 4). A century later, the chapbook publishers adapted them back into book form in 24-page editions for country buyers. This dialectic between song and book versions reflected changes of audience and growing literacy within each social group.

Even when such stories were not attached to a tune they could still be

---

[1] Henry Parrot, 'The mastive, or young-whelpe of the olde-dogge', *Epigrams and satires* (1615); quoted in Natascha Wurzbach, *Die englische straßenballade 1550–1650* (Munich, 1981), p. 398.

[2] George Puttenham, *The arte of English poesie* (1589). (See above, p. 13.)

[3] 'Gui de Warewic', survives from *c.* 1232–42; 'Morte Arthure' from *c.* 1360. (Lee C. Ramsey, *Chivalric romances: popular literature in medieval England* (Bloomington, Indiana, 1983), pp. 233–4.) For printed versions see Table 4.

transmitted orally. In 1568 the printer Robert Copland describes how his customers pester him with requests for copies of their favourite ballads and jests:

> Have ye not seene a prety geest in ryme
> Of the seven sorrows that these women have
> When that their husbands be brought to grave.

Copland has not and suggests that he might print it if a copy were brought to him.

> I have no boke, but yet I can you shewe
> The matter by herte, and that by wordes fewe
> Take your penne and wryte as I do say
> But yet of one thyng, hertely I you praye
> Amend the englysh somewhat if ye can.[4]

Oral culture passed into print this way, and printed stories seeped into the oral culture. Even expensive books bought by the country gentry were, according to the author of *Cyvile and uncyvile life* (1579), read aloud on winter nights in the presence of 'our honest neighbours, Yeomen of the Countrey, and good honest fellowes, dwellers there about: as Graziers, Butchers, Farmers, Drovers, Carpenters, Carriers, Taylors & such like men, very honest and good companions'.[5] This description of country recreations is coloured by the author's polemical stance in favour of city life, but there is evidence that parish gentry did mix socially with the local 'middling sort'.[6] Stories might trickle down the social ladder as they were retold by these 'honest neighbours' in inns and alehouses; the centres for the exchange of news, jokes and merry tales. The Coventry mason Captain Cox must have passed on many stories in his library this way, as he was able 'to talk as much without book as any Inholder betwixt Brainford and Bagshot'.[7]

When did stories and news begin to circulate widely in book form, as well as by oral report, amongst the 'Farmers, Drovers, Carpenters, Carriers, Taylors & such like men'? How did reformers make use of the growth of a humble book-reading public for the dissemination of Protestantism? The general question of Protestant use of the printing press is an enormous

---

[4] Robert Copland, ed., *The seven sorowes that women have when theyr husbandes be deade* (1568), prologue.

[5] *Cyvile and uncyvile life. A discourse very profitable, pleasant, and fit to bee read of all nobilitie and gentlemen* (1579), sig.H4–H4v.

[6] B.A. Holderness, 'The parish gentry of England: a neglected element of social history', paper delivered at Cambridge seminar in early modern English economic and social history, 22 January 1987.

[7] Margaret Spufford, *Small books and pleasant histories. Popular fiction and its readership in seventeenth-century England* (1981), pp. 65–7. For more on Captain Cox see below, p. 268.

one, and far beyond the scope of this study. A survey based on sheer volume of output would have to begin with the official prayer book, psalter and catechism, which ran through enormous numbers of repeat editions, with print runs twice the normal size.[8] Unofficial 'best-sellers' included many works which were long and expensive, like Michael Sparke's *Crumms of comfort* (over 300 pages) and Arthur Dent's *Plaine mans pathway* (over 450 pages). But there were also cheap black-letter sermons, like those stocked by Roger Ward in his Shrewsbury bookshop in 1585: ninety sermons valued at 2.5d. each, and another ninety-three at 3d. Ward had a further forty-two 'Dentes sermons', not priced, probably from the pirated edition he put out himself in 1582–3. This profitable tract was Dent's *Sermon of repentaunce* (valued at 2d. in the inventory of another bookseller in York) which had run to an impressive thirty-seven editions by 1638.[9]

The evidence of numbers of editions can be useful, but it is biassed against the cheapest works like broadsides and chapbooks, whose survival rates are low, and whose extant editions are rarely numbered. There is no straight equation between 'popularity' in numerical terms and print for the 'popular' classes. When literacy was weighted at the top of the social scale, reprints of learned and expensive books could be supported by an elite group of readers in London.[10] Meanwhile, of the shortest and cheapest works, many editions (and even whole titles) were lost through use. The first surviving copy of William Perkins' chapbook *Death's knell* (1628) is labelled the '9th edition': had it not been announced as such we would have no knowledge of its popularity.[11]

Sermons, prayer books and aids to devotion may have been increasingly available, as the seventeenth century progressed, in simple language at an affordable price. But sermon writing was not a direct replacement for ballad writing. Our focus in this study has not been on creation of a Protestant culture centred on pulpit and pastor, but on the presentation of religion in 'popular' cultural forms. The godly ballad writers borrowed the tunes and themes of secular balladry, sending out Protestant ideas along the same distribution network. We know that by the late seventeenth century the 'chapbook' had begun to take over from the ballad as the most prevalent form of cheap print. A full third of chapbook publishers' output by the

---

[8] In his *Religious instruction in early modern England c. 1540–1740* (in progress) Ian Green looks at all Protestant works which went through five or more editions in the space of thirty years.

[9] Alexander Rodger, ed., 'Roger Ward's Shrewsbury stock: an inventory of 1585', *The Library*, 5th ser., 13 (1958), pp. 259, 267. STC 6649.5. Robert Davies, *A memoir of the York press* (1868), p. 363.

[10] See David Cressy, *Literacy and the social order. Reading and writing in Tudor and Stuart England* (Cambridge, 1980), p. 47.

[11] STC 19684. (G. Purslowe f.M. Trundle, 1628.)

1680s was made up of 'small godly books', comparable to the religious percentage at the height of Elizabethan godly ballad writing.[12] The task of Part III will be first to chart the development of the chapbook trade, and secondly to look at its use as a vehicle for evangelical energies.

The identification of 'cheap' or 'popular' print in the period before 1640 is far from clear-cut, and demands a careful examination of possible definitions and approaches. We will then discuss the entire trade list of a number of publishers, some of whose stock of godly books was negligible compared with their offerings of merry tales. However, there may be some gains in looking at religion as a minor line of products in the pedlar's pack, amongst the gloves and combs, books of riddles and ballads of Robin Hood. If he carried only one little octavo of *Seven weapons to conquer the devil* and a couple of ballads of 'St Bernard's vision', there is a chance that these reached a different sort of buyer than the sermons and treatises published by mainstream stationers for sale in ordinary bookshops.

Access to books

The first factor determining the accessibility of books was literacy, of which David Cressy's statistics can be only a partial measure. Nevertheless, improvement in the separate skills of reading and writing would have relied generally on the same presence of schoolmasters and foundation of village schools. On the graph of literacy, readers would probably form a dotted line running parallel above writers, so that the two skills followed the same 'dynamics'.

The first half of Elizabeth's reign was a period of 'educational revolution', with advances in ability to sign in all social groups for those schooled between 1560 and 1580. In East Anglia, husbandmen of this generation improved from 10% to 30% fully 'literate', yeomen from 45% to 75% and tradesmen in Norwich from 40% to 60%. From 1580 to 1610 was a period of 'educational recession', followed by a recovery during James' reign and 'pronounced improvement' in the 1630s.[13] The growing specialization of 'cheap-print' publishers coincided with this second phase of 'educational revolution', and may reflect an increasing awareness of lower social groups as a potentially lucrative market for print.

After literacy, the other major factor affecting accessibility of books was the cost. The absence of books from humble inventories tells us nothing here: even valuable books like bibles and Foxe's 'Book of Martyrs' which appeared in wills were not entered separately in the corresponding inventories. Pamphlets and ballads, if they had not perished as lavatory paper or

[12] Spufford, *Small books*, pp. 99–100, 197.
[13] Cressy, *Literacy and the social order*, pp. 168–71.

stops for mustard pots, were never considered worth listing.[14] It is almost impossible to measure what was 'affordable' to an individual, or what sacrifices a craftsman or husbandman was willing to make for a special book. Some might save for a year to buy an octavo bible at 3s.4d. rather than waste the same amount on three or four ballads a month just for amusement.[15] But not everyone had this kind of patience and foresight. There must be some justification in determining a level of 'cheap' print which could be bought on a whim when the money was on hand, from a travelling chapman or a stall in the market, and on a fairly regular basis.

Taking into account the general inflation, books were becoming more affordable during our period. Book prices remained steady from 1560 to 1635, when other commodities more than doubled in price and wages rose by half to two-thirds.[16] In 1560 a building craftsman made 8d. to 10d. a day, and a twopenny book was one fifth to one quarter of his daily wages. In 1600 he made a shilling, and the price of the pamphlet had dropped to one sixth; in 1640 when he made up to 16d., a regular twopenny purchase begins to look more affordable. Labourers in the building trade and in agricultural work improved from 6d. to 10 or 12d. in this period.[17] This tells us little unless we know how much a labourer had to spare after he had fed and clothed himself, and how badly he was squeezed by the general fall of his purchasing power.[18] Keith Wrightson estimates a basic cost of subsistence of around £11–14 for a family in a normal year, while the wages of a labouring man might total only £9–10. Clearly there was little 'surplus' for luxuries like pamphlets. An early seventeenth-century husbandman with an arable holding of 30 acres might have £3-4 'surplus' after

---

[14] Margaret Spufford, *Contrasting communities. English villagers in the sixteenth and seventeenth centuries* (Cambridge, 1974), p. 211; Spufford, *Small books*, pp. 48–50.

[15] In the early seventeenth century a bible in 8vo cost 3s. 4d. unbound, and a 4to bible cost 7s., according to Michael Sparke, *Scintilla* (1641), referring to 'times past' before the monopolists raised the prices. (Quoted in T. H. Darlow and H. F. Moule, *Historical catalogue of printed editions of the English Bible 1525–1961*, 2nd edn., revised and expanded by A.S. Herbert (1968), pp. 182–7.) In Cambridgeshire in the 1660s, bibles were left by Robert Reynolds with goods worth only £18.7s.3d.; Richard Turner, a retired husbandman (who owned no less than four bibles); and John Tolworthy, a barber with goods worth £12.19s.0d. (Spufford, *Contrasting communities*, p. 210.)

[16] Francis R. Johnson, 'Notes on English retail book-prices, 1550–1640', *The Library*, 5th ser. 5 (1950), p. 93. E.H. Phelps Brown and Sheila V. Hopkins, 'Seven centuries of the prices of consumables compared with builders' wage-rates', in Eleanor M. Carus-Wilson, ed., *Essays in economic history II* (1962), pp. 194–5; 'Seven centuries of building wages', in *ibid.*, p. 177.

[17] Phelps Brown and Hopkins, 'Seven centuries of building wages', p. 177. Joan Thirsk, ed., *The agrarian history of England and Wales*, vol. IV: *1560–1640* (Cambridge, 1967), p. 864.

[18] Purchasing power of the agricultural labourer's wages fell from 66 to 47, on a scale where the average price ruling in the period 1450–99 was used as a base. (*Ibid.*, pp. 865, 869.)

food, or an average of 14d to 18d a week.[19] On this scale, a twopenny pamphlet every fortnight or so looks like a possibility, although it might mean sacrificing two quarts of strong beer at the alehouse.[20] A lesser yeoman with £40–50 income a year would hardly have to think twice about buying pamphlets or ballads, and probably represented a more regular market.[21]

In the hand-press period, paper was the largest expense that went into making a book; often about 75% of the total in the sixteenth century.[22] So the cost of the book was, in general, directly proportionate to the number of sheets used. Francis Johnson has collected evidence of pricing from accounts of book buyers, notations in the books themselves, booksellers' bills and invoices, and inventories of stock. Johnson found that from 1560 to 1635, prices for normal new unbound books (printed in pica or larger type) stuck quite closely to the halfpenny per sheet prescribed by the Stationers' Company in 1598.[23] This fact legitimizes the un-literary, almost philistine, activity of mechanically counting pages to establish the likely price and audience of a book.

However, there are a number of complications in the length–cost equation. Illustrated books could cost up to 100% more than other books, although not when printed with old re-used wood-blocks, as is the case with most 'cheap print'. Reprints generally cost less than new books, sometimes as little as 1/5d. per sheet, although 1/3d. seems average. Copies of old favourites like Aesop's *Fables in Englysshe, Sir Bevis of Hampton,* and *Guy of Warwick* can be found for between 4d. and 7d. in bookseller's inventories from Edinburgh and York, although these prices appear to be wholesale.[24]

Lengthy books, then, became more affordable the older they grew. As they fell out of favour with fashionable Londoners they came into favour with social groups who could begin to afford them. Meanwhile, according to Johnson's evidence, the shortest works were relatively more expensive than longer books. The pamphlets in his sample tended to be sold at a price of 1d. per sheet, levelling off to the standard 1/2d. at around four sheets. 'Except for a broadside', Johnson concludes, '2d. seems to have

---

[19] Keith Wrightson, *English society 1580–1680* (1982), pp. 32–4.

[20] Strong beer cost roughly 2.5d. to 3d. per gallon in Norwich in the 1570s; by 1610 prices had risen by one fifth. (Peter Clark, *The English alehouse: a social history 1200–1830* (1983), pp. 103–4.) At Hoveringham in 1617, 'a cake and beer' could be bought for twopence at the alehouse. (*Ibid.*, p. 132.)

[21] Wrightson, *English society*, p. 33.

[22] Philip Gaskell, *A new introduction to bibliography* (Oxford, 1972), p. 177.

[23] Johnson, 'Notes on English retail book-prices', pp. 84, 93.

[24] *Ibid.*, pp. 88, 90, 93, 95, 97. Inventory of John Foster in Robert Davies, ed., *A memoir of the York press* (1868), p. 362. Books at York seem to be valued at two-thirds their usual retail price (see Tessa Watt, 'Cheap print and religion *c.* 1550 to 1640' (Cambridge PhD, 1988), pp. 316–17).

been the minimum price at which a printed work was offered to the public'.[25] However, Johnson's 'pamphlets' are all works pitched at readers with a fairly high level of education, and appreciation of literary fashion. They include several masques, a Marprelate tract, petitions to Parliament, works by Ben Jonson, a *Discourse of Lightnings,* and a *Speache by Mathematicall Lecturer.*[26] There is not a single example of the roughly printed sensational news tract, like *A true relation of Gods wonderfull mercies in preserving one alive which hanged five days,* or *A straunge and terrible wunder in the parish church of Bongey.*[27]

These may have been the sort of stock listed in York as 'one hundred and foure sticht bookes of little work [ie. worth?]' valued at 3s. together, or only 0.35d. each (apparently wholesale). Two 'Robin of Conscience' (2 sheets 4to) were valued at a halfpenny each.[28] Roger Ward had '69 Bookes at pence' in his Shrewsbury shop in 1585.[29] The items which even meticulous booksellers' inventories did not list by title may be more important for our purposes than the named works of contemporary poets and polemicists.

In 1556 the Oxford scholar Julins Palmer was described as 'a jolly writer of three halfpenny bookes', as if this were a standard price and form.[30] Later, however, there is some support for Johnson's claim of twopence as the expected price of a short pamphlet. Near the end of the century, the printer William Barley was brought before the High Commission for selling at Cowdry in Sussex a 'twopenny book' relating to Her Majesty's progress.[31] Almanacs were sold in 1576 for 'only two poor pence, or three pence at the most' although by the 1650s the 'sorts' (standardized almanacs, usually three sheets long) had crept up to as much as 4d.[32] In Durham in the early 1630s, the parson–astrologer John Vaux sold almanacs from the communion table of St Helen Awckland at 2d. each.[33] Even in 1658, John Gadbury's almanac ended with the comment that the countryman

---

[25] Johnson, 'Notes on English retail book-prices', p. 93.

[26] STC 1663, 6264, 6363, 7292, 9246, 12918, 13694, 14762, 14772, 14776, 17887, 24739, 24746, 25170. (In *ibid.,* pp. 96–112.)

[27] John Johnson (of Antwerp), *A true relation* ... (1605), published by E. Allde, 2 sheets 4to. Abraham Fleming, *A straunge and terrible wunder* ... (1577), published by F. Godly, 1 sheet 8vo.

[28] Davies, ed., *Memoir of the York press,* pp. 362, 364. For *Robin Conscience* see below, pp. 286–7.

[29] Rodger, ed., 'Roger Ward's Shrewsbury stock', p. 260.

[30] 'The second examination and accusation of Julins Palmer, at Newbury', 16 July 1556, in John Foxe, *Actes and monuments* (1610 edn), II, p. 1759.

[31] This occurred some time before 1598. R.B. McKerrow, *A dictionary of printers and booksellers in England, Scotland and Ireland, and of foreign printers of English books 1557–1640* (1910), p. 20.

[32] Statement from Securis' *A prognostication for 1576,* sig.B1 cited in Bernard Capp, *Astrology and the popular press 1500–1800* (1979), pp. 41, 397 n. 114.

[33] W.H.D. Longstaff, ed., *The acts of the High Commission within the diocese of Durham,* Publications of the Surtees Society, vol. 34 (Durham, 1858), p. 40.

would never pay more than 2d.: 'Chave liv'd these vorty years, and nere did gei / A varthing more'.[34] Martin Parker describes his 'twopenny customers' in a little work of 1637, only 1.5 sheets long. This was published after a general rise in book prices around 1635, of at least 40%.[35] It may be that lengthier pamphlets were no longer offered at the expected price of twopence, and that these little octavos were able to fill the gap.

What kind of works might have been called 'three halfpenny' or 'twopenny' books? A search through the STC for works of anything from one to four sheets would yield many items which happened to be short, but were aimed at an elite or educated audience; from grammar school texts to pastoral poetry. Works which we might judge to be suitable for a wider audience with rudimentary reading skills would be written in a plain style, without too much in the way of untranslated Latin phrases, unexplained classical allusions, technical or learned terms, or preoccupation with London fashions and literary feuds. Apart from almanacs, the two major kinds of short, simple works we would find could be loosely termed as news 'pamphlets' and 'chapbooks'.

Pamphlets

The term 'pamphlet' can be used in a neutral bibliographical sense as a short unbound book, but in popular usage it often has connotations of a topical, 'ephemeral' subject matter.[36] Pamphlets have been collected into several checklists, and have been the subject of a number of studies, although knowledge about their distribution and audience is vague.[37] They were published by all kinds of stationers: in Shaaber's account of 'popular news' I have counted some forty-two publishers from 1560 to 1622 who produced

[34] Capp, *Astrology and the popular press*, p. 41.
[35] Martin Parker, *Harry White his humour* (1637). Johnson, 'Notes on English retail book-prices', pp. 89–90.
[36] *The Concise Oxford Dictionary* (6th edn) defines a pamphlet as a 'Small usually unbound treatise, esp. in prose on subject of current interest'. In the period pre-1640 the term was used very loosely by authors and printers, sometimes referring to works over sixty pages long (e.g. Joannes Caius, *Of Englishe dogges*, trans. from Latin by A. Fleming (Richard Jones, 1576), 62 pages 4to).
[37] D.C. Collins has found 271 extant news pamphlets published between 1590 and 1610 inclusive, and 95 further titles entered in the Stationers' Register during the same period (excluding ballads). D.C. Collins, *A handlist of news pamphlets 1590–1610* (1943). See also Mattias A. Shaaber, *Some forerunners of the newspaper in England 1476–1622* (Philadelphia, 1929); Sandra Clark, *The Elizabethan pamphleteers. Popular moralistic pamphlets 1580–1640* (1983); Marie-Hélène Davies, *Reflections of Renaissance England: life, thought and religion mirrored in illustrated pamphlets 1535–1640*, Princeton theological monograph series, vol. 1 (Allison Park, Pennsylvania, 1986).

pamphlets on miracles, monsters, witchcraft, unusual weather and sensational murders.[38]

One should not therefore conclude that all of these publishers catered specifically for a 'popular clientèle'; most were solid, mainstream publishers who ran off news as a sideline. 'Ephemeral' or 'popular' pamphlets are often automatically equated with a humble readership, and indeed the proliferation of broadsides with woodcuts of deformed babies, or ditties of criminals' last words would indicate that these themes were popular with anyone who could afford the penny price. But as Sandra Clark has noted, the pamphlets catered for different degrees of literary sophistication, sometimes expecting the audience to recognize rhetorical figures, quotations in Latin and French, and classical references.[39] Many of their clients, too, would no doubt have picked up the news pamphlets as we do a paper: in addition to, rather than as a substitute for, more substantial reading matter.

There are surprisingly few of these pamphlets itemized in the inventories for booksellers in market towns. Roger Ward's Shrewsbury stock of 1585, which included '1 Reame 6 quire ballates' (or about 650) had only two sensational news pamphlets specifically named: '1 popishe monsters' and '1 Disclosing divell in 2 maids'. As was suggested above, some of his unnamed '69 Bookes at pence' could also have been of this type. This is not, however, an impressive number within the list of some 2,500 books in his stock, mostly catechisms, prayer books, Latin texts, sermons, psalters and so on.[40] One answer might be that news pamphlets were carried by petty chapmen, for whom inventories were not normally made. If this is right, it is surprising that most of the surviving pamphlets were published in quarto, often of three sheets or more, which does not suggest they were specially designed for the purpose of carrying in a pack. A contrast is found in the 500 *canards* studied by Jean-Pierre Seguin in France; pamphlets which dealt with the same subjects of crime, miracles, floods, heavenly apparitions and so on. These *canards* had been produced in quarto format before about 1510, but after that the smaller octavo dimensions were adopted. The standard length was between six and sixteen pages; one sheet or less.[41] They were also produced by Paris publishers who specialized in the trade, unlike the haphazard London situation. Roger Chartier has emphasized that these

---

[38] Shaaber, *Some forerunners of the newspaper*, footnotes to ch. 4.
[39] Clark, *Elizabethan pamphleteers*, p. 21.
[40] Rodger, ed., 'Roger Ward's Shrewsbury stock', pp. 252, 257, 260, 262. The unnamed books might just as easily be some cheap school texts, in which Ward specialized.
[41] Jean-Pierre Séguin, 'L'Information en France avant le périodique. 500 canards imprimés entre 1529 et 1631', *Arts et Traditions Populaires*, 11 (1963), pp. 20–32, 119–45, 203–80. Format discussed p. 22.

canards, rather than the better-known 'livrets bleus', were the earliest wide-spread form of reading material after the broadsides.[42]

Some of the smallest English pamphlets were, in fact, ones translated from French or Dutch or German.[43] The tiny one sheet-octavos are rare, and tantalizing. A report on the appearance of the devil in the form of a black dog in Bongay in 1577 bore a picture of 'an horrible shaped thing' on the title-page, and promised to be worth 'hearing and considering'. The printer, 'Frauncis Godly dwelling at the west end of Paules', has left only one other extant work, a ballad of a monstrous child.[44] Perhaps he produced many more of these pamphlets, whose chances of survival were as slim as their size. The search for 'penny chapbooks' (below) has turned up a handful of news pamphlets in the 1- to 1.5-sheet octavo format, but not enough to establish them as a specialized trade.[45] For now the distribution of these sensational pamphlets remains an interesting question mark, and one which would merit further research.

Chapbooks

The most neutral meaning of the term 'chapbook' is simply any book carried by a chapman, a perfectly adequate definition for periods when we have the evidence of wholesale catalogues or contemporary collections. But pre-1640 publishers did not advertise their wares specifically 'for country chap-men', nor have we found a chapman's or bookseller's inventory to shed light on distribution practices.[46] Pedlars of 'small books' were certainly stock figures of the London streets in this period; a print of thirty-six 'criers of London' shows a man with a wooden box of 'Alminaks' hanging from

---

[42] Roger Chartier, 'Culture as appropriation: popular cultural uses in early modern France', in Stephen L. Kaplan, ed., *Understanding popular culture: Europe from the middle ages to the nineteenth century* (Berlin, 1984), pp. 246–7.

[43] Adam Islip published *The most rare strange and wonderful example of almightie God shewed in the citie of Telonne in Provence on a cruell papisticall bishop* (1592) in only 1 sheet 4to. The same size was used for John Danter's *Strange signes seene in the aire about the citie of Rosenberge. Tr. out of the high Dutch* (1594).

[44] Fleming, *A straunge and terrible wunder. A discription of a monstrous chyld, borne at Chychester in Sussex . . . 1562.* (STC 6177.)

[45] These include three 'end and confession' tracts published by Richard Jones (see below). There were two other 'penny-sized' news pamphlets produced by my group of ballad pub-lishers: John Fisher (of Chester), *The copy of a letter describing the wonderfull woorke of God in delivering a mayden within the City of Chester, from an horrible kinde of torment and sicknes* (John Awdeley, 1564, 18 pages 8vo); *A mirrour for murtherers, or a caveat for disobedient children* (John Wright, 1633, 24 pages 12mo).

[46] I have searched the records of the Prerogative Court of Canterbury, the Archdeaconry and Commissary Courts without luck; an unsurprising result given the general paucity of inventories in this period.

his neck.[47] In *The ordinary* (*c.* 1635), William Cartwright mentions the same method of distribution, within the city, for religious tracts and sermons:

> I shall live to see thee
> Stand in a Play-house doore with thy long box,
> Thy half-crown Library, and cry small Books.
> Buy a good godly Sermon Gentlemen –
> A judgement shewn upon a Knot of Drunkards –
> A pill to purge out Popery – The life
> and death of *Katherin Stubs.*[48]

Itinerant book pedlars were also familiar in parts of the countryside as early as the 1570s. In 1578, one such pedlar in Cambridgeshire ventured several miles off the main road to the village of Balsham, where he sold 'lytle bookes' in the churchyard. One of these books was bought by an impoverished patcher of clothes, but unfortunately we have no titles.[49] Book pedlars were also wandering in Shropshire by the seventeenth century. The London stationer Michael Sparke remembered travelling around the county selling Roman Catholic books, during his apprenticeship between 1603 and 1610. Richard Baxter, also from Shropshire, recorded how, around 1630, 'a poor pedlar came to the door that had ballads and some good books: and my father bought of him *Dr. Sibb's Bruised Reed*'.[50]

After the Restoration, Pepys and Wood collected the wares of contemporary publishers whom they knew from their own observations to be producing popular reading matter, distributed by chapmen. For the period before 1640, searches through the catalogues of such collections as the Pepys, Wood, Lauriston Castle, New York Public Library and the Osbourne Early Children's Books have produced almost nothing.[51] And when someone like Wood did venture into these dark ages before the Commonwealth, it was

---

[47] Hind, III, p. 367 and pl. 212. BL Prints (Authorities for Artists, Vol. II, period V). The plate appears to date from the reign of Charles I. It was recut after the Restoration, and sold by I. Overton at the White Horse. The rat-catcher who occupied the large central panel in the pre-1640 plate was replaced with a man holding books, and a scroll labelled 'Buy a new Booke'. (The almanack seller still remained as one of the thirty-six smaller figures.) The alteration appears to reflect the burgeoning of the 'small book' trade after the Restoration, as described in Spufford, *Small books.*

[48] William Cartwright, *The ordinary, a comedy* (written *c.* 1635), III, v, in *The plays and poems of William Cartwright,* ed. G. Blakemore Evans (Madison, 1951), p. 317. The speaker in this passage is Vicar Catchmey, 'a cathedral singing-man', mocking Rimewell the poet. 'Katherin Stubs' was one of the stock publications of the ballad seller Richard Jones, and, later, John Wright. (See below, pp. 283–4.) John Mico, *A pill to purge out popery,* was first published in 1623. (*Ibid.,* p. 644.)

[49] This pedlar appears 'to have caused no special remark'. Spufford, *Contrasting communities,* p. 208.

[50] [M. Sparke], *A second beacon fired by Scintilla* (1652), pp. 5–6. R. Baxter, *Reliquiae Baxterianae* (1696), pp. 3–4. I owe these references to Paul Morgan.

[51] These collections are held in the Bodleian Library, Oxford; Magdalene College, Cambridge; the National Library of Scotland; New York Public Library; Toronto Public Library.

as an antiquarian, whose opinion of a 'chapbook' is not necessarily authoritative.[52]

Without collections to guide us, the pre-1640 chapbook has tended to be defined by a certain kind of subject matter. If pamphlets were topical, chapbooks were timeless: chivalric romances and favourite jests. The library of Captain Cox the mason of Coventry, recorded in a letter of 1575, has been used as the first important list of reading matter for the people.[53] Cox owned many of the titles published as 'small books' a century later, which are also the titles mocked as 'popular' by educated commentators of Cox's day. 'King Arthur, Bevis and Sir Guye' are some of the book titles which reappear again and again in the period as evidence of unlearned or old-fashioned taste (from the point of view of the literati) and of 'witless' or 'vain' pursuits (from the perspective of some Protestant reformers).

An approach to 'popular literature' through contemporary eyes is not without merit. In Table 4, I have listed ten works which appear as favourite titles in various commentaries, in Captain Cox's library, and a century later in Pepys' collection of chapbooks. Most of these works were in print right from the beginning of the sixteenth century, from the shops of Caxton, De Worde and Pynson. Four of them appeared also in broadside ballad form during Elizabeth's reign. As was mentioned above, the familiarity of a figure like Guy of Warwick did not necessarily imply ownership of books. These titles are of interest especially for what they tell us about the oral culture which may have been widely transmitted by minstrels or amateur story telling. This relatively unscientific sample could be extended in a longer study to provide a list of the 'stock' of stories which endured over generations and approached what we might call 'folk stories', just as some of the 'stock' ballads became 'folksong'.

It would not necessarily, however, provide a list of the titles which were widely accessible in book form throughout this period. There is a large discrepancy between little books like *The fryar and the boy*, at two sheets quarto, and great chronicles like *The four sons of Aymon*, over 100 sheets folio. Some of the medium-sized works like *Guy* and *Bevis* were moving down-market as they were reprinted. But Parrot's 'country farmer' who bought *King Arthur* would have to be at least a prosperous yeoman to afford the price of roughly 9s. There is no evidence before 1640 of an *Arthur* in 24-page quarto, like the edition published by Francis Coules in

[52] Wood collected several sixteenth-century items, including an octavo pamphlet on *The execution of the late popish traitors* (1581); Thomas Nashe, *The unfortunate traveller. Or, the life of Jacke Wilton* (1594) and *The strange fortune of two excellent princes* (1600). The last were both quartos of over 60 pages. (Wood 284(3); Wood C31(3); Wood 321(1).)

[53] Frederick J. Furnivall, ed., *Captain Cox, his ballads and books; or, Robert Laneham's letter* (1871). Spufford, *Small books*, pp. 51, 66, 67 etc.

1660, although we must keep in mind the possibility of abridged versions which have not survived.[54]

When we do separate the short and cheap from the long and pricey, there is still the problem of identifying the audience. These little books need to be seen within a social and economic context, not as isolated artefacts. The problem of defining the chapbook only by its properties (content, size and price), rather than its context, can be illustrated by looking at two booksellers separated by 130 years.

John Dorne, bookseller in Oxford, sold 'chapbooks' for a penny, twopence and threepence each. For entertainment he offered merry tales like *Syr Eglamour*, *Robert the devill* and *The Nutbrown mayde*. For the pious he stocked the *Jesus Psalter*, *The Complaint of Saint Magdalene* and the lives of saints Barbara, Margaret, Katherine, Erasmus and others. Surviving copies of these little books are in black letter, and range from eight pages (sold at a penny) to over fifty pages (sold at 2d. or 3d.).[55]

John Andrews, bookseller at Pye Corner in London, also sold 'chapbooks' for twopence and threepence. His merry titles included *Dick of Kent* and *Cupids master-piece*. For the godly he offered *The black book of conscience* and *The plain mans' plain path-way to heaven*. These were mostly black-letter octavo chapbooks of twenty-four pages each.[56]

The records for John Dorne come from the year 1520, when he kept a day-book in his Oxford shop, and at the St Fridiswyde and Austen fairs. In an entire year he sold only one or two copies of each of his two dozen 'chapbook' titles; 'st. katrine lyf' breaking all records at four copies. In the countryside of 1520, less than one third of yeomen and one twentieth of husbandmen were fully 'literate'.[57] Most of Dorne's 'chapbook' buyers would probably have been the local gentry, and the Oxford scholars taking a break from their Latin and Greek.

John Andrews published and sold his books 130 years later, from 1651 to 1663. By this time at least three-quarters of yeomen and one quarter of husbandmen could write their names, and many more are likely to have been able to read.[58] We do not know exactly how many copies Andrews

---

[54] Spufford, *Small books*, p. 96.

[55] F. Madan, ed., 'The day-book of John Dorne, bookseller in Oxford 1520', *Collectanae*, Proceedings of the Oxford Historical Society, 1st series (1885), pp. 71–178. Extant copies include *Here begynneth the lyfe of the gloryous vyrgyn and marter saynt Barbara* (Julian Notary, 1518, 8 pages 4to), sold at 1d.; *Here begyneth the lyfe of the moast myscheuoust Robert the devyll* (Wynkyn de Worde, [1517?], 56 pages 4to), sold at 3d.

[56] Extant copies include *A new dialogue between Dick of Kent* (1654 edn); *Cupids master-piece* (1656 edn); Andrew Jones, *The black book of conscience* (1658 edn); John Hart, *The plain mans plain path-way to heaven* (1659).

[57] Cressy, *Literacy and the social order*, pp. 160, 162 (graphs 7.10 and 7.13, both from the diocese of Norwich).

[58] *Ibid.*, same graphs plus p. 168 comments on East Anglia as a whole.

Table 4. *Ten favourite titles*

Title		Book	Ballad	Length/cost?[a]
King Arthur (STC 801) A,C,E,F,G	1	Caxton (1485)	?ent. R. Jones (1565–6)	*c.* 312 sheets fol.
	2	T. East (1578)	ent. E. Allde (1603)	= 9s.
	3	W. Stansby f. J. Bloome (1634)	ent. partners (1624) W. Jones? (*c.* 1620)	
Foure Sonnes of Amon (STC 1007) A,C,D	1	Caxton (1490)	–	*c.* 112 sheets fol.
	2	W. Copland f. T. Petet (1554)		= 3s. 3d.
	3	W. Copland f. R. Toye (1554)		
Adam Bell (STC 1805.7) A,B,C,F,G	1	W. de Worde (*c.* 1505)	Child no. 116	2.5 sheets 4to = 1–2d.?
	2	W. Copland (*c.* 1565)		
	3	London (*c.* 1640)		
Bevis of Hampton (STC 1987) A,B,C,E,F	1	W. de Worde (1500)	–	*c.* 18 sheets 4to = 6d.
	2	W. Copland (1565?)		
	3	R. Bishop (1639?)		
Book of riddles (STC 3288.5) A,D,F,G	1	W. Rastall (1530?) a few repr. in:	–	*c.* 3 sheets 8vo = 2d.?
	2	f. R. Jackson (1617)		
	3	f. M. Sparke (1629)		
King and the tanner (STC 7503) A,G	1	ent. W. Griffith (1564–5)	ent. E. White (1582)	1.5 sheets 4to 1 sheet 8vo
	2	J. Danter (1596)	ent. J. Trundle (1615)	= 1–2d.?
	3	W. White (1613)	ent. partners (1624)	

Table 4. *cont.*

Title		Book	Ballad	Length/cost?[a]
Guy of Warwick (STC 12540) B,C,D,E,F,G	1	R. Pynson (1500?)	ent. R. Jones (1592)	*c.* 34 sheets fol. = 12d.
	2	in Lothbury W. Copland (*c.* 1565)	ent. partners (1624) f. J. Wright (*c.* 1640)	
	3	in Lothbury W. Copland (*c.* 1565)		
Robin Hood (STC 13688) A,C,F,G	1	R. Pynson (1500?)	ent. J. Alde (1562–3)	*c.* 8 sheets 4to = 3–4d.?
	2	W. Copland? (*c.* 1565?)	ent. partners (1624)	
	3	f. E. White (*c.* 1590)	+ other versions	
Fryar and the boy (STC 14522) A,F	1	W. de Worde (1510–13)	–	2 sheets 4to = 1–2d.?
	2	E. Allde (1584–9)		1.5 sheets 8vo
	3	E. Allde (1626)		
100 merry tales (STC 23663) A,D	1	J. Rastall (1526?)	–	*c.* 24 sheets fol. = 8d.
	2	R. Copland? (1548?)		
	3	R. Copland? (1548?)		

[a] Cost estimated at rate for reprints of 0.35d./sheet (except pamphlets under 4 sheets). Approximate length applies to all three editions listed.

Sources to Table 4

A Frederick J. Furnivall, ed., *Captain Cox, his ballads and books* (1575), 1871.
B George Puttenham, *The arte of poesie* (1589), ed. G. D. Willcock and A. Walker, 2nd end, Cambridge, 1970.
C Edward Dering, *A briefe and necessary instruction*, 1572.

D *Cyvile and uncyvile life*, 1579.
E Henry Parrot, *Epigrams and satires*, 1615.
F Pepys collection (1680s).
G William Thackeray's trade list (1689), printed in Spufford, *Small books*, pp 262–7.

Publication history

1 First known edition.
2 Captain Cox edition (closest to 1575).
3 Last pre-1640 edition.

sold, but *The black book of conscience* was in its '13th edition' in 1660, within four years of the day Andrews registered it.[59] *The plain mans plain path-way to heaven* (an abridgement of Dent's classic) reached 'the seventeenth edition' in only three years.[60] If this enumeration was correct, these two titles could represent some 30,000 copies or more; even at half that number the volume is impressive. Andrews' readers may have been tradesmen, yeomen, husbandmen, and even some agricultural labourers and servants.

How can we tell if the chapbook was reaching a wide rural market? The approach in this study will be to focus on the trade list of the group of publishers who apparently commanded a wide distribution network: the ballad publishers. We know that the chapbook trade after the Restoration was closely connected with the ballad trade. We know that from the second half of the sixteenth century ballads were distributed in the countryside.[61] This distribution was apparently the primary function and skill of the ballad partnership formed in 1624. The ballad publishers had access to a network of chapmen; at what point did they begin to distribute chapbooks along this network as well?

An eye to the post-Restoration trade should also help in a more precise definition of a format by which to recognize the chapbook. By the time Pepys was collecting in the 1660s, their identical format enabled him to bind up all the little books together as 'penny merriments' and 'penny godlinesses'. This standard 'penny' size format was twenty-four pages or less, in octavo or duodecimo.[62] Pepys also collected an assortment of longer works which he called 'Vulgaria': these included 24-page quartos called 'double-books' (costing 3d. or 4d.) and longer quartos called 'histories' (costing 6d. or more).[63] We will pay some attention here to the predecessors of the 'double-books', although the 24-page octavo 'penny books' will be our primary focus.

---

[59] Registered 30 July 1656 (Eyre, II, p. 76). The author was Andrew Jones.

[60] Registered 22 April 1656 (Eyre, II, p. 53). The 'author' was John Hart. An edition of 1674 for William Thackeray and Thomas Passinger was labelled the '57th', although we should be skeptical about the accuracy of this claim (Wing 959B).

[61] In 1553, a ballad against 'maistres mass' was being shown around at the alehouse in Orwell, Cambridgeshire (Spufford, *Contrasting communities*, p. 208); and by 1570 ballads were 'cast in the streetes' of Northampton. (Collmann, p. 171.) For further examples see ch. 1.

[62] In 8vo, 24 pages uses 1.5 sheets of paper. Works of 36 pages 12mo and 48 pages 16mo also used 1.5 sheets and should have cost the same to the printer, although these formats were not so often used. Longer 12mo and 16mo works have been included at the end of the 'penny godly' list.

[63] Spufford, *Small books*, pp. 130–1, 150–1.

In addition to its cheapness (requiring only 1 to 1.5 sheets), the 'penny' format was ideally designed for chapmen, who could have carried large numbers of these small books in their packs. This was to remain the standard format through the eighteenth and nineteenth centuries. The introduction to the collection in the New York Library defines the chapbook as 'anything from a broadside to a good-sized book – anything printed – that was carried for sale by a chapman into villages, hamlets, towns'. But it goes on to describe the 'poorer penny ones of popular taste': 'most were about 5.5 × 3.5 inches in size and contained from 4 to 24 pages'.[64] This falls in line with the description used by Victor Neuberg; 'paper-covered books, approximately 3.5 × 6 in., consisting usually of twenty-four pages including woodcut illustrations'.[65]

The term 'penny chapbook' is useful as a description of the precise format which we know had emerged by the Restoration, and whose origins we wish to trace. The fact that Pepys' 'penny merriments' and 'penny godlinesses' actually cost twopence did not prevent him from using 'penny' books as a generic term. The label 'twopenny books' would beg the question of cost: the evidence for a standard price of twopence comes from 1637 onwards, after the 40% rise in book prices which occurred around 1635.[66] I will therefore follow Pepys in the use of the term 'penny books', as a description of an unmistakable size and format, rather than a precise statement about price.[67]

The rest of this study is an attempt to chart the development of a specialist 'cheap print' trade by looking at the output of those who commanded the right distribution network, the ballad publishers. I will look in particular for the format of 24-page octavo or smaller, but also at short pamphlets or old quarto chapbooks of up to four sheets, as precursors of the 'double-books', and as potential reading matter in their own right. It seems very likely that the ballad publishers, who, later in the century, were also the unchallenged chapbook publishers, must have been responsible for the genesis and nurturing of the trade. If this hypothesis is correct, then a search through the output of the early ballad publishers should uncover the origins of the 'penny chapbook'.

---

[64] Harry B. Weiss, *A catalogue of the chapbooks in the New York Public Library* (New York, 1936), p. 3.

[65] Victor E. Neuberg, *The Batsford Companion to popular literature* (1983), p. 51.

[66] Martin Parker describes his 'twopenny customers', in *Harry White his humour* (1637). John Andrews, bookseller, lists seven books at 2d. in the back of John Hart, *The plain mans plain path-way to heaven* (1659). Johnson, 'Notes on English retail book-prices', pp. 89–90.

[67] For further discussion of these terms see Watt, 'Cheap print and religion', p. 331 n. 82.

The STC search

In the absence of any ready-made contemporary collections, I have embarked on a selective search through the revised STC. This approach has not by any means uncovered all 'penny books' and their publishers; however, I believe it gives an outline of the general development of the trade.

I have looked at the entire non-ballad output of eight ballad publishers, three from the sixteenth century and five from the seventeenth century, searching for any 'penny books' in their lists.[68] This output includes all extant works listed in the revised STC (except single sheets) which were printed by or for, sold by, registered or assigned to one of my publishers.[69] For one major publisher from each period (Richard Jones and John Wright) I have examined each work, noting number of pages, quality of printing, woodcuts, writing style, prefatory remarks, general theme, the presence or absence of the trappings of learned culture (Latin, complex theology, classical illusions, etc.); and, of course, reading any very short pamphlets and 'penny books'.

For the other six publishers (William Pickering, John Awdeley, John Trundle, Henry Gosson, Francis Coules and Francis Grove) I have copied the title and bibliographical details of each work, and have looked at a representative sample of the genres in which each one specialized. Then I looked specifically only at those works whose subject was not obvious from the title, and at those which could possibly be 'penny chapbooks'.

In the sixteenth century, Richard Jones was the obvious choice: he produced the largest number of ballads (164 titles entered in the Stationers' Register) and spanned a period from 1564, within six years of the inception of the Company, to 1602. Two Elizabethan publishers with a smaller output have also been chosen, with an eye to the particular focus of this study on *godly* chapbooks. William Pickering had a high religious percentage (55–66%) in his ballad output and operated on London Bridge in the earliest years of the Stationers' Company, from 1557 to 1575, covering the period before Jones. John Awdeley (1559–75) is of special interest because he wrote some of his thirty ballads himself. The sincerity of his religion is confirmed by the very lengthy, very Protestant preamble to his will.[70] With his personal

---

[68] This was done with the aid of Paul G. Morrison, *Index of printers, publishers and booksellers in Pollard and Redgrave STC* (Charlottesville, 1950), updated with the information to appear in the forthcoming revised printers' index. I am extremely grateful to Katherine Pantzer of the Houghton Library, who copied from file cards by hand the new items for my publishers.

[69] One exception is a very large assignment to John Wright and J. Haviland in 1638: none of these titles were printed for Wright before 1640, and they are mostly long, expensive works having nothing to do with Wright's usual publishing habits.

[70] PRO, Prerogative Court of Canterbury, Prob. 11. 57.

evangelical motives, we might expect him, if anyone, to be an innovator in the sixteenth-century godly print trade.

In the seventeenth century, as we have seen, there were no specialists in godly ballads, but publishers have been chosen for their role in the ballad partnership, and also with an eye to their links with the late seventeenth-century ballad and chapbook partners (Fig. 6). John Wright (1602–46) was a founding member of the 1624 partnership, whose apprenticeship line leads directly through William Gilbertson, Charles Tias and Thomas Passinger (1), to John Back, Josiah Blare and Thomas Passinger (2); all familiar names from the chapbook imprints in Margaret Spufford's *Small books and pleasant histories*. Henry Gosson (1603–41) was another senior 'partner' whose line does not appear to lead anywhere, but who is of interest as the largest single producer of ballads: some seven dozen broadsides survive with his imprint, as compared with two dozen for John Wright.[71]

Francis Coules (1624–63) joined the 'partners' in 1626, and has left over four dozen ballads with his imprint before 1640. Coules was himself a chapbook publisher by the 1660s. His line of influence leads through John Wright (2) to Jonah Deacon, Thomas Vere and John Wright (3); again, important chapbook figures in the Pepys era.[72] John Trundle (1603–26) had dealings with the 'partners' but remained an independent agent in the ballad trade. He published some interesting single-sheet woodcuts, and was infamous in his day as a publisher of ephemeral literature, including a poached copy of *Hamlet*, and numerous sensational news pamphlets.[73] His widow Margery carried on the business for two years, but on 1 June 1629 she transferred her copyrights to the 'ballad partners'.[74] Trundle, too, can be linked with a Restoration chapbook 'partner' John Clarke, via the Commonwealth ballad publisher Richard Harper (Trundle's apprentice). Francis Grove (1624–63) had trade descendants including John Andrews (the earliest chapbook publisher found by Margaret Spufford), William Thackeray and Phillip Brooksby. He gained his freedom in 1623, and appears in the 1630s as the publisher of several Martin Parker chapbooks on my list of 'penny merriments'.

The results of this search have been summarized in Appendices H and I. It is immediately apparent that there were very few books of 'penny'

[71] R.S. Thomson also claims for Gosson the greatest impact on folksong pre-1640. (Thomson, 'The development of the broadside ballad trade and its influence upon the transmission of English folksongs' (Cambridge PhD, 1974), p. 57.)

[72] John Wright (2) was the cousin of John Wright (1) (the publisher who features here). John Wright (3) was the son of John Wright (2). I am grateful to Sheila Lambert for information on the Wrights.

[73] Gerald D. Johnson, 'John Trundle and the book-trade 1603–1626', *Studies in Bibliography*, 39 (1986), pp. 177–99.

[74] William A. Jackson, ed., *Records of the Court of the Stationers' Company 1602 to 1640* (1957), p. 210.

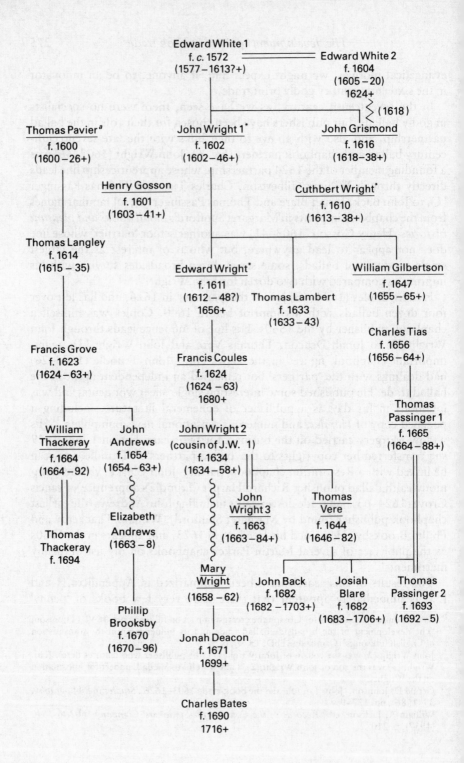

Edward White 1
f. c. 1572
(1577 – 1613?+)

Edward White 2
f. 1604
(1605 – 20)
1624+

(1618)

Thomas Pavier[a]
f. 1600
(1600 – 26+)

John Wright 1*
f. 1602
(1602 – 46+)

John Grismond
f. 1616
(1618 – 38+)

Henry Gosson
f. 1601
(1603 – 41+)

Cuthbert Wright*
f. 1610
(1613 – 38+)

Thomas Langley
f. 1614
(1615 – 35)

Edward Wright*
f. 1611
(1612 – 48?)
1656+

William Gilbertson
f. 1647
(1655 – 65+)

Thomas Lambert
f. 1633
(1633 – 43)

Francis Grove
f. 1623
(1624 – 63+)

Francis Coules
f. 1624
(1624 – 63)
1680+

Charles Tias
f. 1656
(1656 – 64+)

Thomas
Passinger 1
f. 1665
(1664 – 88+)

William
Thackeray
f. 1664
(1664 – 92)

John
Andrews
f. 1654
(1654 – 63+)

John Wright 2
(cousin of J.W. 1)
f. 1634
(1634 – 58+)

Thomas
Thackeray
f. 1694

Elizabeth
Andrews
(1663 – 8)

John
Wright 3
f. 1663
(1663 – 84+)

Thomas
Vere
f. 1644
(1646 – 82)

Mary
Wright
(1658 – 62)

John Back
f. 1682
(1682 – 1703+)

Josiah
Blare
f. 1682
(1683 – 1706+)

Thomas
Passinger 2
f. 1693
(1692 – 5)

Phillip
Brooksby
f. 1670
(1670 – 96)

Jonah Deacon
f. 1671
1699+

Charles Bates
f. 1690
1716+

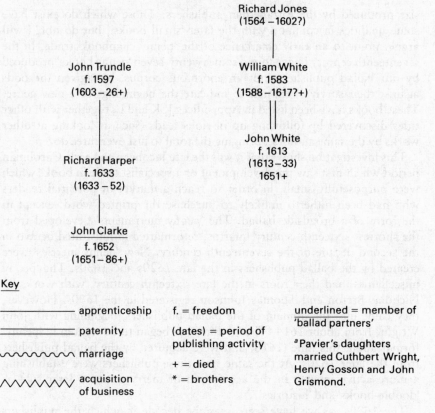

Fig. 6   Genealogy of the ballad publishers

Sources
Cyprian Blagden, 'Notes on the ballad market in the second half of the seventeenth century', *Papers of the Bibliographical Society of the University of Virginia*, 6 (1953–4), pp. 161–80.

D. F. McKenzie, *Stationers' company apprentices 1605–1640* (1961).

D. F. McKenzie, *Stationers' company apprentices 1641–1700* (1974).

R. B. McKerrow, *A dictionary of printers and booksellers in England, Scotland and Ireland, and of foreign printers of English books 1557–1640* (1910).

Katherine Pantzer, unpublished notes for forthcoming Dictionary of Publishers.

H. R. Plomer, *A dictionary of the booksellers and printers who were at work in England, Scotland and Ireland from 1641 to 1667* (1907).

Margaret Spufford, *Small books and pleasant histories. Popular fiction and its readership in seventeenth-century England* (1981), ch. 4.

R. S. Thomson, 'The development of the broadside ballad trade and its influence upon the transmission of English folksongs' (Cambridge PhD, 1974), p. 61 and unpublished chart.

size produced by the Elizabethan publishers. Those which do exist have some qualities in common with the later 'small books', but do not, I will argue, point to an early emergence of the 'penny chapbook' trade. In the seventeenth century I have found some twenty-seven 'penny books' produced by our ballad publishers: not an enormous corpus, but (given the odds against their survival) enough to indicate the beginnings of a new genre. These books have been listed in Appendices J, K and L, together with other titles discovered by following up obvious leads (such as looking at other works by the same authors), bringing the total to just over three dozen.

This investigation shows that it was the late Jacobean and early Carolinian period which first saw the development of a specialist trade in books which were purposefully small, in order to reach a market of potential readers who had been hitherto unlikely to purchase the printed word, except in the form of a broadside ballad. The 'penny merriments' developed from the shortest sixteenth-century quartos, reformatted in illustrated octavo in the second decade of the seventeenth century. New 'penny merries' were created by the ballad publishers in the late 1620s and 1630s. The 'penny miscellanies' had their roots in the late sixteenth century, with works by Nicholas Breton and Thomas Johnson registered in the 1590s. However, they came into the domain of the ballad publishers, beginning with John Wright, from about 1614. The 'godlinesses' began to be written in 'penny' format about this time (1616) and were acquired by the ballad publishers from the later 1620s. At the same time these publishers were establishing a more active interest in the acquisition of merry quartos, later sold as 'double-books' and 'histories'.[75]

The 1620s, as we have seen, was the decade in which the publishers organized themselves into a specialized syndicate for distribution of broadside ballads. The combined evidence also points to this as the period when ballad publishers began consciously to acquire the copyrights to these small books, which they could sell to the same wide market as their ballads.

THE BALLAD PUBLISHERS AND THEIR NON-BALLAD OUTPUT

The sixteenth century

The 'penny chapbooks' will be the subject of chapter 7, but here we will look more broadly at the output of the eight ballad publishers. What other printed matter did they produce alongside their broadsides? What kinds of cheap pamphlet might have reached some of their customers along the same routes of distribution? What does the absence of 'penny chapbooks' from the earlier presses tell us about the chronology of the trade?

Richard Jones was by Elizabethan standards a 'popular' printer: he pro-

---

[75] See William Thackeray's trade list of 1689, in Spufford, *Small books*, pp. 266–7.

duced only two works in Latin, and none of the staple textbooks for the schools and universities: he catered for 'lay' rather than 'learned' culture.[76] Yet his clientèle consisted, it appears, of gentry and wealthy London merchants. Almost half his corpus was made up of full-length books, many addressed to 'young gentlemen', 'young courtiers', 'To the Gentlemen Readers' or to specific members of the court and city elite.[77] A debate over *Cyvile and uncyvile life* (1579) claims to be fit for 'all Nobilitie and Gentlemen': it compares the country gentleman with the city courtier, not the average yeoman with the London tradesman. Some of Jones' authors claimed to write for 'everie man from the highest to the lowest: from the Richest to the poorest', but did so in works of over 300 pages, which would have cost a minimum of 10d. unbound.[78]

A large group of Jones' works I have listed under 'history and geography': mostly books about foreign lands such as *The voyage and travaile of M. Caesar Frederick, merchant of Venice, into the East India*, which was translated partly for 'the commoditie that Merchants and other my Countrimen may reape of it'.[79] The same readers would buy what I have called Jones' 'sober' news pamphlets, to keep themselves informed about political events in England and the Continent.[80] For entertainment these readers bought play texts (usually at least nine sheets quarto) and verse collections; usually retellings of classical myths, tangled in Renaissance allegories and conceits, which do not strike one as poetry for the rudimentary reader. One of the 'penny-sized' works fits into this category: William Hubbard, *The tragicall and lamentable historie of two faythfull mates: Ceyx Kynge of Thracine and Alcione his wife: drawen into English Meeter* (1569).[81] Only a couple of the Jones pamphlets approach the category of 'small merries': *Orpheus his journey to Hell* (1595) and *The mylner of Abyngton* [c. 1575]. These are quartos of about four sheets each (i.e. 4d. or less); simple narratives of the type that appealed to all social groups, but too few to constitute a special line for a different clientèle than Jones' more erudite works.[82]

---

[76] Jones' Latin titles were George Dicker, *Discors concordia papae* (1595); *Continens Conticum Canticorum Salomonis* (1597).

[77] STC 3631, 21593, 20402, 16674, 3633, 19880.

[78] John Norden, *A sinful mans solace* (1585), 336 pages = 21 sheets 8vo.

[79] Trans. Thomas Hickock, 1588.

[80] These pamphlets included straight translations of edicts from the Prince of Parma [1579?], the Archbishop of Cologne (1583) and the King of France (1585). (STC 333, 11694, 13092.5.)

[81] Other short verse pamphlets include Thomas Lodge, *Scillaes metamorphosis: enterlaced with the unfortunate love of Glaucus* (1589). Longer collections include Thomas Procter, *A gorgious gallery of gallant inventions* (1577); Nicholas Breton, *A floorish upon fancie* (1577), and Anthony Copley, *Wits fittes and fancies* (1595).

[82] *A right pleasant and merye historie of the mylner of Abyngton ... Whereunto is adioyned another merye jest, of sergeaunt that would have learned to be a fryar*, partly by Sir T. More, was originally printed by Wynkyn de Worde.

More promising, but equally rare, are Jones' little octavo tracts reporting the 'end and confession' of various traitors, and news of murderers and monstrous births. In at least one case he acted as part author, elaborating on the report and drawing out the moral conclusions.[83]

Jones' religious publications fit into the category of practical spirituality and morality described by Louis B. Wright in *Middle-class culture in Elizabethan England*.[84] These works laid out duties, virtues and basic Christian doctrine for the godly merchant and gentry classes; or anyone who could not only read, but afford books costing up to a shilling or more unbound.[85] Jones did print several godly pamphlets, short enough to cost 3d. or less. Some deal with contentious elements of the new Protestant doctrine, rather than more simply calling for repentance and amendment of life as the later 'penny godlinesses' do. Others seem to aim at a genteel or London-based public. However, they are of interest to look at in more detail, as forerunners of the 'penny godly', and showing at least some of its characteristics.

The most straightforward of these are the moral diatribes against particular social evils such as drunkenness and whoredome, unsurprising since so many Elizabethan ballads printed by Jones and others called for this reformation of morals. In *A delicate Diet, for daintiemouthde Droonkardes* (1576, 48 pages i.e. 3 sheets 8vo), George Gascoyne expresses concern with the behaviour of the meaner sort of people, but it is not they themselves he expects to be reading his pamphlet:

> shall we see the unthriftye Artificer, or the labourer, permitted to syt bybbing and drinking of Wine in every Taverne ... But it were folly to stand so much upon these mean personages, who for lacke of wytte or good education, maye easily be enclyned to thinges undecent. I would (for God) that our gentrie, and the better sort of our people, were not to much acquainted with quaffing, carowing, and drinking of harty draughtes.[86]

Other moral pamphlets were aimed especially at a city audience. A tract by 'R.C. Citizen', *The blasinge of bawdrie* (1574, 24 pages 8vo, i.e. 'penny size') was addressed to the parish and ward officials responsible for rooting

[83] *The several confessions of T. Norton & C. Norton* (1570); John Partridge, *The ende and confession of J. Felton* (1570); R.B., *The severall executions & confessions of J. Slade & J. Bodye: traitours* (1583). This genre is discussed in J.A. Sharpe, '"Last dying speeches": religion, ideology and public execution in seventeenth-century England', *Past and Present*, 107 (1985), pp. 147–65. Jones addresses the reader in *A most straunge, and true discourse; of the wonderfull judgement of God. Of a monstrous deformed infant, begotten by incestuous copulation* (1600).

[84] Louis B. Wright, *Middle-class culture in Elizabethan England* (Ithaca, 1958 edn), pp. 228–96.

[85] For example, 'W.B.', *The maner to dye well* (1578); Thomas Pritchard, *The schoole of honest and virtuous lyfe* (1579); Bartholomew Chappell, *The garden of prudence* (1595).

[86] Gascoyne, *Delicate diet*, sig.C3.

out prostitutes, although all classes in London would supposedly profit: 'Geven for a New yeares Gyfte, as well to all such in whose charge, the due punishment thereof is committed: As also to all other that may reap comodytte by lothyng their practises, either by readyng, or hearyng of the same.'[87] A broad spectrum of evils applying particularly to London are attacked in *The will of the devill, with his x. detestable commaundements* (1566?, 24 pages 8vo, i.e. 'penny size'), first published around 1548. The devil leaves bad wares in his will to help goldsmiths, pewterers, vintners, pie-bakers and other tradesmen with their malpractices; the mercers are given 'a subtyle lyght, to make all their wares shew fyne'.[88] The usual timeless social evils (whoring, dicing, usury, etc.) are also favoured by the devil. But the topical bite of the pamphlet is its anti-papism: 'And I give Constantine, all the whole Images of my Churches: My Belles to Sabianus; my Popish Hymnes to Pope Leo.'[89] This pamphlet belongs in the 'satirical sub-genre of the Protestant hell vision', related to the 'pasquinade' tradition and to the ballad epistles to and from Rome.[90] Jones printed further editions of this work in [1567?] and [1580?], so the mock testament format must have been popular.[91] However, it did not last into the seventeenth century: its Edwardian and early Elizabethan outcry against idols, ceremonies, corrupt clergy and other popish trappings was somewhat dated; the anti-papist element seems virtually to have disappeared from the bottom end of the religious print spectrum by the Jacobean period.

Jones' relatively up-market readers were commonly offered their moral lessons in the form of an extended metaphor (such as the devil's last will and testament) unlike the twopenny customers of a century later. The writers of Pepys' 'penny godlinesses' opted, without exception, for the direct approach: straight preaching without the benefit of subtle or clever allegory. However, this may be as much a function of the sensibilities of the writers as of the changed nature of the audience: the later 'penny godly' writers were non-conformist ministers with a puritan taste for plain speaking, and without literary experience.[92] Jones' godly pamphlets, on the other hand, were often written by gentlemen and poets, such as Nicholas Breton's *A smale handfull of fragrant flowers, selected and gathered out of the lovely garden of sacred scriptures, fit for any honorable or woorshipfull gentle-*

---

[87] R.C., *Blasinge of bawdrie*, title-page.

[88] *Will of the devyll*, sig.A4.

[89] *Ibid.*, sig.A2v.

[90] See above, p. 88. John King, *English Reformation literature: the Tudor origins of the Protestant tradition* (Princeton, 1982), p. 380.

[91] Mock testaments were a common form of parody across Europe; not only the devil's, but also the pope's, the cock's, Philip II's, and so on. (Peter Burke, *Popular culture in early modern Europe* (1978), p. 122.)

[92] Eamon Duffy, 'The godly and the multitude in Stuart England', *Seventeenth Century Journal*, 1 (1986), pp. 47–8.

woman to smell unto (1575, 16 pages 8vo). This 'penny sized' verse pamphlet listed twenty virtues (constancy, modesty, humility, and so on), together with flowers to remember them by. While this pamphlet was supposedly for 'gentlewomen', Jones had published a similar mnemonic verse in more accessible broadside form, with the flowers as the holy men of the Bible.[93]

Other allegorical situations could come from the more male-oriented worlds of politics and law, such as *A new yeres gift, or an heavenly acte of parliament: concerning how every true Christian should lyve: made and enacted, by our soveraigne lorde God, and all the whole clergie in heaven consenting to the same* (1569, 30 pages i.e. 2 sheets 8vo). The Lords in this Parliament were 'Christ Jesus Vicegerent [*sic*]', 'John the Evangelist, Lorde Secretarie', 'Moses the Speaker of the Parliament' with other equally illustrious members. William Pickering published a 'penny-sized' work parodying the contemporary news pamphlets which reproduced the texts of foreign royal edicts: *The general pardon, geven longe agone, and sythe newly confyrmed by our Almightie Father, with many large privileges, grauntes, and bulles graunted for ever, as it is to be seen here-after* [1570?].[94] The text included injunctions against popish belief in Purgatory, indulgences and images, and a grant of the liberty to read the Bible in every language. A similar little printed drama, printed by William White in 1617, is one of our first seventeenth-century penny godlinesses. John Andrewes' *A subpoena from the high imperiall court of heaven* (24 pages 8vo) went through at least five editions by 1632. The text consisted of speeches in verse by Justice, Death and Mercy, not unlike a medieval morality play.[95]

A couple of Richard Jones' godly pamphlets did receive the ultimate seal of commercial success, by lasting through many editions well into the seventeenth century and beyond 1640. These were Francis Seager's *The schoole of vertue* (1593) and Philip Stubbes' *A christal glasse for Christian women* (1591), both transferred to another ballad publisher Edward White in 1601, and then to the 'ballad partners' Thomas Pavier and John Wright in 1620.[96] Seager's work was for children, setting out directions for behaviour from the practical (washing and dressing in the morning) to the social (humble attitude to elders, decorum in church, no filthy talking or lying) to the religious (prayers and graces for various times of day). Some of the instructions for serving at table, delivering messages and behaviour at school suggest

---

[93] John Symon, 'A pleasant poesie, or sweete nosegay of fragrant smellyng flowers gathered in the garden of heavenly pleasure, the holy and blessed bible; to the tune of Black Almayne' (1572), Lilly, p. 5.

[94] Trans. from French by Wyllyam Hayward. 24 pages 8vo.

[95] Andrewes made no further attempts of this kind: his later godlies were straightforward puritan repentance tracts (see below, pp. 306–11).

[96] 46 pages 8vo (3 sheets); 22 pages 4to (3 sheets), i.e. 'double-book' size. John Wright was Edward White's apprentice.

an affluent context; however, if the work was originally written for the children of gentry and wealthy merchants, there is no reason why it could not, over time, have reached a wider market. Evidence that it had begun to do so by 1601 is found in the port books recording imports to Ireland, where an entry of 22 May lists '2 doz. p'vis libris called the *School of Virtue*'.[97] In 1616, the York bookseller John Foster had 'Twelve School of Vertues' (stitched and unbound) valued at 15d., or a penny-farthing each.[98]

While this strict and humourless work was no doubt more popular with parents than children, *A cristal glasse for Christian women* must have been more encouraging and inspiring for its intended audience; as, indeed, its twenty-five editions would suggest.[99] This was Philip Stubbes' account of the life of his wife Katherine, who died in childbirth at the age of twenty. The first part tells the basic story: her parentage and marriage, her virtuous life, her sickness in childbirth; and various visions, prayers and meditations which came to her as death approached. The second part consists of her confession of faith, neatly summarizing all the basic tenets of Christianity, with special emphasis on Protestant interpretations such as 'Neither the Bread nor Wine changed in the Lords Supper' and 'Christ is our only Mediator'. The last part dramatizes her final moments: the conquest of her soul over Satan, her last words and her death. 'The life and death of Katherin Stubs' was, according to William Cartwright's satire of *c.* 1635, one of the 'small Books' sold from a wooden box outside playhouse doors, along with 'A judgement shewn upon a Knot of Drunkards' and 'A pill to purge out Popery'.[100]

This pamphlet of Katherine Stubbes, although physically unlike a 'penny godly' because of its very neat quarto format, has elements foreshadowing the death-bed chapbooks which were so popular after the Restoration.[101] Like the ballads of the Duchess of Suffolk and Anne Askew, it presents an idealized Protestant heroine, yet unlike these, it also functions as a practical handbook for those who would wish to emulate her, with its prayers

---

[97] The custom paid was 2d. This was normally 5% of the valuation given in the books of rates, therefore the books must have been valued at 1s.8d. per dozen, or 1.7d. each; suggesting a wholesale price of 2d. each. (Information from Bob Hunter of the University of Ulster.)

[98] Davies, ed., *Memoir of the York press,* p. 363.

[99] STC 23381. *A cristal glasse for christian women. Contayning an excellent discourse of the life and death of Katherine Stubbes.* 1591. The copyright was assigned to John Wright on 13 December 1620. 'Katherine Stubs' lived on as a 'double-book' sold by William Thackeray in 1689. (Spufford, *Small books,* p. 266.)

[100] William Cartwright, *The ordinary, a comedy* (written *c.* 1635), III, v, in *The plays and poems of William Cartwright,* ed. Evans, p. 317. Passage quoted above, p. 267.

[101] Titles include *The dying man's last sermon* and *The mother's blessing.* (Spufford, *Small books,* pp. 201–2.)

and synopsis of doctrine. *A christal glasse* offers a role model for all would-be godly women to follow. It is the literary equivalent of the pictures of godly people kneeling in prayer which began to adorn broadside ballads in the seventeenth century.[102] If visual icons of saints were no longer allowed, neither were printed lives of saints like those little black-letter tracts published by Julian Notary and Wynkyn de Worde. Instead of worshipping ancient saints, the reader was invited to join a contemporary 'saint' in worship. If Protestant women in labour could no longer appeal to Saint Margaret or the virgin Mary in childbirth, they had the companionship and inspiration of Katherine Stubbes.

Another Protestant heroine was presented in William Pickering's pamphlet, *An epistle of the ladye Jane to a learned man of late falne from the truth of Gods word* (ent. 1569–70).[103] Her popularity was confirmed by the reprinting of this pamphlet in 1615, 1629 and 1636 by John Wright (3 sheets 4to).[104] The dramatic narrative of a woman's martyrdom was again used as a forum for a defence of Protestant doctrine and an anti-papist diatribe. The four discourses 'written with her own hands' included a catechism emphasizing that there were two sacraments rather than seven, that the Eucharist was not the real body of Christ, and so on. Like Katherine Stubbes, her 'last words' are the epitome of godliness, courage and strength.

The need for human role models was also recognized by the makers of the post-Restoration 'penny godlies', whose message was very frequently placed in the mouth of a mother, father, brother or godly pastor; always on their death-bed. Not only did this add drama and interest, but it must also have brought an aura of authenticity to the message, in the same way that news stories of horrible crimes and monstrous births had to purport to describe real events. And the death-bed testimonies were expected to be 'new' as well as 'true': the 1646 edition of *A chrystall glasse for Christian women* claimed that Katherine Stubbes 'departed this life at Burton upon Trent in Staffordshire, the 14th Dec. 1645', thus updating her story by over half a century.[105]

Jones is a springboard to a variety of Elizabethan 'popular' printed material, including a handful of early forms of the 'small godly'. It has been necessary to look at him in detail, because of the importance of the negative evidence. The largest ballad publisher in the sixteenth century was not running a sideline in 'penny chapbooks'. This negative evidence is as

---

[102] See p. 149.
[103] *An epistle of the ladye Jane ... Wherunto is added the communication that she had with master Feckenham. Also another epistle to her sister, with the words she spake upon the scaffold.* MDLiiii [J. Day? 1554?]. Pickering's edition does not survive.
[104] STC 7281. Wright's version was retitled *The life, death and actions of the lady Jane Gray. Containing foure discourses written with her owne hands* (1615 etc.).
[105] Wing S6074.

crucial as any positive discovery in the attempt to chart the chronology of the 'penny chapbooks' trade. Its development came after Jones' death, and did not affect the character of the Elizabethan cheap print industry which Jones had dominated.

A glance at the extant trade list of John Awdeley and William Pickering in Appendix I confirms this impression for two smaller stationers. Pickering's extant corpus is mostly topical and ephemeral, but not 'penny-sized'. There are four extant almanacs from his press; no doubt this was one of his staple products, of which other examples have disappeared. He published several news pamphlets on witches, floods and gallows-speeches;[106] as well as one moral play called *A newe enterlude of godly queene Hester* (1561). A couple of his godly pamphlets have been discussed above in conjunction with similar works in the Jones corpus: *The general pardon, geven longe agone* ([1570?], 'penny size'), and *An epistle of the ladye Jane* (ent. 1569–70). Both of these are artefacts of early Elizabethan Protestantism, with its urgent need to convey reformed doctrine, the sense of the papist enemy not yet vanquished, and the mood of struggle, inspiration and martyrdom. They belong more within the context of Reformation polemic than alongside the genre of edifying, soul-saving 'penny godlies' which developed later.

While Pickering dealt mostly in almanacs and news, John Awdeley produced a preponderance of religious works, as we might expect from the personal convictions expressed in his will (see above). Awdeley was the zealous publisher who penned many of his own godly ballads. But his non-ballad output shows little of this popular character: the religious works are long and learned. Awdeley's stock is strong evidence against the existence of a godly chapbook trade in this period, since we would expect him, of all stationers, to have fostered it. There are eight sermons of at least forty pages each, and twelve full-length books. Such treatises as Heinrich Bullinger's *The Christian state of matrimony* (1575), Henry Bennet's *A famous and godly history, contayning the lyves of three reformers* (1561) and *Certen godly, learned a. comfortable conferences betwene D.N.Ridley and M.H.Latymer* (1574) contain 150 to 200 pages each. Awdeley's secular output is mostly weighty history and geography of the Richard Jones variety. Exceptions are a couple of old merry quartos (mentioned below), a 'penny-sized' news pamphlet about a Chester maiden possessed by the devil and

---

[106] John Phillips, *The examination and confession of certaine wytches at Chensforde in the countie of Essex* (1566). Thomas Knell, *A declaration of such tempestious, and outragious fluddes, as hath been in England* (1570). Sampson Davie, *The end and confession of T. Norton and C. Norton rebels who died the 27th of May 1570* (ent. 1569–70). No copy of the latter survives with Pickering's imprint, but the extant edition is 16pp. 8vo. i.e. 'penny size'.

a piece of rogue literature called *The fraternitie of vacabondes* (1565) written by Awdeley himself.[107]

In only one or two of Awdeley's publications is there any attempt to spread reformed ideas to a wide public, and to follow up the work of his godly ballads. Awdeley printed the first known copy of *Robin Conscience*, a classic little verse pamphlet of sixteen pages quarto (therefore short, but not 'penny size'), which highlights again the differences between the moral pamphlets of the sixteenth century and the 'small godly books' of the seventeenth century.[108] It presented reformed ideas in a palatable narrative form, and became one of the most popular pamphlets of the Elizabethan and Jacobean period (judging by the evidence of stationers' inventories). The godly Robin chastises his father Covetousnesse for extortion, his mother Newgise for vain apparel, and his sister Proud Beauty for her wantonness. But more than a morality tale, it is a Protestant manifesto; a conflict between old religion and new religion. The family swears 'By the Masse' while Robin urges them to 'have a respect unto Christ's Testament'. The vanity of his sister is associated with the vanity of Rome: her gold chains and embroidered hair are 'the decking and balming of proud living Idols.'[109] The father warns his son:

> By the masse, yf thou to the Scripture incline,
> Be sure that I wyll never do the pleasor
> Nor yet never helpe the, with none of my treasor.[110]

This paternal diatribe is described in the margin as 'the rebuke and admonicion of the generacyon of Satan'. As a generational conflict, with Protestant doctrine in the mouth of the son rebuking his parents, *Robin Conscience* supports the association of the mid-sixteenth-century Reformation with 'novelty, youth, insubordination and iconoclasm'.[111]

In 1630, the ballad writer Martin Parker updated the tale for seventeenth-century tastes.[112] Gone is the Protestant content, gone is the generational

---

[107] How the plowman lerned his pater noster and The proude wyves pater noster were both entered to Awdeley in 1560, but his editions do not survive. John Fisher, *The copy of a letter describing the wonderfull woorke of God in delivering a mayden within the City of Chester* (1564), 18pp. 8vo.

[108] *The book in meeter of Robin Conscience* [c. 1565?]. Another edition printed by Edward Allde [1590?]. The 'second booke with ij songes in iiij partes' was entered to John Wally 3 August 1579, but is now lost. The original is reprinted in W. Carew Hazlitt, ed. *Remains of the early popular poetry of England* (4 vols., 1864–6), III, pp. 225–47.

[109] 'Robin Conscience', in Hazlitt, ed., *Remains of the early popular poetry of England*, III, pp. 225–47, original printed marginal notes, lines 296–300.

[110] *Ibid.*, lines 71–3.

[111] Patrick Collinson, *From iconoclasm to iconophobia: the cultural impact of the second English Reformation*, Stenton lecture 1985 (Reading, 1986), p. 4.

[112] *Robin Conscience, or, conscionable Robin* (f. F. Coules, 1635). Entered to M. Sparke 20 April 1630; assigned to F. Coules 13 June 1631.

conflict: in this story, morality is linked to social responsibility, as the 'Conscience' figure visits people from various walks of life and is turned away. The setting in named places around London ('Smithfield', 'Pye corner', 'Southwark') gives the moral a topical, contemporary feel; yet it is only in the country that 'Conscience' is finally welcomed. Not with the gentry or yeomanry (who refuse to give up their corn for the poor), but with the labourers:

> Mongst honest folks that have no lands,
> But get their living with their hands,
> These are his friends that to him stands,
>   and's guiding.[113]

By 1630, Parker seems to be appealing directly to an audience at the bottom levels of rural society. The commercial potential of this audience was increasing as literacy progressed: the second wave of Cressy's 'educational revolution' reached its peak in the 1630s.[114] Just as the ballads were being more widely distributed and more effectively 'marketed', with woodcuts and named tunes, the publishers were finding a formula for little books to sell to the same readers.

The distribution of the original *Robin Conscience*, despite its longevity, appears to have been fairly limited. Roger Ward's Shrewsbury shop in 1585 contained '20 bookes of Robin consciens & suche'.[115] 'And suche' probably refers to several other short verse quartos of two or three sheets, mostly merry tales like *How the plowman lerned his pater noster* and *The proude wyves pater noster that wold go gaye*; both entered to John Awdeley in 1560, though with roots as far back as the Wynkyn de Worde press.[116] Awdeley also owned the copyrights to *The 100 merye tales*, *Adam Bell* and *A Pennyworth of witte*, but his editions have not survived.[117] Together with Jones' *Mylner of Abyngton* (also descended from the de Worde press), these jests from the early sixteenth century are the titles which were probably most appealing to the same public who bought ballads. Yet these old quartos were not a major part of the stock of our Elizabethan ballad publishers. The favourite 'merry' titles were valued copyrights owned by various mainstream publishers, not yet the preserve of specialized 'cheap-print' publishers.

The Elizabethan publishers also produced very few works in 'penny-sized' format, and none which seem pitched for a humble audience like the small books later designed to be carried by chapmen to the rural backwaters

---

113 *Ibid.*, p. 15.
114 Cressy, *Literacy and the social order*, pp. 168–71.
115 Rodger, ed., 'Roger Ward's Shrewsbury stock', p. 252.
116 *How the plowman* ... was published by Wynkyn de Worde in 1510. Hazlitt collected many of them in his *Remains of the early popular poetry*.
117 On the travels of *Adam Bell*, from the early sixteenth to the late seventeenth centuries, see Watt, 'Cheap print and religion', p. 351 n. 137

of England. This negative evidence supports the hypothesis that the trade did not appear in any organized form until the second and third decades of the seventeenth century.

The seventeenth century

After 1600, the overall output of the ballad publishers began to shift, with a concentration on ephemeral or 'popular' material such as news pamphlets and plays (see App. I). The publication of cheap print was becoming a more specialized activity. Our major publisher, John Wright, was in fact the most substantial of the seventeenth-century ballad publishers I have looked at, putting out fewer ballads and more full-length books. Yet less than half his non-ballad works ran to four sheets or more, as opposed to almost two-thirds for Richard Jones (see App. H). Ten of Wright's works were plays, including works by Christopher Marlowe, Thomas Dekker and Thomas Heywood. Another group of ten were news pamphlets; not the sober political reports published by Jones, but more sensational stories of murders, earthquakes and monstrous births, complete with title-page wood-cuts.[118] Wright was still publishing and/or selling solid religious guidebooks by Arthur Dent, Thomas Draxe, Roger Cotton, Robert Hill, John Dod and Robert Cleaver.[119] He also published several single sermons, including two by the popular Dent, both of which he saw through their seventh edition.[120] It may be that Wright's experience of the popularity of longer religious works and sermons, together with his involvement in the more frivolous ballad trade, made him realize the potential of a 'penny-sized' godly for the same market.

For, in fact, the largest single category on Wright's trade-list was this new form of print: the 'penny godly'. By 1640 there were a dozen 'penny godly' titles in Wright's corpus. 'Penny chapbooks' in general account for one quarter of his total surviving non-ballad output; after 1620 over half his new non-ballad publications were 'penny books'. Here, indeed, is the evidence of the emergence of the trade which we have been searching for. The 'penny books' will be described in detail in chapter 8; at this point I will do no more than outline the rough chronology of their development.

Wright's new line began with the publication of tiny miscellanies by Nicholas Breton in 1614 to 1617, which he re-issued in the 1620s and 1630s (see App. J).[121] The prototype for these collections of aphorisms was Breton's

---

[118] For example, STC 4768, 6553, 12630, 18786, 25840.
[119] STC 5868, 6619, 6977, 7183, 7187, 13477.
[120] *Christes miracles, delivered in a sermon* (1608); *A sermon of Gods providence* (1609). Both were three sheets octavo.
[121] *The figure of four. The second part* (1614). *Crossing of proverbs* (1616). *Crossing of proverbs. The second part* (1616). *Soothing of proverbs* (1617).

Figure of four (1597) which Wright revived in 1631. Meanwhile, he began to add the 'penny godlies', starting with John Andrewes' *Humble petition* in 1623. In the early 1630s, Wright acquired the copyrights to another half-dozen works by the popular Wiltshire preacher (see App. K).[122] Some were transferred from Andrewes' first publisher Nicholas Okes (and reduced to 'penny size' if necessary); others seem to have been obtained straight from the preacher–author himself. 'Penny-sized' works by Henry Smith and William Perkins were added in the late 1620s, with Perkins' popular *Death's knell* reaching its '16th edition' by 1637.[123]

Although one most often associates chapbooks with merry stories, there are very few of these 'penny merriments' surviving from this period (see App. L). Wright published only two of them: *Tom Thumb* (1630) and *Patient Grissell* (*c.* 1640). However, several old merry quartos, reprinted in octavo by the printers Edward Allde and William White, may have provided the inspiration for the entire 'penny book' genre.[124] It may be that the new 'penny merries' developed last because the still-thriving trade in broadside ballads satisfied the public demand for stories. The 'penny godlies' developed earlier, filling a hole in the market where the old godly ballads had been. John Wright was apparently the leader in this new trade, although others like Henry Gosson and Francis Coules added a handful of titles to the pre-1640 list.

The output of the other publishers supports the impression of a 'penny chapbook' trade emerging in the 1620s. John Trundle died in 1626, before this new trade was properly off the ground, and contributed no 'penny book' titles. He did, however, publish a popular little moral work called *Keepe within compass* (1619) which he may have written himself, and which, with its aphoristic advice and octavo size, came close to the 'penny chapbook' formula. John Wright acquired the copyright in 1623 and turned it from 8vo to 16mo (making it more pocket-sized, though still forty-eight pages long). The rest of Trundle's output was topical and ephemeral, including some thirty ballads, ten plays and fourteen news pamphlets. He was notorious for the publication of sensational news items from every conceivable source, such as the story of the headless bear in *A miracle of miracles* (1614) which was a reprint of a 1584 pamphlet. His output has already been discussed at length in an article by Gerald D. Johnson.[125]

Francis Coules, apart from his fifty-odd broadsides, produced only two

---

[122] *A most necessary caveat from God, Andrewes repentance, Andrewes resolution, A soveraigne salve,* all acquired from Nicholas Okes in 1630. *Andrewes caveat* and *Andrewes golden chaine* both registered to Wright in 1631. *A subpoena* sold by Wright in 1632.

[123] Henry Smith, *The trumpet of the soule* (sold by Wright, 1626). William Perkins, *Death's knell* (acquired by Wright and partners, 1629).

[124] See below, pp. 297–8.

[125] Johnson, 'John Trundle and the book-trade'.

dozen works before 1640.[126] But Coules opened shop in 1624, when the
'penny chapbooks' were just beginning, and he was soon involved in this
new trade. His output confirms the appearance and profitability of small
godly books. In 1627–8 he published three 'penny godly' tracts which appear
to be by the same author, George Shawe: *A looking glasse for drunkards*
(1627), *The doctrine of dying well* (2nd edn, 1628) and *Seven weapons
to conquer the devil* [1628?]. In 1635 he acquired a John Andrewes work
(*A celestial looking-glasse*), and there is evidence for other Coules godlies
which have disappeared.

For example in the *Looking glasse for drunkards*, the author refers us
to another of his works which is now lost: 'See Drunkards cup, pag.17.
line 33.'[127] Since neither of these works on drunkenness was registered,
there may have been further 'penny godlies' published by Coules of which
we have no record. The Stationers' Company Register does record a few
works which were transferred to Coules in the late 1620s which may have
been 'penny godlies'. In 1626 Henry Gosson assigned over the titles 'Highway
to heavenly happiness' and 'Cobhead his catechisme'. The next year, Gosson
again transferred to Coules 'A sweet nosegaye for Gods saintes to smell
to, or an ABC for everye true Christian to use, being the first and seconde
parte, with a short discourse [how] to conquer the devil'.[128] The last part
of this entry may be Shawe's *Seaven weapons to conquer the devil*, indicating
that Coules split the longer work up into small godlies of 'penny size'. The
transfer of the copies suggests that while Gosson had no particular interest
in small godlies (as, indeed, none survive with his imprint), Francis Coules
was collecting these titles in the 1620s, for his own special line in 'penny
books'.[129]

Coules also published a 'penny merry', Martin Parker's *Robin Conscience*
(1635 and 1640 editions) and a 'penny miscellany', Thomas Johnson's
Dainty conceits (1630), in partnership with Henry Gosson. We know that
his line in small books continued to grow, for by 1656 he was publishing
them in partnership with the younger arrivals John Wright (3), Thomas
Vere and William Gilbertson.[130] Francis Coules confirms the emergence

---

[126] These included several merry quartos (see below), and an edition of Shakespeare's *Venus and Adonis* (1636 edn).

[127] *Looking glasse*, sig.AB.

[128] 7 February 1626 (Arber, IV, p. 151). 3 December 1627 (Arber, IV, p. 189). I have been unable to find any surviving copy of the two parts of the 'nosegaye', or the other works acquired from Gosson; nor any original registration of these Gosson titles.

[129] One more pre-1640 penny godly survives with Coules' imprint: this is a 1635 copy of *Christ in the clouds, or Gods comming to judgement*. It is an unremarkable repentance alarum, written by one John Warner, according to the Stationers' Register entry of 25 March 1630.

[130] Spufford, *Small books,* pp. 94, 265.

of the 'penny books' we saw in John Wright's output, and provides a direct link with the Commonwealth and Restoration trade.

Henry Gosson did little on his own in the chapbook line. There is the Johnson miscellany mentioned above, and another fascinating 'penny-sized' pamphlet called *The kings medicines for the plague. Prescribed for the yeare 1604. by the whole colledge of physitians* (1630 and 1636 edns), also done in partnership with Coules, who was responsible for its sale. Like the plague broadsides, the pamphlet recommends a combination of 'bodily' and 'spirituall' medicines involving herbs, bramble leaves, vinegar, patience, prayer and hope.[131] It would seem that Gosson's time was taken up with the ballad trade: he was the biggest single ballad producer, and over eighty separate ballad titles bear his imprint. Apart from ballads, and seventeen news pamphlets, Gosson specialized in the works of one author: John Taylor the 'Water Poet'. Gosson's thirty pamphlets by Taylor (from 1612 on) averaged about three sheets in quarto or octavo (thus costing about 3d.), although they could be as short as one sheet, or as long as five or more.[132]

It appears from Taylor's own *Carriers cosmographie* that his pamphlets were readily available across the realm.[133] But if the Water Poet's works were bought in the countryside, it was not necessarily by humble readers. Some of his works are so full of literary conceits, classical references, topical satire and in-jokes, that they could have made little more sense to the remote rural reader without connections to the London or gentry elite, than to the uninitiated historian.[134] There was enough demand from wealthy Taylor readers to justify a folio volume in 1630 containing *All the works of John Taylor the water poet: being sixty and three in number*. In 1619 he obtained 1,650 signatures of sponsors for a trip by foot to Scotland: these people could be expected to afford at least 12d. for a book about the travels (presumably bound).[135] Although almost half refused to pay up, Taylor's complaint against them indicates the economic status of some of the readers:

> They took a booke worth 12 pence, & were bound
> To give a Crowne, an Angell, or a pound.
> A Noble, piece, or halfe piece, what they list ...
> Foure thousand, and five hundred bookes I gave.[136]

---

[131] See the 'Lord have mercy upon us' series on pp. 227–9, with remedies based on Michael Sparke, *Crumms of comfort* (1627 edn). Since the *King's medicines* were originally 'prescribed' in 1604 (although no copies survive from before 1630), they may have been the source of inspiration for Sparke's spiritual remedy.

[132] *The great O Toole* (1622), 1 sheet. *The complaint of Christmas* (1631), 5 sheets.

[133] See above, pp. 76–7.

[134] For example, *Laugh, and be fat, or a commentary upon the Odcombyan blanket* (1612); *The great O Toole* (1622).

[135] John Taylor, *Pennilesse pilgrimage* (1619).

[136] *A kicksey winsey, or a lerry come-twang* (1619), in *All the works of John Taylor the Water Poet 1630* (facs. edn. 1973), pt 2, p. 39.

But some Taylor works were more accessible than others in language and content, such as *Wit and mirth. Chargeably collected out of tavernes, ordinaries, innes, bowling-greenes and allyes, alehouses, tobacco-shops, highwayes, and water-passages* (1626).[137] This is full of anecdotes; simple merry tales like a traditional jest-book.[138] *The old, old very old man* (1635), about a Shropshire man who lived to be 150 years old, would probably have had the same wide appeal as other marvellous news stories.[139] It was reprinted two centuries later by nineteenth-century chapbook publishers.[140]

Taylor even tried his hand at a kind of 'small godly' pamphlet which harks back to the pre-Reformation 'lives of saints'. *The life and death of the virgin Mary* (1620) was passed from John Trundle's widow to John Wright and the 'ballad partners' in 1629, indicating the continued appeal of this earliest form of biblical biography. The pamphlet, complete with title-page woodcut of the virgin and child, was based on an old Catholic tract Taylor found in Antwerp:

Out of which I have (like a Bee) suckt the sacred honey of the best authorities of Scriptures, and Fathers which I best credited, and I have left the poyson of Anti-christianisme to those where I found it ... I know this work will be unrelished in the pestiferous pallats of the dogmatical Amsterdammatists, but I doe, must & will acknowledge a most reverent honor & regard unto the sacred memory of this blessed Virgin Mary.

Within the poem itself, Taylor was careful to make clear his Protestant orthodoxy; stating, for example, that no prayers for intercession should be made to the virgin Mary. But it is not surprising that he was attacked for 'popish' views in 1641 (along with Martin Parker and George Herbert) in a work called *The popish proclamation*.[141] Taylor's virgin Mary represents the other end of the spectrum from the usual penny godlies, which were written by those 'dogmatical Amsterdammatists' he abhorred. Like the nativity ballads in the 'partners' stock, and the woodcut 'Christus natus est', this pamphlet suggests that the virgin birth could still play an important part in post-Restoration piety.

Pamphlets like *Wit and mirth* and *The virgin Mary* are closer to the simple, timeless appeal of the chapbook than are Taylor's more topical flytings. The Water Poet himself claimed to court a humble audience as well as a high one: 'There is no degree of man or woman, whatsoever, from the Court to the Cottage, or from the Pallace to the Plough, but may make good use of this Poem.'[142] Although such authorial comments should

---

137 Printed for H. Gosson, sold by E. Wright. It ran through five further editions.
138 Such as *A, C, mery talys* (1526?).
139 Printed for H. Gosson, 4 sheets 4to.
140 National Library of Scotland, Lauriston Castle 3007 (2).
141 Replied to by Martin Parker in *The poet's blind mans bough* (1641).
142 *The water cormorant* (1622), preface, in *All the works of John Taylor*, pt 3, p. 1.

always be taken with a pinch of salt, Taylor's corpus does seem to occupy an ambiguous place similar to those sensational news pamphlets described earlier, probably coming into some degree of contact with both the highest and the lowest levels of literate society. In the 1620s and 30s Henry Gosson and others may have been sending these sensational and satirical pamphlets further out into the countryside (via itinerant chapmen or the regular carriers Taylor describes) helping to expand a reading public which would be more deliberately targeted with the 'penny chapbooks'.

The 'penny books' described in chapter 8 are the forerunners of what were the cheapest and most widespread chapbooks by the 1680s, the 'small godly books' and 'small merry books' which were sold at 2d. But before 1640, chapbooks in longer formats were more important numerically within our publishers' stock: the sort of titles which would later be sold as 'double-books' and 'histories' on William Thackeray's trade list of 1689, and collected by Pepys as 'Vulgaria'. The double-books were twenty-four page quartos and cost 3d. or 4d.; the histories were longer quartos costing from 6d. to 1s. or more.[143]

Many of these longer chapbooks were the favourites of Captain Cox, and were sold (as we saw earlier) by a variety of mainstream publishers. Their movement down market was a gradual process which cannot be pin-pointed too precisely. However, there are some signs of the ballad publishers actively acquiring quarto jests, romances and supernatural tales, particularly from the 1620s on.

The strongest interest in merry quartos seems to have come from the ballad publishers who began their careers in the 1620s, Francis Coules and Francis Grove. Both were in the business until 1663, and provide personal links with the post-Restoration trade. In the late 1620s and through the 1630s they were busy acquiring a stake in many of the titles which were later sold as 'double-books' and 'histories'. Some of these works were sold by Coules or Grove for other stationers, presumably again because they had access to the right sort of market.

Francis Coules sold jest-books of the early seventeenth century, a neo-chivalric adventure written by Richard Johnson in the 1590s, and one early sixteenth-century chivalric tale.[144] Francis Grove's stock consisted almost entirely of entertaining works and handbooks between two and eight sheets in length, including clerical jest-books like *The historie of frier Rush* (5 sheets 4to) and *The famous history of Friar Bacon*, a seventeenth-century

---

[143] Spufford, *Small books*, pp. 130–1, 150–1.
[144] Samuel Rowlands, *Doctor Merrie-man: or nothing, but mirth* (1607); *Pasquils jests, mixed with Mother Bunches merriments* [by W. Fennor?, 1632? edn]; R. Johnson, *The most pleasant history of Tom a Lincolne* (1599); *Adam Bell, Clim of the Clough and William of Cloudesle* (1632 edn). For post-Restoration editions see Spufford, *Small books*, pp. 53, 266–7.

best-seller.[145] *Robin Goodfellow his mad prankes, and merry jests*, registered in 1627, included songs to popular ballad tunes like 'The Spanish Pavin' and 'The Joviall Tinker'. Broadside versions of 'The mad-merry prankes of Robin Good-fellow' were published from *c.* 1625 for Henry Gosson, illustrating again the transfer of successful stories and characters between ballad and chapbook forms.[146]

Magic tricks, if less spectacular than those of the Goodfellow and the friars, were available to the amateur in *Hocus pocus junior. The anatomie of legerdemain* sold by Grove in 1638. The pamphlet could apparently be bought at the same fairs where one was likely to see these sleight-of-hand tricks performed by gypsies or 'divers vagrant English':

Would you know whence it first came? why, from Bartholomew Faire: would you know whither it's bent? for the Faire againe; its a straggler, a wanderer, & as I said, as it lightly comes, so it lightly goes; for it means to see not only Bartholomew Faire, but all the Fairs in the kingdom also.[147]

A more practical handbook offered by Grove in 1634 was Richard Hawes' *The poore-mans plaster-box* (6 sheets 4to) written for 'the poore and plaine people, such as cannot (for their remote living) get a Chirurgion, or else (dwelling where they may be had) want meanes to pay them for their paines'.[148] While appeals to 'the poor' from educated writers were often superficial or unrealistic, Hawes shows a consistent concern for the particular accidents and illnesses of the husbandman or labourer. Wounds are likely to be caused by scythe or sickle; bruises when 'men in building fall from off the house' or 'in felling of trees'. And 'if the man faln or bruised be so poore that he hath no bed to sweat in' then one must 'set him for to sweat in horse dung up to the chin'.[149] Like Martin Parker's version of *Robin Conscience*, this is directly and realistically aimed at readers from the lower levels of rural society. Writers of the 1630s, and their publishers, were increasingly aware of these new readers as literacy progressed.

One of Grove's most successful works, apparently aimed at a similar market was a handbook of 1632 called *Cupids schoole: wherein, yongmen and maids may learne divers sorts of complements. Newly written, and never any written before in the same kinde* (3 sheets 8vo). This claim may indeed be true, as this appears to be the earliest example of the courtship manuals and lovers' dialogues which made up one of the largest groups

[145] STC 21451, 1182.7–1184. Spufford, *Small books*, p. 155 n. 47. Charles C. Mish, 'Best-sellers in seventeenth-century fiction', *Papers of the Bibliographical Society of America*, 47 (1953), p. 368.
[146] STC 12016–17, 12018, 12018.3.
[147] *Hocus pocus junior*, sig. A3, A4.
[148] Hawes, *Poore-mans plaster-box*, sig. A2.
[149] *Ibid.*, sig. A2, B1v, B2v.

of Pepys' 'penny merriments', or sixteen titles.[150] The idea seems to have come from a longer handbook called *Cupids messenger: or a trusty friend stored with sundry sorts of letters* (8 sheets 4to) sold by Grove in 1629. The shorter *Cupids schoole* adapted the idea for an audience which might not be able to write, but would deliver these 'amorous words' in person. The book was 'necessary both in the City and Country', and included such scenes as 'The Servingman's wooing of Susan a chamber-maid': 'have wee not seene many Couples, whose whole stocke could hardly purchase a wedding Ring, and a Licence, who yet afterward by their owne indeavours have liv'd more contentedly than those great money matches, which seldom prosper'.[151]

These humble wooing dialogues must have met with instant success, for a second part was entered by Grove the next year (1633), and by the 1680s Grove's prototype had spawned a whole genre in Cupid's name: 'Cupid's posies', 'Cupid's Masterpiece', 'Cupid's Court of Salutations', 'Cupid's Soliciter of Love', 'Cupid's Love-Lessons'; as well as other twopenny courtship books with titles like 'The Lover's Academy' or 'A Pleasant Dialogue between Honest John and Loving Kate'.[152] *Cupids schoole* is an indication of the inroads being made in the 1620s and 30s by Francis Grove and the other ballad publishers into a new kind of market.

---

[150] Spufford, *Small books*, pp. 136, 157.
[151] *Cupids schoole*, sig.C3.
[152] Spufford, *Small books*, pp. 156–70 and notes.

8

Penny books and marketplace theology

THE PENNY CHAPBOOKS

During the second and third decades of the seventeenth century, several London stationers were developing a new 'publishing formula': a range of books to distribute to the same audience as their ballads.[1] The formula which united the French *bibliothèque bleue*, which evolved during the same period, was based on the very low price, the outward similarity afforded by the blue paper covers, and various typographic and structural devices which made the texts manageable for basic readers. In France, the length was not a consistent factor; nor was subject matter. As Roger Chartier has pointed out, the texts 'all had earlier careers in print, either brief or lengthy, before their publication in the *bibliothèque bleue* series, and they came from all genres, all epochs, and all styles'.[2]

In England, however, as in Spain, the size of the books was to be an integral part of the formula, and a standardized feature.[3] As we have already seen, most of the English chapbooks were, by the later seventeenth century, sold either as 24-page quarto 'double-books', or (even more commonly) as 24-page octavo 'small books' or 'penny' books. Like Chartier, we have used 'material and economic characteristics' to identify the beginnings of this chapbook trade, keeping to a minimum assumptions about the 'popular' nature of the texts.[4] Nevertheless, now that we have identified our list of pre-1640 titles, we can see that the content of the early 'penny' books did fit broadly into three publishing strategies.

The 'penny merriments' offered abridged and illustrated versions of chivalric tales and jests which had been old favourites of prosperous laymen for years, often since the early sixteenth century. The 'penny miscellanies', as I have called them, were aphoristic collections which threw together an

[1] The phrase is used in Roger Chartier, *The cultural uses of print in early modern France*, trans. Lydia C. Cochrane (Princeton, 1987), p. 252.
[2] *Ibid.*, pp. 248–9, 252, 256, 346.
[3] The Spanish *pliegos de cordel* were usually 8 or 16 pages quarto. *Ibid.*, p. 253.
[4] *Ibid.*, p. 346.

unabashed mixture of the sacred and the profane. In some of them, merry riddles and proverbs predominated. Others were more heavily moralistic and even catechetical, merging with the 'godlies' at the other end of the scale. Finally, the 'penny godliness' proper was usually a fire-and-brimstone repentance tract. Evangelical and commercial motives joined to create the figure of the popular preacher–author, whose name became a trademark and signpost to the buyer.

Penny merriments

The 'penny merriments' were most closely associated with the ballad trade, growing out of the same themes and authors. The history of the 'penny merries' is related to the short merry quartos dating back to the earliest decades of the printing press. Octavo versions of these old favourites seem (from the extant evidence) to have been the first kind of 'penny-sized' books to emerge. However, no *new* 'penny merries' were written until the 1630s, when Martin Parker's abridged stories were pitched directly at the expanding bottom end of the reading public.

The original innovators in the merry book trade were William White and Edward Allde, both among the printers of ballads officially sanctioned from 1612 to 1620. The story of *King Edward the fourth, and a tanner of Tamworth* had been circulating in quarto form since 1564–5, and in ballad form since 1586.[5] In 1613, William White squeezed the quarto into a single sheet of octavo, and increased the number of woodcuts.[6] The jest of *The fryar and the boy*, was published in 1510–13 by Wynkyn de Worde, entered to John Allde in 1568–9 and printed by Edward Allde in 1584–9. This edition of Edward Allde's was virtually identical to the original De Worde format: a quarto of two sheets, with one woodcut on the title-page showing the boy playing his pipe and the friar dancing in the bushes. But for Allde's next known copy of 1617 he switched from quarto to octavo format, making the tale run twenty-four pages (standard 'penny' size). He added four more woodcuts: one repeat of the title-page, one 'factotum' of a man and woman in early Tudor dress, and two which appear to have been cut specially for the story.[7] In this same year, William

---

[5] Quarto: STC 7503, ent. to W. Griffith 1564–5; assigned by widow Danter to W. White, 6 October 1600. Ballad: STC 7505, ent. to E. White, 1 August 1586; assigned by widow Danter to W. White, 6 October 1600; ent. to J. Trundle, 9 December 1615; ent. to 'partners', 14 December 1624.

[6] John Danter's 1596 version (STC 7503) was 1.5 sheets quarto, with four woodblocks used to produce six pictures. White's octavo had six blocks used on ten occasions. In both editions most of the cuts depict generic knights or courtiers on plumed horses.

[7] One shows Jack shooting with his special bow and the friar behind; the other Jack setting off into the fields with his cow.

White printed the first of the 'penny godlinesses' in 24-page octavo form.[8] There may well have been other 'penny books' printed by White or Allde in the second decade of the seventeenth century, but, if so, they have not survived.[9]

These octavo versions of old tales seem to have provided the model for the 'penny merriments' published in the 1630s, mostly by Coules and Grove. Stories like *Tom Thumb*, *Robin Conscience* and *Robin Hood* were all abridged and rewritten versions of old favourites. But the handful of 'penny merriments' listed in Appendix L were, at least visually, something new and distinctive: these pocket-size books were filled with woodcuts. Some, like most of those in *Tom Thumb*, were specially cut to illustrate the story; others, like most of the *Patient Grissel* pictures, were generic lords and ladies used often on the 'partners' ballads. In both cases, these were the very crude and simple pictures one associates with the seventeenth-century ballads; however, this was the first time that pictures had been available in very short, cheap books. The sensational news pamphlets usually had a picture of similar quality on their title-pages, but it was usually only in long, expensive books like *Reynard the Fox* (1481) and the *Foure Sonnes of Amon* (1490) that the reader had been treated to pictures throughout (in these cases Continental woodcuts acquired by Caxton). The sudden proliferation of pictures in these earliest 'penny merries' suggests they might have passed through the hands of many who could not actually read the text, for the friends and families of the literate would surely be fascinated with this visual novelty.

In *Harry White his humour* (1637), Martin Parker describes the sale of his little books, showing that they were hawked by pedlars in the same manner as ballads, and that their price was twopence:

Harry White is glad at the heart to see the young men laughing, the maides smiling, some drawing their purses, others groping in their pockets, some pretty lasses feeling in their bosomes for odde parcells of mony wrapt in clouts: for these are evident presages of his good fortune: ah what dulcid musick it is to his eares, when he heares his audience cry, joyntly, give me one, give me two: change my mony says one, here is a single twopence says another.[10]

In Parker's preface (addressed to his character Harry) he even suggests the number of copies to be sold, although this may only be an arbitrary artistic

---

[8] John Andrewes, *A subpoena from the high imperiall court of heaven* (1617).

[9] I have checked the STC for all titles printed by William White and Edward Allde from 1612 to 1620, the period in which they were the official printers of ballads. They printed a number of merry quartos (mostly for the ballad publishers we have been examining) but no 'penny' chapbooks other than those described in this chapter.

[10] Parker, *Harry White*, sig.B2v.

invention: 'thus wishing that thy humour may be satisfied with tenne thousand two peny customers, I commit thee to thy humour'.[11]

Martin Parker was the most popular and prolific of seventeenth-century ballad writers, and the first ballad hack to try his hand at writing merry tales in pamphlet form.[12] Parker's involvement with these little books suggests they were aimed at the same public as the ballads. Indeed, the chapbook was sometimes merely a ballad text printed over a number of pages. *The pleasant and sweet history of patient Grissell* was first registered as a broadside in 1565–6, and reappeared on the lists of ballad 'stock' in 1624, 1674, 1712 and 1754.[13] It told the story of Grissel, a poor girl married to a noble marquess, who tested her by taking away her babies and sending her back to her father's cottage for sixteen winters. As in all the versions of the story, which dates back to before Boccaccio's *Decameron*, Grissel bears all this 'most milde and patiently' and is eventually reunited with her 'gracious lord'.

Around 1640, the 'partner' John Wright took the ballad text, spread it out over 24 pages octavo, and adorned it with seven woodcuts, mostly 'factotum' cuts of gentlemen with plumed hats and ladies with fans. For the 'penny book', a prose introduction and conclusion were added, persuading 'all Women in Generall' to learn patience, humility and obedience from Grissel's example. The verse text was divided into little chapters with headings: 'How patient Grissell was sent for the wedding, and of her great humility and patience' (and so on). The editorial policy of chopping longer works into small units with headings was also followed by the publishers of the French *bibliothèque bleue*, apparently on the understanding that readers with only basic literacy skills 'would rely on short, easily deciphered self-contained segments, and would require explicit signposts'.[14] *Patient Grissel* demonstrates concretely the movement of the ballad from oral into print culture. The song which had been frozen into broadside form for commercial distribution had now moved a step further into book form, to be read rather than sung.

Once established, however, the ballad–chapbook relationship could also work the other way round: Martin Parker's 'penny merry' *The king and a poore northerne man* (1633) was abridged for a broadside a couple of

---

[11] *Ibid.*, sig.A4.
[12] A number of earlier ballad journalists wrote news pamphlets. The prolific Elizabethan balladeer William Elderton wrote only one work that was not a broadside: *A new merry newes, as merry can bee, from Italy, Barbary, Turkie, and Candee* (1606).
[13] Arber, I, p. 296; IV, p. 131. Eyre, II, p. 498. Norris and Brown 1712. Dicey catalogue 1754. STC 12384: 'A most pleasant ballad of patient Grissell' [*c.* 1600].
[14] Chartier, *The cultural uses of print*, p. 249.

years after its appearance.[15] This was the story of a poor Northumberland
man who, being cheated by a lawyer, went to the king himself to have
things set right. Like Parker's *Robin Conscience* (described in chapter 7),
it is set in a seventeenth-century world dealing with specific, topical social
ills (in this case wicked lawyers), and with the plain rural people as the
heroes.

Penny miscellanies

One of Parker's little books, *Harry White his humour* (1637) crosses the
boundary into a different genre I have called 'penny miscellanies' (App.
J). These are little collections of aphorisms, ranging from pure humour
to pure moralizing and catechizing; most of the examples including a curious
assortment of both, with no sense of incongruity. Martin Parker put his
brand of street wisdom into the mouth of the Harry White character, who
spouted puns and anti-female humour, but who also gave practical advice
(such as how to stay out of debt), and showed a social conscience: 'Item:
He would have fewer bawdy houses, and more almshouses: also he wisheth
that rich people were more charitable: or that the poore had lesse neede.'[16]
Did people buy these miscellanies in order to be told what to think? Parker
suggested a more critical response from his readers:

> In his one humour many are compriz'd
> Then take your choice, as every man shal find
> In his owne heart: what here's epitomis'd
> You may exemplifie in your owne mind.[17]

If Parker is right, his readers wanted to see their own opinions reflected
in print, perhaps packaged more cleverly by a popular poet. In a society
still mostly oral, wit was more collective than individual. Readers must
have digested new sayings from print, adding them to their stock of old
proverbs, riddles and memory aids.[18]

Some of these miscellanies had more practical use than others, such as
the 'books of conceits' by Thomas Johnson, written in the 1590s, but
acquired by the 'ballad partners' in 1629.[19] Johnson was undoubtedly writing for a country public, with practical tips on 'How to order Oxen when

---

[15] RB repr. I, p. 521 [*c.* 1635]. The ballad, like the chapbook, was published by Francis
   Grove.
[16] Parker, *Harry White*, sig.A5v.
[17] *Ibid.*, sig.B3.
[18] On habits of mind in oral and partially literate societies, see Walter Ong, *Orality and
   literacy: the technologizing of the word* (1982).
[19] *Dainty conceits, with a number of rare and witty inventions* (1630); *A new booke of new
   conceits* (1630). The latter entered to J. Danter, 8 March 1594; both parts entered to
   the 'partners', 7 December 1629.

they are newly unyoaked comming from Labour', 'How to have Peaches sooner by two moneths then other', 'To make Walls or Floores, that neither Snaile, Weasle, Cat, Mouse, or Werrill, will come neere, to destroy either Corne, or other thing'.[20] Writing in the 1590s, he seems to have intended an audience amongst the gentry and prosperous yeomanry, for he included such advice as how to gild one's silver inexpensively, and how to make gold letters for writing.[21] However, with the wealth of more down-to-earth advice on farming, cooking and mending, there is no reason why these twopenny pamphlets would not have sold well with lesser yeomen and literate husbandmen by the time the 'ballad partners' were marketing them.

Nicholas Breton was another miscellany writer who had catered to the Elizabethan gentry. He was responsible for several of the long collections of verse published by Richard Jones, which were mostly love poems and pastoral allegories.[22] But the 'penny miscellanies' published by John Wright, like *The crossing of proverbs* (1616) were rooted in more simple folk wisdom. Here, Breton set up a popular proverb, and then contradicted it with a 'cross':

P. There is nothing so sure as death.
C. Yes, life to the Faithfull.
P. Newes are like fish.
C. Not so, for then they would stinke when they are stale.
P. The Mistris Eye makes the Capon fatt.
C. Not so, it is the good cramming of them.[23]

Here we see the sacred mixed haphazardly with the profane. Later on comes a biblical quiz set up much like a catechism, but using the Bible more for its entertainment value than for edification. It runs like a biblical version of the *Guinness Book of World Records*:

Q. Who was the best wrestler that ever there was?
A. Jacob, when he wrestled with the Angell.[24]

Success with the two parts of the *Crossing of proverbs* led to the *Soothing of proverbs* (entered to John Wright in 1617). Meanwhile the progenitor was still part of the 'penny chapbook' stock in 1670, when William Whitwood sold *Crossing of proverbs*: 'A merry book which will yield comfort to the hearer: merriment to the reader, pleasure to the buyer, and profit to the seller.'[25]

---

[20] Johnson, *Dainty conceits*, sig.A2v, B1, A2.
[21] *Ibid.*, sig.A8v, B2.
[22] *A floorish upon fancie* (1577); *Britton's bowre of delights* (1591); *The arbor of amorous devises* (1597).
[23] *Crossing of proverbs. The second part* (1616), sig.A3v.
[24] *Ibid.*, sig.A6v.
[25] Now 16 pages octavo.

Another miscellany by Breton, *The figure of four*, parented a whole line
of 'penny miscellanies': *The figure of three* (anon., 1636), *The figure of
five* (Martin Parker, 1645?), *The figure of six* (by 'D.N.', 1652), *The figure
of seven* (Martin Parker, 1647), and *The figure of nine* (by Samuel Smithson,
1662).[26] Francis Coules also put out a broadside called 'Choice of inventions, or severall sorts of the figure of three' (1632?). The standard twopenny
price of these little books is again confirmed in the preface to *The figure
of six*:

> This Book is like a Paire of Dice
> That doth run still upon the sice,
> And two pence of it is the price.
> The Figure of six is liked well
> For tis six to one but it will sell.

These verses had been written by 1647, when Martin Parker indicated on
the title-page to *The figure of seven* that the number six had already been
used. He also commented on the vendibility of the little books:

> Three; Foure, Five, Six, sufficient proofe have given
> Of their acceptance; what should hinder seven?

The sales appeal of these books may have lain in the tidy thought-packages
they presented (much like the godly tables of chapter 6), deriving a special
authority from the use of numbers, which still held a quasi-mystical power
in the seventeenth-century mind. As in the other miscellanies, there were
common-sense sayings, practical advice, puns and anti-female jokes: 'Three
things will not prove well without beating: a Walnut tree, an Asse, and
a Woman.'[27] But in all cases there was a large religious content too: not
anti-papism or controversial doctrine, but simple injunctions for the daily
living of a Christian life. Remember death, fear God, be sorry for your
sins, avoid sloth and gluttony, be sober and chaste (especially if you are
female): above all, *be good* is the message of the miscellanies. Most of
this might have been written before the Reformation, although the basics
of Protestant doctrine are there. The advice in *The figure of six* steers just
clear of good works:

Six hard steps lead to Heaven: Crosses, Afflictions, Troubles, Contempt of men,
Want and Povertie.

Six helps there are to climbe these steps: Prayer, Patience, Humility, Faith, Zeale,
and hope in God.[28]

---

[26] Published by R. Bird, [unknown], John Wright (2), Francis Coules, Thomas Vere. Later
editions of these were included among Pepys' penny merriments.

[27] *Figure of three*, sig.B2.

[28] D.N., *Figure of six*, sig.B1.

The author of *The figure of three* puts more emphasis on the elect, and the central position of faith in Christ; beginning his book:

The knowledge of God is threefold: Generall, Speciall, and Singular. Generall, as the Philosophers: Special, as of the Christians: and singular, as of them that are blessed.

The sweetnesse of this Name Jesus consists in three things: It is honey to the mouth, Melodie to the Eare, and joy to the Hearr [*sic*].[29]

These writers were poets, not preachers, and their little books may reflect the moderate religion of the majority of the literate public: those who would buy godly advice mixed with merry jests, but might not venture their two-pence for a purer dose of the fire-and-brimstone found in the more puritanical 'penny godlies'.[30] The religion in these miscellanies is very similar to that in the aphoristic ballads like the 'Proverbs of Solomon', with their conservative series of biblical and common-sense injunctions. The same type of public may have bought the post-Restoration 'sententious' chapbooks which Eamon Duffy has described as 'heavily moralistic, even pelagian, emphasizing the virtues of loyalty to family, good neighbourliness, charity to the poor, with little or no reference to Christ or faith'.[31]

Penny godlinesses

This moderate readership was also the target of *Keep within compasse: or the worthy legacy of a wise father to his beloved sonne* (1619).[32] The format was still aphoristic, like the miscellanies, but the context of a mono-logue from father to son relates it to the later 'penny godlies' with their death-bed advice from father, mother, pious Christian and so on (discussed above). This was John Trundle's most popular work: in contrast to his one-off pamphlets of miraculous happenings, it went through six editions in his own hands, reaching its tenth for John Wright after Trundle's death. The author, 'John T.', may have been Trundle himself; a publisher whose trade list shows no evidence of religious zeal. The keynote of his philosophy is moderation. The golden mean is to be sought out in Religion, Conversa-tion, Dyet and Apparell: falling 'out of compasse' leads to Atheisme, Luxury, Gluttony and Prodigality. The religious content is platitudinous: again, the

---

[29] *Figure of three*, sig.A3.
[30] On the moderate religion of 'honest householders' at all levels of society, see Martin Ingram, *Church courts, sex and marriage in England, 1570–1640* (Cambridge, 1987), discussed below on pp. 325–6.
[31] Eamon Duffy, 'The godly and the multitude in Stuart England', *Seventeenth Century Journal*, 1 (1986), p. 44.
[32] The original is slightly long for a penny book at 48 pages 8vo. However, John Wright's edition of *c.* 1630 is 48 pages 16mo (1.5 sheets), which should have cost the same as a 24-page 8vo according to the prescribed rates.

issue seems to be religion versus irreligion, not one interpretation of religion versus another. Prayer 'in thy chamber' is urged; on the other hand, it seems no love is lost with over-zealous precisians: 'He that hath too quicke a beliefe hath ever too rash a judgement.'[33] A woodcut on the title page illustrates the 'compass'; over the page another small cut of a clock face is used as a diagrammatical guide to basic Christian tenets, in the same manner as the mnemonic broadsides. The 'hours' of the clock are explained in verse:

> I One, God, one Baptism, and one Faith
>   One truth there is, the Scripture saith
> II Two Testaments the Olde and New,
>   We must acknowledge to be true.
> III Three Persons in the Trinitie
>   Doe make one God in Unitie.[34]

The successful formula was repeated in *The mothers counsell, or live within compasse. Being the last will and testament to her dearest daughter* [1630?], entered to John Wright in 1623, and presumably commissioned to go with the male version he acquired from Trundle on the same day. A similar woodcut adorns the title-page, but now we have the feminine qualities of chastity, humility, temperance and beauty. The book begins with twelve points of 'Good Counsell to the Christian Reader', revealing a new author of somewhat hotter religion than John T. 'M.R.' recommends:

That you stirre up your selve to liberalitie to Gods Saints. That you looke daily for the comming of our Lord Jesus Christ for your full deliverance out of this world.

That you acquaint your selves with some godly person, with whom you may conferre of your Christian estate, and open your doubts, to the quickening of Gods graces in you.[35]

It may be that literate women were considered to be a more pious market than men, although one should be wary of reading too much into the subtler alterations in the patchwork of these godly sayings. Often the aphorisms were inconsistent; cobbled together from various sources by professional hacks. This inconsistency may in fact reflect a large segment of popular religious belief, better than the well-thought-out positions of evangelical ministers.

There is one little work which belies these generalizations, venturing firm and consistent positions on contentious issues of Protestant doctrine. It uses the same formula of godly aphorisms within the narrative framework of familial advice: *A brothers gift: containing an hundred precepts, instructing all sorts of people to a godly, honest and morall life* (1623), by Humphrey

[33] *Keep within compasse*, sig.A8v.
[34] *Ibid.*, sig.A3v.
[35] M.R., *Mothers counsell*, sig.A3v.

Everinden, published by John Wright. Everinden was also the author of another 'penny godliness', *The reward of the wicked*, a fire-and-brimstone tract of only fourteen pages which reached its fifth edition in 1635. Here Everinden explains that people may be allured to the love of God by instructions, by consolations or by threats; and that this particular pamphlet will unabashedly make use of the latter method.[36] *A brothers gift* is slightly long to be listed as a 'penny godly' (40 pages 8vo, or 2.5 sheets) and there are no signs of popularity in further editions or transfers of copyright, indicating that its concern with issues of church policy may be the exception to prove the rule. The author seems to be aiming especially at apprentices and journeymen, writing of 'thy master' and 'thy fellow servants', but within the context of 'Trade' and 'being skillful', suggesting a craft rather than domestic service.[37]

Everinden is certainly 'the hotter sort of Protestant' in some ways, but a staunch supporter of the Church of England. He does not mind the label 'precisian': 'Flatter not thy selfe that it is but a foolery to be in thy life precise and careful: for as there is a difference betweene heaven and hell, so there must be between the professors of either.'[38] Yet he is a declared enemy of dissent and schism: 'Be not hasty to reveale the infirmities of thy brethren, especially of the Clergie: for wheras therin thou thinkest to doe justly, thou mayst notwithstanding doe very wickedly in causing a scandell to arise at Religion which cannot so soone be healed.'[39] He urges the young godly to attend the sermons in their own parish, to receive the sacrament often, and to obey the magistrates and clergy.[40] Most interesting is his defence of the church line on kneeling for communion, an issue which had not yet been brought to the fore by the Laudian reforms.

Receive the Sacrament of the Lords Body and Bloud, always humbly kneeling: thinke not that so doing thou adorest the Bread, for thou maist adore the Bread as well sitting or standing: and if thy heart be free from superstition, the three gestures are all in themselves free, obey thy Prince in that one of them, that he commanded for conscience sake.[41]

This sober advice is placed in the mouth of a 'brother', perhaps the best way for the author to endear himself to a young audience; that is, as a peer, rather than an authority figure.

As I have argued earlier, the fiction of advice from a parent or sibling emphasized the veracity of the godly lesson: it came out of an event in the real world, not just the abstract, self-contained world of print. The

---

[36] *The reward of the wicked*, 2nd edn (1625), sig.A1v.
[37] Everinden, *Brothers gift*, sig.A5, B3, B3v.
[38] *Ibid.*, sig.B6.
[39] *Ibid.*, sig.C2.
[40] *Ibid.*, sig.A4, C1v.
[41] *Ibid.*, sig.A4.

newly literate public may have been uncomfortable with the idea of a distant anonymous author, unless some kind of personal relationship was established. Another way to achieve this could be a letter format, as in *A Letter sent by D. Sprint, to a man seaven yeares grievously afflicted in Conscience, and fearefully troubled in Mind* (1623), which promised to be 'Very comfortable and commodious to withstand the assaults of Satan.'[42] The letter is an excuse for a rousing piece of prose encouraging the faith of the godly in the face of temptation: 'Every temptation of a Christian, is a ground of strong consolation, because Sathan's Onsets argue, that wee are none of his; for his Dragon strikes not his owne souldiers.'[43] The reader, having thus established his membership in the elect, is given practical advice for warding off the devil: 'Next if Sathan seeke to lay your sins before your eyes, therto you must lay the sufferings of Christ before your eyes; If he accuse you, tell him, the accuer [*sic*] of the Brethren is cast out.'[44] With this little godly book we have moved from the moderate, platitudinous Christianity of *Keep within compasse* to the passionate Protestantism which inspires the main bulk of the 'penny godlies'.

THE PENNY GODLY AUTHORS

John Andrewes, marketplace theologian

This genre seems in its early stages to have been shaped by one author, whose history deserves closer examination. The list of early 'penny godlinesses' is dominated by an unfamiliar name: John Andrewes, 'Minister and Preacher of the word of God at Barricke Basset in the County of Wiltes'.[45] Anthony à Wood associated him with a John Andrews from Somerset who entered Trinity College, Oxford, in 1601, aged eighteen and graduated with an MA.[46] However, the Wiltshire preacher was in the 'autumn or declining of my age' in 1614, an unlikely description for a thirty-one-year-old man.[47] The Trinity graduate was probably the John Andrews who wrote *The anatomie of basenesse* (1615), a thirty-six-page verse satire bearing no resemblance

---

[42] Printed for Samuel Rand. I found this via a later copy in a box of chapbooks, mostly post-1640, described below. (BL Cup.408.d.8 (13).) I have checked all of Rand's titles recorded in Paul G. Morrison, *Index of printers, publishers and booksellers in Pollard and Redgrave STC* (Charlottesville, 1950), and found no other penny books. The author was John Sprint, vicar, who wrote no other works of this size.

[43] *Letter sent by D. Sprint*, sig.A4v.

[44] *Ibid.*, sig.A6.

[45] John Andrewes, *Christ his crosse* (1614).

[46] Alexander B. Grosart, ed., *Miscellanies of the Fuller Worthies' Library* (4 vols., Blackburn, 1871), II, p. 6. Grosart is used as the source for the entry in *DNB*.

[47] Andrewes, *Christ his crosse*, sig.A4. He uses this phrase again in *Andrewes humble petition* (for J. Wright, 1623), title-page.

to the Andrewes godlinesses.[48] There was a third John Andrewes, who claimed never to have been in print before 1621, when he wrote *The brazen serpent: or, the copie of a sermon.*[49] This man, a minister at St James Clerkenwell in Middlesex, gives us an idea of the reputation of our 'penny godly' author:

For another there is, who writes both his Names as I do, and hath published divers Books, (as Petitions, Subpoena's, Christ-Crosses &c) ... I doe hereby certifie thee, that I am not the man: For I never saw the kingdome of Ireland in all my life, but in Bookes; nor the County of Wilts ... And for my part, howsoever I be the meanest among the many thousands that are called to the Sacred Priesthood; yet I may truly protest, that I never played the Circumforanean Theologaster: Istos enim Circulatores, qui Sacram Philosophiam honestius neglixissent, quam vendunt, semper exosus habui.[50]

In other words, by 1621, our Andrewes was known as a 'marketplace theologian' whose books were peddled around the countryside by those chapmen of dubious character of whom reformers had complained in connection with the ballads.

John Andrewes of the small godlies gives us his own clues as to how he came to be a marketplace author. In his first work he claims to be something of a born-again Christian:

it is the only motive, that I might in all humblenesse of duty, with these or such-like meditations, end and spend the rest of my time in the divine service of my Lord Jesus, that hath called me from teaching of Schoole, and brevity in writing, to become a Minister, for to instruct and labour in the vineyard of the Lord. Wherefore (Gentle Reader) if I, that spent the whole prime of my youth in that forme or faculty, be now applyed unto better labours, thinke though it be Sero ... yet it is Serio.[51]

With his experience of school teaching, Andrewes must have been aware of increasing literacy at the lower social levels during James' reign; indeed, he helped to foster it himself. He may well have noticed the need for simple black-letter tracts of the kind he would later write, aimed at the kind of readers he used to teach.

Andrewes' first work is a long treatise of ten sheets quarto, dealing in systematic point-by-point form with the act of meditation on Christ's passion: the motives for undertaking it, the frame of mind necessary, the philosophical nature of this meditation ('literall', 'spirituall', 'exemplariall'

---

[48] Reprinted in Grosart, ed., *Miscellanies of the Fuller Worthies' Library*, II. I disagree with Grosart's claim that the snippets of bad verse included in Andrewes' godly tracts provide evidence for his authorship of the satire.

[49] Two further clerical 'John Andrews' are mentioned by Paul S. Seaver (*The Puritan lectureships. The politics of religious dissent 1560–1662* (Stanford, 1970), pp. 141, 290), neither of whom match our Wiltshire preacher.

[50] 'I never played the Marketplace Theologian: I have always detested those pedlars who neglect the sacred philosophy which they sell.' Andrewes, *Brazen serpent*, sig.A3.

[51] Andrewes, *Christ his crosse* (1614), sig.A4.

and 'allegorical'). This is not food for simple folk, but Andrewes was already
taking an unusual initiative, as verses at the back of the book tell us:

> My Author did the impression buy
> And from the presse he did me take
> That none should sell me certinly
> But he himselfe which did me make
> Except it be his nearest friend
> Which may me sell, both give and lend.[52]

This unusual venture into marketing could have been to avoid the vice-ridden
chapmen; however, it was more likely prompted by the need to raise money
by keeping a larger percentage of the profits. For Andrewes had no regular
living in Wiltshire: he was not the incumbent at Berwick Bassett, and must
instead have been an occasional preacher or puritan lecturer.[53] In *Andrewes
humble petition* he tells us of his impecunious position:

It is well known (gentle Reader) unto many, besides my licence of absence, which
I John Andrewes the author of this work have to shew, that by the handy-work
of God in sending contrary windes, I have lost to the value of three-score pounds
by the yeare in spirituall livings within the Realme of Ireland, to the utter impoverish-
ing of me, my wife and children for ever, except God in his mercy open the harts
of well disposed Gentlemen, and others, by their good liking of these my labors
to relieve me in these my present wants, that thereby I may attaine unto some
better estate againe.[54]

The ill-fated trip to Ireland was taken some time before 1 September
1617, on which date a London stationer Bernard Alsope was fined for printing the *Humble petition* without registration.[55] This work may have been
Andrewes' first small godly, although no copies survive before 1623. On
the title-page is a variation on the verses quoted above ('My Author did
the impression buy ...'), indicating that Andrewes was again acting as his
own salesman. He was also part-publisher: the 1621 *Celestiall looking-glasse*
was 'imprinted at my own cost and charges', although in 1630 the printer,
Nicholas Okes, owned the copyright (which he assigned over to his son
John that year).[56] The early works printed by Okes ran to two-and-a-half
sheets 12mo (56–60 pages); however, as they came into the hands of the

---

[52] *Ibid.*, sig.L2v.
[53] Grosart, ed., *Miscellanies of the Fuller Worthies Library*, II, p. 6.
[54] *Andrewes humble petition* (for J. Wright, 1623 edn), sig.A4.
[55] Court-Book C, p. 461 in William A. Jackson, ed., *Records of the Court of the Stationers'
Company 1602 to 1640* (1957).
[56] I have looked at a sample of works published by Nicholas Okes, all of which turned out
to be lengthy: he was not a specialist in cheap print. The son, John, did publish in 1639
two of the early 'small merry' books in the Wood Collection (Bodleian): Thomas Heywood,
*A true relation of the lives and deaths of the two most famous English pyrats, Purser
and Clinton, who lived in the reign of Queen Elizabeth* (1639) in two parts of 22 pages
octavo each. Wood 284(4a), 284(4b).

ballad publishers they were printed more compactly.[57] John Wright first got hold of the *Humble petition* in 1623, and from then on printed Andrewes' works only in the 24-page 12mo format.

From the beginning, Andrewes' personal concern with the marketing of his books led him to develop a written sales patter to be included in the introduction or on the back page, not unlike the stanzas sometimes included in broadside ballads for the benefit of the ballad monger:

> Go thou my Booke with the zeale of my hart
> To all that shal come view thee:
> When thou hast past from the press and art print
> Cry daily, 'come peruse me . . .'[58]

In *A soveraigne salve* (1624) the Book addresses the Reader:

> If I had tongue to speake with voyce,
> Oh then most loude still should I cry,
> All those that heare me would reioyce,
> Now for to buy me presently.
> Each greater booke of price more deare
> Which you may buy cannot containe
> Effectual physicke which is here,
> Soules health from sinne for to regaine.[59]

This sales pitch, deliberately reminiscent of a pedlar of potions and 'salves', makes one wonder how literally Andrewes' label 'marketplace theologian' should be taken. Perhaps he sold his little books from a box after a rousing session of preaching. Whatever his own techniques in Wiltshire, by the 1620s Andrewes' books were being distributed along John Wright's ballad network, and selling so well that their author remarked on the phenomenon in 1630:

whereas I have formerly published unto the view of the world, many small bookes for the setting forth of Gods glory ... now seeing that my former bookes are so vendible, and so well likeing unto the children of God, that in short time there have been divers impressions printed, I have therefore now set foorth another booke, intituled *Andrewes Repentance*[60]

Andrewes' story is not unlike the pattern for later godly chapbook writers shown by Eamon Duffy: that is, ejected non-conformist ministers who turned to evangelical writing as a substitute for the usual pastoral duties.[61] But Andrewes appears to be the first of this line. Perhaps by accident, he discovered the small format, then came into the hands of a publisher with

---

[57] *A celestiall looking-glasse* (1621), *Andrewes resolution* (1621).
[58] *Humble petition*, sig.B4.
[59] *Soveraigne salve*, sig.A2v. This was originally an acrostic on Andrewes name, as in *Andrewes resolution* (1621 edn).
[60] *Andrewes repentance* (1631 edn), sig.A2.
[61] Duffy, 'The godly and the multitude', pp. 47–8.

a wide country market, and with a combination of zeal and business initiative they created the 'penny godliness' genre.

What were these small books which proved so 'vendible'? All were variations on one theme, as Andrewes said himself:

And I which am the unworthiest of all men, have wrote (for the benefit of others, as well as my selfe) almost all the books that ever I made, concerning repentance: and the longer I have written of it, the more tender my heart is, and the more earnest my desire is to returne unto my God by repentance, and amendment of life.[62]

Sometimes Andrewes focusses on the first step of repentance, the fire-and-brimstone 'alarum' to the unconverted sinner:

Heare, oh therefore, heare all you that walke after the lusts of your owne hearts, and depart from Bethel the house of God, to starve your soules in Bethauen, the den of iniquity: It is sinne, oh! it is your unrepented sinne that drawes Gods anger towards you, that makes your eyes more dry than the stony rocke, and your hearts more hard than the Adament.[63]

But Andrewes dwells more often on the next step of the repentance process; offering encouragement to the penitent man, already converted but needing practical advice and reassurance of his salvation. If, says Andrewes, Satan shows you your sins and tempts you to despair, tell him 'Oh, thou hellish fiend, I say againe, Depart, I doe utterly defie thee, O take thy ugly sinnes againe, which thou hast caused me to commit; and lay them not unto my charge, for I am a member of my Lord and Saviour Jesus Christ.'[64]

Andrewes' style is always immediate and informal. Much of his appeal must have lain in the very personal tone; the way he includes himself as a companion in the reader's predicament: 'Repent yee ... These two words are ... as needfull to direct me that made this booke, as you that reade it.'[65] Several works take the form of personal pleas from Andrewes himself directly to God, which he suggests the readers may also use 'in their daily prayers.'[66] With an eye to the practical problems of devotion, he provides an emotional outpouring for which the reader on his own might not find the words: 'Oh therefore sweet Jesu, whom my soule longeth for, let me see thee, O light of mine eyes, O come Lord Jesu, Come quickly, come Jesus my Saviour, my life, and my comfort.'[67] The personal element – the rapport between reader and preacher – seems to have been an important element in the later, post-Restoration chapbooks. Some of Pepys' 'penny godlinesses' included a generic woodcut of the godly pastor, bearded and

---

[62] *Andrewes repentance* (1631), sig.B1v.
[63] *Andrewes caveat to win sinners* (f.J. Wright, 1631), sig.A6.
[64] *Andrewes repentance* (1631), sig.A7.
[65] *Ibid.*, sig.B2.
[66] *Andrewes humble petition* (1623); *Andrewes golden chaine* (1637), both on title-page.
[67] *Humble petition*, sig.B2.

holding a book, presumably making the presence of the author more imme-diate.[68] Andrewes' books are notable for so often including his name in the title, as if for a loyal following waiting for his next 'penny godly' to appear. Like the practice of claiming chapbooks as genuine death-bed testi-monies, this was another way of making godly exhortations more personal. Perhaps for a newly literate audience, unused to the third-person distance of written discourse, it was especially necessary to put this human face on the printed word. Andrewes himself gave some indication that he felt his audience would include those on the fringes of literacy: he addressed himself to hearers as well as readers. 'If thou dost reade or heare this worke . . .'; 'Gentle Readers, or Hearers, whosoever yee are, that are the Children of God. . . .'.[69] In his early works he had included epistles soliciting the patronage of eminent persons with godly reputations – the High Chancellor of England and the Marchioness of Buckingham (with whom, he said, he was not personally acquainted).[70] But later he dispensed with these aspi-rations, perhaps finding his audience further down the social scale; he addressed himself only to the spiritual elite, to 'all the Elect Children of God'.[71] Andrewes' public did certainly include readers of at least gentry status, such as the Staffordshire lady, Frances Wolfreston (discussed below). But her copy of *A golden trumpet* gives the best indication that not all of Andrewes' readers were as well-read and well-off as herself: in 1648, the *Golden trumpet* had reached its 'nine and twentieth Impression'.[72]

Ministers of God's word

John Andrewes, preacher, and John Wright, publisher, may indeed have invented the 'penny godly'; however, in the late 1620s another partnership tried a similar formula. In 1627–8 Francis Coules published three anony-mous 'penny-sized' works which seem to have been written by one author. Apart from compatibility of subject and tone, the most notable common point is the author's characteristic method of introducing references to scrip-tural or patristic authority:

It is well said of an ancient Father, heere his words which hee saith: The Devill (saith he) is a slippery serpent . . .

Heere what St. Chrisostome speaketh to this purpose, If thou, saith he, shouldest come into a loathsome prison . . .

[68] Pepys Library, Penny Godlinesses (10), (26), (27), (34).
[69] *Humble petition*, title-page; *Converted man's new birth*, sig.A2.
[70] *Andrewes resolution*, sig.A3; *Celestial looking-glass*; both 1621.
[71] *Celestial looking-glass, Converted mans new birth*, etc., on title-pages.
[72] Printed for Edward Wright. This work was written before 1630 when N. Okes assigned it to John Wright. However, there are no surviving copies before 1641.

Heere what Saint Austen saith to this purpose: Drunkennesse is a flattering Devill
... Another saith well, heare his words what he saith ...[73]

The orality of this phrasing is conspicuous since the texts were almost certainly composed as written works, not as sermons.[74]

One of the three titles, *The doctrine of dying-well* was registered as a
work by 'George Shawe minister of Gods word' to M. Flesher and G. Elderton in 1621.[75] Like Andrewes' works, it is a combination of repentance
alarum and practical encouragement for the godly, and its title-page, like
Andrewes', appeals to would-be members of the elect: 'Wherein is briefly
comprised a short view of the glorious estate of God's Saints in the Kingdome
of Heaven. Together with. The Meanes to obtaine, the Markes to know,
and the Motives to urge us to prepare our selves for Christ, before our
soules be unbodied, lest Heavens gate be shut against us.' *Seaven weapons
to conquer the devil* is another plain rousing tract to buttress the faith of
the godly. It is structured around St Paul's images of divine warfare in the
Epistle to the Ephesians 6:13–17. The seven parts of the 'armour of God'
are taken directly from this passage: 'the girdle of verity', 'the Breastplate
of righteousnesse', 'feete shod with the preparation of the Gospell of peace'.
This tract retains the sense of a combat between the forces of good and
evil in the world; a vision which had informed the early Elizabethan reforming ballads, but which was largely absent from the commercial godly ballad
stock and the milder aphoristic chapbooks.

Besides the very basic theme of repentance and faith, Shawe also writes
on the specific social symptoms of sinfulness, in particular, drunkenness.
A looking glasse for drunkards is in the best tradition of moral diatribes,
racy in style and full of physical images: 'For as wet and foggy grounds
in the summer time doe ingender multitudes of frogs and Toads, and other
venomous vermine: So doth drunkenness produce and ingender multitudes
of diseases in the body of man.'[76] More than Andrewes, Shawe loves the
shock-technique of graphic descriptions of hell: 'Oh that all the revell rout
of beastly drunkards, would seriously think of this ... your drink shall
be lakes of fire and brimstone, your musicke shall be howling and weeping,
and gnashing of teeth, in the company of devils for evermore.'[77] This is

---

[73] *Seven weapons to conquer the devil* [1628?], sig.A2. George Shawe(?), *The doctrine of
dying-well* (1628), sig.B2. *A looking-glasse for drunkards* (1627), sig.A2v.

[74] Not only is there no mention of a place of delivery, as is usually the case with sermon
texts, but *The doctrine of dying-well* and *Seven weapons* are set up in a numbered point-by-
point format intended for the printing press, not the pulpit.

[75] There were many works on this theme, from the first 'ars moriendi' published by Caxton
in 1491 (STC 786 sqq. *Here begynneth a lytell treatyse called ars moriendi, the craft to
deye for the health of mannes soule*). However, M. Flesher was also the printer of the
copy published by Francis Coules.

[76] *Looking glasse*, sig.A4.

[77] *Ibid.*, sig.B2.

quite unlike the 'delicate Diet' offered to 'daintiemouthde Droonkardes' by George Gascoyne in 1576 (see above). Gascoyne complained of the drunkard in dry third-person prose; in contrast with Shawe's head-on attack. However, Shawe also shows a practical awareness of the social customs which cause drunkenness: if a man out drinking with his friends pleads that he has had enough 'then the drunken rout will wind him in, by drinking healths to one great personage or another'.[78]

Our first 'penny' publisher, John Wright, was also in this period laying his hands on other godly titles besides those of our leading 'penny' preacher John Andrewes. In 1629, he and the other 'partners' acquired the copy to *Death's knell or the sicke mans passing-bell* by William Perkins. The first extant copy, printed for Margery Trundle (John Trundle's widow) in 1628, was already the 'ninth edition'; in John Wright's hands it had reached its sixteenth edition by 1637.

One selling point must have been the woodcut on the title-page: a crude picture also used on ballads from about 1625. It is a bed-side scene with the skeleton-figure of Death pulling at the rope of a bell, and aiming his arrow at the man in the bed.[79] Perkins' text itself lacks none of the power and persuasion of the 'penny' repentance alarum, relying especially, like Shawe, on simple concrete images. He conjures up the scene of the reader's dying moments: 'if thou layest panting for shortnesse of breath, sweating a fatall sweat, and tyred with struggling against deadly pangs; O, how much then wouldst thou give for a dayes contrition, an houres repentance, or a minutes amendment of life?'[80] If the reader is unmoved by fear, perhaps he will be inspired by the description of Christ at the last Judgement 'clothed in white linnen, through which, his body shining like precious stones, his eyes like burning Lampes, his face like lightning, his Armes and Legs like flaming Brasse, and his Voice as the shout of a multitude'.[81] If the godly reader is successfully moved to repent, Perkins offers practical aid at the end in the form of two 'prayers for private Households at all times'.[82] Perkins seems to have missed his true calling as a 'penny godly' writer, since I have found no other works by him of this size.[83]

In 1626 John Wright sold a work by another well-known godly author,

---

[78] *Ibid.*, sig.A7.
[79] Used by Henry Gosson on 'Death's Dance' [*c.* 1625], RB repr. I. p. 283. Later used by William Thackeray, RB repr. VII, p. 40. Margery Trundle's 1628 copy of *Death's knell* uses the cut, but I have not been able to check the editions printed for John Wright, now in the Folger Library.
[80] Perkins, *Death's knell*, sig.A5.
[81] *Ibid.*, sig.A5v.
[82] *Ibid.*, sig.B3v.
[83] I have checked those 8vo and 12mo works by Perkins which went through large numbers of editions. Most of his work ran from 100 to 500 pages long, with the shortest (such as *A graine of musterd-seed*, (1597) at 72 pages (or 3 sheets 12mo).

Henry Smith, *The trumpet of the soule sounding to judgement*. The first edition, printed in 1591 by Edward Allde, was indeed only 24 pages octavo, but in neat Roman type, and later editions had wide border margins which extended them to 40 pages.[84] This lack of concern for economy is untypical of 'penny godly' publishing, and it seems likely that only when Wright sold the work was it distributed to a more humble market. The audience which Smith originally anticipated came mainly from the affluent merchant and gentry classes, as we see by the sins he thought them likely to commit: 'The Judge setteth downe all in the Table of remembrance and his Scrole reacheth up to heaven. Item, for lending to usury: Item, for racking of Rents ... Item, for thy yellow starcht Ruffe: Item, for curling thy Hayre: Item for selling of Benefices: Item for starving of Soules.'[85]

It was, in fact, the printed version of a sermon preached at St Paul's Cross, focussing in sermon style around one text (Eccles. 11:9), and retaining all the original phrases like 'while I preach to you here ...'.[86] If it was ever distributed as a 'penny godly', it was by the initiative of the publishers, not the conscious design of the author.

Henry Smith brings us back to the problem of defining the godly chapbook: although 'penny godlies' sometimes began as sermons, a short printed sermon was not necessarily a 'penny godly', and must be seen in the context of its publication history. However, the approach via the ballad publishers could be complemented by checking the corpus of best-selling authors like Henry Smith. Could any of the prolific Tudor–Stuart religious writers have been producing small godlies with stationers unconnected to the ballad trade? I have tried a sample check on Henry Smith, looking at all of his single works which reached three or more editions. *The trumpet of the soule* was the only work of the right size with any longevity: it continued on, through its nine editions, until 1640. There were four other works of two sheets octavo or less (i.e. thirty-two pages) which did not survive into the seventeenth century: they ran their course in the early 1590s, before the development of the 'penny godly'.[87] These works are simply the printed by-products of Smith's sermons, which focussed on specific scriptural texts, and dealt with nicer and subtler points of devotion than the fire and brimstone of the late 'penny godlies'. While the chapbooks rarely bring in biblical events and characters other than the most familiar, Smith elucidates less well-worn passages for an audience which knows its own bible well: 'You heard the last Sabaoth, how Zaccheus the Publican was called to be a Chris-

[84] STC 22706, 22710.
[85] Smith, *Trumpet of the soule* (1632 edn), sig.B2v.
[86] *Ibid.*, sig.A6v.
[87] *The sinners confession* (1594 edn), *The sinners conversion* (1594 edn), *Three prayers, one for the morning, another for the evening: the third for a sick-man* (1591), *The wedding garment* (1591 edn).

tian: Now you shall heere the fruite of his conversion.'[88] These sermons were also printed, not in black letter, but in a very neat Roman font: not proof, but an indication that the audience was not at the humblest end of the reading public.[89]

Similar checks on such religious writers as Samuel Smith, Arthur Dent and William Worship have failed to turn up any surprise enclaves of 'penny godly' production. Ian Green has compiled a list of all Protestant 'best-sellers' which reached five editions between 1558 and 1640. Only nine works on this list are of 24 pages or less, of which four are catechisms. The others are all in our appendix of 'penny godlinesses': Everinden's *Reward of the wicked*, Perkins' *Death's knell*, Smith's *Trumpet*, Sprint's *Christian sword*; together with Stubbes' *Christal glasse* in quarto. This provides further confirmation that the study of the 'ballad partners' has accurately located the source of the 'penny godly' genre. It would seem that the 'penny godly' was a product of the 1620s, and that its first prolific writer was the Wiltshire preacher and ex-schoolmaster John Andrewes.

FRANCES WOLFRESTON, CHAPBOOK COLLECTOR

Some confirmation of this outline comes from a last source I have not discussed: not the godly author or publisher, but the collector. While Pepys and Wood may be responsible for the earliest chapbook collections which remain intact, there was an earlier collector whose library was dispersed at auction in 1856. This was Frances Wolfreston (1607–77), a Staffordshire lady whose copies of important contemporary poetry, drama, romance and criticism remained in the family for 200 years, practically all uncut and unbound.

Frances was born near Birmingham and began collecting books after her marriage in 1631 to Francis Wolfreston, son of a gentry family settled at Statfold, near Tamworth. Bibliographers have noticed Frances for her Shakespearean quartos and other literary treasures, marked out with the inscription 'frances wolfreston hor [or her] bouk' on the first page.[90] Some of her 'better quality' books may have been purchased from booksellers

[88] Smith, *Sinners confession*. The earlier sermon is the *Sinners conversion*.

[89] Charles C. Mish, 'Black letter as a social discriminant in the seventeenth century', *Publications of the Modern Language Association*, 68 (1953), pp. 627–30.

[90] J. Gerritsen, 'Venus preserved: some notes on Frances Wolfreston', *English Studies Presented to R. W. Zandvoort*, Supplement to *English Studies*, 45 (1964), pp. 271–4. Paul Morgan, 'Frances Wolfreston and "hor bouks": a seventeenth-century woman book-collector', *The Library*, 6th ser., 11 (1989), pp. 197–219. I am grateful to Paul Morgan for access to an earlier version of this paper before publication.

in Coventry or Birmingham, or on visits to London.[91] But she also appears to have purchased from travelling chapmen. In the Sotheby's sale catalogue appear the titles of some fifty 'penny godlinesses' and sixteen small merry books which the bibliographers have overlooked.[92]

Frances' 'merriments' were published from the 1640s to the 1660s by Francis Coules, Francis Grove, William Gilbertson, Thomas Vere, John Andrews and Richard Harper: all of them specialist ballad and chapbook publishers. Titles which we have seen before 1640 included Parker's *Robin Conscience* (for F. Coles, 1662) and the anonymous *Cupids schoole* (R. Cotes, 1642).[93] Frances also collected quartos distributed by the ballad publishers, such as *A pleasant history of the life and death of Will Sommers* (for F. Grove, 1637), Philip Stubbes' *A chyrstall glasse for Christian women* (for J. Wright, 1646), and a dozen works by John Taylor.[94] It seems likely that she relied upon chapmen travelling the midlands for reading material between visits to more substantial bookshops.

Frances had only half as many religious works as literary, but a much larger proportion of these were 'penny size'.[95] At her death she left them to her youngest son Stanford, instituted as Vicar of Wootten Wawen (War-wickshire) a few months earlier: 'And I give my son Stanford all my phisicke bookes, and all my godly bookes, and all the rest conditionally if any of his brothers and sisters would have them any tyme to read, and when they have done they shall returne them to their places againe, and he shall carefully keepe them together.'[96] Most of her books are now scattered among differ-ent libraries, but there is one box of godlinesses in the British Library, still kept together.[97] It is startling to open the box and find the sixteen unbound little books; all of the 24-page octavo format, and recognizable beyond doubt as a distinctive 'penny chapbook' genre.

Frances began collecting in 1631, and her signed books date from 1589.[98]

---

[91] John Cartwright was established as a bookseller in Coventry (17 miles from Stratfold) by 1635, followed by John Brooke before 1669. Birmingham, a similar distance away, had Thomas Simmons in 1652. Frances is known to have gone to London with her daughters in 1657. (Morgan, 'Frances Wolfreston and "hor bouks"', pp. 208–9.)

[92] BL Sotheby C.S.413(3). 24 May 1856. Some of the Wolfreston books were sold off before 1856, but these are likely to have been works of more recognizable commercial worth than the chapbooks. The figure for the 'merry books' is approximate.

[93] *Cupids schoole* was 3 sheets 8vo, longer than 'penny size'. *Babes in the wood* (E. Crouch for F. Grove, 1670) and *The life and death of the famous champion of England St. George* (for F. Coles, T. Vere and W. Gilbertson [1658–64]) were old ballad favourites (both in the 1624 stock), sold in chapbook form after the Restoration.

[94] Five of these were published by Henry Gosson: STC 23726, 23729, 23743, 23786, 23799.

[95] Paul Morgan estimates from the titles in the sale catalogue that her library was 48% 'English literature' and 24% 'theology'. Other categories include 'history', and 'medicine'. (Morgan, 'Frances Wolfreston and "hor bouks"', p. 204.)

[96] Quoted in Morgan, 'Frances Wolfreston and "hor bouks"', pp. 200–1.

[97] BL Cup.408.d.8 (1–16).

[98] Gerritsen, 'Venus preserved: some notes on Frances Wolfreston', p. 272.

Yet her pre-1640 'penny godlinesses' number only five out of a total of fifty: of these, four are by John Andrewes and one by John Warner (all on our list of 'penny godlinesses').[99] She then collected five 'penny godlies' from the 1640s, eight from the 1650s and twenty from the 1660s. (A further dozen were listed in the sales catalogue as 'and one other', or titled but without date: most of these were lumped together with post-1660 books and probably date from that period.)[100]

It is possible that Frances' collecting habits reflected nothing but the state of her own interest in the chapbooks; however, it does seem unlikely that a lukewarm interest of several decades should suddenly blossom into fascination in the 1660s without outside cause. One is tempted to think that she bought most of the 'penny godlies' which came her way, and that her collection faithfully reflects the snowballing growth of the trade; just as Pepys' attention may have been caught by a further upswing in the 1680s.[101] If the Wolfreston collection is representative, there were a few new godly books in the 1640s and early 1650s, but no prolific writers like our John Andrewes of Wiltshire, whose works continued to be reprinted. Andrewes' *A golden trumpet sounding* reached its 'twenty-ninth edition' for Edward Wright in 1648: an achievement which was no doubt beyond all expectations of the 'marketplace theologian' when he first started selling his little books.[102]

The ballad publishers were apparently distracted from developing their new line in chapbooks by the events of the 1640s. Francis Coules published a deluge of topical and political publications in 1641–6; John Wright died in 1646; and his cousin John Wright (2) was soon busy as official printer to the House of Lords.[103] However, when the partnership of Coules, Wright, Vere and Gilbertson were required to register their stock in 1656, they entered 'ten little bookes', most of whose titles we have already seen.[104] The list included early penny books like 'Tom Thumb', 'Death's knell', and 'The history of the noble marques' (that is, 'Patient Grissel'), as well as a few titles which survive only in broadside form before 1640: '100

---

[99] Andrewes, *Subpoena* (1620), *Humble petition* (1623), *Soveraigne salve* (1624), *Celestial looking-glasse* (1639 edn). Warner, *Christ in the clouds* (1635).

[100] It is also very rare for a pre-1640 chapbook to have no date in the imprint.

[101] Margaret Spufford, *Small books and pleasant histories, Popular fiction and its readership in seventeenth-century England* (1981), p. xx.

[102] Wing A3118.

[103] Post-1640 search using Paul G. Morrison, *Index of printers, publishers and booksellers in Donald Wing's short-title catalogue of books printed in England, Scotland, Ireland, Wales and British North America and of English books printed in other countries 1641–1700* (Charlottesville, 1955). Information on the Wrights was given to me by Sheila Lambert.

[104] Eyre, II, p. 55.

godly lessons' and 'St. George'. One of the titles, 'The exhortation that a father gave his children', survives in a copy printed in 1648 for Francis Coules. It is just sixteen pages in octavo, with a scene of a martyr at the stake on the title-page, and a plethora of 'factotum' woodcuts throughout. The text is the same as 'Rogers will' (one of the parental-advice ballads described in chapter 3), recorded by Foxe as the last words of a prisoner awaiting martyrdom.[105] The chapbook 'partners' of the 1650s were thus relying on some very old stock, but their entry of 1656 is one of the first signs of them collecting together these 'little books' and registering them as a special genre.

The final stage in the development of the trade was to advertise these chapbooks as a separate trade list. The first to reach this stage seems to be John Andrews the bookseller (not to be confused with the preacher of the same name), whose shop, not surprisingly, was located at Pye-Corner, in the Smithfield area. In 1658 and 1659 he advertised 'other small books, all of them very godly' on the back page of the books themselves.[106] (It was only about 1650 that booksellers in general began to print trade lists in their books.)[107] Unlike the contemporary chapbook business of Coules and his partners, who relied on old stock, Andrews seems to have been busy signing up new best-selling authors. In 1656, he registered titles by John Hart and Andrew Jones, two authors whose numerous 'small godlies' were to remain part of the stock-in-trade of chapbook publishers right through the 1680s.[108] In 'John Hart Doctor of Divinity' we at last have another penny godly author of a stature and success to rival that of the Wiltshire preacher John Andrewes. The bookseller Andrews, and later his widow Elizabeth, published at least eighty-one editions of Hart's works between 1656 and 1668: from *A warning-piece to the sloathful* (evidently not popular) to *The dying mans last sermon* (at least eight editions) to *The dreadful character of a drunkard* (ten editions or more). Elizabeth's 1665 edition of Hart's *The plain mans plain path-way to heaven* (an abridgement of Arthur Dent's classic) claimed to be the thirty-fourth edition. If

---

105 *The exhortation that a father gave to his children, which he wrot a few dayes before his burning. Being godly admonitions, fit for all christians to follow* (1648). (BL Ch.640/1.) The text was included with four other godly pieces in a 'little booke' registered to John Arnold as far back as 1577. (Arber, II, p. 319.) Other items in the 1577 book included 'a song of Caine and Abbell', and 'the saienge of master Hooper that he wrote the nighte before he suffered upon a wall with a Cole in the newe Inne in Gloucester'.

106 Andrew Jones, *The black book of conscience*, 6th edn (1658). John Hart, *The plain mans plain path-way to heaven* (1659 edn). The latter lists seven books at 2d. and two at 3d. Andrews the bookseller is noted in Spufford, *Small books*, p. 94.

107 Philip Gaskell, *A new introduction to bibliography* (Oxford, 1972), p. 183.

108 For example, John Hart, 'The charitable christian', in Eyre, II, p. 59. Andrew Jones, 'The black book of conscience', in Eyre, II, p. 76. Later published by William Thackeray *et al.* (see Wing H923B and Wing J904).

this was an exaggeration, it was not entirely haphazard, since her next surviving edition from two years later is labelled the thirty-fifth.[109] By the time Pepys was collecting, the penny godliness was clearly an established vehicle for 'marketplace theologians' trying to earn a living outside the ecclesiastical mainstream. As Eamon Duffy has shown, most of Pepys' chapbooks were written by ejected non-conformist clergy.[110] Without a parish to absorb their evangelical energies, they addressed themselves to the wider, if more anonymous public of the chapbook readers.

The development of the specialized 'penny godly' trade appears to have come in broadly three stages. The first was the *ad hoc* publication of short works by godly authors: instruction for children by Francis Seager, inspiration for women by Philip Stubbes, Protestant morality by the author of *Robin Conscience*, repentance sermons by preachers like Henry Smith. The second stage was the systematic collection by ballad publishers of the copyright to small works (in conjunction with small 'merries' and 'miscellanies'), the standardization of the 'penny-sized' format and price of 2d. and the more deliberate involvement of authors like John Andrewes and George Shawe. The third was the development of the trade to a degree of self-consciousness where 'small books' were advertised for chapmen and readers as a special genre with separate trade lists.

The development of the 'penny godly' in the 1620s coincided with the final phase of decline for the production of new religious ballads. In 1624, the large 'ballad partners' entry of Elizabethan stock was still one third religious titles, but after that date the godly proportion of ballads trailed off to under one tenth.[111] If the evidence of extant chapbooks is correct, the 'penny godly' emerged in significant numbers before the 'penny merry', perhaps precisely because there was this gap in the market to fill. There were plenty of new merry ballads on offer, but less in the way of cheap, widely distributed religious print, for which (as the success of the 'penny godlies' shows) there was a ready public.

This gap was filled by evangelical ministers like John Andrewes and George Shawe, who would perhaps have written ballads in the 1560s. Now they had a new outlet, without the same dangers of a dubious reputation; although (as we have seen) a clergyman with the same name as our John Andrewes made derogatory remarks about the profanity of the pedlars who carried the little tracts. The themes in the evangelical 'penny books' were some of the same ones harped upon in the early Elizabethan ballads: the sins of society, repentance alarums, and comfort to converts. However, the anti-papism and Protestant patriotism had gone; the seventeenth-century

109 Wing H960A, H945F, H943A, H957, H958.
110 Duffy, 'The godly and the multitude', pp. 47–8.
111 See above, p. 47.

chapbooks seem to have taken the basic Protestant context for granted, concentrating on the individual's redemption and social behaviour. The chapbooks were not, one would have to argue, as adaptable to oral and visual uses as the broadsides; they could not be sung for recreation at bride-ales, transmitted in the performances of minstrels or pasted up on the wall. The fact that the authors now chose a wholly literate form, which had severed its musical ties with the oral culture, may be an indication of how literacy in the countryside was progressing.

CONCLUSION

In 1626, John Taylor the Water Poet compiled his collection of *Wit and mirth*. He claimed to have heard the anecdotes in inns and alehouses, taverns and tobacco shops, and along highways and waterways. Even if many of them were chestnuts from old jest-books, given Taylor's popularity the stories were likely to end up in these places once the printed collection appeared. Some of the mirth touched on matters of religion.

A Poore Country may [man] praying devoutly superstitious before an old Image of S.Loy, the Image suddenly fell downe upon the poore man, and bruised his bones sorely, that hee could not stirre abroad in a moneth after; in which space the cheating Priests had set up a new Image: the Country man came to the Church againe, and kneeled a farre off to the new Image, saying, Although thou smilest and lookest faire upon mee, yet thy father plaid me such a knavish pranke lately, that Ile beware how I come too neere thee, lest though shouldst have any of thy Fathers unhappy qualities.[1]

There were several jokes about sleeping in church :

A diligent and learned Preacher on a Sunday in the afternoone was preaching, whilest most of the zealous vestry men (for their meaner edification) were fast asleepe in their pues : in the meane space a young child cryed somewhat aloud at the lower end of the Church, which the Preacher hearing, called to the Nurse, and said, Nurse, I pray thee still thy childe, or else it may chance to awaken some of the best men in our parish.[2]

John Taylor's audience was amused by the backward image-worshipper, but equally happy to laugh at the zealous vestry men. Both the new Protestant culture of the word, and the traditional culture of the image, were familiar reference points. Like the vestry men in the anecdote, most of Taylor's readers were less likely to be hostile to the Protestant preacher than simply bored by the sermon. Like the country man, they had less faith than they

---

[1] *All the works of John Taylor the Water Poet 1630* (facs. edn, 1973), sig.Qq2v.

[2] *Ibid.*, sig.Rrl. Sleeping in church was said to be a 'very generall' practice. In 1624 a Wiltshire girl described her minister's sermons as 'such a deale of bible babble that I am weary to heare yt and I can then sitte downe in my seat and take a good napp'. (Keith Wrightson, *English society 1580- 1680* (1982), pp. 213, 219.)

321

used to in the power of icons (probably through education against idolatry, rather than the 'knavish pranks' of a statue), but the artefacts of this older system of belief were still part of their visual vocabulary.

The sort of buyers we have identified for the cheap religious print in our study were not the minority of godly 'elect', but the ordinary parishioners. If the sermon was soporific, and the old images of saints no longer worked, the godly ballads and chapbooks caught the attention of some of the audience which gathered around the pedlar in the churchyard or marketplace.

Why should the historian be interested in these ephemeral pedlar's wares? The development of 'cheap print' is important as a chapter in publishing history; acting both as an instrument and a measure of 'typographic acculturation' in rural England.[3] These paper artefacts also have insights to offer us on some of the wider questions of the period, especially on the impact of Protestantism, and of print, on traditional culture. We will begin here with a brief summary of the development and specialization of the 'cheap print' trade, before going on to address some of the larger historical issues.

During the first quarter of the seventeenth century, a group of London stationers developed publishing strategies which were increasingly responsive to the demands of the buyers, as they assembled and pruned a stock of successful ballads and chapbooks, according to commercial dictates. The nature of the ballad trade was transformed, as the 'ballad partners' organized themselves for efficient production and distribution. They increased the use of woodcuts, standardized the naming of tunes, and collected the copyrights to favourite titles, registered in 1624. Meanwhile, they translated some of the themes of the rising copper print trade into the cheaper medium of woodcut, producing large poster-size pictures which survive from about 1613. Most significantly for later generations of readers, they began to develop a new line of little books, to send along the same distribution network as the ballads. In the second and third decades of the century, they collected miscellanies and godlies in 'penny' size; as well as the merry quartos which would later be sold as 'double-books' and 'histories'. Finally, from the late 1620s, they began to stock new versions of these old merry tales, specially written or abridged for the 24-page octavo format.

Certain salient themes recurred in the successful ballads, broadsides and chapbooks, flowing freely between the different media. Partial substitutes for the outlawed saints were provided by new archetypes: Protestant martyrs and heroines like the Duchess of Suffolk and Anne Askew, Old Testament

---

[3] Term used by Roger Chartier in *The cultural uses of print in early modern France*, trans. Lyda C. Cochrane (Princeton, 1987), p. 159.

or apocryphal figures like wise Solomon and constant Susanna, pious women such as Katherine Stubbes or the Lady Jane Grey. Handy rules for social behaviour were available in the ballad of 'Solomon's Sentences', in tables for the wall like 'Finch his alphabet' and in the portable chapbook format of *Keep within compasse*. The fear of death was omnipresent, whether as the medieval vision of St Bernard, the secularized image of the skeleton in the 'dance of death' woodcut or the Protestant faith and repentance preached by John Andrewes, and practised by the clerk of Bodnam. The miraculous element of religion was still present in carols and woodcuts of the nativity and of Christ's miracles, as well as in ballads of Doctor Faustus, chapbook tales of magical friars and woodcuts of strange creatures ominously interpreted as divine portents.

These themes were packaged in forms which were suitable for the rudimentary reader, and attractive to an audience on the fringes of literacy. Ballads were set to catchy tunes, and given decorative woodcuts, which carried them beyond their readers to 'illiterate' singers and viewers. Tables and chapbooks used mnemonic tricks adopted from oral habits of thought: numerical groupings like the 'figure of three'; aphorisms, proverbs and short chunks of narrative (like the tiny chapters in *Patient Grissel*) which were easily digested and remembered. The structure of printed wares could also imitate familiar visible objects, such as the points, gloves and garters which may have been sold by the same petty chapmen who brought the broadsides into the countryside.

The new 'publishing formula' of the chapbook was not an equation devised in the abstract. It was a response to the growing market of readers created by the rise of literacy. The specialization of 'cheap print' coincided with the second phase of 'educational revolution' which affected the school generations of James' and Charles' reigns. The publishers in London were not isolated from such developments, but linked to the rest of the country by a network of communications, which included the authors and the distributors of their products.

Even at the beginning of our period, the minstrel Richard Sheale followed a route between the Earl of Derby's household in Lancashire, the markets of Staffordshire and the shops of London tradesmen. His travels indicate the great distances covered, both geographically and socially, by the performers and pedlars who disseminated the ballads in oral or printed form. Sheale brought his account of the Countess of Derby's funeral from Ormskirk to the London press, and probably carried back a new repertory culled from broadside ballads, including 'Remember man thy frayle estate' and 'Chevy Chase'.

This two-way cultural flow between London and the country, and between printed texts and oral tradition, is confirmed elsewhere. The publisher

Robert Copland printed 'pretty jests' copied down from customers who had learnt them 'by heart'.[4] The London pamphleteer John Taylor travelled by foot all the way to Scotland, no doubt keeping his ears open for stories to use in his collections of anecdotes and jests.[5] Martin Parker, who apparently made a living as an alehouse-keeper, was well placed to pick up stories and songs, to try out his own on the clientèle, and to judge what would be popular in cheap printed form.[6] His 'penny-sized' books of the 1620s and 30s seem to address a new kind of reader: the 'honest folks that have no lands', the young maids feeling in their bosoms for twopence 'wrapt in clouts'. John Andrewes was a very different sort of author, but he, too, knew his audience well : both from school teaching, and from selling his own little books around Wiltshire.

Of course, Andrewes' 'vendible' books were soon taken over by the cheap-print publishers, and sent out across the country with their chapmen to readers he would never see. When he was long dead, the 1689 trade list of the chapbook publisher, William Thackeray, included 'Andrew's Golden Chain' and 'Andrew's Golden Trumpet'; it also offered Parker's version of 'Robin Conscience' and his 'King and Northern Man'. These titles were now part of the chapbook 'stock', and (like the ballad stock of 1624) divorced from the intentions of their original authors. The buyers themselves may be said to have played a part in the creation of this popular 'stock', through their collective choices, and through the agency of the commercially minded publisher.

This study has raised questions about the effects of two related forces in the century after the Reformation: Protestantism and print. Both have been credited with enormous, disruptive and even 'revolutionary' impact on traditional English culture. According to Wrightson and Levine's study of Terling in Essex, a militant Protestantism 'inserted a cultural wedge' in village society, as 'distinctions of religious outlook, education and manners' were 'superimposed on the existing distinctions of wealth, status and power'. The godly parish notables led the attack on 'a popular culture of communal dancings, alehouse sociability and the like' which 'retreated before a more sober ideal of family prayer, neighborly fellowship, and introspective piety'.[7] Other historians have focussed on the logo-centrism of this new Protestant culture; its emphasis on 'the invisible, abstract and didactic word:

[4] Robert Copland, *The seven sorowes that women have when theyr husbandes be deade* (1568), prologue. See above, pp. 257–8.
[5] John Taylor, *Pennilesse pilgrimage* (1619).
[6] Susan Aileen Newman, 'The broadside ballads of Martin Parker : a bibliographical and critical study' (Birmingham PhD, 1975), I, p. 2.
[7] Keith Wrightson and David Levine, *Poverty and piety in an English village, Terling, 1525–1700* (1979), pp. 162, 171.

primarily the word of the printed page.' Thus, around 1580, according to Patrick Collinson, the English people crossed a watershed 'from a culture of orality and image to one of print culture: from one mental and imaginative "set" to another'.[8]

The evidence of cheap religious print does not contradict the cultural importance of either Protestantism or the printed word, but it does suggest that the confrontational models sketched above are unsatisfactory. In studying the relationship between these new forces and the existing culture, we need to see not only points of conflict and displacement, but also areas of consensus and gradual integration. Even to write of Protestantism or print as 'forces' is misleading: we need to see them not as coherent and unchanging entities (one a set of doctrines, the other a technology), but as inseparable from and constantly modified by the cultural contexts in which they are found.

There were also, of course, points of disjuncture or disruption; situations and events in which conflicts flared. The sources to which historians have access tend to record these points of confrontation. Protestant tracts reveal a deliberate crusade against traditional visual images. Quarter sessions, assize and church court records document local conflicts over sexual morality, ale-selling and sabbath-day festivities. However, this bias in the sources can lead us to ignore areas of culture where these conflicts were either resolved or unarticulated. In some media, such as the narrative 'stories' for walls, Bible-centred Protestantism and traditional visual piety found common ground. In other cultural forms, such as the ballads on death and salvation, old and new beliefs rubbed elbows without apparent sense of contradiction. These sources provide an oblique approach to the area of unconscious or semi-conscious values and assumptions; to the fragmentary mosaic of 'commonplace mentalities.'

The attempt to interpret cheap print in terms of consensual values, shared at many levels of society, is supported by Martin Ingram's investigation of church court records in Wiltshire during the same period. Ingram argues that the church courts enforced values which were 'broadly consensual' and in line with the wide 'spectrum of unspectacular orthodoxy' within which the beliefs of most villagers can be categorized.[9] He argues that 'the notion that religious commitment was conditioned by social class must be treated with caution'. Rebellion against the church and its moral standards was more often a matter of youth culture than of economic standing, and estab-

---

[8] Patrick Collinson, *The birthpangs of Protestant England. Religious and cultural change in the sixteenth and seventeenth centuries* (1988), p. 99.

[9] Martin Ingram, *Church courts, sex and marriage in England, 1570–1640* (Cambridge, 1987), pp. 124, 94.

lished householders at all levels were normally guided by a sense of social morality. The church and religion

were important as markers of status, respectability and belonging, if for nothing else; and though this may have been most true for the middle to upper strata of parish society (the groups from which churchwardens were usually recruited and which were most likely to possess family pews), it probably applied also to many 'honest householders' of the poorer sort, who had a definite, albeit modest stake in the community.[10]

Ingram criticizes Geoffrey Quaife's picture of an amoral 'peasantry' concerned only with the economic consequences of their sexual conduct, pointing out that 'economic ideas were suffused with moral values and conceived in ethical terms'. The 'village whores' and bigamous vagrants were a small and marginalized group. Far more significantly, the numerous cases of sexual slander show the widespread concern amongst the ranks of the middling and poor with sexual 'credit' and 'honesty' as the touchstones of respectability.[11]

This evidence of a core of 'honest householders', dominating village society at all social levels, indicates a solid market for the godly broadsides and chapbooks of the present study. The moderate piety of '100 godly lessons' or the woodcut 'Christus natus est' would not seem out of place in the households (whether poor or prosperous) of Martin Ingram's Wiltshire village. It is less easy to see where they would belong in Wrightson and Levine's Essex village of Terling, where the atmosphere in the early seventeenth century was one of 'strain and conflict' between the parish notables who tried to impose their values of 'order and godliness' on the community, and the labouring poor who were indifferent, if not hostile, to the innovative Protestant culture.[12] The evidence of cheap print questions the rigidity of this 'polarization' of experience between godly and ungodly, elite and poor. In these cheapest of printed wares, Protestant doctrine and conservative piety were integrated, and 'religion' continued to have a place in the world of popular songs and alehouses, which were supposedly the preserve of the irreligious multitude.

There is no doubt that religious and moral issues could often serve as a focus for parish rivalries. But, as Martin Ingram argues, these social diversions 'were as much vertical as horizontal'.[13] Of course, the attempt to measure degrees of 'conflict' and of 'consensus' in the early seventeenth century is a particularly loaded one, because of its implications for the nature of the Civil War. The 'revisionist' interpretation emphasizes harmony and

[10] *Ibid.*, p. 123.
[11] *Ibid.*, pp. 159–60, 165.
[12] Wrightson and Levine, *Poverty and piety*, p. 176.
[13] Ingram, *Church courts, sex and marriage*, p. 118.

consensus in early Stuart political and religious culture, finding the causes of the war in personalities and accidents of fate. The critics of revisionism reassert the importance of long-term developments, stressing the existence of deep social divisions.[14] The interpretation of cheap godly print in terms of consensual values should not necessarily be seen as evidence for either of these political views. The ballads and chapbooks studied here are biassed toward the *longue durée*, and exclude sources like slanderous rhymes which would reveal more topical, contentious and divisive concerns.[15]

However, while historians continue to argue over the correct ratio of conflict and consensus, even the exponents of the 'polarized' society (such as Keith Wrightson) are agreed on the existence of 'canons of good neighbourliness', 'minimum standards' of behaviour and a 'moral community' within which village society had to operate.[16] The godly ballads, broadsides and chapbooks are artefacts of the process by which these standards were articulated, disseminated, absorbed, modified, adapted and reflected. They are the products of a dialogue between Protestant norms and traditional practices; between a centralized press and localized experience; between authors and consumers, through the profit-conscious publisher as middleman.

We need, then, to see belief-formation as a process: not a simple replacement of Catholic with Protestant doctrine, but a gradual modification of traditional piety. The resulting patchwork of beliefs may be described as distinctively 'post-Reformation', but not thoroughly 'Protestant'. Piety retained a visual dimension, even if Christ in glory was now more remote, banished to the windows or roof of the parish church, or to the tiny woodcuts along the top of a ballad. Religious emotion still attached itself to heroic archetypes, even if these were increasingly Protestant martyrs rather than Catholic saints. Morality still meant good neighbourly behaviour, and hell was still the same fiery place, a final threat as direct punishment for sins committed in this world.

'Religion' cannot just be measured in terms of knowledge of particular doctrines, or attendance at church, or even adherence to the increasingly strict Protestant norms of sexual conduct. We must also look at the hazier area of images, emotions and fears; of the rules by which people ordered their lives (even if these were looser than the mostly 'godly sort' might wish); and of how people placed themselves in history and the universe. Most historians would agree that the early sixteenth-century villager's representation of the world was inseparable from a Christian framework, even if

---

[14] Richard Cust and Ann Hughes, 'Introduction: after Revisionism', in Cust and Hughes, eds., *Conflict in early Stuart England. Studies in religion and politics 1603–1642* (1989), pp. 1–46.

[15] See, for example, Richard Cust, 'News and politics in England', *Past and Present*, 112 (1986), pp. 60–90.

[16] Wrightson, *English society*, pp. 53–4, 205.

this was infused with beliefs we would call 'magical' or 'pagan'. The Protestant Reformation removed large chunks of the imagery and the festival calendar which had reinforced this framework, but the 'mental set' was not so easily dismantled.

'Religion', even in Protestant England, was not a category isolated from other aspects of experience. If reformers abandoned their ambitious mid-sixteenth-century programme to create a Protestantized 'popular culture' of song and imagery, this did not mean a sudden divorce of religion from these media. Artisans and writers could not help but continue to embed their products with religious values and themes. Even the broadside ballads written by the early Elizabethan reformers had a life of their own well into the seventeenth century, and sometimes beyond. A hardening of 'puritan' attitudes in some places may well have alienated the young, the indigent or the transient from the parish churches, but we cannot assume that even these marginalized groups had no religious opinions. We must not think of religion as the exclusive preserve of the church, but look for ways in which 'religious' beliefs in the broadest sense were encountered throughout local society: in popular songs, in cloths on alehouse walls, in tables pasted up in cottages, or in accounts of grisly executions chanted out in the marketplaces.

Just as Protestantism should not be seen as a coherent set of doctrines which simply replaces older belief, so print and literacy were not unchanging technologies which unilaterally replaced other forms of communication. Researchers on literacy in a twentieth-century context have criticized the 'autonomous model' of literacy as a 'neutral' technology. According to this model, literacy alters the processes of thought in certain universal ways, facilitating the capacity for 'rationality' and for 'abstract context-free thought'. Brian Street has argued that we need an 'ideological model' which stresses that 'the processes whereby reading and writing are learnt are what construct the meaning of it for particular practitioners'. He also criticizes Jack Goody and others for an approach which 'polarizes the difference between oral and literate modes of communication in a way that gives insufficient credit to the reality of "mixed" and interacting modes'.[17]

This attempt to look at literacy in specific cultural contexts, and at 'mixed' modes of communication, is appropriate to the evidence of cheap print in early modern England. The meaning of a printed ballad was not only in its text, but also in the melody of the tune it was sung to; its tempo and instrumentation; the location of the performance; the talent, character

---

[17] Brian V. Street, *Literacy in theory and practice* (Cambridge, 1984), pp. 2, 8, 5.

and social status of the singer; the people in the audience; the other songs sung before and after; even the other songs sung to the same tune, which resonated in the ears of the listener. The meaning could also be in the woodcuts along the top of the broadside; its location on the alehouse or cottage wall; the other ballads or painted cloths in the room; and the stained glass windows or paintings in the local church which recurred in the mind's eye of the viewer.

The 'consumers' of cheap print brought certain habitual ways of seeing, reading, and remembering to the broadsides and chapbooks, such as the tendency to conceptualize morality in aphoristic packages, or to think of printed texts in terms of familiar objects like gloves and garters. Our interest in cultural 'mentalities' on a broad societal level need not imply a deterministic attitude to the individual consumer. Unfortunately, we rarely have documents like those used by Carlo Ginzburg to show how a sixteenth-century miller constructed his own meaning from the books he read, filtered through the primarily oral culture he lived in.[18] But by approaching obliquely, through an exploration of the various ways print could be used, we can suggest contexts in which an individual might encounter and interpret a given text. A crude woodcut of the holy family might trigger a visual response related to a favourite window in the parish church. A ballad of godly 'Susanna' or the 'Duchess of Suffolk' might be subsumed into a singer's stock of heroes and heroines; memorized and stored along with 'Bonny Barbara Allen' and 'The bailiff's daughter of Islington'.[19]

Indeed, whether or not the text was a song, it may have been treated as something to be *learnt*. Reading was taught as a form of rote-learning, with an emphasis on the ability to memorize set forms of words, such as the Creed, Lord's Prayer, Ten Commandments and catechism. Even when a pupil left school with what we would call full reading skills, this learning process may have helped to inculcate a habit of 'intensive' reading: that is, contact with a restricted number of texts, which were slowly and closely perused, frequently re-read and often rendered aloud.[20] A Bordeaux lawyer Pierre Bernaudau described this kind of reading amongst the French peasants of the late eighteenth century, whose reading matter consisted primarily of Books of Hours, almanacs and the *bibliothèque bleue*: 'They have a mania for going back over these miserable books twenty times, and when

---

[18] Roger Chartier, *The cultural history of print in early modern France*, trans. Lydia C. Cochrane (Princeton, 1987), pp. 39–40. Carlo Ginzburg, *The cheese and the worms: the cosmos of a sixteenth-century miller*, trans. John and Anne Tedeschi (Baltimore, 1980).

[19] James Kinsley, ed., *The Oxford book of ballads* (Oxford, 1982 edn.), nos. 94, 90.

[20] R.A. Houston, *Literacy in early modern Europe, Culture and education 1500–1800* (1988), pp. 57, 195-6.

they talk with you about them (which they do eagerly), they recite their little books word for word, so to speak.'[21]

Roger Chartier is sceptical of Bernadau's portrait of peasant reading, suggesting that it falls within an idealized literary tradition. Nevertheless, the study of cheap print in the early modern period does suggest that the relationship of reader to text was not the same as that of a twentieth-century literate scanning the morning paper. It appears often to have been more like the relationship of singer to song text, with the printed artefact acting as an aid to memory. The 'godly tables' and painted sayings on walls were there to remind the viewer of things already known, not to bring new information. The ballads and chapbooks of Robin Hood, Patient Grissel and Guy of Warwick retold stories which had long been circulating orally, and were simply given a fixed form in print. Of course, we would not want to exaggerate this point: new stories of northern farmers, west-country tailors and London whores were constantly being added to the stock of timeless chivalric tales. But these acquisitions from print continued to enrich the oral culture, rather than simply replace it.

Literacy and print were not only 'agents of change', but could also be forces for cultural continuity.[22] Lucien Febvre and Henri-Jean Martin have shown how printing could reinforce a traditional world view:

Although printing certainly helped scholars in some fields, on the whole it could not be said to have hastened the acceptance of new ideas or knowledge. In fact, by popularising long cherished beliefs, strengthening traditional prejudices and giving authority to seductive fallacies, it could even be said to have represented an obstacle to the acceptance of many new views.[23]

A striking example of this persistence of old-fashioned beliefs is the length of time it took for the general reading public to take any interest in the discovery of the New World. Throughout the first half of the sixteenth century, works on the Americas circulated only within a small circle, and travel books continued to perpetuate a distorted picture of the world.[24] This conservatism can be seen again and again in the ballads and chapbooks of the present study, which reprinted medieval chivalric stories and pre-Reformation visions of the after-life well into the eighteenth century.

We have been describing the conservatism of print in terms of the mental habits of orality: reading as remembering, reader as speaker or singer. The continuity of orality was, on the whole, accepted, unquestioned and ideologi-

---

[21] Quoted and discussed in Chartier, *Cultural history*, pp. 163–4.
[22] Elizabeth L. Eisenstein, *The printing press as an agent of change* (2 vols. in 1, Cambridge, 1980 edn.). R.A. Houston provides a balanced evaluation in *Literacy in early modern Europe*, pp. 230–4.
[23] Lucien Febvre and Henri-Jean Martin, *The coming of the book. The impact of printing 1450–1800*, trans. David Gerard (1976 edn.), p. 278.
[24] *Ibid.*, pp. 278–82.

cally unproblematic. Hearing and reading were both means of access to words; an oral sermon or a printed tract could bring an audience to the Word; and the Bible was the medium of revelation whether in printed form or read aloud.[25] However, the continuity of the visual dimension was a more contentious matter. Here, in printed word and image, were two different ways of seeing, which seemed (from the extreme iconoclast's point of view) to be two incompatible ways of conceptualizing religious belief.

At the end of the sixteenth century, some reformers and writers in England became acutely aware of a tension between the verbal and the visual; between the iconic impulse of their inherited culture from Rome, and the iconoclastic implications of their new logo-centric religion.[26] At its strongest, this awareness of cultural tension was directed inward, causing individuals to reflect on their sensory intake and on the value given to things read or heard, and things seen, in their construction of the world and its meaning.[27] However, it would be a mistake to project this preoccupation of an educated minority onto the society as a whole. If there was a gradual suppression of the visual dimension in English culture, relative to the growing value placed on verbal or literate communication, it did not occur in one generation, nor even in several generations. The iconic and the verbal continued to exist in fruitful tension in the seventeenth century, finding new life in hybrid forms like the emblem, and in simpler 'tables' which combined picture and text to meet the needs of a semi-literate audience.

How can we logo-centric historians conceptualize that fragmentary, heterogeneous patchwork of images which made up 'commonplace' or 'popular' religious belief? Perhaps we might bring back the visual dimension by following the example of the 'art of memory' practitioners, projecting the collective early seventeenth-century mind out onto the external representation of a building. Not a grand hall or cathedral, since we are in post-Reformation England, but an ordinary village alehouse.

This is not the luxurious inn where 'Civis' and 'Uxor' would stay, but an 'honest alehouse' where established householders, whether poor or relatively prosperous, could respectably be seen.[28] Above the entrance is a very Protestant painted cloth which reads 'Feare God', almost illegible from the

---

[25] The need to 'hear and read' the Word was a constant refrain of reformers. See, for example, Richard Baxter quoted in Margaret Aston, *England's iconoclasts. vol. I: Laws against images* (Oxford, 1988), p. 355.

[26] For an exploration of this tension in literature, see Ernest B. Gilman, *Iconoclasm and poetry in the English Reformation. Down went Dagon* (Chicago, 1986).

[27] See particularly John Donne's sermons and poetry, discussed in *ibid.*, pp. 117–48.

[28] 'Civis' and 'Uxor' visit their emblematic alehouse in William Bullein, *A dialogue bothe pleasaunte and pietifull, wherein is a goodly regimente against the fever pestilence* (1564), sig.H6. A rather idealized 'honest Alehouse' is described in Izaak Walton, *The complete angler; or, the contemplative man's recreation* (1653), facs. edn. (1876), p. 49.

ravages of smoke. On the same wall has been nailed a rather Catholic-looking woodcut of the nativity scene, surrounded by the arms of the passion. The long back wall is crudely painted with the story of the prodigal son in four scenes, with a black-letter text below. The third wall is hung with a plain cloth upon which is pinned a row of ballads decorated with woodcuts, including various figures kneeling in prayer, and a small faded scene which might be the resurrection. The final wall is dominated by the hearth, above which hangs a wooden plaque with rows of wise sayings: 'Save us o Lord from heathens sword', 'An evill woman is like a scorpion' and so on.

What happens if we move forward to the mid-eighteenth century? The wall painting and painted cloths are gone, but instead there is a wide selection of woodcut pictures from the press of Dicey and Marshall, available from chapmen across the country.[29] There are still tables of godly sayings: 'The Christian's Dial', 'The Lord's Prayer, finely ornamented', 'King Charles's Rules'. For narrative biblical stories, we have the history of the prodigal son in four paper sheets, or we may choose Susanna and the Elders, or Abraham offering Isaac. And for more direct piety, the nativity scene remains unchanged, while the image of Christ is now available in a great range of scenes – the last supper, the crucifixion, the resurrection, the ascension – each on a large sheet of fine royal paper.[30]

Of course, we are exaggerating the piety of this metaphorical alehouse: perhaps there are only one or two religious images in a room full of knights on woodcut horses, portraits of royalty, scatalogical political satires, and placards of strange fish or deformed pigs. Nevertheless, this is precisely the point. The profane and the pious, the verbal and the visual : all were accommodated within the same room, the same mind, the same experience. It is only the historian who, like an iconoclast, wants to rip down all the images on the walls which do not seem to fit. We need to recognize how the culture could absorb new beliefs while retaining old ones, could modify doctrines, could accommodate words and icons, ambiguities and contradictions. There may have been Reformation and Civil War, riot and rebellion, but the basic mental decor did not change as suddenly or completely as historians would sometimes lead us to believe.

[29] Cluer Dicey and Richard Marshall, *A catalogue of maps, prints, copy-books, drawing-books, histories, old ballads, patters, collections &c* (1764).
[30] *Ibid.*, pp. 15–19, 62–5.

Appendix A The godly ballad 'stock'

Format

'Title in Stationers' Register entry' [Title of extant edn if different]
    author and date of composition if known; date of Stationers' Register entries
    first extant broadside edition: STC or Wing no. if listed; location; printer; date
    (If no broadside survives, an appearance in manuscript or printed collection is
    cited.)

STC conventions are used for publication details.

Listed in chronological order of first appearance (Stationers' Register entry, surviving
copy, or mention in another source).

THE 'PARTNERS' 1624 ENTRY

These are the religious ballads registered to the 'partners' on 14 December 1624.
(Arber, IV, pp. 131–2.)

UNIDENTIFIED BALLADS
'In the beginning God made men'
'Harke Harke alas my brethren'
'O Lord my God which way shall I'
'Such as doe for theire sinnes'
'O saviour Christ I must confesse'
'Jesus punishment'
'Wrapped in woeful sorrowes'
'O man in desparation' (ent. 15 au. 1586. The ballad is lost, but gives its name
to the tune in Simpson, p. 535.)

EXTANT BALLADS
  1 'Susanna' [The ballad of constant Susanna]
      ent. 1562–3; 14 de.1624; 8 se.1592; 1 mr.1675
      STC 23435a.5; Pepys, I, 33; [G. Purslowe f.] H. Gosson [c. 1625]
  2 'Rogers will' [The exhortacion of Robert Smith, unto his children, commonly
    set out in the name of maister Rogers]
      ?ent. 14 se.1564; ?1 au.1586; 14 de.1624; ?1 my. 1656
      Foxe, *Actes and monuments* (1563), sig.3U2–3U2v
  3 'John Carelesse' [A godly and vertuous songe or ballade, made by the constant
    member of Christe, John Carelesse . . .]
      ent. 1 au.1586; 14 de.1624; ?9 fe.1635

Coverdale, *Certain most godly, fruitful, and comfortable letters* (1564), pp. 634–8

4 'Patient Job' [A pleasant ballad of the just man Jobe, shewing his patience in extremitie]
> ent. 1564–5 (twice); 14 de.1624
> BM Addit. MS 15,225, fols. 16v–17; repr. Rollins, *Old English ballads*, p. 209

5 'From sluggish sleepe' [The belman's good morrow, beginning 'From sluggish sleep and slumber']
> ?ent. 1568–9; 21 no. 1580; 14 de.1624
> Shirburn, p. 182

6 'David and Bethsheba' [The story of David and Berseba]
> ?ent. 1569–70; 14 de.1624; 1 mr.1675; 20 se.1712; Dicey catalogue 1754
> STC 6317; RB orig. I, 88–9; RB repr. I, p.270; [Eliz. Allde?] f. J. Wright (snr), [*c*. 1635]

7 'When Jesus Christ was 12' [first line of: A new ditty, shewing the wonderful miracles of our lord (and saviour) Jesus Christ . . .]
> ent. 11 se.1578; 8 au.1586; 14 de.1624; 1 mr.1675
> STC 6922.7; Pepys, I, 58; f. H. G[osson, *c*. 1625]

8. 'Christians ABC' [A right godly and Christian A,B,C/ Shewing the duty of every degree]
> ?ent. 19 au.1579; 14 de.1624
> STC 22; RB orig. I, 492; RB repr. III, p. 160; f. H. Gosson, [1625]

9. 'Harke man what I thi God [shall speak]' [first line of: A passing bell towling to call us to mind, Our time evill spending, a plague now we find . . .]
> ent. 30 oc.1582; 14 de.1624
> STC 19460; Wood 276 B(103) [torn copy]; repr. Hyder E. Rollins, *A Pepysian Garland* (Cambridge, 1922) p. 185; [London, 1625?]

10 'Proverbs of Salomon' [? A most excellent new dittie, wherein is shewed the sage sayings, and wise sentences of Salomon . . .]
> ent. 1 au.1586; 14 de.1624; 1 mr.1675
> STC 22900; Collmann no. 84; W.W[hite] for T.P[avier], [*c*. 1615]

11 'Good Lord what a wicked world' [first line of: A most excellent godly new ballad: shewing the manifold abuses of this wicked world]
> ent. 1 au.1586; 14 de.1624
> STC 1328.7; Manchester, I, 4; repr. Hyder E. Rollins, *The Pack of Autolycus* (Cambridge, Mass., 1927), p. 3; R.B[lower, *c*. 1615]

12 'It was a ladies daughter' [first line of: A rare example of a vertuous maid in Paris . . .]
> ent. 1 au.1586; 15 au.1586; 14 de.1624
> Pepys II, 24–5; J. Clarke, W. Thackeray and T. Passinger, [1684–6]

13 'When faire Jerusalem did stand' [first line of: A warning or lanthorne to London. A dolefull destruction of faire Jerusalem . . .]
> ?ent. 15 au.1586; 8 jn.1603; 14 de.1624
> Shirburn, p. 32

14 'I am a poore sinner' [first line of: A Christian conference betweene Christ and a sinner . . .]
> ent. 7 no.1586; 14 de.1624
> STC 14544; RB orig. I, 493; RB repr. III, p. 164; assignes of T. Symcocke, [1628–9]

15 'Resurrection of Christ' [A most godly and comfortable ballad of the glorious resurrection of our lord Jesus Christ . . .]
 ?ent. 4 mr.1588; 14 de.1624; 1 mr.1675
 STC 14553.3; RB orig. I, 258–9; RB repr. I, p. 388; f. F. Coules, [1640?]

16 'Christs teares over Jerusalem' [Christes teares over Jerusalem. Or, a caveat for England, to call to God for mercy . . .]
 composed [c. 1593?]; 14 de.1624; ent. 1 mr.1675
 STC 14543; BL Cup.651.e(26); f. H. Gosson, [c. 1640]

17 'Doctor Faustus' [The judgment of God shewed upon John Faustus, Doctor of Divinitye]
 ent. 1589; 14 de.1624; 1 mr.1675; Dicey catalogue 1754
 Wing J1178; RB orig. II, 235; RB repr. VI, p. 703; A. M[ilbourne, 1693?]

18 '100 godly lessons' [An hundred godly lessons that a mother on her death-bed gave to her children . . .]
 ?ent. 26 no.1590; 14 de.1624; 13 mr.1656; 1 mr.1675; 20 se.1712
 Pepys, II, 16–17; f. W. Thackeray and T. Passinger, [1686–8]

19 'All careful Christians' [All careful Christians, marke my song = first line of: A right excellent and godly new Ballad, shewinge the uncertainetye of this present lyfe . . .]
 ent. 3 my.1591; 14 de.1624
 Shirburn, p. 40

20 'O mortall man bedrencht' [first line of: A new ballad intituled A myrrour or lookinge glasse for all sinners]
 ?ent. 18 my.1595; 14 de.1624
 Shirburn, p. 149

21 'Duchesse of Suffolke' [The most rare and excellent history of the Dutchesse of Suffolkes calamity]
 [anon.] by Thomas Deloney [c. 1602]; ent. 14 de.1624; 1 mr.1675; Dicey catalogue 1754
 STC 6557.8; RB orig. I, 94–5; RB repr. I, p. 287; f. E. Wright, [c. 1635]

22 'Jerusalem my happie home' [first line of: The zealous querister's songe of Yorke, in the prayse of heaven, to all faithful singers and godlye readers in the world]
 by F.B.P. [c. 1601]; ent. 14 de.1624
 Rawlinson 566(4to), fol. 167; F. Coles, T. Vere, J. Wright [1663–74]

23 'Jeffa Judge of Israell' [A proper new ballad, intituled when Jepha judge of Israell]
 composed by 1603; ent. 14 de.1624
 STC 14498.5; Manchester, II, 56; T. Langley, [c. 1620]

24 'Who viewes the life of mortall [men]' [first line of: A proper new ballad, devised upon the theam I know not what . . . 1614]
 ent. 14 de.1624
 Shirburn, p. 50

25 'Good people all repent [with speed]' [first line of: A warninge to worldlings to learne them to dye]
 ent. 14 de.1624; 1 mr.1675
 Shirburn, p. 25 [pre-1616]

26 'Tobias of Ninive' [A pleasant new ballad of Tobias, wherein is shewed the wonderfull things which chanced to him in his youth]
 ent. 14 de.1624; 1 mr.1675; 20 se.1712; Dicey catalogue 1754
 STC 24094; RB orig. I, 420–1; RB repr. II, p. 621; f. F. Coules, [c. 1640]

27 'Joseph and Marye' [A most excellent ballad of Joseph the carpenter and the

sacred virgin Mary . . .]
  ent. 14 de.1624; 1 mr.1675
  Pepys, II, 27; f. F. Coles, T. Vere, J. Wright, J. Clarke, W. Thackeray and
  T. Passinger [1678–80]
28 'In slumbering sleepe I lay' [first line of: A comfortable new ballad of a dreame
  of a sinner, being very sore troubled with the assaults of Sathan]
  ent. 14 de.1624
  STC 1328; Pepys, I, 39; [A. Mathewes] f. E. Wright, [1625?]
29 'I am a poore woman and blinde' [A ballad of Anne Askew, intituled: I am
  a woman poor and blind]
  ent. 14 de.1624; 1 mr.1675
  STC 853.5; Manchester, I, 54; [A. Mathewes?] f. T.P[avier, 1624?]
30 'Table of good nurture' [A table of good nurture: wherein is contained a schoole-
  masters admonition to his schollers to learne good manners: the father to his
  children to learne virtue: and the houshoulder to his servants to learne godlinesse]
  ent. 14 de.1624
  STC 23635; RB orig. I, 402–3; RB repr. II, p. 570; f. HG[osson, 1625?]
31 'Clarke of Bodnam' [A very godly song, intituled, the earnest petition of a faithfull
  Christian, being earnest clarke of Bodnam, made upon his death-bed, at the instant
  of his transmutation]
  ent. 14 de.1624; 1 mr.1675
  STC 3194.5; Pepys, I, 48–9; f. H.G[osson, 1624?]
32 'sore sicke deare freinds' [first line of: The deadmans song, whose dwelling was
  neere unto Basing Hall in London]
  ent. 14 de.1624; 1 mr.1675; 20 se.1712
  STC 17229.5; Pepys, I, 55; f. E. Wright, [1625?]
33 'O Lord my God I come to thee' [first line of: The sorrowful lamentation of
  a penitent sinner]
  ent. 14 de.1624
  RB orig. III, 37; RB repr. VIII, p. 99 (also IV, p. 365); F. Coles, T. Vere,
  I. Wright, [1663–74]
34 'Dozen of pointes' [A godly new Ballad, intituled, A dozen of poynts]
  ent. 14 de.1624
  Wing G937A; Euing no.126; F. Coles, T. Vere, W. Gilbertson, [1658–64]

OTHER GODLY BALLADS LASTING TWENTY-FIVE YEARS OR MORE IN BROADSIDE FORM

These are godly ballads not included in 1624 list, but showing evidence of long-lasting
popularity in broadside form (twenty-five years or more).

35 Even in the twinkling of an eye
  ent. 1561–2
  Wing E3525; Pepys, II, 27; F. Coles, T.Vere, I. Wright, I. Clarke, W. Thackeray, T. Passenger [1678–80]
36 The historie of the prophet Jonas. The repentance of Ninivie that great Citie.
  ?ent. 1562–3; ?1567–8
  STC 14716; Pepys, I, 28–9; E. A[llde, *c.* 1620]
37 A most excellent and famous ditty of Sampson judge of Israell, how he wedded
  a Philistine's daughter.
  ?ent. 1563–4; 15 au.1586

STC 21688.5; Pepys, I, 32; [London, *c.* 1625]
38 A new ballad; declaring the excellent parable of the prodigal child
?ent. 1570–1; 13 mr.1656
Wing N557C; RB orig. I, 346–7; RB repr. II, p. 393; A.M[ilbourne, 1690?]
39 A new ballad intituled, A bell-man for England ... [begins: Awake! Awake! Oh Englande!]
composed before 1580; ent. 6 de.1586; 1 mr.1675
STC 1848.5; Pepys, I, 54; f. H.[Gosson, *c.* 1620]
40 Two pleasant ditties, one of the birth, the other of the passion of Christ
composed by 1616; ent. 24 ap.1640; 1 mr.1675
STC 14577; RB orig. I, 394–5; RB repr. II, p. 549; assignes of T. Symcocke, [1628–9]
41 The wandering Jew; or, the shooemaker of Jerusalem ...
?ent. 21 au.1612; 9 oct.1620; 13 mr.1656; 1 mr.1675
Pepys, I, 524–5; J.Clarke, W.Thackeray and T. Passinger [1684–6]
42 An excellent song wherein you shall finde / Great consolation for a troubled minde [known by first line: 'Ayme not too hie']
ent. 13 mr.1656
STC 22918.7; RB orig. I, 106–7; RB repr. I, 325; assignes of T. Symcocke, [1628–9]
43 The sinner's redemption. Wherein is described the blessed nativity of our lord Jesus Christ
ent. 13 jn.1634; 26 mr.1656; 20 se.1712
STC 22576; RB orig. I, 374–5; RB repr. II, p. 486; [f. J. Wright?, 1634?]
44 The dying tears of a penitent sinner. Which was written as he lay on his death-bed, according to his own direction ...
ent. 24 de.1638; 1 mr.1675
Wing D2958; RB orig. II 113; RB repr. IV, p. 362; F. Coles, T. Vere, I. Wright, I. Clarke, W. Thackeray, T. Passinger, [1675]
45 The angel Gabriel: his salutation to the blessed virgin Mary [first line: 'When righteous Joseph wedded was ...']
?ent. 22 fe.1639
Wing A3163; Pepys, II, 30; W. Thackeray and T. Passinger, [1686–8]
46 St Bernard's vision
ent. 13 mr.1656; 1 mr.1675; 20 se.1712; Dicey catalogue 1754
STC 1910; RB orig. I, 376–7; RB repr. II, p. 491; f. J. Wright, [*c.* 1640]

Appendix B All other godly ballads surviving in broadside copies 1550–1640

Format

Title; author (if known); entry date (if earlier than extant edn); STC no.; date of extant edn.

Listed in chronological order of first appearance (extant copy or Stationers' Register entry).

1 An ABC to the christen congregacion / Or a patheway to the heavenly habitacion; by T[homas] Knell; STC 15029; [1550?].

2 The husbandman. Let us lyft up our hartes all ... [A ballad of Luther, the pope, a cardinal and a husbandman]; STC 14008.5; [c. 1550?].

3. Of misrules contending with Gods worde by name, And then of ones judgement that heard of the same; by Wyllyam Kethe; STC 14941; [1553?].

4 An Ave Maria in commendation of our most vertuous queene; by L[eonard] Stopes; STC 23292; [1553?].

5 A new ballade of the marigolde; by William Forrest; STC 11186; [1553?].

6 An exclamation upon the erronious and fantasticall sprite of heresy, troubling the unitie of the church ...; STC 10615; [1553?].

7 Remember man both night and day, Thou must nedes die, there is no nay; STC 17236; [1554–8].

8 Susteine, absteine, kepe well in your minde ...; STC 23446; [c. 1555].

9 A newe balade made by N. Balthorp which suffered in Calys the xv daie of Marche M.D.L.; by N[icholas] Balthorp[e]; STC 1342; [1557?].

10 The wonders of England; by J[ohn] A[wdeley]; STC 996; 1559.

11 A prayer or supplycation made unto God by a yonge man ...; by John Pyttes [Pits]; STC 19969.4; 1559.

12 A newe ballade, O dere lady Elysabeth ...; by R.M.; STC 17147; [1560?].

13 The cruel assault of Gods fort; by J[ohn] A[wdeley]; STC 989; [c. 1560].

14 A balade declaryng how neybourhed, love and trew dealyng is gone; by John Barker; STC 1419; [1561].

15 The maner of the world now a dayes; ?ent. 1561–2; STC 17255; [c. 1590].

16 A ballad against slander and detraction; by John Heywood; STC 13290; [1562].

17 Against filthy writing, and such like delighting; by Thomas Brice; STC 3725; [1562].

18 The complaint of a sinner, vexed with paine, desyring the joye, that ever shall remayne; by William Birch; STC 3076; [1563].

19 A complaynt agaynst the wicked enemies of Christ in that they have so tyrannusly

handled the poore chrystians; STC 14545; [1564].

20 The reedifying of Salomons temple, and the laborers thereof; STC 22902; [1564?].

21 The refuge of a sinner, wherein are briefly declared the chiefest poinctes of true salvation; by Rober Burdet esq.; STC 4104; 1565.

22 A warning to England, let London begin: / To repent their iniquitie, and flie from their sin; by William Birch; STC 3080; [1565].

23 Almightie God I pray his holy spirite to send, The just mannes hart stedfast to stay, and wicked lives to amend [+ a song against the mass, on same sheet]; by Christopher Wilson; STC 25766; 1566.

24 A godly ballad declaring by the scriptures the plagues that have insued whordom; by A.I.; STC 14046; 1566.

25 A proper new balad of the bryber Gehesie. Taken out of the fourth boke of kinges, the v chapter; by George Mell; STC 17802; [1566].

26 Of the horyble and woful destrucion of Jerusalem. And of the sygnes and tokens that were seene before it was destroied . . . ; by John Barker; STC 1420; [1569?].

27 A new yeres gift, intituled, a christal glas for all estates to looke in, wherein they may plainly see the just rewarde, for unsaciate and abhominable covetous-nesse; by W. Fering; STC 10821; 1569.

28 Of the endes and deathes of two prisoners, lately pressed to death in Newgate; STC 18492; 1569.

29 Of the horrible and wofull destruction of Sodome and Gomorra; ent. 1568-9; STC 22890; [1570].

30 Ecclesi.xx. Remember death, and thou shalt never sinne; by Joh[n] Awd[eley]; STC 990; 1569.

31 A godly ditty or prayer to be song unto God for the preservation of his Church, our queene and realme, against all traytours, rebels and papisticall enemies; by John Awdeley; STC 995; [1569?].

32 The mirror of man's lyfe made by a modest virgine Fransisca Chauesia a nonne of the clyster of S. Elizabeth in Spain burned for the profession of the gospell; STC 5104; 1570.

33 A lamentation from Rome, how the pope, doth bewayle, That the rebelles in England can not prevayle; by Thomas Preston, dramatist; STC 20289; 1570.

34 A ballad intituled, A newe well a daye, as playne, maister papist, as Donstable waye; by W[illiam] E[lderton]; STC 7553; [1570].

35 The plagues of Northumberland; by John Barker; STC 1421; [1570?].

36 A ballad intituled, Prepare ye to the plowe; by William Elderton; STC 7555; [1570].

37 A ballad rejoysinge the sodaine fall Of rebels that thought to devower us all; STC 1326; [1570].

38 A ballat intituled Northomberland newes, Wherein you may see what rebelles do use; by William Elderton; STC 7554; [1570].

39 A description of Nortons falcehod of Yorke shyre, and of his fatall farewel; by William Gibson; STC 11843; [1570].

40 Newes from Northumberland; by William Elderton; STC 7560; [1570].

41 The end and confession of John Felton who suffred in Paules Churcheyeard in London, the viii of August, for high treason. 1570; by F.G.; STC 11493; [1570].

42 A balade of a priest that loste his nose, For sayinge of masse, as I suppose; STC 1324; [1570?].

43 Other thus it is, or thus it should bee; STC 7550; [1570?].

44 O marvelous tydnges, both wonders old and new, The devyll is endited, yf many mens wordes be tru; STC 24066; [*c.* 1570]

45 A newe Ballade, intituled, Agaynst rebellious and false rumours; by Thomas Bette; STC 1979; 1570.

46 An answer to a papisticall byll, cast in the streetes of Northampton, and brought before the judges at the last syses. 1570; [by Thomas Knell]; STC 15030; 1570.

47 The braineles blessing of the bull; STC 19974.1; [1570].

48 A balad intituled, A cold pye for the papistes . . . ; by John Phillip[s]; STC 19863; [1570?].

49 A free admonition without any fees To warne the papistes to beware of three trees; by G.B.[William Birch]; STC 3077; 1571 (12 de.).

50 An admonition to Doctor Story beeing condemned of high treason, sent to him before his death . . . ; by John Cornet, Minister; STC 5772; [1571].

51 A letter to Rome, to declare to y[e] pope, J. Felton his freend is hangd in a rope: And farther, a right his grace to enforme, He dyed a papist, and seemd not to turne; by Steven Peele; STC 19549; [1571].

52 The pope in his fury doth answer returne, To a letter y[e] which to Rome is late come; by S[teven] P[eele]; STC 19550; [1571].

53 A proper new balande expressyng the fames, Concerning a warning to al London dames; by Steven Peele; STC 19551; [1571].

54 A new ballad intituled, Daniels siftyng in these our dayes: aptly applyed to the true preachers of the Gospell; STC 6235; 1572 (22 oc.).

55 A pleasant poesie, or sweete nosegay of fragrant smellyng flowers gathered in the garden of heavenly pleasure, the holy and blessed bible; by John Symon; STC 23589; 1572.

56 A balad intituled, the dekaye of the duke; by William Elderton; STC 7552.5; [1572].

57 A new balade or songe, of the lambes feast [+ an other, out of Goodwill, on same sheet]; 'per W.S. Veritatis Amatorem'; STC 21529; [Cologne, N. Bohmberg], 1574.

58 A prayer, and also a thankesgiving unto God, for his great mercy, in giving, and preserving our noble Queene Elizabeth . . . to be sung the xvii day of November 1577; by I. Pit, minister [John Pits]; STC 19969.2; [1577].

59 A warning to London by the fall of Antwerp; by Rafe[Ralph] Norris; STC 18656; [1577?].

60 A good exhortation to every man what he should doo when he goeth to bed and when he riseth; STC 10627; [1580?].

61 A triumph for true subjects, and a terrour unto al traitours: By the example of the late death of Edmund Campion, Ralphe Sherwin, and Alexander Bryan, Jesuites and seminarie priestes . . . ; [by William Elderton?]; STC 7564; 1581.

62 A declaration of the death of John Lewes, a most detestable and obstinate hereticke, burned at Norwich the xviii daye of September, 1583 . . . ; not found in STC; 1583.

63 A godlie dittie to be song for the preservation of the Queene's most excelent majestie's raigne; by R. Thacker; STC 23926; 1586.

64 The lamentation of follie; by William Elderton; STC 7557; [1588?].

65 A spiritual songe of thankes giving unto God, for his grace and power. Written by a close prisonner (with a coale) for his owne comforte; STC 22923; 1592.

66 The heartie confession of a Christian, devised for his own comfort, written

for his remembrance, and now published for the use of M.H. and others his faithfull and private friends only; STC 5152; 1593.

67 The shamefull downefall of the popes kingdome. Contayning the life and death of Steven Garnet, the popes chiefe priest in England . . . ; STC 11620.5; [1606?].

68 Calebbe Shillocke, his prophesie: or, the Iewes prediction; STC 22434; [1607].

69 A prophesie of the judgment day. Being lately found in Saint Denis church in France, and wrapped in leade in the forme of an heart; STC 20440; [1620?].

70 A scourge for the pope; by Martin Parker; STC 19268; [1624].

71 A song or psalme of thanksgiving, in remembrance of our deliverance from the gun-powder treason the fift of November, 1605; by T.S.; STC 21522; 1625.

72 Death's dance; STC 6444; [*c.* 1625].

73 A New-yeeres-gift forthe [*sic*] pope. Come see the difference plainly decided, betweene truth and falshood; STC 20112; [*c.* 1625].

74 A discourse of man's life; STC 6907; f. H. Gosson, [1629?].

75 Glad tydings from heaven: or Christs glorious invitation to sinners; STC 24065; [*c.* 1630].

76 The sinner's supplication. Confessing his sins; STC 22579; [*c.* 1630].

77 The Iudgement of Salomon: In discerning the true mother from the false, by her compassion, giving sentence to divide the childe; STC 22898; [*c.* 1630].

78 Good admonition Or to al sorts of people this counsell I sing, That in each ones affaire, to take heed's a faire thing; STC 150.5; [*c.* 1630].

79 A godly song, entituled, A farewell to the world, made by T. Byll, being the parish clerke of West-Felton [Shropshire], as he lay upon his death-bed [+ The soul's petition at heaven's gate]; by Thomas Byll; STC 4241; [*c.* 1630?].

80 Solomon's sacrifice. With his prayer in Gibeon; STC 22904; [*c.* 1635, orig. probably Elizabethan].

81 The confession of a paenitent sinner; STC 5627; [*c.* 1635].

82 The complaint of a sinner; STC 5608.5; [*c.* 1635].

83 Bee patient in trouble; by L[aurence] P[rice]; STC 20312; [1636].

Appendix C Godly ballads registered 1557–1640, surviving in manuscripts and printed collections

These are religious titles entered in the Stationers' Register 1557–1640, which can be identified with ballads surviving in manuscripts or in printed collections. (Manuscript ballads are *only* included where there is evidence that they appeared in broadside form.)

MANUSCRIPT SOURCES

British Museum

Addit. MS 15,225.	Compiled *c*. 1616, apparently by a Catholic.
Sloane MS 1896.	Protestant ballads, compiled before 1576.
MS Cotton Vesp.A.XXV.	Collection of Henry Savile of Banke (1568–1617), probably recusant, Yorkshire provenance, mainly *c*. 1576.

Bodleian

MS Ashmole 48	Copied mainly from broadsides *c*. 1557–65. Contains five pieces attributed to minstrel Richard Sheale.
MS Rawlinson Poet. 185.	Copied from broadsides *c*. 1592.

Shirburn Castle, Oxfordshire

Shirburn Ballads	Copied from broadsides dating between 1585 and 1616.

BALLADS

Format

Title and/or first line; author (if known); date of probable entry; location (MS or printed collection)

In chronological order of first Stationers' Register entry.

1 [beg.:] Aryse and wak, for Christes sake ...; ?ent.1557–8; MS Ashmole 48; repr. Wright no.52.
2 Dives and Lazarus [beg.: As it fell out upon a day ...]; ?ent. 1557–8, 1570–1; Child no.56.

3 [beg.:] Awake, rych men, for shame, and here ...; by Henry Spooner; ?ent. 1558–9; MS Ashmole 48; repr. Wright no.33.

4 [beg.:] Consideryeng Godes mercye greate ...; by Henry Spooner; ?ent. 1558–9; MS Ashmole 48; repr. Wright no.32.

5 [beg.:] Thys myserable world in dede ...; by Henry Spooner; ?ent. 1561–2; MS Ashmole 48; repr. Wright no.25.

6 [beg.:] To pass the place where pleasure is ...; ent. 1561–2, 1564–5; Addit. MS 15,225; repr. Rollins, *Old English ballads*, p. 213.

7 A pretie dittie and a pithie intituled O mortall man; by Mr Thorne; ent. 1563–4; MS Rawlinson Poet.185; repr. Rollins, *Old English ballads*, p. 265.

8 [beg.:] Wysdom woold I wyshe to have ...; ent. 1563–4; MS Ashmole 48; repr. Wright no.64.

9 [beg.:] Who lovithe to lyve in peas, and merkithe every change ...; ent. 4 se.1564; MS Ashmole 48; repr. Wright no.19.

10 I myghte have leved meryly morralysed [beg.:] I might lived merelie if I had sinned never ...; 1564–5; Addit. MS 15, 225; repr. Rollins, *Old English ballads*, p. 216.

11 Aballett of Adam & eve [beg.:] What tyme that god his holy hande ...; ent. 1564–5, ?1 au.1586; MS Cotton Vesp.A.XXV; repr. Seng no.23.

12 A notable Instrucyon for all men to bewaire the abuses of dycce wynne & women; ent. 1565–6, 17 se.1578; MS Cotton Vesp.A.XXV; repr. Seng no.41.

13 The pittiful lamentation of a damned soule [beg.:] As I walked forth in a morninge tyde ...; ent. 1565–6, 1 au.1586; Shirburn, p. 260.

14 The overthrow of proud Holofernes, and the triumph of vertuous Queene Iudith; by Thomas Deloney; ent. 1566–7, 23 mr.1588; Deloney, *The garland of good will* (1631), repr. in Mann, ed., *Works of Deloney*, p. 355.

15 [beg.:] After mydnyght, when dremes dothe fawll ...; ?ent. 1568–9; MS Ashmole 48; repr. Wright no.11.

16 The sinner, dispisinge the world and all earthly vanities, reposeth his whole confidence in his beloved saviour, Jesus Christ [beg.:] Jesu, my loving spouse ...; ?ent. 1568–9, ?1570–1; Shirburn, p. 84.

17 [beg.:] Awak, all fethfull harttes, awake ...; by Henry Spooner; ?ent. to Alex Lacy 1568–9; MS Ashmole 48; repr. Wright no.30.

18 [beg.:] Ould Tobie calde his lovinge sonne ...; ?ent. 1568–9; Addit. MS 15,225, fols. 19–20; repr. Rollins, *Old English ballads*, p. 219.

19 Justice. Zaleuch and his Sonne [beg.:] Let rulers make most perfect lawes ...; by Richard Edwards; ent. 1568–9; Edwards, *The paradyse of daynty devises* (1576), sig.G1v.

20 A carroll of the birthe of christ [beg.:] The golden tyme ys nowe at hande ...; ?ent. 1569–70; MS Cotton Vesp.A.XXV; repr. Seng no.33.

21 A ballet declaring howe everye Christian ought to prepaire them selffe to warre & for to fight valiantly under the banner of his capton christ; ent. 1569–70; MS Cotton Vesp.A.XXV; repr. Seng no.31.

22 A ballett of the last dayes [beg.:] Who wislye wyll with gostlye eye ...; by T.Tayler; ?ent. 1569–70; MS Cotton Vesp.A.XXV; repr. Seng no.30.

23 The prayer of Daniel turned into metre and applied unto our tyme. Daniel. ix. [beg.:] O Lorde thou hygh & fearful God ...; by Thomas Cottesforde; ent. 1569–70; Cottesford, trans., *The accompt rekenynge and confession of the faith of H.Zwinglius* (1555), sig.I2v–I4.

24 A ballad from the countrie sent to showe how we should fast this lent [beg.:]

Prepare yourselves to fast this lent . . . ; by Thomas Preston (dramatist); ?ent. 1569–70; MS Rawlinson Poet.185; repr. Shirburn, p. 347.

25 Of the three wise sentences, which three yong men of the guarde of King Darius presented him; by Anthony Munday; ?ent. 20 no.1577; Munday, *A banquet of daintie conceits* (1588); repr. Thomas Park, ed., *Harleian miscellany* (10 vols., 1808–13), IX, p. 241.

26 Another song of T.pereson doing [beg.:] O man Refraine thie vile desyre . . . ; ?ent. 9 se.1578; MS Cotton Vesp.A.XXV; repr. Seng no.37.

27 Fortitude. A young man of AEgypt. and Valerian [beg.:] Eche one deserves great prayse to have . . . ; by Richard Edwards; ent. 5 mr. 1579; Edwards, *The paradyse of daynty devises* (1576), sig.G1.

28 [beg.:] When Father Adam first did flee . . . ; ?ent. 18 mr.1579; Forbes, *Cantus* (1666), no.21.

29 A godly and good examyle [*sic*] to avoyde all Inconveniences as hereafter followeth [beg.:] Why should not mortall men awake . . . ; by R.D.; ?ent. 19 au.1584, ?1 au.1586; MS Rawlinson Poet.185; repr. Rollins, *Old English ballads*, p. 245.

30 A warning unto repentaunce and of Christes comming unto judgement [beg.:] What meanes this carelesse world to vance . . . ; ?ent. 1 au.1586; Sloane MS 1896; repr. Rollins, *Old English ballads*, p. 240.

31 A dialogue betwene Christe and the pore oppressed synner [beg.:] Alas, how long shall I bewaile . . . ; ent. 1 au.1586; Sloane MS 1896; repr. Rollins, *Old English ballads*, p. 270.

32 A dittie, delivering a freendlie admonition to women, to have care of theyr own estates . . . and, after the example of Sara, to order themselves in all their actions [beg.:] List awhile, fair ladies . . . ; by Anthony Munday; ?ent. 15 au.1586; Munday, *A banquet of daintie conceits* (1588); repr. Park, *Harleian miscellany*, IX, p. 228.

33 [beg.:] A Jollie sheppard that sate on Sion hill; ent. 15 au.1586; Addit. MS 15,225; repr. Rollins, *Old English ballads*, p. 101.

34 A hartie thankes givinge to god for our queenes most excellent maiestie [beg.:] Prepare with speed, crist commyng is at hand . . . ; ent. 15 au.1586; MS Rawlinson Poet.185; repr. F.J.Furnivall and W.R. Morfill, eds., *Ballads from manuscripts* (2 vols., 1868–73), II, p. 109.

35 A pleasant Dialogue betweene plaine Truth and blind Ignorance; by Thomas Deloney; ent. 23 mr.1588; Deloney, *The garland of good will* (1631), repr. in Mann, ed., *Works of Deloney*, p. 351.

36 The table of good Counsell with a singuler salve for the syck soule [beg.:] O man that runneth heere thy race . . . ; ent. 11 de.1596, 7 my.1599; Addit. MS 15,225; repr. Rollins, *Old English ballads*, p. 229, 405.

37 The translation of the blessed S. Barnards verses, conteining the unstable felicitie of this wayfaring world [beg.:] Why doth eache state apply it selfe to wordly prayse; ent. 22 jn.1602; Edwards, *The paradyse of daynty devises* (1576), sig.A3.

38 Miraculous newes from the cittie of Holdt in Germany, where there were three dead bodyes seene to rise out of their graves upon the twentieth day of September last 1616, with other strange things that hapned [beg.:] The dreadfull day of doome drawes neere . . . ; ent. 20 oc.1616; Shirburn, p. 76.

Appendix D Religious broadsides or 'tables' 1550–1640

These include broadsides with nothing but text, as well as engravings and woodcuts where the text is dominant.

Excluded are official proclamations and statutes of church or state; petitions; almanacs; epitaphs; items not in English.

STC 674. A true and plaine genealogy or pedigree of Antichrist. 1634. Ent. 1561–2.

STC 1335.3. James Balmford. To the maior, aldermen, and inhabitants of N. A dialogue against playing at cardes and tables. [Anon.], [c. 1595].

STC 1335.7. [Another edition]. [1600?].

STC 1858. A benedicite or blessinge to be saide over the table. [By H. Niclas]. [Cologne,] 1575.

STC 2751. To my Christian friend, I.F. ... I composed this Selah or collection of those verses in the psalmes with this word of attention Selah. [c. 1590?].

STC 2756.5. [Selections from the 'Books of Solomon': Proverbs, Ecclesiastes, Wisdom, etc.]. [1550?].

STC 2787.4. The prayer of the prophet Daniel. [1553?].

STC 3090. The lofty bishop, the lazy Brownist, and the loyall author. 1640.

STC 3874.5. Our Lord his line of fathers from Adam. [Anon. by Hugh Broughton]. 1595.

STC 3874.7. [Another edition, Init. H.B.]. 1609.

STC 4273. Londons Lord have mercy upon us. A true relation of five modern plagues in London. [Verse attrib. to H. Crouch]. [1637].

STC 4797.5. A briefe catechism, conteining the most principall groundes of religion. [c. 1615?].

STC 4900.5. William Cecil, Baron Burghley. The counsell of a father to his sonne, in ten severall precepts. Left as a legacy at his death. [Anon.]. [1611].

STC 5208. Feare God [etc.] A psalme of prayer and praise for the prosperous and good estate of our soveraigne lord the king ... for the private use of the poore orphanes in Christs Hospitall. [Before 1610?]. [printed music by J. Farrant].

STC 5208.5. A psalme of thanksgiving, to be sung by the Children of Christs Hospitall ... 1610. [Reports of charities] by T.S.[T.Stint?]. [Printed music by J. Farrant].

STC 5208.7. A psalme of thankes-giving, to be sung ... on Munday in Easter holy dayes ... 1628.

STC 5209. A psalme of thankes-giving, to [be sung] ... on Munday in the [Easter] holy-dayes ... 1634.

STC 5209.3. A psalme of thanksgiving, to be sung ... on Tuesday in the Easter holy-dayes, ... 1636. [Verses init. T.S.]. [Printed music by H. Semper?].

STC 6005.5 The recantation of Thomas Cranmer ... tr. faythfully out of Latin. [1556].

STC 6170.5. I.D. In this table is set forth three principall things: first, mans creation: secondly his misery in Adams fall: and lastly, the happy restoring againe of all the faithfull by Christ. 1629. Ent. 1 au.1586.

STC 6766.5. A divine descant full of consolation. [c. 1620?]. Plate 40.

STC 6798.7. Come ye blessed, &c. Goe ye cursed, &c. [1628?]. Plate 44.

STC 7508. A prayer said in the kinges chappell in the tyme of hys sicknes ... Set forth the .xix. of June M.D.L.III. [1553].

STC 7509. The prayer of kynge Edwarde the syxte, whiche he made the .vi.of July, M.D.L.iii thre houres afore his death. [1553].

STC 7594.5. A prayer meete to be sayd of all true suiectes for our queene Elizabeth and for the present state. Eng.a.Fr. [1586?]. Ent. 22 au.1586. French trans. signed by Jacques Bellot.

STC 10626.5. A godly exhortation, necessary for this present time. 1603. A reworking of STC 10627 (App. B no.60).

STC 10869.5. Finch his alphabet, or, a godly direction, fit to be perused of each true Christian. [c. 1635?]. Plate 43.

STC 11819.5. Charles Gybbon. A premonition for every disposition. 1588. Plate 46.

STC 12092.4. Gerardus Gossenius, trans. The maner and order of proceeding against Christ. [1586].

STC 12561.2. A. H. Another godly letter, written to the same H.H. by his owne sister out of the Countrey, about eighty miles from London. [1625]. Sequel to 15107.3.

STC 12576. [Prayer for assistance against the Armada].s.sh.fol. 1588. Signed Rob. H.

STC 12743. The painefull hand: shall rule the lande. [c. 1630?]. Used as lining paper. Plate 37.

STC 12938.5. Matthew Haviland. A monument of God's most gracious preservation of England from Spanish invasion, Aug.2.1588. and popish treason, Novem.5.1605. [c. 1635?].

STC 13855.2. The coblers thread is cut. Or, the coblers monument: wherein, to the everlasting memory of the folly of Samuel How, his doctrines are detected. 1640.

STC 13855.4. The vindication of the cobler, being a brief publication of his doctrine. Or certaine tenents [sic] collected out of the sermon [13855] of S.How. 1640.

STC 14706. Thomas, Johnson, minister. Stand up to your beliefe, or, a combat betweene Satan tempting, and a Christian triumphing in the comfort of the Creed. Exeter, [1640].

STC 15107.3. I.L., Pastor. A Christian consolatory letter; written by a reverend pastour and minister of Gods Word, to one of his loving parishioners and friends .... [1625]. See also STC 12561.2.

STC 15470a.5. Publius Lentulus, his newes to the Senate of Rome, concerning Jesus Christ. [c. 1625].

STC 15706.5. A lamentable list, of certaine hidious, frightfull, and prodigious signes, which have bin seene, for these 18. yeares last past ... Anno. 1638.

STC 16758.7. London soundes a trumpet, that the countrey may heare it. 1630.

STC 16801.7. A looking-glasse for city and countrey. [With same woodcut as 16758.7]. [1630].

STC 16802.7. A lookinge [glass] ... or a worthy table to be had in every good Christian [house]. [*c.* 1590].

STC 16823. A short interpretation of the Lords Praier: necessary for all householders to learne, and to teach their children and servants. The third impression. 1627.

STC 16824. An instruction for all those that intend to goe to the sacrament of the Lords Supper. 1634.

STC 17294. The map of mortalitie. 1604. Plate 47.

STC 17770.7. The seven soveraigne medicines and salves, to be diligently applied to the seven deadly wounds and sores. 1603.

STC 17773.5. A godly meditation day and night to be exercised. [Engr. William Rogers, *c.* 1600]. Plate 45.

STC 17816.5 Memento mori. Remember to die. [*c.* 1640]. Plate 50.

STC 18548.5. Hendrik Niclas.   All the letters of the a.b.c. by every sondrye letter whereof, ther is a good document set-fourth and taught, in ryme. Tr. out of Base-almaine. [Init. H.N.]. [Cologne, 1575].

STC 19070.5. I. P.   A godlie and zealous prayer ... for the preservation of our most soveraigne Lady Elizabeth. [1586?].

STC 19251.3. Martin Parker.   Lord have mercy upon us. [In verse. Init. M.P.]. [1636]. Plate 39.

STC 19598.2. John Penkethman.   The cities comfort: or, Patridoephilus his theologicall and physicall preservatives against the plague. [Anon.]. [1625?].

STC 20112.5. The popes eschucheon, or coate of armes. [1606].

STC 20190. In the name of almightie God. [*c.* 1595].

STC 20191. Lord omnipotent and moste mercyfull father ... [*c.* 1552].

STC 20192.5. A praier very comfortable and necessary to be used of all Christians every morning and evening, amongst their families. [*c.* 1603].

STC 20197.7. In the time of Gods visitation by sicknesse, or mortality especially, may be used by governours of families. [1607?].

STC 20206. Lord have mercy upon us. Preservatives and medicines as well before infection as afterwards. [1636].

STC 20823. The Red-Crosse: or, Englands Lord have mercy upon us. 1625.

STC 20824. [Another edition]. 1636.

STC 20834.3 Of the publique reformation of a church. [Cambridge?, 1589?].

STC 20875. Lord have mercy upon us. [1636].

STC 20961.5. Mathew Rhodes.   The dismall day, at the Black-fryers. Or, a deplorable elegie, on the death of almost an hundred persons, slaine by the fall of a house in the Black-fryers. 1623.

STC 21307a.1. [The plucking down of the romish church]. 1566 (17 au.).

STC 21533.3. W.S.,   Christ's unworthy minister. To the faithfull Christians [etc.]. 1607.

STC 22378. The confession and declaration of R. sharpe clerke, and other of that secte, tearmed the Familie of love, the .xij. of June. 1575.

STC 23432. A short summe of the trueth which is according to godlines. 1592.

STC 23499. The Christians jewell fit to adorne the hearte and decke the house of every Protestant. [Engr. w. text including verses by W. Grant]. [1624]. Plate 48.

STC 23511.5. Richard Swaine.   A table concerning Christ our advocate, and whether emission of sinnes once obtained, can againe be made frustrate. 1615.

STC 23588.5. Thomas Symmes.   [An invective against such runningate papists that greedily go about to disturb the concord of the church]. 1584 (22 oc.).

STC 23628.5. T.T. [Some f]yne gloves devised for newyeres gyftes to teche yong peo[ple to] knowe good from evyll. [1559–67]. Plate 49.

STC 23633a.5. In this second table is contained the law of God being the second principall part of his heavenly honour. [*c*. 1590].

STC 23634.7. Table observations. [*c*. 1615].

STC 23741.5. John Taylor. Christian admonitions, against the two feareful sinnes of cursing and swearing, most fit to be set up in every house. [*c*. 1630].

STC 23772a.5. John Taylor. A meditation on the passion. 1630. Plate 41.

STC 23812.7. John Taylor. A warning for swearers and blasphemers. 1626.

STC 23819.5. Thomas Taylor. An answer to that question, how farre it is lawfull to flee in the time of the plague; extracted out of a sermon preached in Alderman-bury. [1636?].

STC 23884a.6. Pietro Teramano. The miraculous origin and translation of the church of our B.lady of Loreto. [Anon., tr. R. Corbington]. Loreto, 1635.

STC 23884a.8. [Another trans.]. Loreto, 1635.

STC 24953.3. I. Waker. A breefe of scripture, disproving the principall points of popery. [Init. I.W.]. [Dublin], 1624.

STC 24953.5. [Another edition, w. title:] A table briefly pointing out such places of scripture, as either plainely or by good consequence condemne the principall points of popery. 1625.

STC 24953.7. [Another edition, revised] A table . . . gathered by I. Waker. 1628.

STC 25109.5. Chrisopher Watson. Briefe principles of religion, collected for the exercise of youth. [Init. Chris.Wats.De.]. 1578.

STC 25291.5. Hugh Weston. A prayer made by the deane of Westminster, and delyvered to the chyldren of ye queenes maiesties gramer scole there. [1555].

STC 25365.5. William Whitaker. Antichrist. We will not have this man to rule over us. Luc.19.14. Certaine articles publicklie propounded . . . now enlarged in a table. [Cambridge, 1589?].

STC 25943. Edward Wollay. A new yeres gyft, intituled, a playne pathway to perfect rest: gathered out of sundry godly patriarkes, and prophets. 1571.

STC 26013.5. Thomas Wray. Sundry lawes against swearing, cursing and blaspheming the most holy name of God. 1624.

STC 26038.2. Memento mori. [1636?].

STC 26112.7. Richard Young. The state of a Christian, lively set forth by an allegorie of a shippe under sayle. [Init. R.Y.]. 1636.

Appendix E Religious pictures: woodcuts and engravings 1550–1640

Includes both woodcuts and engravings in which the picture is dominant.

STC 4605. A newe secte of friars called Capichini. [Woodcut]. [c. 1580?].

STC 4643.5. A thankful rememberance of Gods mercie. By G[eorge] C[arleton]. 2nd edn. [Eng. by C. Danckerts]. 1625.

STC 5028. [A petition to the king against the doctrines of Arminius]. [Engr.]. Amstelrodam, H. Laurentz, 1628.

STC 5209.5. Christus natus est. [Woodcut]. 1631. Ent. 18 no.1637. Plate 25.

STC 10671.5 Faiths victorie in Romes crueltie. [Engr.] [c. 1640?].

STC 11227.3 John Foxe. A table of the X. first persecutions of the primitive church. [3 woodcuts]. 1610.

STC 11227.5. John Foxe. A most exact and accurat table of the first ten persecutions of the primitive church. [Engr.]. [c. 1625?].

STC 11228.3. John Foxe. A table of the X. first persecutions ... [3 woodcuts]. 1632.

STC 11930.4. The historie of Joseph, sonne of Jacob. [Series of 6 woodcuts]. [G. Godet, c. 1565?].

STC 11930.6. The historie of S. Paule. [Series of 6 woodcuts]. G. Godet [1563?]. Ent. 1562–3. Plate 29.

STC 11930.8. [The historie of the prodigal son]. [Series of 6 woodcuts]. G. Godet [1566]. Ent. 1565–6. Plate 32.

STC 20113.5. The popes pyramides. The fruites of Rome, thou here portractur'd seest. [Woodcut]. [1624?]. Plate 15.

STC 20917.5. The revells of Christendome. [Engr. by T. Cockson]. [1609].

STC 22636.5. A type of trew nobilitye or ye armes of a xptian emblazoned. Exornavit G. Slatyer. J[acob] v[an] L[angeren] fecit. [Engr.]. [c. 1635].

STC 22824.7. Richard Smith, satirist. The powder treason, propounded, by Sathan. Approved, by Antichrist. Enterprised, by Papists. [Engr. by Michael Droeshout]. [c. 1615].

STC 23018. Michael Sparke. To the glory of God in thankefull remembrance of our three great deliverances. [Anon. engr. by J. Barra]. [1627?]. ?Ent. 30 no.1624.

STC 24179. The travels of time: loaden with popish trumperies, from Great Britaine to Rome: with a dialogue betwixt Time and Truth, Popery and Policy. 1624. [Engr.]. [1624].

STC 25043. Samuel Ward, of Ipswich. 1588. Deo trin-vni Britanniae bis ultori in memoriam ... to God, in memorye of his double deliveraunce from ye invincible navie and ye unmatcheable powder treason. 1605. [Engr.]. Amsterdam, 1621.

NOT IN STC

WOODCUTS

[Pope on a horse. Text begins:] [...] trappings fine ... [imperfect]. BM Prints, Case 270*. Plate 16.

A showe of the Protestants petigrew as ye haue it before at large deducted. Ashmolean Prints (unmounted Douce in box). Plate 14.

[Tree of Catholic church. Text begins:] From Simons ambition and Iudas couetise, This poysonous tree plated in Rome doth rise. BM Prints, Case 270. Plate 13.

ENGRAVINGS

[Martyrdom of the Marian reformers. Text begins:] The lambe speaketh . . . . [Temp. Eliz?]. BM Satires no.10. Repr. Miller, ed., *Religion in the popular prints*, no.1.

[Execution of the conspirators in the Gunpowder Plot]. N. de Visscher fecit. BM Satires no. 69.

A plot without powder. [Depicts pope and priests in conference, under roof labelled 'Black Breed Fe[ter] Lane']. BM Satires no.87. [1620].

No plot, no powder. [Depicts downfall of Catholic chapel in Blackfriars, 1623]. Sold by T. Jenner at the Exchange dore. BM Satires no.95.

[Kings of Sweden, Denmark and England playing cards, dice and tables against three representatives of Rome, 1626]. BM Satires no.101. [Copies STC 20917.5., substituting different monarchs].

Appendix F Secular woodcut pictures 1550-1640

This is a provisional checklist of single-sheet woodcut pictures on themes other than religion. Copper engravings are not included.

Also excluded are maps and perspective views, anatomical sheets, genealogies and coats of arms, technical diagrams.

MONSTROUS CREATURES

STC 1033. H.B. The true discripcion of a childe with ruffes borne in the parish of Micheham, in the countie of Surrey . . . . 1566.

STC 1422. John Barker. The true description of a monsterous chylde borne in the Ile of Wight . . . . [1564].

STC 6117. D. John. A discription of a monstrous chylde, borne at Chychester in Sussex . . . . 1562.

STC 6768. The description of a monstrous pig farrowed at Hamsted . . . . [1562].

STC 6769. The discription of a rare or rather most monstrous fishe, taken on the east cost of Holland . . . . [1566].

STC 6774. The true description of two monsterous chyldren borne at Herne in Kent . . . . [1565].

STC 7565. William Elderton. The true fourme and shape of a monsterous chyld whiche was borne in Stony Stratforde. [1565].

STC 11485. William Fulwood. The shape of ii monsters . . . . [1562].

STC 12186. Timothie Granger. A moste true and marveilous straunge wonder . . . of .xvii monstrous fisshes, taken in Suffolke, at Downam brydge, within a mile of Ipswiche . . . . [1568].

STC 12207. The true reporte of the forme and shape of a monstrous childe borne at Muche [Great] Horkesleye, a village three myles from Colchester, in the countye of Essex . . . . 1562.

STC 17194. The forme and shape of a monstrous child, borne at Maydstone in Kent . . . . 1568.

STC 17803 John Mellys. The true description of two monsterous children, lawfully begotten . . . in the parish of Swanburne in Buckynghamshyre . . . . 1566.

STC 19071. I. P. A mervaylous straunge deformed swyne. [By John Phillips? or John Patridge?]. [1570?].

STC 20126. Le vray purtraict d'un ver monstrueux qui a este trouue dans le coeur d'un chaval qui est mort en Londres . . . . 1586.

STC 20570. C. R. The true discripcion of this marveilous straunge fishe. [1569]. Plate 18.

DEATH

STC 6222. The daunce and song of death. [1569]. Plate 17.

STC 6223. [Dance of death, depicting 'A divine, a soldier, a lady, a lawyer, a labourer and death'. Text begins:] Marke well the effect, purtreyed here in all. [c. 1580?].

HUMOUR

STC 11211.5. Which of these fower, that here you see, In greatest daunger you thinke to be. [A clyent, betweene two lawyers. A maide, betweene two friers, etc.]. 1623.

STC 18599. The welspoken nobody. [Depicts ragged figure with winged cap and skates; broken objects scattered on ground; scroll with inscription 'Nobody is my name that beyreth every bodyes blame']. [c. 1550].

STC 19974.4. The severall places where you may hear news. [Groups of women gossiping 'at the childbed', 'at the market', 'at the aelle hous' etc.]. [c. 1640, woodblock probably Elizabethan. The scene was copied in the following prints:
   Tittle-tattle; or, the severall branches of gossipping. (BM Satires no.61).
   Hollar, Wenceslaus. The market place. (BM Satires no.62).

STC 23757. Fill gut, & pinch belly. 1620. Plate 11.

ROYAL PORTRAITS

This is only a small sample of the extant woodcut portraits. They have been chosen to illustrate what appears to be the cheaper end of the market.

STC 5022.5. England and France, hand-in-hand: triumphing, for the happy contract of marriage, betweene Charles, and the princesse Henrietta Maria. [1624].

STC 5024.3. The high and mighty Prince Charles . . . The manner of his arivall at the Spanish court, his happy returne, the fifth of October, 1623.

STC 7588. Loe here the pearle, whom God and man doth love. [Portrait of Queen Elizabeth]. [G. Godet, 1563].

STC 11360.3. The most illustrious Prince Fredericke, by the grace of God King of Bohemia . . . And of Elizabeth his queene. Dort, 1619.

STC 11360.5. [. . .] high and illustrious king of Bohemia, [wh]ich God hath bestowed upon them in their royall issue. [1622?].

STC 13541.7. William Hockham.   Prince Charles his welcome to the court, or, a true subjects love for his happy returne from Spaine. 1623.

STC 17699.5. James Maxwell.   An English-royall pedigree: Common to the two most noble princes lately maried. [Portrait of Frederick and Elizabeth w. genealogy]. [1613].

STC 17700.5 James Maxwell.   The imperiall and princely pedigree of . . . Friderick . . . and Elizabeth. [1613].

The royall line of kings, queenes, and princes, from the uniting of the two royall houses, Yorke and Lancaster. [1613?]. Plate 10.

CRIMINALS

STC 7627.5. The picture of the unfortunate gentleman, Sir Gervis Elvies Knight, late leiftenant of his Maiesties Tower of London. 1615.

STC 21406. Samuel Rowlands. Sir Thomas Overbury or the poysoned knight's complaint. [1614?].

STC 24341.5. Mistris Turners farewell to all women. [1615].

MISCELLANEOUS

STC 7745.7. The names of the knights, citizens and burgesses of the counties, cities and burrough-townes of England and Wales . . . . 1628.

STC 7745.5. The manner of the sitting of the Lords. [1628].

STC 13526.5. The historie of the life of man. 1616.

STC 13851. The good hows-holder. [Woodcut *c.* 1565, w. verses]. 1607. Ent. to G. Godet, 1564–5. BM Prints (*c.*2.E.6–38). Plate 38.

STC 16751.5. [The cries of London. 12 woodcuts]. [*c.* 1630]. ?Ent. to J. Wolfe 16 my.1599. BM Prints (I.7.–65*). Pepys has an impression [*c.* 1610] of these cuts and 12 others, without verses. Other pre-1640 'cries of London' sheets are engravings, with engraved inscriptions. See Hind, III, pp. 366–9 and pls. 211–14, and BM Prints ('Authorities for Artists', II, period V).

STC 20126.7. The true portraiture of the valiant English soldiers in their proceedings to the wars for the service of their prince; and honour of their countrey.]1588?].

The ark royal. 1588. BM Prints. Repr. Hind, I, pl. 15.

The image of the lyfe of man that was painted in a table by Apelles. BM Prints, Case 270. [9 sheets, which together make a picture of over 5 ft × 3 ft. Depicts 'the house of sorowe', 'the house of health and honor', 'the house of sobriete', etc., each with allegorical figures of virtue and vice within].

Appendix G Woodcut pictures registered to Gyles Godet (1562–8) and Thomas Warren (1656)

Sources
Gyles Godet's pictures registered 1562–3 (Arber, I, pp. 211–12), except those marked as follows:
 * 1564–5 (Arber, I, p. 272)
 ** 1565–6 (Arber, I, p. 300)
 *** 1567–8 (Arber, I, p. 362).
Thomas Warren's pictures registered 4–5 April 1656 (Eyre, II, pp. 46–8). except those marked as follows:
 † 17 April 1656 (Eyre, II, p. 50).

Gyles Godet 1562–8	Thomas Warren 1656
The Tenne Commandementes.	The picture of Moses with ye 10 comandemts [*sic*]. 2 sh.
The Creation of the Worlde.	
The geneolige or lyne of our savyour Christe as touchynge his humanyte from Noee to Davyd.	The generation from Adam to Noah, 3 sh.
The pycture of Saloman the wyse.	A roll of all the kings of Israell, 6 sheets.
The Confyrmation of the old testament.	The historicall parts of the Bible in 42 sheets.
	Jephtha offering his daughter, &c. 1 large sheet.
The pycture of Paule the appostell.	The 12 patriarchs, 4 sheets.
A pycture made upon the vth of saynte Pawle to the Romanynes.**	Christ brought before Pontius Pilate and the elders. 4 large sh.
The historye of the prodigall childe.**	The rich man in ye Gospell. 2 large sh.
The heavenly veryte.	
The fygure of True Religion.	True wisdome throwing ye world behind her.
The pycture of Charyte.	
The pycture of True Sobryete.	A roll of vice and vertue, in 12 severall pourtraictures in 6 sheets.
The example of Justice.	

354

The Rememberaunce to Dye.

The triumph of death.
Six portratures, vizt, A Divine, a Soldier, a Lady, a Lawyer, a Labourer and Death. 1 large sh.

The pycture of the Devell and the pope.

The divell leading the Witch and Usurer in chaines. 1 large sheet.

A Christian exhortation of the good husholder to his chyldren.*

The good householder. 1 large sh.

The instruction of a very faythfull man.

The carefull wife. 1 sh.†

The Dewty of chreldren [sic] towards thayre masters.***

The pourtraicture of a woman with a key in her hand and a basket of fruit lockt. 1 sh.

The Twelve monythes.*

The ffoure quarters of the yeare. 4 sheets.

An abstract of the geneolege and Race of all the kynges of Englonde from the floude of Noe and Brute.

The ages of man. 1 large sheet.

The image of the life of man, by Apelles, in 9 large sheets.

A roll of all the Saxon kings.

A roll of all the kings of England since the conquest, 5 large sh.

A booke containing the true pourtraictures of the countenances and attires of the kings of England from William Conqueror to [. . .] with a briefe report of some of their principall acts.

The pycture of Kynge Henry the Eiyghte.

King Henry 8th in 1 large sheet.

The pycture of kynge Eddwarde ye VI.

King James. 1 large sh.

Queen Ann. 1 large sh.

Lady Elizabeth on horse backe. 1 large sh.

The pycture of Queen Elysabeth.

His Hignesse the Lord Protectour on horse back. 1 large sheet.

The pycture of the kyng of Swathlande.

The king of Denmarke. 1 large sh.

The pycture of the prynce of Condee.

The emperors heads of Rome, being 13 sh. of small paper.

The Armes of Englonde.

The great ship called the Royall Soveraigne. The States Admirall. 2 large sh.

The pourtraictures of 14 soldiers in Spanish garbes upon their march. 4 sheets.

The Carde of London.

The mapp of the citty of London in 7 sheets. †

The mappe of Englonde and Skotlande.

The anatyme of the inwarde partis of man and Woman.

The anatomy of man and woman. 1 large sheet.

The Dyscription of the howse of an harlott.

The iijde Desolatio inter fratres. *

The story of the emporours.

The story of the iii cheldren.

Democritis and Heraclitus with a globe betwixt them. 1 sh.

The severall employments of the people.

A booke of horsmen, beasts and birds in 30 halfe sheets.

Key to Appendices H and I

Format

Books over 6 sheets	= over 48 pages in 4to
	= over 96 pages in 8vo
Long pamphlets 4–6 sheets	= 32–48 pages in 4to
	= 64–96 pages in 8vo
Short pamphlets up to 3.5 sheets	= up to 30 pages in 4to
	= up to 62 pages in 8vo
'Penny' size 1.5 sheets	= 24 pages 8vo
	[= 32 pages 12mo = 48 pages 16mo]

Total number of works

Represents all works printed by or for, sold by, entered or assigned to the publisher, with the following exceptions:

1 Single sheets excluded (i.e. ballads, broadsides, woodcut pictures).
2 Multiple editions counted only once.
3 Works involving more than one publisher recorded only once.
4 A few works missing from App. H which are located in inaccessible libraries and not on microfilm (a dozen titles for Jones and three titles for Wright).

357

Appendix H STC works of ballad publishers

Description	Richard Jones (1564–1602)				John Wright (1602–46)			
	Books	Long pamphlets	Short pamphlets	'Penny' size	Books	Long pamphlets	Short pamphlets	'Penny' size
Edification								
Sermons	3	–	–	–	–	–	4	–
Other religious/moral works	7	6	7	3	9	1	3	12
Entertainment								
Play texts	6	1	–	–	8	2	–	–
Verse & verse collections	6	10	1	1	1	1	–	–
Chivalric/'merry' tales	4	–	2	–	2	1	3	2
Social commentary	5	–	–	–	–	2	1	–
Miscellanies								
Moral/proverbial/practical/humorous	2	1	–	–	3	1	1	5
Learning for laymen								
History/geography/arts & sciences	11	–	3	–	1	–	–	–
Handbooks	2	–	–	–	–	–	–	–
Almanacs	–	–	–	–	–	–	–	–
News								
Sober	–	–	9	–	–	–	1	–
Sensational	–	–	3	3	1	–	8	1
'End and confession' of traitors	–	–	–	–	–	–	–	–
Plague	–	–	–	–	–	–	–	–
Propaganda/polemic								
Patriotic	1	–	5	–	1	–	–	–
Panegyrics	–	1	1	–	–	1	2	–
Female question	–	–	2	–	–	–	–	–
John Taylor, Water Poet	–	–	–	–	–	–	–	–
Total	47 = 44%	19 = 18%	33 = 31%	7 = 7%	26 = 33%	9 = 12%	23 = 29%	20 = 26%

Total number of works: Jones = 106; Wright = 78.

Appendix 1 STC works of ballad publishers

Description	William Pickering (1557–75)		John Awdeley (1559–75)		John Trundle (1603–26)		Henry Gosson (1603–41)		Francis Coules (1624–63)		Francis Grove (1624–63)	
	Books & pamphlets	'Penny' size	Books & pamphlets	'Penny' size	Books & pamphlets	'Penny' size	Books & pamphlets	'Penny' size	Books & pamphlets	'Penny' size	Books & pamphlets	'Penny' size
Edification												
Sermons	3	–	8	–	–	–	1	–	1	–	–	–
Other religious/moral works	–	1	12	–	5	–	5	–	4	4	1	1
Entertainment												
Play texts	1	–	2	–	10	–	1	–	2	–	1	–
Verse & verse collections	–	–	–	–	–	–	–	–	3	–	1	1
Chivalric/'merry' tales	–	–	2	–	3	–	2	–	4	1	7	2
Social commentary	2	–	2	–	5	–	4	–	–	–	3	–
Miscellanies												
Moral/proverbial/practical/humorous	–	–	–	–	–	–	1	2	–	–	1	–
Learning for laymen												
History/geography/arts & sciences	1	–	4	–	1	–	2	–	1	–	–	–
Handbooks	–	–	1	–	–	–	–	–	1	–	5	–
Almanacs	4	–	–	–	–	–	–	–	1	–	–	–
News												
Sober	1	–	1	–	3	–	10	–	–	–	1	–
Sensational	1	1	1	1	11	–	7	–	1	–	2	–
'End and confession' of traitors	1	–	–	–	–	–	1	–	1	–	–	–
Plague	–	–	–	–	–	–	–	1	–	–	–	–
Propaganda/polemic												
Patriotic	–	–	–	–	1	–	1	–	–	–	–	–
Panegyrics	–	–	–	–	–	–	1	–	–	–	–	–
Female question	–	–	–	–	2	–	–	–	–	–	1	–
John Taylor, Water Poet	–	–	–	–	4	–	30	–	1	–	–	–
Total	14	2	33	1	45	–	66	3	19	5	22	4

Total number of works: Pickering = 16; Awdeley = 34; Trundle = 45; Gosson = 69; Coules = 24; Grove = 26.

Appendix J Penny miscellanies (to 1640)

| | Dates | | | Title | Author | STC number | Details | |
First registered	First extant	First edition by ballad publisher	Other extant editions				Format	Woodcuts
1594 (J. Danter. Ass'd to ballad partners 1629)	1630	1630 (Eliz. Allde f. E. Wright a. C. Wright)	–	A new booke of new conceits	Thomas Johnson, miscellaneous writer	14708.5	24pp. 8vo	–
1597 (N. Ling. Ass'd to J. Smethwick 1607)	1631	1631 (Eliot's Court Press f. J. Wright)	–	The figure of four, or a handfull of sweet flowers	Nicholas Breton	3651	22pp. 8vo	–
1614 (J. Wright)	1626	1626 (J. Wright)	1636 (J. Wright)	The figure of four. The second part	Nicholas Breton	3652	22pp. 8vo	–
1616 (J. Wright)	1616	1616 (G. Elderton f. J. Wright)	1631 (J. Wright)	Crossing of proverbs. Cross-answers. And crosse-humours	Nicholas Breton	3643	24pp. or less (copy imp.) 8vo	–
1616 (J. Wright)	1616	1616 (G. Elderton f. J. Wright)	1632 (J. Wright)	Crossing of proverbs. The second part	Nicholas Breton	3644	24pp. or less (copy imp.) 8vo	–
1617 (J. Wright)	1626	1626 (f. J. Wright)		Soothing of proverbs: with only true forsooth. In two parts	Nicholas Breton	3698.5	24pp.? 12mo (Not on micro.)	?
1626 (E. Brewster f. R. Bird)	1636 (J. Beale f. R. Bird)	–	–	The figure of three: or, a patterne of good counsell	Anon.	10865.5	24pp. 12mo	–
1626 (ass'd fr. T. Pavier to R. Bird E. Brewster)	1631 (N. Okes f. R. Bird)	–	–	A booke of merrie riddles	Anon.	3324	22pp. 8vo	–
–	1630	1630 (Eliz. Allde f. H. Gosson a. F. Coules)	–	Dainty conceits, with a number of rare and witty inventions	Thomas Johnson, misc. writer	14708.1	22pp. 8vo	–
1637 (T. Lambert)	1637	1637 (T. Cotes? f. T. Lambert)	–	Harry White his humour	Martin Parker	19242	24pp. 16mo in 8s	2

Appendix K Penny godlinesses (to 1640)

	Dates			Title	Author	Details		
First registered	First extant	First edition by ballad publisher	Other extant editions			STC number	Format	Woodcuts
–	1591 (E. Allde f. J. Perrin)	1626 1st black-letter and penny size (E. Allde f. G. Edwards, sold by J. Wright)	Total of 9 edns 1591–1640	The Trumpet of the Soule Sounding to Judgement	Henry Smith	22706	24pp. 8vo	–
1616 (J. White)	1617 (W. White)	1632 (A. Mathewes, sold by J. Wright)	Total of 5 edns 1617–32	A subpoena from the high imperiall court of heaven [in verse]	John Andrewes	595.6	24pp. 8vo	–
[1617: B. Alsope recv'd fine]	1623	1623 (G. Elderton for J. Wright)	–	Andrewes humble petition unto almighty God, declaring his repentance	John Andrewes	589	24pp. 12mo	–
–	1621 (N. Okes)	1635 (F. Coules)	Total of 4 edns 1621–39	A Celestiall looking-glasse: to behold the beauty of heaven, and the perfect way unto it	John Andrewes	592	56pp. 12mo (1621 edn) 24pp. 8vo (1630 edn)	–
–	1621 (N. Okes)	[Ass'd to J. Wright 1630]	1630 (N. Okes?)	Andrewes resolution: to returne unto God by repentance	John Andrewes	590	60pp. 12mo (1621 edn) 24pp. 8vo (1630 edn)	–
1621 (M. Flesher a. G. Elderton)	1628	1628 (M. Flesher f. F. Coules)	c. 1635 (F. Coules)	The doctrine of dying well. Or the godly mans guide to glory	George Shawe(?)	6934	24pp. 8vo	–
–	1623 (S. Rand)	–	6 edns 1623–36	The Christian Sword and Buckler	John Sprint	23108.2	20pp. 8vo	–
–	1624 (N. Okes, sold by F. Grove)	1636 (J. Wright: copy ass'd from N. Okes 1630)	–	A soveraigne salve to cure a sicke soule, infected with the poyson of sinne	John Andrewes	595.4	24pp. 12mo	–
–	'2nd edn' 1625 (W. Jones f. R. Bird)	–	'5th edn' 1635 (R. Bird)	The reward of the wicked	Humphrey Everinden	10601.9	14pp. 8vo	–

| First registered | First extant | Dates | | Title | Author | Details | | |
		First edition by ballad publisher	Other extant editions			STC number	Format	Woodcuts
–	1627	1627 (M. Flesher f. F. Coules)	–	A looking glasse for drunkards	George Shawe(?)	16802	24pp. 12mo	–
1627?	1628?	1628? (G. Purslowe f. F. Coules)	–	Seven weapons to conquer the devill. With some excellent motives to stirre us up to this conquest	George Shawe(?)	25146	24pp. 8vo	–
–	'9th edn' 1628 (G. Purslowe f. M. Trundle)	[Ass'd to J. Wright & others 1629]	'16th edn' 1637 (J. Wright)	Death's knell: or, the sicke mans passing-bell	William Perkins	19684	24pp. 8vo	1
–	1631 (J. Haviland f. J. Wright)	1631 (copy ass'd to J. Wright by N. Okes 1630)	–	Andrewes repentance, sounding alarum to returne from his sins unto almightie God	J. Andrewes	589.5	24pp. 12mo	–
1630 (F. Coules)	1635	1635 (F. Coules)	–	Christ in the clouds, or Gods comming to judgement	John Warner	25078	24pp. 8vo	–
–	1631	1631 (f. J. Wright)	1636 (f. J. Wright)	Andrewes caveat to win sinners	John Andrewes	588	24pp. 12mo	–
1631 (J. Wright)	1637	1637 (J. Wright)	–	Andrewes golden chaine to linke the penitent sinner unto God	John Andrewes	588.5	22pp. 12mo	[1 v. small]
1619 (J. Trundle 1623 ass'd to J. Wright)	1619 (J. Trundle)	c. 1630 (J. Wright) first in penny format	Total of 10 edns 1619–30	Keepe within compasse: or, the worthy legacy of a wise father to his beloved sonne	John Trundle(?)	14899	48pp. 8vo (1619) 48pp. 16mo in 8s (c. 1630)	2
1623 (J. Wright)	163[0?]	163[0?] (J. Wright)	–	The mother's counsell, or, live within compass	M.R.	20583	48pp. 16mo in 8s	1
–	1627 (N. Okes)	[1630: ass'd from N. Oakes to J. Wright]	–	A most necessary caveat from God to beware of his rod	John Andrewes	595.3	48pp. long 12mo(?) (not on micro)	?
1635 (J. Okes)	1629 (N. Okes a. J. Norton)	–	1634 (J. Norton) 1639 (N. a. J. Okes)	The converted mans new birth: describing the direct way to heaven	John Andrewes	595	48pp. 12mo	–

Appendix L Penny merriments (to 1640)

	Dates			Title	Author	Details		
First registered	First extant	First edition by ballad publisher	Other extant editions			STC number	Format	Woodcuts
1557–8 (J. Waley) 1568–9 (J. Allde)	1510–13 (W. de Worde)	1584–9 (E. Allde, printer)	1617, 1626 (E. Allde)	Here beginneth a merry jest, of the fryer and the boy	Anon.	14524.3	16pp. 4to (1510, 1584) 24pp. 8vo (1617, 1626)	5
1564–5 (W. Griffith) 1600 ass'd to White	1596 (J. Danter)	1613 (W. White, printer)	–	A merrie pleasant and delectable historie, betweene King Edward the fourth, and a tanner of Tamworth	Anon.	7504	12pp. 4to (1596) 16pp. 8vo (1613)	10
1628 (F. Coules)	1630	1630 (J. Wright)	–	Tom Thumb, his life and death	Anon.	24115	24pp. 8vo	11
1630 (M. Sparke 1631 ass'd to F. Coules)	1635	1635 (F. Coules)	c. 1640 (F. Coules)	Robin conscience, or conscionable Robin	Martin Parker	19266	16pp. 8vo	1
1632 (F. Grove)	1632?	1632? (T. Cotes f. F. Grove)	Another edition, 1632? (F. Grove)	A true tale of Robin Hood	Martin Parker	19274.5	24pp. 8vo	3
1633 (R. Cotes)	1633	1633 (T. Cotes f. F. Grove)	1640 (F. Grove)	The King and a poore northerne man	Martin Parker	19248	24pp. 8vo	7
1636 (M. Sparke jnr)	1637 (T. Cotes f. M. Sparke jnr)	–	Extant edn claims to be 2nd edn	The country mouse, and the city mouse. Or a merry morrall fable	Wye Saltonstall	21642	24pp. 8vo	1
–	c. 1640	c. 1640 (E. Purslowe f. J. Wright)	Edns in ballad form: 1600, 1624, c. 1635	The pleasant and sweet history of patient Grissell	Verse by T. Deloney?	12386	24pp. 8vo	7

INDEX

Cambridge Studies in Early Modern British History

*Also published as a paperback